Scholars Praise Śrīla Prabhupāda

This life of Śrīla Prabhupāda is pointed proof that one can be a transmitter of truth and still be a vital and singular person, even—in a sense I now feel safe to use—in some ways "original." . . . At what almost anyone would consider a very advanced age, when most people would be resting on their laurels, he harkened to the mandate of his own spiritual teacher and set out on the difficult and demanding voyage to America. Śrīla Prabhupāda is, of course, only one of thousands of teachers. But in another sense, he is one in a thousand, maybe one in a million.

Harvey Cox
Professor of Divinity
Harvard University

Seldom before have we had such an intimate and detailed account of a spiritual master bringing forth a new religious movement, and probably never has there been such a wealth of contemporary data to back it up. Those of us who are historians of religion will be working this rich vein for years to come.

Dr. Thomas J. Hopkins
Chairman
Department of Religious Studies
Franklin and Marshall College
Lancaster, Pennsylvania

Perhaps more than anything else, this volume reveals those extraordinary personal attributes of Śrīla Prabhupāda that elicited such deep reverence and affection from his disciples. Besides being a man of deep moral strength, humility, and holiness, he was genuinely renounced. Unlike many modern *gurus,* he was content to live as his disciples did. . . . Śrīla Prabhupāda's life, as it is revealed here, is the epitome of his ideal, and ideal that he set forth for others to follow. In an age of pervasive hypocisy and cynicism, it is this kind of rare model that we need.

Dr. J. Stillson Judah
Professor Emeritus, History of Religions
Graduate Theological Union and Pacific
School of Religion
Berkeley, California

In . . . Bhaktivedanta Swami's biography, one of the central lessons taught the astute reader is the complexity and depth of the *guru*-disciple relationship. Much of the criticism from parents and anticult groups centers on the authoritarian demand of "cult" leaders for absolute submission from their followers. It is assumed that the leader has personal motives (e.g. power or monetary gain) that drive him to control others, while the surrendered disciples are manipulated, in an unthinking state, by the capricious whim of the spiritual master. In this volume of the life of Bhaktivedanta Swami, we see the foolishness of such an analysis. What springs from page after page is the willing devotion of young men and women to a man whom they admire for his deep faith and humility, not his autocratic or forceful demands. This is a fascinating chronicle I urge you to read.

Dr. Larry D. Shinn
Danforth Professor of Religion
Oberlin College
Oberlin, Ohio

Readers of Swami Bhaktivedanta's biography will be fascinated. It provides rich data for understanding the growth of a religious movement new to Westerners. It provides documentation more extensive than that available for any other such movement.

Of particular significance is that this book shows ISKCON to be not merely a "new" religion concentrated on the two coasts of North America, but a movement deeply rooted in India while reaching throughout the world. It is an Indian religious movement in that it originated in India and continues to live and grow in modern India.

Dr. Robert D. Baird
Professor, History of Religions
School of Religion
University of Iowa

These pages tell the story of a visionary spiritual teacher who understood the chaos of present-day civilization and who resuscitated spiritual values in the face of the materialistic values of consumerism and hedonism now dominating society. We meet in this volume a saint, indiscriminately inspiring the humanity that surrounds him with purpose of life, and offering them not a mere theory but a practical way of living.

Shaligram Shukla
Professor of Linguistics
Georgetown University

Prabhupāda

He Built a House in Which the Whole World Can Live

By

Satsvarūpa Dāsa Goswami

The Bhaktivedanta Book Trust

Los Angeles • London • Paris • Mumbai • Sydney • Hong Kong

Readers interested in the subject matter of this book are invited by The Bhaktivedanta Book Trust to correspond with its Secretary at the following address:

The Bhaktivedanta Book Trust
Hare Krishna Land
Juhu, Mumbai 400 049
India

Previous printings in India: 10,000 copies
Third Printing, December 1998: 5,000 copies

Published by Narmada Goswami for The Bhaktivedanta Book Trust, Hare Krishna Land, Juhu, Mumbai 400 049 and printed at Srinivas Fine Arts (P) Ltd., 35-A, Velayutham Road, Sivakasi-626 123, India.

ISBN 0-89213-127-6

Contents

INTRODUCTION

The worldwide fame of His Divine Grace A. C. Bhaktivedanta Swami, later known as Śrīla Prabhupāda, was to come after 1965—after he arrived in America. Before leaving India he had written three books; in the next twelve years he was to write more than sixty. Before he left India he had initiated one disciple; in the next twelve years he would initiate more than four thousand. Before he left India, hardly anyone had believed that he could fulfill his vision of a worldwide society of Kṛṣṇa devotees; but in the next decade he would form and maintain the International Society for Krishna Consciousness and open more than a hundred centers. Before sailing for America, he had never been outside India; but in the next twelve years he would travel many times around the world propagating the Kṛṣṇa consciousness movement.

Although his life's contribution may appear to have come in a late burst of revolutionary spiritual achievements, the first sixty-nine years of his life were a preparation for those achievements. And although to Americans Prabhupāda and his teachings were an unknown sudden appearance—"He looked like the genie that popped out of Aladdin's lamp"—he was the stalwart representative of a centuries-old cultural tradition.

Śrīla Prabhupāda was born Abhay Charan De on September 1, 1896, in Calcutta, India. His father was Gour Mohan De, a cloth merchant, and his mother was Rajani. His parents, in accordance with Bengali tradition, employed an astrologer to calculate the child's horoscope, and they were made jubilant by the auspicious reading. The astrologer made a specific prediction: when this child reached the age of seventy, he would cross the ocean, become a great exponent of religion, and open 108 temples.

Abhay's home at 151 Harrison Road was in the Indian section of north Calcutta. Abhay's father, Gour Mohan De, belonged to the aristocratic *suvarṇa-vaṇik* merchant community. He was related to the wealthy Mullik family, which for hundreds of years had traded in gold and salt with the British. Originally the Mulliks had been members of the De family, a *gotra* (lineage) that traces back to the ancient sage Gautama; but during the Mogul period of pre-British India, a Muslim ruler had conferred the title Mullik ("lord") on a wealthy, influential branch of the Des. Then, several generations later, a daughter of the Des had married into the Mullik family, and the two families had remained close ever since.

An entire block of properties on either side of Harrison Road belonged to Lokanath Mullik, and Gour Mohan and his family lived in a few rooms of a three-story building within the Mullik properties. Across the street from the Des' residence was a Rādhā-Govinda temple where for the past 150 years the Mulliks had maintained worship of the Deity of Rādhā and Kṛṣṇa. Various shops on the Mullik properties provided income for the Deity and for the priests conducting the worship. Every morning before breakfast, the Mullik family members would visit the temple to see the Deity of Rādhā-Govinda. They would offer cooked rice, *kacaurīs,* and vegetables on a large platter and would then distribute the *prasādam* to the Deities' morning visitors from the neighborhood. Among the daily visitors was Abhay Charan, accompanying his mother, father, or servant.

Gour Mohan was a pure Vaiṣṇava, and he raised his son to be Kṛṣṇa conscious. Since his own parents had also been

Vaiṣṇavas, Gour Mohan had never touched meat, fish, eggs, tea, or coffee. His complexion was fair and his disposition reserved. At night, before locking his cloth shop, he would set a bowl of rice in the middle of the floor to satisfy the rats, so they wouldn't gnaw the cloth in their hunger. On returning home he would read from *Caitanya-caritāmṛta* and *Śrīmad-Bhāgavatam* (the main scriptures of Bengali Vaiṣṇavas), chant on his *japa* beads, and worship the Deity of Lord Kṛṣṇa. He was gentle and affectionate and would never punish Abhay. Even when obliged to correct him, he would first apologize: "You are my son, so now I must correct you. It is my duty. Even Caitanya Mahāprabhu's father would chastise Him. So don't mind."

A picture always remained in Prabhupāda's memory of his father's devotional worship of Lord Kṛṣṇa. He would recall how his father used to come home late at night from the cloth shop and faithfully perform his worship of Lord Kṛṣṇa before the home altar. "We would be sleeping," Prabhupāda recalled, "and father would be doing *ārati.* We would hear the ding, ding, ding—we would hear the bell and wake up and see him bowing down before Kṛṣṇa."

Gour Mohan wanted Vaiṣṇava goals for his son; he wanted Abhay to become a servant of Rādhā and Kṛṣṇa, to become a preacher of the *Bhāgavatam,* and to learn the devotional art of playing the *mṛdaṅga* drum. He regularly received sadhus in his home, and he would always ask them, "Please bless my son so that Śrīmati Rādhārāṇī will grant him Her blessings." When Abhay's mother said she wanted her son to become a British lawyer when he grew up (which meant he would have to go to London to study), one of the boy's uncles thought it was a good idea. But Gour Mohan would not hear of it; if Abhay went to England he might be influenced by European dress and manner. "He will learn drinking and woman-hunting," Gour Mohan objected. "I do not want his money."

From the beginning of Abhay's life, Gour Mohan introduced his plan. He hired a professional *mṛdaṅga* player to teach Abhay the standard rhythms for accompanying *kīrtana.* Rajani was skeptical: "What is the purpose of teaching such a young child to play the *mṛdaṅga*? It is not important." But Gour Mohan had his dream of a son who would grow up singing *bhajanas,* playing *mṛdaṅga,* and speaking on *Śrīmad-Bhāgavatam.*

Abhay's mother, Rajani, was thirty years old when he was born. Like her husband, she came from a long-established Gaudiya Vaiṣṇava family. She was darker-skinned than her husband, and whereas his disposition was cool, hers tended to be fiery. Abhay saw his mother and father living together peacefully; no deep marital conflict or complicated dissatisfaction ever threatened home. Rajani was chaste and religious-minded, a model housewife in the traditional Vedic sense, dedicated to caring for her husband and children. Abhay observed his mother's simple and touching attempts to insure, by prayers and vows, that he continue to live.

Like Gour Mohan, Rajani treated Abhay as the pet child; but whereas her husband expressed his love through leniency and plans for his son's spiritual success, she expressed hers through attempts to safeguard Abhay from all danger, disease, and death. At Abhay's birth, she vowed to eat with her left hand until the day her son would notice and ask her why she was eating with the wrong hand. When one day little Abhay asked, she immediately stopped. It had been just another prescription for his survival, since she thought that by the strength of her vow he would continue to grow at least until he asked her about the vow. His mother would often take him to the Ganges and personally bathe him. When he got dysentery, she cured it with hot *purīs* and fried eggplant with salt. Sometimes when he was ill, Abhay would show his obstinacy by refusing to take any medicine. But just as he was stubborn, his mother was determined, and she would forcibly administer medicine into his mouth. When Abhay had been unwilling to attend school, his father had remained lenient, while Rajani insisted, and even hired a man to escort him to the school.

Throughout northern India, Lord Kṛṣṇa is accepted by the great majority of people as the supreme form of God. This version of Kṛṣṇa is actually in accordance with the Vedic scriptures, especially the *Bhagavad-gītā,* which is the most widely read Vedic literature. Naturally, therefore, Abhay imbibed Kṛṣṇa consciousness from his very birth. Moreover, his father was particularly religious, and in later years Prabhupāda would refer to him as "a pure devotee of Kṛṣṇa." Gour Mohan used to take his son, even before the child was old enough to walk, to a nearby temple of Rādhā-Kṛṣṇa, known as Rādhā-Govinda Mandir. Prabhupāda later recalled "standing at the doorway of the Rādhā-Govinda temple saying prayers to Rādhā-Govinda *mūrti* for hours together. The Deity was so beautiful with His slanted eyes."

Abhay was also enamored with the Ratha-yātrā festival of Lord Jagannātha, held yearly in Calcutta. The biggest Calcutta Ratha-yātrā was held at the Rādhā-Govinda Mandir, with three separate carts bearing the deities of Jagannātha (Kṛṣṇa), Balarāma, and Subhadrā. Beginning from the Rādhā-Govinda temple, the carts would proceed down Harrison Road for a short distance and then return. The temple managers would distribute large quantities of Lord Jagannātha's *prasādam* to the public on this day.

Ratha-yatrā was held in cities all over India, but the original Ratha-yātrā, attended each year by millions of pilgrims, took place three hundred miles south of Calcutta at Jagannātha Purī. For centuries at Purī, three wooden carts forty five feet high have been towed by the crowds along the two-mile parade route, in commemoration of one of Lord Kṛṣṇa's eternal pastimes. Abhay heard how Lord Caitanya Himself, four hundred years before, had danced and led ecstatic chanting of Hare Kṛṣṇa at the Purī Ratha-yātrā festival. Abhay would sometimes look at the railway timetable or ask about the fare to Purī, thinking about how he would collect the money and go there.

Abhay wanted to have his own cart and perform his own Ratha-yātrā, and naturally he turned to his father for help. Gour Mohan bought him a used, three-foot-high replica of a *ratha* (cart), and father and son together constructed supporting columns and placed a canopy on top, resembling as closely as possible the ones on the big carts at Purī. Abhay engaged his playmates in helping, especially his sister Bhavatarini, and he became their natural leader. Responding to his entreaties, amused mothers in the neighborhood agreed to cook special preparations so that he could distribute *prasādam* at this Ratha-yātrā festival.

Like the festival at Purī, Abhay's Ratha-yātrā ran for eight consecutive days. His family members gathered, and the neighborhood children pulled the cart in procession, chanting and playing drums and *karatālas*.

When Abhay was about six years old, he asked his father for a Deity of his own to worship. Since infancy he had watched his father doing *pūjā* at home and had been regularly seeing the worship of Rādhā-Govinda and thinking, "When will I be able to worship Kṛṣṇa like this?" Gour Mohan purchased a pair of little Rādhā-Kṛṣṇa Deities and gave Them to his son. From then on, whatever young Abhay ate he would first offer to Rādhā and Kṛṣṇa, and imitating his father and the priest of Rādhā-Govinda, he would offer his Deities a ghee lamp and put Them to rest at night.

When in the late 1960s Śrīla Prabhupāda began introducing large Ratha-yātrā festivals in U.S. cities and when he began installing Deities of Rādhā-Kṛṣṇa in his ISKCON temples, he said that he had learned all these things from his father. The only very important item of Kṛṣṇa consciousness that he had not learned from his father, he said, was the importance of printing and distributing transcendental literature. That he learned exclusively from his spiritual master, whom he met later in his youth.

During Abhay's college years, his father arranged for his marriage, selecting Radharani Datta, the daughter of a merchant family with whom he was associated. For several years Abhay lived with his family, and she with hers; so his marital responsibilities of supporting a family were not immediate. First he had to finish college.

But during his fourth year of college Abhay began to feel reluctant about accepting his degree. He had become a sympathizer to the nationalist cause, which advocated national schools and self-government.

In the class one year ahead of Abhay was a very spirited nationalist, Subhas Chandra Bose, who was later to become the leader of the Indian National Army, formed to overthrow the British rule of India. When Subhas Chandra Bose urged the students to support the Indian independence movement, Abhay listened. He liked Bose's faith in spirituality, his enthusiasm and determination. Abhay wasn't interested in political activity, but the ideal of the independence movement appealed to him. The call to *svarāj,* independence, although covert, attracted virtually all the students, and Abhay among them.

Abhay was especially interested in Mohandas K. Gandhi. Gandhi always carried a *Bhagavad-gītā* and spoke of being guided by the *Gita* above all other books. He was pure in his personal habits, abstaining from intoxication, meat-eating, and illicit sex. He lived simply, like a sadhu, yet he seemed to have more integrity than the begging sadhus Abhay had seen so many times. Abhay read Gandhi's speeches and followed his activities. Maybe Gandhi, he thought, could carry spirituality into the field of action.

Gandhi called on Indian students to forsake their studies. The foreign-run schools, he said, instilled a slave mentality; they made one no more than a puppet in the hands of the British. Still, a college degree was the basis of a life's career. Abhay weighed the choices carefully and in 1920, after completing his fourth year of college and passing his examination, refused to accept his diploma. In this way, he registered his protest and signalled his response to Gandhi's call.

After the killing at Jallianwalla Bagh, where British soldiers had shot to death hundreds of unarmed Indians who had gathered for a peaceful meeting, Gandhi called for complete noncooperation and boycott of everything British. In refusing his degree, Abhay was moving to align himself more closely with Gandhi's independence movement. Although Abhay's father was disturbed, he didn't resent his son's action. He was more concerned for Abhay's future than for the destiny of India's politics. He therefore arranged for good employment for Abhay through a prominent friend of the family, a Dr. Kartick Chandra Bose. Dr. Bose, a distinguished surgeon and chemical industrialist, had his own establishment, Bose's Laboratory, in Calcutta, and he gladly accepted Abhay as a department manager in his firm.

Often throughout his life, Śrīla Prabhupāda would feelingly recall his first meeting in 1922 with his spiritual master, Bhaktisiddhānta Sarasvatī Ṭhākura. At first Abhay didn't want to meet him, having been unimpressed by the so-called sadhus who used to visit his father's house. But a friend of Abhay's had insisted, escorting him to the quarters of the Gaudiya Math, where they were brought onto the roof and into the presence of Bhaktisiddhānta Sarasvatī.

No sooner did Abhay and his friend respectfully bow before the saintly person and prepare to sit than he said to them, "You are educated young men. Why don't you preach Lord Caitanya's message throughout the whole world?"

Abhay was very surprised that the sadhu had immediately asked them to become preachers on his behalf. Impressed by Bhaktisiddhānta Sarasvatī, he wanted to test him with intelligent inquiries.

Abhay was dressed in white *khādī* cloth, which at that time in India proclaimed one to be a supporter of Gandhi's cause for political emancipation. In the spirit of Indian nationalism, therefore, Abhay inquired, "Who will hear your Caitanya's message? We are a dependent country. First India must become independent. How can we spread India's culture if we are under British rule?"

Śrīla Bhaktisiddhānta replied that Kṛṣṇa consciousness didn't have to wait for a change in Indian politics, nor was it dependent on who ruled. Kṛṣṇa consciousness was so important that it could not wait.

Abhay was struck by his boldness. The whole of India was in turmoil and seemed to support what Abhay had said. Many famous leaders of Bengal, many saints, even Gandhi himself—men who were educated and spiritually minded—all might well have asked the same question, challenging this sadhu's relevance.

But Śrīla Bhaktisiddhānta contended all governments were temporary; the eternal reality was Kṛṣṇa consciousness, and the real self was the spirit soul. No man-made political system could help humanity. This was the verdict of the Vedic scriptures and the line of spiritual masters. Real public welfare work, he said, should go beyond concerns of the temporary and prepare a person for his next life and his eternal relationship with the Supreme.

Abhay had already concluded that this was certainly not just another dubious sadhu, and he listened attentively to the arguments of Śrīla Bhaktisiddhānta and found himself gradually becoming convinced. Bhaktisiddhānta Sarasvatī quoted Sanskrit verses from *Bhagavad-gītā,* wherein Lord Kṛṣṇa declares that a person should give up all other religious duties and surrender unto Him, the Supreme Personality of Godhead. Abhay had never forgotten Lord Kṛṣṇa and His teachings in *Bhagavad-gītā,* and his family had always worshiped Lord Caitanya Mahāprabhu, whose mission Bhaktisiddhānta Sarasvatī was espousing. But he was astounded to hear those teachings presented so masterfully.

Abhay felt defeated in argument. But he liked it. When the discussion was completed after two hours, he and his friend walked down the stairs and onto the street. Śrīla Bhaktisiddhānta's explanation of the independence movement as a temporary, incomplete cause had made a deep impression on Abhay. He felt himself less a nationalist and more a follower of Bhaktisiddhānta Sarasvatī. He also thought it would have been better if he weren't married. This great personality was asking him to preach; he could have immediately joined. But to leave his family, he felt, would be an injustice.

"He's wonderful!" Abhay told his friend. "The message of Lord Caitanya is in the hands of a very expert person."

Śrīla Prabhupāda would later recall that on that very night he had actually accepted Bhaktisiddhānta Sarasvatī as his spiritual master. "Not officially," Prabhupāda said, "but in my heart. I was thinking that I had met a very nice saintly person."

After his first meeting with Bhaktisiddhānta Sarasvatī, Abhay began to associate more with the Gaudiya Math devotees. They gave him books and told him the history of their spiritual master. Śrīla Bhaktisiddhānta Sarasvatī was the son of Bhaktivinoda Ṭhākura, another great Vaiṣṇava teacher in the disciplic line from Lord Caitanya. Before the time of Bhaktivinoda, the teachings of Lord Caitanya had been obscured by teachers and sects falsely claiming to be followers of Lord Caitanya but deviating in various drastic ways from His pure teachings; the good reputation of Vaiṣṇavism had been compromised. Bhaktivinoda Ṭhākura, however, through his prolific writings and through his social position as a high government officer, had reestablished the respectability of Vaiṣṇavism. He preached that the teachings of Lord Caitanya were the highest form of theism and were intended not for a particular sect or religion or nation but for all the people of the world. He prophesied that Lord Caitanya's teachings would go worldwide, and he yearned for it.

Śrīla Bhaktisiddhānta Sarasvatī was teaching the conclusion of Lord Caitanya's teachings, that Lord Kṛṣṇa is the Supreme Personality of Godhead and that the chanting of His holy name should be stressed above all other religious practices. In former ages, other methods of attaining to God had been available, but in the present age of Kali only the chanting of Hare Kṛṣṇa would be effective. On the authority of scriptures such as *Bṛhan-nāradīya Purāṇa* and the *Upaniṣads,* Bhaktivinoda Ṭhākura and Bhaktisiddhānta Sarasvatī had specifically stressed the importance of the *mahā-mantra:* Hare Kṛṣṇa, Hare Kṛṣṇa, Kṛṣṇa Kṛṣṇa, Hare Hare/ Hare Rāma, Hare Rāma, Rāma Rāma, Hare Hare.

Abhay knew these scriptural references, he knew the chanting, and he knew the conclusions of the *Gītā.* But now, as he eagerly read the writings of the great *ācāryas,* he had fresh realizations of the scope of Lord Caitanya's mission. Now he was discovering the depths of his own Vaiṣṇava heritage and its efficacy for bringing about the highest welfare for people in an age destined to be full of troubles.

For business purposes, Abhay and his wife and family moved to Allahabad, and it was there, in 1932, that he received initiation and became a disciple of Bhaktisiddhānta Sarasvatī. The story of the next thirty years of his life in India is the story of a single, growing desire to preach Kṛṣṇa consciousness worldwide, as his spiritual master had ordered him.

Abhay's family responsibilities and his preaching, however, seemed to conflict. His wife was religious at home, but didn't like the idea of working to spread Kṛṣṇa consciousness. Even when Abhay attempted to hold gatherings in their home and speak from *Bhagavad-gītā,* she preferred to stay upstairs drinking tea. Still, despite her obstinacy, Abhay remained patient and tried to include her.

As a pharmaceutical salesman, Abhay did a lot of traveling by rail, especially in northern India. He thought that if he could become wealthy, he could then use his money for propagating the mission of Bhaktisiddhānta Sarasvatī, and this thought encouraged him in his business.

Abhay was unable to travel with his spiritual master or to see him often, but whenever possible he tried to time a business trip to Calcutta when his spiritual master was also there. Thus over the next four years he managed to see his spiritual master about a dozen times. Although Śrīla Bhaktisiddhānta Sarasvatī was so strong in argument against other philosophies that even his own disciples were cautious about approaching him if he were sitting alone, and although Abhay's contact with him was quite limited, still Śrīla Bhaktisiddhānta would always treat him kindly. Prabhupāda would later recall, "Sometimes my Godbrothers would criticize because I would talk a little freely with him, and they would quote this English saying, 'Fools rush in where angels fear to tread.' But I would think, 'Fool? Well, maybe. But that is the way I am.'

My Guru Mahārāja was always very, very affectionate to me."

In 1935, on the occasion of Śrīla Bhaktisiddhānta Sarasvatī's sixty-second birthday, Abhay submitted a poem and an essay at a meeting of his Godbrothers in Bombay. The writings were well received and were consequently published in the Gaudiya Math magazine, *The Harmonist.* One of his Godbrothers informally dubbed Abhay as *kavi,* "learned poet." For Abhay, however, the glory of his first published writing came when the poem reached Bhaktisiddhānta Sarasvatī and gave him pleasure. One stanza specifically made Śrīla Bhaktisiddhānta so happy that he made a point of showing it to all of his guests:

Absolute is sentient
Thou hast proved,
Impersonal calamity
Thou hast moved.

Somehow, in this simple couplet Abhay had captured the essence of his spiritual master's preaching against impersonalist philosophies, and Śrīla Bhaktisiddhānta took it as an indication of how well Abhay knew the mind of his gurudeva. Śrīla Bhaktisiddhānta also found Abhay's essay pleasing, and he showed it to some of his confidential devotees. "Whatever he writes," he instructed the editor of *The Harmonist,* "publish it."

One of Abhay's most significant meetings with his spiritual master took place in Vṛndāvana in 1935. Abhay was no longer a newcomer, but a bona fide disciple, doing his best within the context of a householder's life. One day as Śrīla Bhaktisiddhānta was walking by the sacred lake of Rādhā-kuṇḍa with Abhay and several other disciples, he began speaking confidentially to Abhay. Some of his leading disciples had been quarreling, he said, and this distressed him very much. The disciples had been fighting over who would use various rooms and facilities at the Gaudiya Math headquarters in Calcutta. If they were quarreling even now, what would they do after their spiritual master passed away?

Abhay had no part in these matters and did not even know the details of what was involved. But as he listened to his spiritual master, he also became distressed.

Deeply concerned, Śrīla Bhaktisiddhānta said to Abhay, "There will be fire." One day there would be fire in the Calcutta Gaudiya Math, and that fire of party interest would spread and destroy. Abhay heard but did not know what to make of it. "It would be better," said Bhaktisiddhānta Sarasvatī, "to take the marble from the walls of the temple to secure money. If I could do this and print books, that would be better."

Śrīla Bhaktisiddhānta Sarasvatī then said directly to Abhay, "I had a desire to print some books. If you ever get money, print books." Standing by Rādhā-kuṇḍa and beholding his spiritual master, Abhay felt these words deeply enter his life—"If you ever get money, print books."

Śrīla Bhaktisiddhānta departed from the mortal world in December 1936. One month before his departure, Abhay wrote him a letter. He was thinking that as a *gṛhastha* he couldn't fully serve his spiritual master, and he wanted to know what more he could do. Thus he inquired, "Is there any particular service I can do?"

Two weeks later Abhay received a reply:

> I am fully confident that you can explain in English our thoughts and arguments to the people who are not conversant with the languages [Bengali and Hindi] . . . This will do much good to yourself as well as your audience. I have every hope that you can turn yourself into a very good English preacher.

Abhay at once recognized this to be the same instruction he had received at his first meeting with Śrīla Bhaktisiddhānta, in 1922. He took it as a confirmation. He now had no doubt as to the purpose of his life.

"The fire in the *maṭha*" Śrīla Bhaktisiddhānta had predicted broke out almost immediately. Some senior disciples quarreled about succession of leadership in the *maṭhas*, and matters soon degraded into legal disputes over temple proprietorship. As a *gṛhastha* businessman, Abhay had taken little part in the Gaudiya Math activities, and now that was in his favor. He was at a distance from the fray, but lamented that his spiritual master's order for his disciples to work cooperatively was being disregarded and his united institution of temples and printing presses was collapsing.

Another, much greater dispute soon erupted—World War II. By their tactic known as the "denial policy" the British sank many Indian boats carrying food and destroyed much of east India's rice crop, fearing that the food would fall into the hands of the enemy. This left Indians starving and without the boats they needed for trade. The famine that ensued was the worst to hit Bengal in 150 years.

Abhay managed to purchase just enough for his own family to survive, but month after month he saw the footpaths and open spaces congested with beggars, cooking their food on improvised stoves and sleeping in the open or beneath trees. He saw starving children rummaging in the dustbins for a morsel of food. From there it was but a step to fighting with the dogs for a share of the garbage, and this also became a familiar sight in the Calcutta streets.

Abhay comprehended the sufferings of famine through the teachings he had heard from Śrīla Bhaktisiddhānta. By God's arrangement the earth could produce enough food; the trouble was man's greed and mismanagement. "There is no scarcity in the world," Śrīla Bhaktisiddhānta Sarasvatī had said. "The only scarcity is of Kṛṣṇa consciousness." Now, more than ever, this spiritual vision seemed relevant, and Abhay grew anxious for a way to apply what he knew to be the remedy for all ills. Convinced that he had an urgent message for the war-weary citizens of the world, he considered starting a publication that would present the world's crises through the eyes of the scripture in the same bold style as had his spiritual master. There was no shortage of ideas, and he had been saving money from his business for this very purpose.

From the front room of his apartment in Calcutta, Abhay conceived, wrote, edited, and typed the manuscript for a magazine. He gave it the name *Back to Godhead:* "Edited and founded under the direct order of His Divine Grace Sri Srimad Bhakti Siddhanta Saraswati Goswami Prabhupada, by Mr. Abhay Charan De."

Repeatedly, however, he had to plead with government officials for permission to use paper to print his journal. Although he was only one voice out of billions, with no backing or money or following, he was confident in his guru and in Lord Kṛṣṇa. He had the conviction of his important message; therefore, even during the war, in between explosions and deaths, he released his first issue, "because there is a great need of a literature like this."

Large national events continued to play across the worldly stage throughout the 1940s in India. In 1947 India gained her long-sought independence from Britain. But the national happiness was soon followed by horror as hundreds of thousands died in the fighting that followed the partition of the nation into India and Pakistan. As Prabhupāda would later recall, "We have seen in 1947, Hindu-Muslim fighting. One party was Hindu, the other party was Muslim. They fought, and so many died. And after death there was no distinction who was Hindu or who was Muslim—the municipal men gathered the bodies together in piles to throw them somewhere."

Abhay was not hopeful about promises for peace, nor did he consider Indian independence the solution. Unless the leaders were God conscious, what change would there be? In *Back to Godhead,* in his article "Gandhi-Jinnah Talks," he wrote, "Fighting will go on between Hindu and Mohammedan, between Christians and Christians, between Buddhist and Buddhist till the day of annihilation." His point: as long as people are possessed of selfish interests and desires for sense gratification, they will continue fighting. Real unity was possible only on the platform of spiritual understanding and service to the Supreme.

Even when Abhay was unable to raise enough money to

publish regular issues of *Back to Godhead,* he continued writing. His most ambitious project was a commentary on the *Bhagavad-gītā,* but he also preached Lord Caitanya's message through letters. He wrote to many leaders in government, to respectable acquaintances, and to people whose articles he had read or whose activities had caught his eye in the newspaper. Presenting himself as a humble servant, he would explain his ideas on how to apply India's original Kṛṣṇa conscious culture as the successful solution to all manner of dilemmas. Sometimes his letters drew replies from government offices and secretaries, but largely they were ignored.

That Abhay would think of engaging Mohandas Gandhi in devotional service was inevitable. Because of his lifetime of courageous, ascetic, and moral activities on behalf of his countrymen, Gandhi had great power to influence the Indian masses. Besides, Abhay had a special feeling for him, having been a follower of his as a young man. On December 7, 1947, Abhay wrote a long letter to Gandhi in New Delhi. He was aware that Gandhi was at odds with many of his former followers, who had taken leadership of the nation and were neglecting his doctrines of Hindu-Muslim unity and agrarianism. Hindus and Muslims alike were critical of him. At seventy-eight years, he was physically weak and melancholy.

Abhay knew that his letter would probably never reach Gandhi, but he sent it nonetheless. Addressing himself as Gandhi's "unknown friend," he wrote, "I tell you as a sincere friend that you must immediately retire from active politics if you do not desire to die an inglorious death." Although warmly acknowledging Gandhi's honor and prestige, he said that it would all amount to illusion unless Gandhi retired from politics and engaged in understanding and preaching *Bhagavad-gītā.* Especially now that Gandhi was at the end of his life, Abhay warned, he should quit the political field and approach the Absolute Truth. At least for a month, Abhay requested, Gandhi should retire and engage with him in discussing *Bhagavad-gītā.*

Abhay never received a reply to his letter, and one month

later, on January 30, Gandhi met his death. Abhay's letter of the previous month suddenly read like a prophecy.

While Abhay's involvement in writing and preaching intensified, his business and family affairs dwindled. He felt that a particular verse spoken by Lord Kṛṣṇa in *Śrīmad-Bhāgavatam* applied to him: "When I feel especially merciful toward someone, I gradually take away all his material possessions. His friends and relatives then reject the poverty-stricken and most wretched fellow"—leaving him only Kṛṣṇa. When Abhay's business in Allahabad went deeply into debt, he tried to open a factory in Lucknow. At first it appeared profitable, but eventually it also lost money and had to be closed.

While continuing to maintain his wife and children in an apartment in Calcutta, Abhay mostly lived away from them. He moved back to Allahabad, but he was putting less and less energy into selling pharmaceutical products. He was more interested in preaching.

When a hospital customer in the city of Jhansi invited Abhay to lecture at the Gita Mandir, he gladly accepted. His lecture was well received by the Jhansi audience, which was made up largely of young medical students and professionals. Their appreciation, however, was mostly social and cultural. They were accustomed to hearing from many speakers, whom they invited to their lecture programs, and they never intended that Abhay try to establish a permanent center in Jhansi. But Abhay was visionary and ambitious. Leaving his Allahabad affairs in the hands of his son, he tried to create a spiritual movement in Jhansi.

Abhay was 56, and he thought that he must now begin very seriously manifesting the orders of his spiritual master. As he told one of the men in Jhansi, "The whole world is waiting, Mr. Mitra, for spiritual revolution." Since his spiritual master's institution, the Gaudiya Math, had become ineffectual due to fights and permanent factions, he attempted to start a movement of devotees with worldwide activities. Although he had only one or two active helpers, he obtained the use of an abandoned temple and began working toward what he envisioned as a kind of spiritual United Nations. He wrote a charter and legally registered his movement as the League of Devotees.

But while absorbed in these affairs, one day Abhay received a telegram that his business in Allahabad had been burglarized. His servants had stolen his money, medicine, and anything else of value. On reading the news, he was silent, but then laughed and uttered the *Bhāgavatam* verse: Kṛṣṇa's mercy was to crush the material success of a sincere devotee. When one of Abhay's Jhansi friends advised him to return to Allahabad, he replied, "No, this is good for me. First I was sad to see this, but I can see that one great attachment has come to an end, and my life is now fully surrendered and dedicated to Śrī Śrī Rādhā-Kṛṣṇa."

On a visit to his family in Calcutta, Abhay made the final break from his family responsibilities. He still had a small business there, and he had gone to try and raise funds for his missionary work in Jhansi. But inevitably he was plunged again into family responsibilities: some of his children were still unmarried, rent and bills had to be paid. Even if he were to develop his Calcutta medical shop, the family would demand whatever he earned, and even if he were to accede to his family's demands and live at home, the greatest difficulty would still remain: they weren't serious about devotional service.

What was the use, he thought, if they wouldn't become devotees? His wife and relatives were not interested in his Jhansi preaching but wanted him to spend more time in business and family affairs. His father-in-law complained, "Why are you always talking about God?" But when friends came to visit, Abhay continued preaching and speaking on *Bhagavad-gītā,* just as he had done in Jhansi. And as before, his wife and the rest of the family would take tea in a separate room. Prabhupāda would later recall, "I wanted as much as possible to get her to work with me in spreading Kṛṣṇa consciousness, to get her help. But she was very determined.

So finally, after thirty years, I could understand—she would not be any assistance to me."

Abhay always advised his wife not to drink tea: it was not the practice of a strict Vaiṣṇava family. Finally he said, "You have to choose between me or tea. Either the tea goes or I go." Abhay's wife replied jokingly, "Well, I'll have to give up my husband then."

Then one day she made a serious mistake. She traded her husband's copy of *Śrīmad-Bhāgavatam* for tea biscuits. When Abhay came home and looked for the sacred book, she told him what had happened. Abhay was shocked, and the incident pushed him to leave his family for good. In a mood of stark determination, he left his family and business.

The 1950s proved very difficult years for Abhay. He returned to Jhansi, but he had to leave his building when the governor's wife insisted that it be used for a ladies' club instead of the League of Devotees. Without a place to stay and with no real support, he left Jhansi—but not his plan to start a worldwide association of devotees. After moving to an *āśrama* in Delhi and living for a while with some of his Godbrothers, he was on his own again, a mendicant, staying from week to week in various temples or in the homes of whatever wealthy, pious people would receive him. In terms of food, clothing, and shelter, these were the most difficult times he had ever gone through. Since his childhood he had always had proper food and good clothes, and there had been no question of where he would live. He had been the pet child of his father, and he had received special guidance and affection from Śrīla Bhaktisiddhānta Sarasvatī. But during the 1950s Abhay was alone.

He spent his time writing and approaching donors, to whom he preached *Bhagavad-gītā*. His goal wasn't to find a permanent residence but to print his transcendental literature and to establish a powerful movement for spreading Kṛṣṇa consciousness. And for this he needed money. So he was calling on wealthy men in their offices and homes, presenting his manuscripts and explaining his mission. But few responded. And when they did, the donation was usually only five or ten rupees. Eventually, however, he collected enough to again print *Back to Godhead.*

Lacking money to buy even proper clothes, Abhay went through the chilly Delhi winter without a jacket. He would regularly walk to the printer's to read the latest proofs of *Back to Godhead.* When the printer asked him why he was intent on producing his newspaper under such hardships, he replied, "It is my mission." He managed to pay the printer small amounts at intervals.

After picking up the copies from the printer, Abhay would walk around the city selling them. He would take a seat at a tea stand, and when someone sat beside him he would ask him to please take a copy of *Back to Godhead.* Through his articles and editorials, Abhay criticized the materialistic and atheistic tendencies of modern civilization. He also drew on his personal experiences. Responding to the resistance (polite and impolite) that he met while selling *Back to Godhead,* he wrote an article, "No Time, a Chronic Disease of the Common Man." His writing was never shrill, strident, or fanatical, despite his desperate poverty and the urgency of his message. He wrote expecting to find his reader prepared to hear sound philosophy and willing to accept the truth, especially when presented logically, relevantly, and authoritatively.

In addition to selling *Back to Godhead* at tea stalls and delivering copies to donors, Abhay also mailed out free copies—both within India and abroad. For years, the vast audience of English-speaking readers outside India had concerned him, and he wanted to reach them. Having gathered addresses of libraries, universities, and cultural and government outlets outside India, he mailed as many *Back to Godheads* as he could afford. He prepared a letter for his Western readers, suggesting that they should be even more receptive than his countrymen.

On the home front, Abhay sent copies of *Back to Godhead* to the president of India, Dr. Rajendra Prasad, along with a letter warning him of the perilous fate that awaits a society conducted by the godless—"Please therefore save them from the great falldown." He requested His Excellency at least to glance over the headlines of the enclosed copies of *Back to Godhead* and to consider granting the editor an interview. "I am crying alone in the wilderness at the present moment," wrote Abhay. His Excellency never replied.

Even through the heat of the New Delhi summer, when the temperatures rose to 114 degrees, Abhay continued to go out daily to sell his fortnightly publication. Once he suffered heat stroke and reeled in the streets, until a friend picked him up in his car and took him to a doctor. Another time he was gored by a cow and lay for some time unattended by the roadside. At times like this, he sometimes wondered why he had left home and business, and why, since he was now surrendered to Kṛṣṇa, everything had become so difficult. But years later, when his Kṛṣṇa consciousness mission was established in many countries with many disciples, he would say, "At the time I couldn't understand. But now I realize all those difficulties were *assets*. It was all Kṛṣṇa's mercy."

While keeping up his effort of printing and selling *Back to Godhead* in Delhi, Abhay decided to take up residence in Vṛndāvana, eighty miles south of New Delhi. Gauḍīya Vaiṣṇavas consider Vṛndāvana to be the most sacred spot in the universe, because of Lord Kṛṣṇa's childhood pastimes there during His incarnation five thousand years ago. The chief followers of Lord Caitanya had gone to Vṛndāvana five hundred years ago, written books, established temples, and located the places of Kṛṣṇa's many pastimes in the forests, pastures, and along the riverbanks. Abhay's idea was to write his essays in the peaceful, spiritual atmosphere of Vṛndāvana and commute to Delhi to distribute his literature and seek donations from respectable patrons. He took a simple, very inexpensive room in the Vaṁśī-gopālajī temple, located on the bank of the Yamunā River, and there he entered the special quality of life in Vṛndāvana.

Abhay didn't see Vṛndāvana as would an ordinary person. As a pure devotee of Kṛṣṇa, he felt great bliss simply in walking down a dirt lane or in seeing the Deity forms of Kṛṣṇa, which appeared on every street, in thousands of temples and homes. From his small rooftop room, he could see the Yamunā flowing before him and extending into a broad curving sheet of river that shimmered in the afternoon sun. In the evening, he enjoyed the cooling breezes from the Yamunā and heard devotees chanting their evening prayers at the Keśi-ghāṭa. He would hear temple bells ringing throughout the town, and sometimes he would cease from his writing and walk into the busy areas, amidst the residents and pilgrim visitors. He heard the chanting of Hare Kṛṣṇa everywhere, and many passersby would greet him with the customary "Jaya Rādhe!" and "Hare Kṛṣṇa."

As Vṛndāvana was Kṛṣṇa's abode, so Abhay was Kṛṣṇa's servant. In Vṛndāvana he felt at home. Naturally, he continued to think of preaching, hankering for others to know the intimate peace and ecstasy of Vṛndāvana. Kṛṣṇa, the Supreme Personality of Godhead, was inviting all souls to join Him in His eternal abode; yet even in India, few understood. And outside India, people knew nothing of Vṛndāvana or of the Yamunā or of what it meant to be free of material desires. Abhay thought, Why shouldn't people all over the world have this? This was the abode of peace, yet no one knew anything of it, nor were people interested. But this was what they were actually hankering for.

Driven by the desire to broadcast the glories of eternal Vṛndāvana, Abhay worked almost constantly in Vṛndāvana to produce each issue of *Back to Godhead.* Commuting, however, became difficult. He would take the morning train into Delhi and, having nowhere to stay, return to Vṛndāvana the same night. That didn't give him much time in the city, and it was expensive. Sometimes a pious gentleman would give him a place to stay, but even with his minimal personal expenses, Abhay had difficulty raising enough donations to cover traveling, printing, and mailing. After producing twelve consecutive fortnightly editions of *Back to Godhead,* Abhay again ran out of money. The printer said he could not print simply out of friendship. Returning to Vṛndāvana, Abhay continued writing, but with no plan for publication.

One day, in a renounced and solitary mood, Abhay composed a Bengali poem, entitled "Vṛndāvana-bhajana." Its opening stanzas were especially self-reflective and personal.

1

I am sitting alone in Vṛndāvana-dhāma.
In this mood I am getting many realizations.

I have my wife, sons, daughters, grandsons, everything,
But I have no money, so they are a fruitless glory.
Kṛṣṇa has shown me the naked form of material nature;
By His strength it has all become tasteless to me today.
Yasyāham anugṛhṇāmi hariṣye tad-dhanaṁ śanaiḥ:
"I gradually take away all the wealth of those upon whom I am merciful."
How was I able to understand this mercy of the all-merciful?

2

Everyone has abandoned me, seeing me penniless—
Wife, relatives, friends, brothers, everyone.
This is misery, but it gives me a laugh. I sit alone and laugh.

In this *māyā-saṁsāra,* whom do I really love?
Where have my loving father and mother gone now?
And where are all my elders, who were my own folk?
Who will give me news of them, tell me who?
All that is left of this family life is a list of names.

One night Abhay had a striking dream, the same dream he had had several times before, during his days as a householder. Śrīla Bhaktisiddhānta Sarasvatī appeared, just as Abhay had known him, the tall, scholarly sannyasi, coming directly from the spiritual world, from Kṛṣṇa's personal entourage. He called to Abhay and indicated that he should follow. Repeatedly he called and motioned. He was asking Abhay to take sannyasa. Come, he urged, become a sannyasi. Abhay awoke in a state of wonder. He thought of this instruction as another feature of the original instruction Śrīla Bhaktisiddhānta Sarasvatī had given him at their first meeting in Calcutta, the same instruction that his spiritual master had later solidified in a letter: become an English preacher and spread Kṛṣṇa consciousness throughout the Western world. Sannyasa was for that end; otherwise, why would his spiritual master have asked him to accept it? In the standard Vedic social system, a man is supposed to leave his family at fifty and become a renounced monk, a sannyasi, and thus dedicate his remaining days to chanting, hearing, and preaching the glories of the Lord. Abhay reasoned that his spiritual master was saying, "Now take sannyasa and you will actually be able to accomplish this mission. Formerly the time was not right."

Abhay deliberated cautiously. By accepting sannyasa, a Vaiṣṇava dedicates his body, mind, and words totally to the service of the Supreme Personality of Godhead, renouncing all other engagements. Abhay was already doing all those things, but he felt that by accepting the sannyasa order, he could solidify his position and gain even more impetus for the great work that still lay ahead. The Vedic standard and the example set by the previous *ācāryas* was that if one wanted to lead a preaching movement, sannyasa was required. At first Abhay had resisted, but now he was reconsidering. He turned to a Godbrother, Keśava Mahārāja, in Mathurā, who stressed that Abhay take sannyasa immediately.

In later years Prabhupāda would recall, "I was sitting alone in Vṛndāvana, writing. My Godbrother insisted to me, 'Bhaktivedanta Prabhu, you must do it. Without accepting the renounced order of life, nobody can become a preacher.' It was my spiritual master who insisted through this Godbrother. So, unwillingly, I accepted."

After a formal sannyasa ceremony in Vṛndāvana, Abhay's name became Abhay Caraṇāravinda Bhaktivedanta Swami. Yet his basic problems remained. He wanted to preach Kṛṣṇa consciousness, but few were willing to listen. Such things hadn't been changed with his becoming a sannyasi.

One change took place, however: Bhaktivedanta Swami decided to write books. When a librarian advised him to write books (they were permanent, whereas newspapers were read once and thrown away), Bhaktivedanta Swami took it that his spiritual master was speaking through this person. Then an Indian Army officer who liked *Back to Godhead* suggested the same thing. In both cases Bhaktivedanta Swami took the advice as a revelation from his spiritual master.

Bhaktivedanta Swami considered *Śrīmad-Bhāgavatam,* because it was the most important and authoritative Vaiṣṇava scripture. Although *Bhagavad-gītā* was the essence of all Vedic knowledge, presented in a brief ABC fashion, *Śrīmad-Bhāgavatam* was elaborate. Śrīla Bhaktisiddhānta Sarasvatī and Bhaktivinoda Ṭhākura had both written Bengali commentaries on the *Bhāgavatam.* In fact, most of the great Vaiṣṇava *ācāryas* of the past had commented on *Śrīmad-Bhāgavatam,* "the spotless Vedic scripture." An English translation and commentary for this book could one day change the hearts of the entire world. And if Bhaktivedanta Swami could publish even a few books, his preaching would be enhanced; he could go abroad with confidence and not appear empty handed.

Bhaktivedanta Swami returned to Delhi with new purpose. The paper and printing capital of India was in the Chandni Chowk section of Old Delhi, and Bhaktivedanta Swami thought it best to somehow locate himself there to regularly negotiate for printing books. Through an old printing contact, he met a temple owner who gave him a free room in his Rādhā-Kṛṣṇa temple near Chandni Chowk. The neighborhood was called Chippiwada, a congested, mixed Hindu-Muslim quarter. Now Bhaktivedanta Swami could work either in Vṛndāvana or Delhi. With new enthusiasm, he picked up a few donations and began again publishing *Back to Godhead* while at the same time beginning his translation and commentary of *Śrīmad-Bhāgavatam.*

He contemplated the size of the project he was attempting. The *Bhāgavatam* contained eighteen thousand verses, in twelve cantos, which he figured would come to at least sixty volumes. He thought he might be able to finish it in five to seven years: "If the Lord keeps me physically fit," he wrote, "then in the fulfillment of Srila Bhaktisiddhanta Sarasvati's will I could complete this work."

Bhaktivedanta Swami's accepting sannyasa, his idea to write and publish *Śrīmad-Bhāgavatam,* and his desire to preach in the West all were interrelated. To preach, he would have to have books, especially if he were to go to the West. There were millions of books in the West, but nothing like this, nothing to fill the spiritual vacuum in people's lives. He would not merely write, however, but he would personally take the books to the West, present them, and teach people—through the books and in person—how to develop pure love of God.

Although he was known as an English preacher, Bhaktivedanta Swami knew his presentation in a foreign language had many technical flaws; and he had no editor to correct them. But such technical faults would not keep him from printing *Śrīmad-Bhāgavatam.* This was an emergency. "When there is fire in the house," he wrote, "the inmates of the house go out for help from the neighbours who may be foreigners to such inmates and yet without adequate language the victims of the fire express themselves, and the neighbours understand the need even though not expressed in adequate language. The same spirit of cooperation is needed in the matter of broadcasting this transcendental message of Srimad-Bhagavatam throughout the whole polluted atmosphere of the present day."

Bhaktivedanta Swami was presenting *Śrīmad-Bhāgavatam* unchanged, with the greatest respect for Śrīla Vyāsadeva, the author. And that was Bhaktivedanta Swami's cardinal virtue. Certainly he was adding his own realizations, but not in a spirit of trying to surpass the previous spiritual masters. In the all-important matter of presenting the subject strictly in *paramparā,* Bhaktivedanta Swami suffered from no "faulty and broken technicalities." He knew that without remaining faithful to the disciplic succession, the *Bhāgavatam* purports would not have value.

At his room in the Chippiwada temple, he typed day and night at his desk beneath the small light that dangled on its cord from the ceiling. He sat on a thin mat on the floor, his typewriter before him on a trunk. Pages accumulated, and he kept them in place with stones. Food and sleep were only incidental. He was completely convinced that *Śrīmad-Bhāgavatam* would create a revolution in a misdirected civilization. Thus he translated each word and wrote each purport with exacting care and concentration. But it had to be done as quickly as possible.

Bhaktivedanta Swami had moved his Vṛndāvana residence to the Rādhā-Dāmodara temple. Now without even leaving his room, he could look out and see the altar and the four-foot-high form of Vṛndāvana-candra, the black marble Kṛṣṇa Deity worshiped hundreds of years ago by Kṛṣṇadāsa Kavirāja. This was superior to his room at the Vaṁśī-gopālajī temple, because now he was living in the temple of Jīva Gosvāmī, where great souls like the Gosvāmīs Rūpa, Sanātana, Raghunātha, and Jīva had all gathered, taken *prasādam,* chanted, and discussed Lord Kṛṣṇa and Lord Caitanya. This was the best place to work on *Śrīmad-Bhāgavatam.*

While staying at the Rādhā-Dāmodara temple, Bhaktivedanta Swami would prepare his own meals. And as he sat to take *prasādam,* he could see through the latticework the *samādhi* tomb of Rūpa Gosvāmī. Feeling Rūpa Gosvāmī's presence, he would think of his own mission for his spiritual master. Bhaktivedanta Swami's spiritual master and the previous spiritual masters in the disciplic succession had wanted the Kṛṣṇa consciousness movement to spread all over the world, and as Bhaktivedanta Swami daily gathered inspiration, sitting before Rūpa Gosvāmī's *samādhi,* he prayed to his spiritual predecessors for guidance. The intimate direction he received from them was an absolute dictation, and no government, no publisher, nor anyone else could shake or diminish it. Rūpa Gosvāmī wanted him to go to the West; Śrīla Bhaktisiddhānta Sarasvatī wanted him to go to the West; and Kṛṣṇa had arranged that he be brought to the Rādhā-

Dāmodara temple to receive Their blessings. At the Rādhā-Dāmodara temple, he felt he had entered an eternal residence known only to pure devotees of the Lord. Yet although they were allowing him to associate intimately with them in the place of their pastimes, he felt they were ordering him to leave—to leave Rādhā-Dāmodara and Vṛndāvana and to deliver the message of the *ācāryas* to forgetful parts of the world.

Writing was only half the battle; the other half was publishing. The publishers, however, were not interested in the sixty-volume *Bhāgavatam* series, and Bhaktivedanta Swami was not interested in anything less. To publish his books, therefore, he would have to solicit donations and publish at his own expense.

A printing contact advised Bhaktivedanta Swami to travel to Gorakhpur and show his manuscript to Hanuman Prasad Poddar, the famous religious publisher. Bhaktivedanta Swami took the five-hundred-mile trip and obtained a donation of four thousand rupees to be used toward the publication of his first volume of *Śrīmad-Bhāgavatam.*

Bhaktivedanta Swami would read and correct the proofs himself, and even as the first volume was being printed, he was still writing the last chapters. When the proofs were ready at O.K. Press, he would pick them up, return to his room at Chippiwada, correct the proofs, and then return them.

In 1962, he was walking daily back and forth between his room and the printers. The neighborhood was a blend of commercial business and tenement life, with children playing in the hazardous street. Bhaktivedanta Swami, a gentle-looking yet determined figure, would walk amidst this milieu. As he moved past the tenements, the tile sellers, the grain sellers, the sweet shops, and the printers, overhead would be electrical wires, pigeons, and the clotheslines from the tenement balconies. Finally he would arrive at O.K. Press, directly across from a small mosque. He would come to deliver the corrected proofs and to anxiously oversee the printing.

When the printing was completed, Bhaktivedanta Swami went out to sell his books, much as he had done with his *Back to Godhead* newspaper. He soon obtained favorable reviews of the work from Hanuman Prasad Poddar and from the renowned Hindu philosopher Dr. Radhakrishnan. The prestigious *Adyar Library Bulletin* gave a full review, noting "the editor's vast and deep study of the subject." His scholarly Godbrothers also wrote their appreciations. He even managed to secure an order for eighteen copies from the U.S. Embassy, to be distributed in America through the Library of Congress. Institutional sales were brisk, but then sales slowed. As the only agent, Bhaktivedanta Swami was spending hours daily just to sell a few copies. Also, he was entirely responsible for raising funds for the next volume. In the meantime, he continued translating and writing the purports. But at the present rate, with sales so slow, he would not be able to complete the work in his lifetime.

Bhaktivedanta Swami sent copies to leading politicians and received favorable reviews from Sri Biswanath Das, governor of Uttar Pradesh, and Dr. Zakir Hussain, the vice-president of India. He also received a personal interview with Dr. Hussain, and a few months later got the opportunity to meet the prime minister, Lal Bahadur Shastri.

This was a formal occasion in the garden of the Parliament Building, where the prime minister, surrounded by his aides, received the elderly sadhu. Bhaktivedanta Swami, looking scholarly in his spectacles, stepped forward and introduced himself and his book, *Śrīmad-Bhāgavatam*. As he handed the prime minister a copy of Volume One, a photographer snapped a photo of the author and the prime minister smiling over the book.

The next day, Bhaktivedanta Swami wrote to Prime Minister Shastri. Soon he received a reply, personally signed by the prime minister:

> Dear Swamiji, Many thanks for your letter. I am indeed grateful to you for presenting a copy of "Srimad Bhagwatam" to me. I do realise that you are doing valuable work. It would be good idea if the libraries in the Government Institutions purchase copies of this book.

Using favorable reviews as advertisements, Bhaktivedanta Swami visited prospective donors as he tried to raise funds for further volumes. Finally, with his manuscript in hand and with money to print it, he again entered the printing world—purchasing paper, correcting proofs, and keeping the printer on schedule so that each book would be finished on time. Thus, by his persistence, he who had almost no money of his own managed to publish his third large hardbound volume within a little more than two years.

At this rate, with his respect in the scholarly world increasing, Bhaktivedanta Swami might soon become a recognized figure amongst his countrymen. But he had his vision set on the West. And with the third volume now printed, he felt he was at last prepared. He was sixty-nine, and he would have to start soon. It had been more than forty years since Śrīla Bhaktisiddhānta Sarasvatī had first asked a young householder in Calcutta to preach Kṛṣṇa consciousness in the West. At first the young Abhay Charan had thought it impossible. The obstacle of family responsibilities, however, was now gone, and he was free to travel West, although penniless.

With most difficulties removed, travel fare and certain items of government permission remained as the last serious restrictions. Then, rather suddenly in 1965, the final impediments were removed one after another.

In Vṛndāvana Bhaktivedanta Swami met Mr. Agarwal, a Mathura businessman, and mentioned to him in passing, as he did to almost everyone he met, that he wanted to go to the West. Although Mr. Agarwal had known Bhaktivedanta Swami for only a few minutes, he volunteered to try to get him a sponsor in America by asking his son Gopal, an engineer in Pennsylvania, to send back a sponsorship form. When Mr. Agarwal volunteered to help in this way, Bhaktivedanta Swami urged him to please do so.

Bhaktivedanta Swami returned to Delhi, pursuing the usual avenues of bookselling, looking for whatever opportunity might arise. One day, to his surprise, he was contacted by the Ministry of External Affairs and informed that his No Objection certificate for traveling to the U.S. was ready. Since he had not instigated any proceedings for leaving the country, he had to inquire from the ministry about what had happened. They showed him the Statutory Declaration Form signed by Mr. Gopal Agarwal of Butler, Pennsylvania; Mr. Agarwal solemnly declared that he would bear the expenses of Bhaktivedanta Swami during his stay in the U.S.

Now Bhaktivedanta Swami had a sponsor. But he still needed a passport, visa, P-form, and travel fare. The passport was simple. Now, with passport and sponsorship papers, Bhaktivedanta Swami went to Bombay, not to sell books or raise funds for printing, but to seek assistance in getting to America. He approached Sumati Morarji, the head of the Scindia Steamship Line, who had helped him with a large donation for printing Volume Two of *Śrīmad-Bhāgavatam.* He showed his sponsorship papers to her secretary, Mr. Choksi, who was impressed and went to Mrs. Morarji on his behalf.

"The swami from Vṛndāvana is back," he told her. "He has published his book on your donation. He has a sponsor, and he wants to go to America. He wants you to send him on a Scindia ship." Mrs. Morarji said no, the Swamiji was too old to go to the United States and expect to accomplish anything. Mr. Choksi conveyed to him Mrs. Morarji's words, but Bhaktivedanta Swami listened disapprovingly. She wanted him to stay in India and complete *Śrīmad-Bhāgavatam.* Why go to the United States? she had argued. Finish the job here.

But Bhaktivedanta Swami was fixed on going. He told Mr. Choksi to convince Mrs. Morarji and even coached him on what to say: "I find this gentleman very inspired to go to the States and preach Lord Kṛṣṇa's message to the people there. . . ." But when Mr. Choksi told Mrs. Morarji she again said no; the Swami was not healthy. Besides, people in America were not so cooperative, and they would probably not listen to him.

Exasperated with Mr. Choksi's ineffectiveness, Bhaktivedanta Swami demanded a personal interview. It was granted, and a gray-haired but determined Bhaktivedanta Swami presented his emphatic request: "Please give me one ticket."

Sumati Morarji was concerned: "Swamiji. You are so

old—you are taking this responsibility. Do you think it is all right?"

"No," he reassured her, lifting his hand as if to reassure a doubting daughter. "It is all right."

"But do you know what my secretaries think? They say, 'Swamiji is going to die there.' "

Bhaktivedanta Swami made a face as if to dismiss a foolish rumor. Again he insisted that she give him a ticket. "All right," she said. "Get your P-form, and I will make an arrangement to send you by our ship." Bhaktivedanta Swami smiled brilliantly and happily left her offices, past her amazed and skeptical clerks.

Following Mrs. Morarji's instructions, the secretary made final arrangements. Since Bhaktivedanta Swami had no warm clothes, Mr. Choksi took him to buy a wool jacket and other woolen clothes. At Bhaktivedanta Swami's request, Mr. Choksi printed five hundred copies of a small pamphlet containing the eight verses written by Lord Caitanya and an advertisement for *Śrīmad-Bhāgavatam.*

Mrs. Morarji scheduled a place for him on one of her ships, the *Jaladuta,* which was sailing from Calcutta on August 13. She had made certain that he would travel on a ship whose captain understood the needs of a vegetarian and a *brāhmaṇa,* and she told the *Jaladuta's* captain, Arun Pandia, to carry extra vegetables and fruits for the Swami. Mr. Choksi spent the last two days with Bhaktivedanta Swami in Bombay picking up the pamphlets at the press, purchasing clothes, and driving him to the station to catch the train for Calcutta.

A few days before the *Jaladuta's* departure, Bhaktivedanta Swami arrived in Calcutta. Although he had lived much of his life in the city, he now had nowhere to stay. It was as he had written in his "Vṛndāvana-bhajana": "I have my wife, sons, daughters, grandsons, everything,/ but I have no money, so they are a fruitless glory." Although in this same city he had been so carefully nurtured as a child, those days were gone forever. He stayed with a slight acquaintance and, the day before his departure, traveled to nearby Māyāpur to visit the *samādhi* tomb of Śrīla Bhaktisiddhānta. Then he returned to Calcutta. He was ready.

He had only a suitcase, an umbrella, and a supply of dry cereal. He didn't know what he would find to eat in America; perhaps there would be only meat. If so, he was prepared to live on boiled potatoes and the cereal which he carried with him. His main baggage, several trunks of his books, was being handled separately by Scindia Cargo. Two hundred three-volume sets—the very thought of the books gave him confidence.

When the day came for him to leave, he needed that confidence. He was making a momentous break with his previous life, and he was old. He was going to an unknown and probably unwelcoming country. To be poor and unknown in India was one thing. Even in these Kali-yuga days when India's leaders were rejecting India's culture and imitating the West, it was still India; it was still the remains of the Vedic civilization. He had been able to see millionaires, governors, the prime minister—simply by showing up at their doors and waiting. A sannyasi was respected; *Śrīmad-Bhāgavatam* was respected.

In America, however, it would be different. He would be no one, a foreigner. And there was no tradition of sadhus, no temples, and no free *āśramas*. But when he thought of the books that he was bringing—transcendental knowledge in English—he became confident. When he met someone in America, he would give him a flyer: " 'Srimad-Bhagwatam,' India's Message of Peace and Goodwill."

It was August 13, just a few days before Janmāṣṭamī, the appearance day anniversary of Lord Kṛṣṇa. During these last years, he had been in Vṛndāvana for Janmāṣṭamī. Many Vṛndāvana residents would never leave there; they were old and at peace in Vṛndāvana. Bhaktivedanta Swami was also concerned that he might die away from Vṛndāvana. That was why all the Vaiṣṇava sadhus and widows had taken vows not to leave, even for Mathurā—because to die in Vṛndāvana was the perfection of life. And the Hindu tradition was that a sannyasi should not cross the ocean and go to the land of the *mlecchas*. But beyond all that was the desire of Bhaktisiddhānta Sarasvatī, and his desire was nondifferent from that of Lord Kṛṣṇa. And Lord Caitanya Mahāprabhu had predicted that the chanting of Hare Kṛṣṇa would be known in every town and village of the world.

He took a taxi down to the Calcutta port, carrying with him his luggage, an umbrella, and a Bengali copy of *Caitanya-caritāmṛta,* which he intended to read during the crossing. Somehow he would be able to cook on board. Or if not, he would starve—whatever Kṛṣṇa desired. He checked his essentials: passenger ticket, passport, visa, P-form, sponsor's address. Finally it was happening.

As Prabhupāda would often recall later, "With great difficulty I got out of the country! Some way or other by Kṛṣṇa's grace, I got out so that I could spread the Kṛṣṇa consciousness movement all over the world. Otherwise, to remain in India—it was not possible. I wanted to start a movement in India, but I was not at all encouraged."

The black cargo ship, small and weathered, was moored at dockside, a gangway leading from the dock to the ship's deck. Indian merchant sailors curiously eyed the elderly saffron-dressed sadhu as he spoke last words to his companion in the taxi then walked determinedly toward the boat.

Chapter One

Struggling Alone

Calcutta
August 13, 1965

The *Jaladuta* is a regular cargo carrier of the Scindia Steam Navigation Company, but there is a passenger cabin aboard. During the voyage from Calcutta to New York in August and September of 1965, the cabin was occupied by "Sri Abhoy Charanaravinda Bhaktivedanta Swami," whose age was listed as sixty nine and who was taken on board bearing "a complimentary ticket with food."

The *Jaladuta,* under the command of Captain Arun Pandia, whose wife was also on board, left at 9:00 a.m. on Friday, August 13. In his diary, Bhaktivedanta Swami noted: "The cabin is quite comfortable, thanks to Lord Sri Krishna for enlightening Sumati Morarji for all these arrangements. I am quite comfortable." But on the fourteenth he reported: "Seasickness, dizziness, vomiting—Bay of Bengal. Heavy rains. More sickness."

On the nineteenth, when the ship arrived at Colombo, Ceylon (now Sri Lanka), Bhaktivedanta Swami was able to get relief from his seasickness. The captain took him ashore, and he traveled around Colombo by car. Then the ship went on toward Cochin, on the west coast of India. Janmāṣṭamī, the appearance day of Lord Kṛṣṇa, fell on the twentieth of

August that year. Bhaktivedanta Swami took the opportunity to speak to the crew about the philosophy of Lord Kṛṣṇa, and he distributed *prasādam* he had cooked himself. August 21 was his seventieth birthday, observed (without ceremony) at sea. That same day the ship arrived at Cochin, and Bhaktivedanta Swami's trunks of *Śrīmad-Bhāgavatam* volumes, which had been shipped from Bombay, were loaded on board.

By the twenty-third the ship had put out to the Red Sea, where Bhaktivedanta Swami encountered great difficulty. He noted in his diary: "Rain, seasickness, dizziness, headache, no appetite, vomiting." In two days he suffered two heart attacks. He tolerated the difficulty, meditating on the purpose of his mission, but after two days of such violent attacks he thought that if another were to come he would certainly not survive.

On the night of the second day, he had a dream. Lord Kṛṣṇa, in His many forms, was rowing a boat, and He told Bhaktivedanta Swami that he should not fear, but should come along. Bhaktivedanta Swami felt assured of Lord Kṛṣṇa's protection, and the violent attacks did not recur.

The *Jaladuta* entered the Suez Canal on September 1 and stopped in Port Said on the second. Bhaktivedanta Swami visited the city with the captain and said that he liked it. By the sixth he had recovered a little from his illness and was eating regularly again for the first time, having cooked his own *kicharī* and *purīs*. He reported in his diary that his strength renewed little by little.

> Friday, September 10
>
> Today the ship is plying very smoothly. I feel today better. But I am feeling separation from Sri Vrindaban and my Lords Sri Govinda, Gopinath, Radha Damodar. The only solace is Sri Chaitanya Charitamrita in which I am tasting the nectarine of Lord Chaitanya's lila [pastimes]. I have left Bharatabhumi [India] just to execute the order of Sri Bhaktisiddhanta Saraswati in pursuance of Lord Chaitanya's order. I have no qualification, but I have taken up the risk just to carry out the order of His Divine Grace. I depend fully on Their mercy, so far away from Vrindaban.

The ocean voyage of 1965 was a calm one for the *Jaladuta*. Captain Pandia said that never in his entire career had he seen such a calm Atlantic crossing. Bhaktivedanta Swami replied that the calmness was Lord Kṛṣṇa's mercy. Mrs. Pandia asked Bhaktivedanta Swami to come back with them so that they might have another such crossing. Bhaktivedanta Swami wrote in his diary, "If the Atlantic would have shown its usual face, perhaps I would have died. But Lord Krishna has taken charge of the ship."

After a thirty-five-day journey from Calcutta, the *Jaladuta* reached Boston's Commonwealth Pier at 5:30 a.m. on September 17, 1965. The ship was to stop briefly in Boston before proceeding to New York City.

Bhaktivedanta Swami had to pass through U.S. Immigration and Customs in Boston. His visa allowed him a two-month stay, and an official stamped it to indicate his expected date of departure. Captain Pandia invited Bhaktivedanta Swami to take a walk into Boston, where the captain intended to do some shopping. They walked across a footbridge into a busy commercial area with old churches, warehouses, office buildings, bars, tawdry book shops, nightclubs, and restaurants. Bhaktivedanta Swami briefly observed the city, but the most significant thing about his short stay in Boston, aside from the fact that he had now set foot in America, was that at Commonwealth Pier he wrote a Bengali poem, entitled "Mārkiṇe Bhāgavata-dharma" ("Teaching Kṛṣṇa Consciousness in America"). Some of the verses he wrote on board the ship that day are as follows:

> My dear Lord Kṛṣṇa, You are so kind upon this useless soul, but I do not know why You have brought me here. Now You can do whatever You like with me.
>
> But I guess You have some business here, otherwise why would You bring me to this terrible place?
>
> Most of the population here is covered by the material modes of ignorance and passion. Absorbed in material life they think themselves very happy and satisfied, and therefore they have no taste for the transcendental message of Vāsudeva [Kṛṣṇa]. I do not know how they will be able to understand it.
>
> But I know that Your causeless mercy can make everything

possible, because You are the most expert mystic.

How will they understand the mellows of devotional service? O Lord, I am simply praying for Your mercy so that I will be able to convince them about Your message.

All living entities have come under the control of the illusory energy by Your will, and therefore, if You like, by Your will they can also be released from the clutches of illusion.

I wish that You may deliver them. Therefore if You so desire their deliverance, then only will they be able to understand Your message. . . .

How will I make them understand this message of Kṛṣṇa consciousness? I am very unfortunate, unqualified, and the most fallen. Therefore I am seeking Your benediction so that I can convince them, for I am powerless to do so on my own.

Somehow or other, O Lord, You have brought me here to speak about You. Now, my Lord, it is up to You to make me a success or failure, as You like.

O spiritual master of all the worlds! I can simply repeat Your message. So if You like You can make my power of speaking suitable for their understanding.

Only by Your causeless mercy will my words become pure. I am sure that when this transcendental message penetrates their hearts, they will certainly feel gladdened and thus become liberated from all unhappy conditions of life.

O Lord, I am just like a puppet in Your hands. So if You have brought me here to dance, then make me dance, make me dance, O Lord, make me dance as You like.

I have no devotion, nor do I have any knowledge, but I have strong faith in the holy name of Kṛṣṇa. I have been designated as Bhaktivedanta, and now, if You like, You can fulfill the real purport of Bhaktivedanta.

Signed—the most unfortunate, insignificant beggar,
A. C. Bhaktivedanta Swami,
On board the ship *Jaladuta*, Commonwealth Pier,
Boston, Massachusetts, U.S.A.
Dated 18th September 1965

On the nineteenth of September the *Jaladuta* sailed into New York Harbor and docked at a Brooklyn pier, at Seventeenth Street. Bhaktivedanta Swami saw the awesome Manhattan skyline, the Empire State Building, and, like millions of visitors and immigrants in the past, the Statue of Liberty.

Bhaktivedanta Swami was dressed appropriately for a resident of Vṛndāvana. He wore *kaṇṭhi-mālā* (neck beads) and a simple cotton dhoti, and he carried *japa-mālā* (chanting beads) and an old *cādar,* or shawl. His complexion was golden, his head shaven except for the *śikhā* in the back, his forehead decorated with the whitish Vaiṣṇava *tilaka.* He wore pointed white rubber slippers, not uncommon for sadhus in India. But who in New York had ever seen or dreamed of anyone appearing like this Vaiṣṇava? He was possibly the first Vaiṣṇava sannyasi to arrive in New York with uncompromised appearance. Of course, New Yorkers have an expertise in not giving much attention to any kind of strange new arrival.

Bhaktivedanta Swami was on his own. He had a sponsor, Mr. Agarwal, somewhere in Pennsylvania. Surely someone would be here to greet him. Although he had little idea of what to do as he walked off the ship onto the pier—"I did not know whether to turn left or right"—he passed through the dockside formalities and was met by a representative from Traveler's Aid, sent by the Agarwals in Butler, Pennsylvania.

Carrying only forty rupees cash, which he himself called "a few hours' spending in New York," and an additional twenty dollars he had collected from selling three volumes of the *Bhāgavatam* to Captain Pandia, Bhaktivedanta Swami, with umbrella and suitcase in hand, and still escorted by the Traveler's Aid representative, set out for the Port Authority Bus Terminal to arrange for his trip to Butler.

* * *

Bhaktivedanta Swami arrived at the Agarwals' home in Butler, Pennsylvania, at 4:00 a.m., and Gopal invited him to sleep on the couch. Their place, a townhouse apartment, consisted of a small living room, a dining room, a kitchenette, two upstairs bedrooms, and a bath. Here they lived with their two young children. Gopal Agarwal and his American wife, Sally, had lived in Butler for a few years now and felt themselves established in a good social circle. Since their apartment had so little space, they decided that it would be better if the Swami took a room at the YMCA and came to visit them during the day. Of course, living space wasn't the real difficulty—it was *him*. How would he fit into the Butler atmosphere?

Sally: *It was quite an intellectual group that we were in, and they were fascinated by him. They hardly knew what to ask him. They didn't know enough. This was just like a dream out of a book. Who would expect to meet a swami in someone's living room in Butler, Pennsylvania? It was just really tremendous. In the middle of middle-class America. My parents came from quite a distance to see him. We knew a lot of people in Pittsburgh, and they came up. This was a very unusual thing, having him here. But the real interest shown in him was only as a curiosity.*

He had a typewriter, which was one of his few possessions, and an umbrella. That was one of the things that caused a sensation, that he always carried an umbrella. And it was a little chilly and he was balding, so he always wore this hat that someone had made for him, like a swimming cap. It was a kind of sensation. And he was so brilliant that when he saw someone twice, he knew who they were—he remembered. He was a brilliant man. Or if he met them in our apartment and saw them in a car, he would remember their name, and he would wave and say their name. He was a brilliant man. All the people liked him. They were amazed at how intelligent he was. The thing that got them was the way he remembered their name. And his humorous way. He looked so serious all the time, but he was a very humorous person. He was forbidding in his looks, but he was very charming.

He was the easiest guest I have had in my life, because when I couldn't spend time with him he chanted, and I knew he was perfectly happy. When I couldn't talk to him, he chanted. He was so easy, though, because I knew he was never bored. I never felt any pressure or tension about having him. He was so easy that when I had to take care of the children he would just chant. It was so great. When I had to do things, he would just be happy chanting. He was a very good guest. When the people would come, they were always smoking cigarettes, but he would say, "Pay no attention. Think nothing of it." That's what he said. "Think nothing of it." Because he knew we were different. I didn't smoke in front of him. I knew I wasn't supposed to smoke in front of Gopal's father, so I sort of considered him the same. He didn't make any problems for anybody.

On September 22 a feature article appeared in the *Butler Eagle:* "In Fluent English, Devotee of Hindu Cult Explains Commission to Visit the West." A photographer had come to the Agarwals' apartment and had taken a picture of Bhaktivedanta Swami standing in the living room holding an open volume of *Śrīmad-Bhāgavatam.* The caption read, "Ambassador of Bhakti-yoga."

The article began:

> A slight brown man in faded orange drapes and wearing white bathing shoes stepped out of a compact car yesterday and into the Butler YMCA to attend a meeting. He is A. C. Bhaktivedanta Swamiji, a messenger from India to the peoples of the West.

The article referred to *Śrīmad-Bhāgavatam* as "Biblical literature" and to Bhaktivedanta Swami as "the learned teacher." It continued:

> "My mission is to revive a people's God consciousness," says the Swamiji. "God is the Father of all living beings, in thousands of different forms," he explains. "Human life is a stage of perfection in evolution; if we miss the message, back we go through the process again," he believes. . . . Bhaktivedanta lives as a monk, and permits no woman to touch his food. On a six-week ocean voyage and at the Agarwal apartment in Butler he prepares his meals in a brass pan with separate levels for steaming rice, vegetables, and making "bread" at the same time. He is a strict vegetarian, and is permitted to drink only milk, "the miracle food for babies and old men," he noted. . . . If Americans would give more attention to their spiritual life, they would be much happier, he says.

Sally: *When he cooked he used only one burner. The bottom-level pot created the steam. He had the* dāl *on the bottom, and it created the steam to cook many other vegetables. So for about a week he was cooking this great big lunch, which was ready about eleven-thirty, and Gopal always came home for lunch about twelve. I used to serve Gopal a sandwich, and then he would go back to work. But it didn't take me long to realize that the food the Swami was cooking we'd enjoy too, so he started cooking that noon meal for all of us. Oh, and we enjoyed it so much.*

Our fun was to show him what we knew of America. And he had never seen such things. It was such fun to take him to the supermarket. He loved opening the package of okra or frozen beans, and he didn't have to clean them and cut them and do all those things. He opened the freezer every day and just chose his items. It was fun to watch him. He sat on the couch while I swept with the vacuum cleaner, and he was so interested in that, and we talked for a long time about that. He was so interesting.

So every day he'd have this big feast, and everything was great fun. We really enjoyed it. I would help him cut the things. He would spice it, and we would laugh. He was the most enjoyable man, most enjoyable man. I really felt like a sort of daughter to him, even in such a short time. Like he was my father-in-law, but I really felt very close to him. He enjoyed everything. I liked him. I thought he was tremendous.

Our boy Brij was six or seven months old when the Swami came—and the Indians love boys. The Swami liked Brij. He was there when Brij first stood. The first time Brij made the attempt and actually succeeded, the Swami stood up and clapped. It was a celebration. Another time, our baby teethed on the Swami's shoes. I thought, "Oh, those shoes. They've been all over India, and my kid is chewing on them." You know how a mother would feel.

Almost every night he used to sit in the next-door neighbor's backyard. We sat out there sometimes with him, or we stayed in the living room. One time something happened with our little girl, Pamela, who was only three years old. I used to take her to Sunday school, and she learned about Jesus in Sunday school. Then when she would see Swamiji with his robes on and everything, she called him Swami Jesus. And this one time when it first dawned on us what she was saying, she called him Swami Jesus, and the Swami smiled and said, "And a little child shall lead them." It was so funny.

Bhaktivedanta Swami spoke to various groups in the community, including the Lions Club. He also gave a talk at the Y and at St. Fidelis Seminary College in Herman, Pennsylvania, and he spoke regularly to guests at the Agarwal home. He saw that the prospects for preaching to the Americans were good, but he felt he would need support from India.

At any rate, after spending one month in Butler he now had one month left in America. So he decided to go to New York City and try to preach there, before his time was up. But first he wanted to visit Philadelphia, where he had arranged a meeting with a Sanskrit professor, Dr. Norman Brown, at the University of Pennsylvania.

As a sannyasi, Bhaktivedanta Swami was used to picking up and leaving one place for another. As a mendicant preacher, he had no remorse about leaving behind the quiet life of the Butler YMCA. And he had no attachment for the domestic habitat where he would cook and talk with Sally Agarwal about vacuum cleaners, frozen food, and American ways.

But his stay in Butler had been helpful. He had gotten first-hand experience of American life, and he had gained confidence that his health was strong and his message communicable. He was glad to see that America had the necessary ingredients for his Indian vegetarian diet and that the people could understand his English. He had learned that casual one-time lectures here and there were of limited value, and that although there would be opposition from the established religions, people individually were very much interested in what he had to say.

On October 18, he left Butler, via Philadelphia, for New York City.

Sally: *After a month I really loved the Swami. I felt protective in a way, and he wanted to go to Philadelphia. But I couldn't imagine—I told him—I could not imagine him going to Philadelphia for two days. He was going to speak there, and then to New York. But he knew no one in New York. If the thing didn't pan out in Philadelphia, he was just going to New York, and then there was no one. I just couldn't imagine. It made me sick.*

I remember the night he was leaving, about two in the morning. I remember sitting there as long as he could wait before Gopal took him to Pittsburgh to get on that bus. Gopal got a handful of change, and I remember telling him how to put the money in the slot so that he could take a bath at the bus station—because he was supposed to take a bath a few times a day. And Gopal told him how to do that, and told him about the automats in New York. He told him what he could eat and what he couldn't eat, and he gave him these coins in a sock, and that's all he left us with.

* * *

Bhaktivedanta Swami knew no one in New York City, but he had a contact: Dr. Ramamurti Mishra. He had written Dr. Mishra from Butler, enclosing a letter of introduction that a friend had given him in Bombay. He had also phoned Dr. Mishra, who welcomed Bhaktivedanta Swami to join him in New York.

At the Port Authority Bus Terminal, a student of Dr. Mishra's met him as he arrived from Philadelphia and escorted him directly to an Indian festival in the city. There Bhaktivedanta Swami met Dr. Mishra as well as Ravi Shankar and his brother, the dancer Udai Shankar. Bhaktivedanta Swami then accompanied Dr. Mishra to his apartment at 33 Riverside Drive, beside the Hudson River. The apartment was on the fourteenth floor and had large windows overlooking the river. Dr. Mishra gave Bhaktivedanta Swami a room to himself. Dr. Mishra was a dramatic, showy personality, given to flashing glances and expressive gestures with his hands. He regularly used words like "lovely" and "beautiful."

Presenting an artfully polished image of what a guru should be, he was what some New Yorkers referred to as "an uptown swami." Although a sannyasi, he did not wear the traditional saffron dhoti and *kurtā*, but instead wore tailored Nehru jackets and white slacks. His complexion was dark, whereas Bhaktivedanta Swami's was golden, and he had thick, black hair. At forty-four, he was young enough to be Bhaktivedanta Swami's son. Dr. Mishra had been suffering from bad health when Bhaktivedanta Swami came into his life, and Bhaktivedanta Swami's arrival seemed the perfect medicine.

Ramamurti Mishra: *His Holiness Prabhupāda Bhaktivedanta Gosvāmījī really knocked me down with love. He was really an incarnation of love. My body had become a skeleton, and he really brought me back to life—his cooking, and especially his love and his devotion to Lord Kṛṣṇa. I was very lazy in the matter of cooking, but he would get up and have ready.*

Dr. Mishra appreciated that Bhaktivedanta Swami, cooking with the precision of a chemist, would prepare many dishes, and that he had a gusto for eating.

Ramamurti Mishra: *It was not bread he gave me—he gave me* prasādam. *This was life, and he saved my life. At that time I was not sure I would live, but his habit to eat on time, whether I was hungry or not—that I very much liked. He'd get up and say, "All right, this is* bhagavat-prasādam," *and I would say, "All right."*

Bhaktivedanta Swami would sometimes discuss with Dr. Mishra the aim of his visit to America, expressing his spiritual master's vision of establishing Kṛṣṇa consciousness in the West. He requested Dr. Mishra to help him, but Dr. Mishra would always refer to his own teaching work, which kept him very busy, and to his plans for leaving the country soon. After a few weeks, when it became inconvenient to maintain Bhaktivedanta Swami at the apartment, Dr. Mishra shifted him to his hatha yoga studio on the fifth floor of 100 West Seventy-second Street, near Central Park. The large studio was located in the center of the building and included an office and an adjoining private room, where Bhaktivedanta Swami stayed. It had no windows.

Philosophically at complete odds with Bhaktivedanta Swami, Dr. Mishra accepted the Absolute Truth in the impersonal feature (or Brahman) to be supreme. Bhaktivedanta Swami stressed the supremacy of the personal feature (or Bhagavān), following the Vedic theistic philosophy that the most complete understanding of the Absolute Truth is personal. The *Bhagavad-gītā* says that the impersonal Brahman is subordinate to Bhagavān and is an emanation from Him just as the sunshine is an emanation from the sun planet. This conclusion had been taught by the leading traditional *ācāryas* of ancient India, such as Rāmānuja and Madhva. Dr. Mishra, on the other hand, followed Śaṅkara, who taught that the impersonal presence of the Absolute Truth is all in all and that the Personality of Godhead is ultimately an illusion. Whereas Bhaktivedanta Swami's theistic philosophy accepted the individual spiritual self (*ātmā*) as an eternal servant of the supreme spiritual being (Bhagavān), Dr. Mishra's view accepted the spiritual self as not an individual. Rather, his idea was that since each person is identical with God, the Supreme Brahman, there is no need to worship God outside oneself. As Dr. Mishra would put it, "Everything is one."

Bhaktivedanta Swami challenged: If each of us is actually the Supreme, then why is this "Supreme" suffering and struggling in the material world? Dr. Mishra would counter that the Supreme is only temporarily covered by illusion and that through hatha yoga and meditation one would become enlightened, understanding, "It is all the Supreme." Bhaktivedanta Swami would again challenge: But if the Supreme could be covered by illusion, then illusion would be greater than God, greater than the Supreme.

Bhaktivedanta Swami considered Dr. Mishra a "Māyāvādī" because of his inadvertent acceptance that maya, illusion, is greater than the Absolute Truth. For Bhaktivedanta Swami not only was the impersonal philosophy unpalatable, it was an insult to the Personality of Godhead.

A mendicant, Bhaktivedanta Swami was temporarily dependent on the good will of his Māyāvādī acquaintance, with whom he regularly ate and conversed and from whom he accepted shelter. But what a great inconvenience it was! He had come to America to speak purely and boldly about Kṛṣṇa, but he was being restricted. In Butler he had been confined by his hosts' middle-class sensibilities; now he was silenced in a different way. He was treated with kindness, but he was considered a threat. Dr. Mishra could not allow his students to hear the exclusive praise of Lord Kṛṣṇa as the Supreme Personality of Godhead.

On November 8, Bhaktivedanta Swami wrote to his Godbrother Tīrtha Mahārāja, who had become the president of the Gaudiya Math, to remind him that their spiritual master, Śrīla Bhaktisiddhānta Sarasvatī, had a strong desire to open preaching centers in the Western countries. Śrīla Bhaktisiddhānta had several times attempted to do this by sending sannyasis to England and other European countries, but, Bhaktivedanta Swami noted, "without any tangible results." Bhaktivedanta Swami pointed out that there were certain Māyāvādī groups who had buildings but were not attracting many followers. But he had talked with Swami Nikhilananda of the Ramakrishna Mission, who had given the opinion that the Americans would be inclined to bhakti yoga.

If the leaders of the Gaudiya Math would consider opening their own branch in New York, Bhaktivedanta Swami would be willing to manage it. But without their own house, he reported, they could not conduct a mission in the city. Bhaktivedanta Swami wrote that they could open centers in many cities throughout the country if his Godbrothers would cooperate. He repeatedly made the point that although other groups did not have the genuine spiritual philosophy of India, they were buying many buildings. The Gaudiya Math, however, had nothing.

Three weeks later Bhaktivedanta Swami received Tīrtha Mahārāja's reply. Bhaktivedanta Swami had explained his hopes and plans for staying in America, but he had stressed that his Godbrothers would have to give him their vote of confidence as well as some tangible support. His Godbrothers had not been working cooperatively. Each leader was interested more in maintaining his own building than in working with the others to spread the teachings of Lord Caitanya around the world. So how would it be possible for them to share Bhaktivedanta Swami's vision of establishing a branch in New York City? They would see it as his separate attempt. Yet despite the unlikely odds, he appealed to their missionary spirit and reminded them of the desires of their spiritual master, Śrīla Bhaktisiddhānta Sarasvatī Ṭhākura. Their Guru Mahārāja wanted Kṛṣṇa consciousness to be spread in the West. But when Bhaktivedanta Swami finally got Tīrtha Mahārāja's reply, he found it unfavorable. His Godbrother did not argue against his attempting something in New York, but he politely said that the Gaudiya Math's funds could not be used for such a proposal.

* * *

In his solitary wanderings in Manhattan, Bhaktivedanta Swami made acquaintances with a number of local people. There was Mr. Ruben, a Turkish Jew, who worked as a subway conductor. Mr. Ruben met Bhaktivedanta Swami on a park bench and, being a sociable fellow and a world traveler, sat and talked with the Indian holy man.

Mr. Ruben: *He seemed to know that he would have temples filled up with devotees. He would look out and say, "I am not a poor man, I am rich. There are temples and books, they are existing, they are there, but time is separating us from them." He always mentioned "we" and spoke about the one who sent him, his spiritual master. He didn't know people at that time, but he said, "I am never alone." He always looked like a lonely man to me. That's what made me think of him like a holy man, Elijah, who always went out alone. I don't believe he had any followers.*

On January 30 the East Coast was hit by severe blizzards. Seven inches of snow fell on the city, with winds up to fifty miles an hour. The City of New York offered warm rooms and meals for people living in tenements without heat. JFK Airport was closed, as were train lines and roadways into the city. For the second time within eight days, a state of emergency was declared because of snow.

As a lone individual, Bhaktivedanta Swami could not do anything about the snow emergency or about the international warfare he read about in the headlines—he saw these as mere symptoms of the Age of Kali. Always there would be misery in the material world. But if he could bring Rādhā and Kṛṣṇa to a building in New York . . . Nothing was impossible for the Supreme Lord. Even in the midst of Kali-yuga a golden age could appear, and people could get relief. If Americans could take to Kṛṣṇa consciousness, the whole world would follow. Seeing through the eyes of the scriptures, Bhaktivedanta Swami pushed on through the blizzard and pursued the thin trail for support of his Kṛṣṇa consciousness mission.

Seeing him from a distance—a tiny figure walking Manhattan's streets and avenues among many other tiny figures, a foreigner whose visa had almost run out—we come upon only the external appearance of Bhaktivedanta Swami. These days of struggle were real enough and very difficult, but his transcendental consciousness was always predominant. He was not living in Manhattan consciousness, but was absorbed in dependence upon Kṛṣṇa, just as when on the *Jaladuta* he had suffered his heart attacks, his reading of *Caitanya-caritāmṛta* had supplied him "the nectarine" of life.

He had already succeeded. Certainly he wanted to provide Rādhā-Kṛṣṇa a temple in New York, but his success was that he was remembering Kṛṣṇa, even in New York City in the winter of 1965–66, whether the world recognized him or not. Not a day went by when he did not work on Kṛṣṇa's book, *Śrīmad-Bhāgavatam*. And not a day went by when he did not offer food to Kṛṣṇa and speak on Kṛṣṇa's philosophy of *Bhagavad-gītā*.

Lord Kṛṣṇa says in *Bhagavad-gītā*, "For one who sees Me everywhere and sees everything in Me, I am never lost to him, and he is never lost to Me." And Kṛṣṇa assures His pure devotees that, "My devotee will never be vanquished." There was never any doubt about this for Bhaktivedanta Swami. The only question was whether Americans would take notice of the pure devotee in their midst. At this point it seemed that no one was going to take him seriously.

On February 15, Bhaktivedanta Swami moved from Dr. Mishra's yoga studio to a room of his own two floors down—room 307—in the same building. According to Dr. Mishra, he moved so he could have his own place, independent of the Mishra Yoga Society.

Room 307, however, was never meant for use as a residence or *āśrama* or lecture hall. It was only a small, narrow office without furniture or telephone. Its door held a large pane of frosted glass, the kind common in old offices; above the door was a glass-paned transom. Bhaktivedanta Swami placed his blankets on the floor before his metal footlocker, which now became a makeshift desk where he wrote. He slept on the floor. There were no facilities here for cooking or even for bathing, so daily he had to walk to Dr. Mishra's apartment.

When Bhaktivedanta Swami had lived in room 501 at Dr. Mishra's *yoga-āśrama,* Dr. Mishra had financed his needs. But now he was on his own, and whatever he could raise by selling his books, he would have to use for his daily maintenance and for the monthly rent of seventy-two dollars. He noted that for a little powdered chili the West End Superette charged twenty-five cents, ten times what he would have paid in India. He had no guaranteed income, his expenses had increased, and his physical comforts had reduced. But at least he had his own place. Now he was free to preach as he liked.

He had come to America to speak about Kṛṣṇa, and even from the beginning he had found the opportunity to do so, whether at an informal get-together in the Agarwals' living room or before a formal gathering at the Butler Lions Club, Dr. Norman Brown's Sanskrit class, or Dr. Mishra's Yoga Society. But he did not attach much importance to lecturing where the people who gathered would hear him only once. This was the main reason he wanted his own building in New York: so that people could come *regularly,* chant Hare Kṛṣṇa, take *prasādam* in his company, and hear him speak from *Bhagavad-gītā* and *Śrīmad-Bhāgavatam.*

Moving out of the yoga studio into the small office downstairs gave Bhaktivedanta Swami what he was looking for—his own place—but not even euphemistically could that place be called a temple. His name was on the door; anyone seeking him there could find him. But who would come there? By its opulence and beauty, a temple was supposed to attract people to Kṛṣṇa. But room 307 was just the opposite: it was bare poverty. Even a person interested in spiritual topics would find it uncomfortable to sit on the rugless floor of a room shaped like a narrow railroad car.

One of Dr. Mishra's students had donated a reel-to-reel tape recorder, and Bhaktivedanta Swami recorded some of his solitary *bhajanas,* which he sang to his own accompaniment of hand cymbals. He also recorded a long philosophical essay, *Introduction to Gītopaniṣad.* "Even if no one attends," Śrīla Bhaktisiddhānta Sarasvatī had told him, "you can go on chanting to the four walls." But since he was now free to speak his message in the new situation God had provided, he decided to lecture three evenings a week (Monday, Wednesday, and Friday) to whoever would come.

His first audiences consisted mainly of people who had heard about him or met him at Dr. Mishra's yoga studio. And despite the poverty of his room, the meetings became a source of new life for him.

The Paradox, at 64 East Seventh Street on the Lower East Side, was a restaurant dedicated to the philosophy of Georges Ohsawa and the macrobiotic diet. It was a storefront below street level with small dining tables placed around the candlelit room. The food was inexpensive and well reputed. Tea was served free, as much as you liked. More than just a restaurant, the Paradox was a center for spiritual and cultural interests, a meeting place reminiscent of certain Greenwich Village or Paris cafes in the 1920s. A person could spend the whole day at the Paradox without buying anything, and no one would complain. The crowd at the Paradox was a mystical congregation, interested in teachings from the East. When news of the new swami uptown at Dr. Mishra's reached the Paradox, the word spread quickly.

Harvey Cohen, a free-lance artist, and Bill Epstein, a worker at the Paradox, were friends. After Harvey had been to Bhaktivedanta Swami's place at Dr. Mishra's yoga studio a few times, he came by the Paradox and began to describe all about the new swami to Bill and other friends.

Bill Epstein was a dashing, romantic person, with long, wavy dark hair and a beard. He was good-looking and effervescent and took upon himself a role of informing people at the restaurant of the city's spiritual news. Once he became interested in the new swami, he made him an ongoing topic of conversation at the restaurant.

The new group from the Paradox was young and hip, in contrast to the older, more conservative uptown people who had been attending Bhaktivedanta Swami's classes. In those days, it was still unusual to see a young man with long hair and a beard, and when such people started coming to the Swami's meetings on the West side, some of the older people were alarmed. As one of them noted: "Swami Bhaktivedanta began to pick up another kind of people. He picked them up at the Bowery or in some attics. And they came with funny hats and gray blankets wrapped around themselves, and they startled me."

David Allen, a twenty-one-year-old seeker who came up from the Paradox, had just moved to the city, optimistically attracted by what he had read about experimentation with drugs. He saw the old group as "a kind of fussbudgety group of older women on the West Side" listening to the Swami's lectures.

David: *We weren't known as hippies then. But it was strange for the people who had originally been attracted to him. It was different for them to relate to this new group. I think most of the teachers from India up to that time had older followers, and sometimes wealthy widows would provide a source of income. But Swamiji changed right away to the younger, poorer group of people. The next thing that happened was that Bill Epstein and others began talking about how it would be better for the Swami to come downtown to the Lower East Side. Things were really happening down there, and somehow they weren't happening uptown. People downtown really needed him. Downtown was right, and it was ripe. There was life down there. There was a lot of energy going around.*

Someone broke into room 307 while Bhaktivedanta Swami was out and stole his typewriter and tape recorder. When Bhaktivedanta Swami returned to the building, the janitor informed him of the theft: an unknown burglar had broken the transom glass, climbed through, taken the valuables, and escaped. As Bhaktivedanta Swami listened, he became convinced that the janitor himself was the culprit. Of course, he couldn't prove it, so he accepted the loss with disappointment.

Bhaktivedanta Swami had lost his spirit for living in room 307. Although some friends had offered replacements for his old typewriter and tape recorder, what would prevent the janitor from stealing again? Harvey Cohen and Bill Epstein had advised him to relocate downtown and had assured him of a more interested following among the young people there. It had been an attractive proposal.

Now Harvey was going to leave New York and go to California, and he offered his loft on the Bowery for the Swami to share with David Allen. Bhaktivedanta Swami accepted.

As he was preparing to leave his Seventy-second Street address, an acquaintance, an electrician who worked in the building, came to warn him. The Bowery was no place for a gentleman, he protested. It was the most corrupt place in the world. The Swami's things had been stolen from room 307, but moving to the Bowery was not the answer. Bhaktivedanta Swami, however, was undaunted.

Bhaktivedanta Swami lived on the Bowery, sitting under a small light, while hundreds of derelicts also sat under hundreds of naked lights on the same city block. He had no more fixed income than the derelicts, nor any greater security of a fixed residence, yet his consciousness was different. He was translating *Śrīmad-Bhāgavatam* into English, speaking to the world through his Bhaktivedanta purports. His duty, whether on the fourteenth floor of a Riverside Drive apartment building or in a corner of a Bowery loft, was to establish Kṛṣṇa consciousness as the prime necessity for all humanity. He went on with his translating and with his constant vision of a Kṛṣṇa temple in New York City. Because his consciousness was absorbed in Kṛṣṇa's universal mission, he did not depend on his surroundings for shelter. Home for him was not a matter of bricks and wood but of taking shelter of Kṛṣṇa in every circumstance. As Bhaktivedanta Swami had said to his friends uptown, "Everywhere is my home," whereas without Kṛṣṇa's shelter the whole world would be a desolate place.

News of the Swami's move to the Bowery loft spread, mostly by word of mouth at the Paradox restaurant, and people began to come by in the evening to chant with him. The musical *kīrtanas* were especially popular on the Bowery, since the Swami's new congregation consisted mostly of local musicians and artists, who responded more to the transcendental music than to the philosophy. Every morning he would hold class on *Śrīmad-Bhāgavatam*, attended by David Allen, a boy named Robert Nelson, and one other boy, and occasionally he would teach cooking to whoever was interested. He was usually available for personal talks with any inquiring visitors or with his new roommate.

Bhaktivedanta Swami held his evening meetings on Mondays, Wednesdays, and Fridays, just as he had uptown. The loft was out of the way for most of his acquaintances, and it was on the Bowery. A cluster of sleeping derelicts regularly blocked the street-level entrance, and visitors would find as many as half a dozen bums to step over before climbing the four flights of stairs. But it was something new; you could go and sit with a group of hip people and watch the swami lead *kīrtana*. The room was dimly lit, and Bhaktivedanta Swami would burn incense. Many casual visitors came and went.

Almost all of Bhaktivedanta Swami's Bowery friends were musicians or friends of musicians. They were into music—music, drugs, women, and spiritual meditation. Because Bhaktivedanta Swami's presentation of the Hare Kṛṣṇa mantra was both musical and meditative, they were automatically interested.

For the Bowery crowd, sound was spirit and spirit was sound, in a merging of music and meditation. But for Bhaktivedanta Swami, music without the name of God wasn't meditation; it was sense gratification, or at most a kind of stylized impersonal meditation. But he was glad to see the musicians coming to play along in his *kīrtanas,* to hear him, and to chant responsively. Some, having stayed up all night playing somewhere on their instruments, would come by in the morning and sing with Swami. He did not dissuade them from their focus on sound; rather, he gave them sound. In the *Vedas,* sound is said to be the first element of material creation; the source of sound is God, and God is eternally a person. Bhaktivedanta Swami's emphasis was on getting people to chant God's personal, transcendental name. Whether they took to it as jazz, folk music, rock, or Indian meditation made no difference, as long as they began to chant Hare Kṛṣṇa.

Despite the bad neighborhood where Bhaktivedanta Swami lived and walked, he was rarely disturbed. Often he would find several Bowery bums asleep or unconscious at his door, and he would have to step over them. Sometimes a drunk, simply out of his inability to maneuver, would bump into him, or a derelict would mutter something unintelligible or laugh at him. The more sober ones would stand and gesture courteously, ushering the Swami into or out of his door at 94 Bowery. He would pass among them, acknowledging their good manners as they cleared his path.

Certainly few of the Bowery men and others who saw him on his walks knew much about the small, elderly Indian sadhu, dressed in saffron and carrying an umbrella and a brown grocery sack.

* * *

Sitting cross-legged, his back to the shelf with its assortment of potted plants, whitish *cādar* wrapped in wide, loose folds across his body, Bhaktivedanta Swami looked grave, almost sorrowful. The picture and an accompanying article appeared in a June issue of *The Village Voice.* The article read:

> The meeting of the mystical West and practical East comes alive in the curious contrast between A. C. Bhaktivedanta Swami and his American disciples. The swami, a cultivated

> man of seventy with a distinguished education, is here for a year to preach his gospel of peace, good will, nearness to God, and, more practically, to raise money for his American church. . . . Like his teachings, the swami is sensible and direct. His main teaching is that mankind may come closer to God by reciting His holy name.
>
> Despite the fact that the swami came to America to seek out the root of godless materialism—a disease, he said, that has already enveloped India—he is a realistic man. "If there is any place on earth with money to build a temple, it is here." The swami wishes to found in America an International Society for Krishna Consciousness, which will be open for anyone—including women.

The article had been written by a reporter named Howard Smith. He had first heard of the Swami by a phone call from a contact who had told him of an interesting holy man from India living in a loft in the Bowery. "Go there any time," Howard's contact had told him. "He's always there. I think you will find it fascinating. I believe he's about to start a major religious movement."

Howard Smith: *So I went down there and went upstairs into this very funky artist's loft. In the back of the loft I noticed a little curtain—an Indian madras type of curtain—and so I decided I'd peer into that area. I looked in, and there was Swami Bhaktivedanta sitting cross-legged in saffron garments, with the markings on his forehead and nose, and his hand in the bead bag. Even though he looked like the real thing, he seemed approachable, and I said, "Hello," and he looked up. I said, "Swami Bhaktivedanta?" and he said, "Yes." I said, "I am Howard Smith."*

Then we sat and talked, and I liked him a lot right away. I mean I'd met a lot of other swamis, and I didn't like them too much. And I don't think it's fair to lump them all together and say, "Those swamis in India." Because he was very, very basic, and that's what I seemed to like about him. He not only made me feel at ease, but he seemed very open and honest—like he asked my advice on things. He was very new in the country.

I thought his ideas stood a good chance of taking hold, because he seemed so practical. His head didn't seem in the clouds. He wasn't talking mysticism every third word. I guess that is where his soul was at, but that isn't where his normal conversational consciousness was at.

Then he said several people had told him that the Voice *would be a very good place to be written up and that basically it would reach the kind of people who already perhaps had a leaning or interest in what he was preaching. And I said that I thought he was correct. He asked me if I had read any books or knew anything about Indian culture, and I said no, I didn't really. We talked a little, and he explained to me that he had these books in English that he had already translated in India. And he handed those to me and said, "If you want more background, you can read these."*

It was obvious to me that I was not talking to some fellow who had just decided that he had seen God and was going to tell people about it. He seemed to be an educated man, much more than myself, actually. And I liked his humbleness. I just plain liked the guy.

He explained everything I wanted to know—the significance of what he was wearing, the mark on his forehead, the bead bag. And I liked all his explanations. Everything was very practical. Then he talked about temples all over the world, and he said, "Well, we have got a long way to go. But I am very patient."

Bhaktivedanta Swami had hope for what the *Voice* article had referred to as "his American church." There was life in his lectures and *kīrtanas,* and at least he was acquiring a small, regular following. But from India there was no hope. He had been regularly corresponding with Sumati Morarji, his Godbrothers, and the Indian Central Government, but their replies had not been encouraging.

If Kṛṣṇa consciousness were ever to take hold in America, it would have to be without assistance from the Indian government or Indian financiers. Kṛṣṇa was revealing His plan to Bhaktivedanta Swami in a different way. He would have to turn all his energy toward the young men and women coming to him in his Bowery loft. He wrote Sumati Morarji:

> I am now trying to incorporate one corporation of the local friends and admirers under the name of International Society for Krishna Consciousness, incorporated.

Of all his friends and admirers, Bhaktivedanta Swami gave his roommate, David Allen, the most personal attention and training. He felt he was giving David a special chance to become America's first genuine Vaiṣṇava. Bhaktivedanta Swami would eventually return to India, and he wanted to take David to Vṛndāvana. He could show him temple worship and train him for future preaching in the West.

"I am very glad to say," Bhaktivedanta Swami said one evening in his lecture, "that our Mr. David says sometimes, 'Swamiji, I want to increase my spiritual life *immediately.*' " Bhaktivedanta Swami laughed as he imitated David's urgency. " 'Take patience, take patience,' I tell him. 'It will be done, of course. When you have got such desire, God will help you. He is within you. He is simply trying to see how sincere you are. Then He will give you all opportunities to increase your spiritual life.' "

At first David and the Swami lived together peacefully in the large hall, the Swami working concentratedly on his side of the partition, David ranging throughout the large, open space. David, however, insisted on taking marijuana, LSD, and amphetamines, and the Swami had no choice but to tolerate. Several times he told David that drugs and hallucinations would not help his spiritual life, but David would look distracted. He was becoming estranged from the Swami.

Bhaktivedanta Swami, however, had a plan to use the loft as a temple—to transform it into New York's first temple of Rādhā and Kṛṣṇa—and he wanted David's cooperation. Although the neighborhood was one of the most miserable in the world, Bhaktivedanta Swami talked of bringing Deities from Jaipur or Vṛndāvana and starting temple worship, even on the Bowery. He thought David might help. After all, they were roommates, so there could be no question of David's not cooperating; but he would have to give up his bad habits.

Bhaktivedanta Swami was trying to help David, but David was too disturbed. He was headed for disaster, and so were Bhaktivedanta Swami's plans for the loft. Sometimes, even not under the influence of a drug, David would pace around the loft. Other times he appeared to be deep in thought. One day, on a dose of LSD, he went completely crazy. As one of the Swami's visitors, Carl Yeargens, put it, "He just flipped out, and the Swami had to deal with a crazy man." Things had been leading up to this—"he was a crazy kid who always took too much"—but the real madness happened suddenly.

Bhaktivedanta Swami was working peacefully at his typewriter when David "freaked out." David started moaning and pacing around the large, open area of the loft. Then he began yelling, howling, and running all around. He went back to where the Swami was. Suddenly, Bhaktivedanta Swami found himself face to face not with David—nice David, whom he was going to take to India to show the *brāhmaṇas* in Vṛndāvana—but a drugged, wild-eyed stranger, a madman.

Bhaktivedanta Swami tried to speak to him—"What is the matter?"—but David had nothing to say. There was no particular disagreement. Just madness. . . .

Bhaktivedanta Swami moved quickly down the four flights of stairs. He had not stopped to gather up any of his belongings or even to decide where he would go or whether he would return. There had been no time to consider anything. He had taken quite a shock, and now he was leaving the arena of David's madness. The usual group of bums was sitting in the doorway, and with their customary flourish of courtesy they allowed him to pass. They were used to the elderly swami's coming in and out, going shopping and returning, and they didn't bother him. But he was not going shopping today. Where was he going? He didn't know. He had come onto the street without knowing where he would go.

He wasn't going back to the loft—that was for sure. But where could he go? The pigeons flew from roof to roof. Traffic rumbled by, and the ever-present bums loitered about, getting drunker on cheap, poisonous alcohol. Although Bhaktivedanta Swami's home had suddenly become an insane terror, the street at its door was also a hellish, dangerous place. He was shaken. He could call Dr. Mishra's, and they might take him in. But that chapter of his life was over, and he had gone on to something better. He had his own classes, young people chanting and hearing. Was it all over now? After nine months in America, he had finally gotten a good response to his preaching and *kīrtana*. He couldn't just quit now.

A. C. Bhaktivedanta Swami Mahārāja, whom everyone knew and respected in Vṛndāvana as a distinguished scholar and devotee, who had an open invitation to see the vice-president of India and many other notables, now had to face starkly that he had not one friend of stature in the United States. Suddenly he was as homeless as any derelict on the street. In fact many of them, with their long-time berths in flophouses, were more secure than he. They were ruined, but settled. The Bowery could be a hell if you weren't on a very purposeful errand—going directly to the store, or back to your place. It was no place to stand wondering where will you live or is there a friend you can turn to. He wasn't on his way to Chinatown to shop, nor was he taking a little stroll, soon to return to the shelter of the loft. If he couldn't go to the loft, he had no place.

How difficult it was becoming to preach in America amid these crazy people! He had written prophetically in his poem the day he had arrived in Boston Harbor, "My dear Lord, I do not know why You have brought me here. Now You can do with me whatever You like. But I guess You have some business here, otherwise why would You bring me to this terrible place?" What about his scheduled classes? What about David; should he go back and try to talk with the boy? This had been David's first fit of violence, but there had been other tense moments. David had a habit of leaving the soap on the floor of the shower stall, and Bhaktivedanta Swami had asked him not to, because it was a hazard. But David wouldn't listen. Bhaktivedanta Swami had continued to remind him, and one day David had gotten angry and shouted at him. But there was no real enmity. Even today's incident had not been a matter of personal differences—the boy was a victim.

Bhaktivedanta Swami walked quickly. He had free passage on the Scindia Line. He could go home to Vṛndāvana. But his spiritual master had ordered him to come here. "By the strong desire of Sri Srimad Bhaktisiddhanta Sarasvati Thakura," he had written while crossing the Atlantic, "the holy name of Lord Gauranga will spread throughout all the countries of the Western world." Before nightfall he would have to find some place to stay, a way to keep up the momentum of his preaching. This is what it meant to be working without government sponsorship, without the support of any religious organization, without a patron. It meant being vulnerable and insecure.

Bhaktivedanta Swami faced the crisis as a test from Kṛṣṇa. The instruction of *Bhagavad-gītā* was to depend on Kṛṣṇa for protection: "In all activities just depend upon Me and work always under My protection. In such devotional service be fully conscious of Me. . . . You will pass over all the obstacles of conditional life by My grace."

He decided to phone Carl Yeargens, one of his regular comers at the evening meetings, and ask him to help. Hearing the Swami's voice on the phone—it was an emergency!—Carl at once agreed that the Swami could move in with him and his wife, Eva. Their place was close by, on Centre Street, five blocks west of Bowery near Chinatown. Carl would be right over.

* * *

When a week had passed and Carl and his friends had not found the Swami a suitable place, Bhaktivedanta Swami suggested that he and Carl take a walk up to Michael Grant's place and ask him to help. Mike, a young musician living on the Bowery, had been coming to the Swami's meetings and had shown inquisitiveness into the teachings. He was resourceful and would probably like to help.

As Mike listened to the Swami's story he felt obligated. So

the next day he went to *The Village Voice,* got the first newspaper off the press, looked through the classified ads until he found a suitable prospect, and phoned the landlord. It was a storefront on Second Avenue, and an agent, a Mr. Gardiner, agreed to meet Mike there. Carl and the Swami also agreed to come.

Mr. Gardiner and Mike were the first to arrive. Mike noted the unusual, hand-painted sign—Matchless Gifts—above the front window. It was a holdover, Mr. Gardiner explained, from when the place had been a nostalgic-gift shop. Mike proceeded to describe the Swami as a spiritual leader from India, an important author, and a Sanskrit scholar. The rental agent seemed receptive. As soon as the Swami and Carl arrived and everyone had been congenially introduced, Mr. Gardiner showed them the small storefront. The Swami, Carl, and Mike carefully considered its possibilities. It was empty, plain, and dark—the electricity had not been turned on—and it needed repainting. It would be good for meetings, but not for the Swami's residence. But at $125 a month it seemed promising. Then Mr. Gardiner revealed a small, second-floor apartment just across the rear courtyard, directly behind the storefront. Another $71 a month and the Swami could live there, although first Mr. Gardiner would have to repaint it. The total rent would come to $196, and Carl, Mike, and the others would pitch in.

Bhaktivedanta Swami had the idea of making Mr. Gardiner the first official trustee of his fledgling Kṛṣṇa consciousness society. During their conversation he presented Mr. Gardiner with a three-volume set of his *Śrīmad-Bhāgavatam,* and inside the front cover he wrote a personal dedication and then signed it, "A. C. Bhaktivedanta Swami." Mr. Gardiner felt flattered and honored to receive these books from their author himself. He agreed to become a trustee of the new society for Kṛṣṇa consciousness, and so pay the Society twenty dollars a month.

Mr. Gardiner took a week to paint the apartment. Meanwhile, Mike arranged for the electricity and water to be turned on and had a phone installed, and he and Carl raised the first month's rent among their friends. When everything was ready, Mike gave the Swami a call at Carl's.

Now it was time to move the Swami into his new place. A few friends who were on hand accompanied the Swami over to the Bowery loft. Maybe they weren't prepared to become his surrendered disciples, but contributing toward the first month's rent and volunteering a few hours of work to help set up his place were exactly the kinds of things they could do very willingly.

At the loft, they all gathered up portions of the Swami's belongings, and then they started out on foot up Bowery. It was like a safari, a caravan of half a dozen men loaded with Swamiji's things. Michael carried the heavy Roberts reel-to-reel, and even the Swami carried two suitcases. They did everything so quickly that it wasn't until they were well on their way and Mike's arm began to ache that he realized, "Why didn't we bring a car?"

It was the end of June, and a hazy summer sun poured its heat down into the Bowery jungle. Starting and stopping, the strange safari, stretching for over a block, slowly trekked along. Swamiji struggled with his suitcases, past the seemingly unending row of restaurant supply shops and lamp stores between Grand, Broome, and Spring streets. Sometimes he paused and rested, setting his suitcases down. He was finally moving from the Bowery. His electrician friend on Seventy-second Street would have been relieved, although perhaps he would have disapproved of the Second Avenue address also. At least he was finished residing on Skid Row. He walked on, past the homeless men outside the Salvation Army shelter, past the open-door taverns, stopping at streetlights, standing alongside total strangers, keeping an eye on the progress of his procession of friends who struggled along behind him.

The Bowery artists and musicians saw him as "highly evolved." They felt that the spirit was moving him and were eager to help him set up his own place so that he could do his valuable spiritual thing and spread it to others. He was depending on them for help, yet they knew he was "on a higher level"; he was his own protector, or, as he said, God protected him.

The Swami and his young friends reached the corner of Bowery and Houston, turned right, and proceeded east. Gazing steadily ahead as he walked, he saw the southern end of Second Avenue, one block away. At Second Avenue he would turn left, walk just one block north across First Street, and arrive at his new home. As he passed the IND subway entrance, the storefront came into view—"Matchless Gifts." He gripped his suitcases and moved ahead. At Second Avenue and Houston he hurried through a break in the rapid traffic. He could see green trees holding their heads above the high courtyard wall, reaching up like overgrown weeds in the space between the front and rear buildings of his new address.

The streetside building housed his meeting hall, the rear building the apartment where he would live and translate. Adjoining the storefront building on its north side was a massive nine-story warehouse. The storefront structure was only six stories and seemed appended to the larger building like its diminutive child. On its southern side, Bhaktivedanta Swami's new temple showed a surface of plain cement and was free of any adjoining structure; there was only the spacious lot of the busy Mobil service station that bordered on First Street. As Bhaktivedanta Swami approached the storefront, he could see two small lanterns decorating the narrow doorway.

There was no certainty of what awaited him here. But already there had been good signs that these American young people, mad though they sometimes were, could actually take part in Lord Caitanya's *saṅkīrtana* movement. Perhaps this new address would be the place where he could actually get a footing with his International Society for Krishna Consciousness.

Chapter Two

Planting the Seed

Bhaktivedanta Swami's new neighborhood was not as rundown as the nearby Bowery, though it certainly was less than quaint. Right across from his storefront, a row of tombstones looked out from the somber, dimly lit display windows of Weitzner Brothers and Papper Memorials. North of Weitzner Brothers was Sam's Luncheonette. Next to Sam's stood an ancient four-story building marked A.I.R., then Ben J. Horowitz Monuments (more gravestones), and finally Schwartz's Funeral Home. On the next block at number 43 a worn canvas awning jutted out onto the sidewalk: Provenzano Lanza Funeral Home. Then there was Cosmos Parcels (importers) and a few blocks further uptown the prominent black-and-white signboard of the Village East Theater.

Up a block, but on the same side of the avenue as the storefront, was the Church of the Nativity, an old three-story building with new blue paint and a gold-colored cross on top. The six-story 26 Second Avenue, its face covered by a greenish fire escape, crouched against the massive nine-story Knickerbocker Fireproof Warehouse.

Second Avenue was a main traffic artery for east Manhattan, and the stoplight at the intersection of Houston and Second pumped a stream of delivery trucks, taxis, and private autos past Bhaktivedanta Swami's door. From early morning until night there would be cars zooming by, followed by the sound of brakes, the competitive tension of waiting bumper to bumper, the impetuous honking, then gears grinding, engines rumbling and revving, and again the zooming by. The traffic was distractingly heavy.

At 26 Second Avenue there were actually two storefronts. The one to the north was a coin laundry, and the one to the south had been a gift shop but was now vacant. Both had narrow entrances, large display windows, and dull paint. Beneath the Matchless Gifts sign was a window, six feet square, that a few weeks before had displayed matchboxes decorated with photos of movie stars of the thirties and forties. The sign—Matchless Gifts—was the only remaining momento of the nostalgic-gift shop that had recently moved out. Below the shop's window, a pair of iron doors in the sidewalk hid stone steps to the cellar and boiler room. The wide sidewalk had been laid down in sections of various shapes and sizes at different times in years past. Certain sections had cracked or caved in, and a fine dust with tiny sparkling shards of glass had collected in the cracks and depressions. A dull-black fire hydrant stood on the curb. Midway between the entrances to the two storefronts was the main entrance to number 26. This door opened into a foyer lined with mailboxes and intercoms, and then a locked door opened into a hallway leading to the stairs or back to the courtyard.

To the left of the gift shop's window was its front door, a dark wooden frame holding a full-length pane of glass. The door opened into the long, narrow storefront, which was now completely bare. Just inside, to the right of the door, a platform extending beneath the display window was just the proper height for a seat. At the far end of the bare, dingy room, two grimy-paned windows covered with bars opened into the courtyard. To the left of the left-hand window was a small sink, fixed to the outside of a very small toilet closet, whose door faced the front of the store. A door on the store's left wall connected to a hallway that led into the courtyard.

The courtyard was paved with concrete geometric sections and encircled with shrub gardens and tall trees. There was a picnic table, a cement birdbath, and a birdhouse on a pole, and near the center of the courtyard were two shrub gardens. The courtyard was bordered north and south by high walls, and front and back by the two tenements. The patch of sky above gave relief.

Overlooking the courtyard from the rear building of 26 Second Avenue was Bhaktivedanta Swami's second-floor apartment, where he would now live, work, and worship. With help from his Bowery friends, he had cleaned and settled into his new home. In the back room—his office—he had placed against one wall a thin cushion with an elephant-print cover and in front of the cushion his unpainted metal suitcase, which served as a desk. He had set his typewriter on the desk and his papers and books on either side. This became his work area. His manuscripts bundled in saffron cloth, his stock of *Śrīmad-Bhāgavatam*s, and his few personal effects he kept in the closet opposite his desk. On the wall above his sitting place he hung an Indian calendar print of Lord Kṛṣṇa. (Kṛṣṇa, as a youth, was playing on His flute with a cow close behind Him. Lord Kṛṣṇa was standing on the planet earth, which curved like the top of a small hill beneath His feet.) There were two windows on the east wall, and the dappled morning sunlight, filtering in through the fire escape, fell across the floor.

The next room was bare except for a fancy coffee table, which became Bhaktivedanta Swami's altar. Here he placed a framed picture of Lord Caitanya and His associates. On the wall he hung an Indian calendar print of four-armed Lord Viṣṇu and Ananta Śeṣa, the celestial snake. And, as in the Bowery loft, he put up a clothesline.

Both rooms were freshly painted, and the floors were clean hardwood parquet. The bathroom was clean and serviceable, as was the narrow, furnished kitchen. Bhaktivedanta Swami would sometimes stand by the kitchen window, gazing beyond the courtyard wall. He had moved here without any prospects of paying the next month's rent.

A few years before Bhaktivedanta Swami's arrival, a new kind of slum-dweller had appeared on the Lower East Side.

Although there have been many sociological and cultural analyses of this phenomenon, it remains ultimately inexplicable why they suddenly came, like a vast flock of birds swooping down or like animals in a great instinctual migration, and why after a few years they vanished.

At first the newcomers were mostly young artists, musicians, and intellectuals, similar to the hip crowd of Prabhupāda's Bowery days. Then came the young middle-class dropouts. Because living space was more available and rents were lower than in nearby Greenwich Village, they concentrated here on the Lower East Side, which in the parlance of the renting agents became known as the East Village. Many even came without finding a place to live and camped in the hallways of tenements. Drawn by cheap rent and the promise of Bohemian freedom, these young middle-class dropouts, the avant-garde of a nationwide youth movement soon to be known in the media as "hippies," wandered to the Lower East Side slums in living protest against America's good life of materialism.

As if responding to an instinctual call, younger teenage runaways joined the older hippies, and following the runaways came the police, counselors, social and welfare workers, youth hostels, and drug counseling centers. On St. Mark's Place a new hip commercialism sprang up, with head shops, poster shops, record shops, art galleries, and bookstores that carried everything from cigarette papers to hip clothes and psychedelic lighting.

The hippies journeyed to the Lower East Side in full conviction that this was the place to be, just as their immigrant predecessors had done. For the European immigrants of another age, New York Harbor had been the gateway to a land of riches and opportunity, as they at long last set their eyes on Manhattan's skyline and the Statue of Liberty. Now, in 1966, American youth thronged to New York City with hopes of their own and feasted on the vision of their newfound mystical land—the Lower East Side slums.

It was an uneasy coexistence, with hippies on one side and Puerto Ricans, Poles, and Ukrainians on the other. The established ethnic groups resented the newcomers, who didn't really *have* to live in the slums, whereas they themselves did. In fact, many of the young newcomers were descended from immigrant families that had struggled for generations to establish themselves as middle-class Americans. Nevertheless, the youth migration to the Lower East Side was just as real as the immigration of Puerto Ricans or Poles or Ukrainians had been, although the motives of course were different.

The hippies had turned from the suburban materialism of their parents, the inane happiness of TV and advertising—the ephemeral goals of middle-class America. They were disillusioned by parents, teachers, clergy, public leaders, and the media, dissatisfied with American policy in Vietnam, and allured by radical political ideologies that painted America as a cruel, selfish, exploitative giant who must now reform or die. And they were searching for real love, real peace, real existence, and real spiritual consciousness.

By the summer of Bhaktivedanta Swami's arrival at 26 Second Avenue, the first front in the great youth rebellion of the sixties had already entered the Lower East Side. Here they were free—free to live in simple poverty and express themselves through art, music, drugs, and sex. The talk was of spiritual searching. LSD and marijuana were the keys, opening new realms of awareness. Notions about Eastern cultures and Eastern religions were in vogue. Through drugs, yoga, brotherhood, or just by being free—somehow they would attain enlightenment. Everyone was supposed to keep an open mind and develop his own cosmic philosophy by direct experience and drug-expanded consciousness, blended with his own eclectic readings. And if their lives appeared aimless, at least they had dropped out of a pointless game where the player sells his soul for material goods and in this way supports a system that is already rotten.

So it was that in 1966, thousands of young people were walking the streets of the Lower East Side, not simply intoxicated or crazy (though often they were), but in search of life's ultimate answers, in complete disregard of "the establishment" and the day-to-day life pursued by millions of "straight" Americans.

That the prosperous land of America could breed so many

discontented youths surprised Bhaktivedanta Swami. Of course, it also further proved that material well-being, the hallmark of American life, couldn't make people happy. Bhaktivedanta Swami did not see the unhappiness around him in terms of the immediate social, political, economic, and cultural causes. Neither slum conditions nor youth rebellions were the all-important realities. These were mere symptoms of a universal unhappiness to which the only cure was Kṛṣṇa consciousness. He sympathized with the miseries of everyone, but he saw the universal solution.

Bhaktivedanta Swami had not made a study of the youth movement in America before moving to the Lower East Side. He had never even made specific plans to come here amid so many young people. But in the ten months since Calcutta, he had been moved by force of circumstances, or, as he understood it, "by Kṛṣṇa's will," from one place to another. On the order of his spiritual master he had come to America, and by Kṛṣṇa's will he had come to the Lower East Side. His mission here was the same as it had been on the Bowery or uptown or even in India. He was fixed in the order of his spiritual master and the Vedic view, a view that wasn't going to be influenced by the radical changes of the 1960s. Now if it so happened that these young people, because of some change in the American cultural climate, were to prove more receptive to him, then that would be welcome. And that would also be Kṛṣṇa's will.

Actually, because of the ominous influence of the Kali millennium, this was historically the worst of times for spiritual cultivation—hippie revolution or not. And Bhaktivedanta Swami was trying to transplant Vedic culture into a more alien ground than had any previous spiritual master. So he expected to find his work extremely difficult. Yet in this generally bad age, just prior to Bhaktivedanta Swami's arrival on the Lower East Side, tremors of dissatisfaction and revolt against the Kali-yuga culture itself began vibrating through American society, sending waves of young people to wander the streets of New York's Lower East Side in search of something beyond the ordinary life, looking for alternatives, seeking spiritual fulfillment. These young people, broken from their stereotyped materialistic backgrounds and drawn together now on New York's Lower East Side, were the ones who were by chance or destiny to become the congregation for Bhaktivedanta Swami's storefront offerings of *kīrtana* and spiritual guidance.

Bhaktivedanta Swami's arrival went unnoticed. The neighbors said someone new had taken the gift shop next to the laundry. There was a strange picture in the window now, but no one knew what to make of it. They didn't know what *Bhagavad-gītā* was, and the few who did thought, "Maybe a yoga bookstore or something." The Puerto Ricans in the neighborhood would look in the window at Harvey Cohen's painting of Lord Caitanya and His associates singing and dancing and then blankly walk away. The manager of the Mobil gas station next door couldn't care less who had moved in—it just didn't make any difference. The tombstone-sellers and undertakers across the street didn't care. And for the drivers of the countless cars and trucks that passed by, Swamiji's place didn't even exist. But there were young people around who had been intrigued with the painting, who went up to the window to read the little piece of paper. Some of them even knew about *Bhagavad-gītā*, although the painting of Lord Caitanya and the dancers didn't seem to fit. A few thought maybe they would attend Swami Bhaktivedanta's classes and check out the scene.

One July morning Howard Wheeler was hurrying from his apartment on Mott Street to a friend's apartment on Fifth Street, a quiet place where he hoped to find some peace. He walked up Mott Street to Houston, turned right and began to walk east, across Bowery, past the rushing traffic and stumbling derelicts, and towards Second Avenue.

Howard: *After crossing Bowery, just before Second Avenue, I saw Swamiji jauntily strolling down the sidewalk, his head held high in the air, his hand in the bead bag. He struck me like a famous actor in a very familiar movie. He seemed ageless. He was wearing the traditional saffron-colored robes of a sannyasi and quaint white shoes with points. Coming down Houston, he looked like the genie that popped out of Aladdin's lamp.*

Howard, age twenty-six, was a tall, large-bodied man with long, dark hair, a profuse beard, and black-framed eyeglasses. He was an instructor in English at Ohio State University and was fresh from a trip to India, where he had been looking for a true guru.

Bhaktivedanta Swami noticed Howard, and they both stopped simultaneously. Howard asked the first question that popped into his mind: "Are you from India?"

Bhaktivedanta Swami smiled. "Oh, yes, and you?"

Howard: *I told him no, but that I had just returned from India and was very interested in his country and the Hindu philosophy. He told me he had come from Calcutta and had been in New York almost ten months. His eyes were as fresh and cordial as a child's, and even standing before the trucks that roared and rumbled their way down Houston Street, he emanated a cool tranquillity that was unshakably established in something far beyond the great metropolis that roared around us.*

Howard never made it to his friend's place that day. He went back to his own apartment on Mott Street, to Keith and Wally, his roommates, and told them and everyone he knew about the guru who had inexplicably appeared within their midst. He told how he and the Swami had stood and talked together and how the Swami had mentioned his place nearby on Second Avenue, where he was planning to hold some classes.

Howard: *I walked around the corner with him. He pointed out a small storefront building between First and Second streets next door to a Mobil filling station. It had been a curiosity shop, and someone had painted the words* Matchless Gifts *over the window. At that time, I didn't realize how prophetic those words were. "This is a good area?" he asked me. I told him that I thought it was. I had no idea what he was going to offer at his "classes," but I knew that all my friends would be glad that an Indian swami was moving into the neighborhood.*

The word spread. Although it wasn't so easy now for Carl Yeargens and certain others to come up from the Bowery and

Chinatown—they had other things to do—Roy Dubois, a twenty-five-year-old writer for comic books, had visited the Swami on the Bowery, and when he heard about the Swami's new place, he wanted to drop by. James Greene and Bill Epstein had not forgotten the Swami, and they wanted to come. The Paradox restaurant was still a live connection and brought new interested people. And others, like Stephen Guarino, saw the Swami's sign in the window. Steve, age twenty-six, was a caseworker for the city's welfare department, and one day on his lunch break, as he was walking home from the welfare office at Fifth Street and Second Avenue, he saw the Swami's sign taped to the window. He had been reading a paperback *Gītā*, and he promised himself he would attend the Swami's class.

Howard had also noticed the little sign in the window that day as he had stood with the Swami before the storefront:

LECTURES IN BHAGAVAD-GITA
A. C. BHAKTIVEDANTA SWAMI
MONDAY, WEDNESDAY, AND FRIDAY
7:00 to 9:00 P.M.

"Will you bring your friends?" Prabhupāda had asked. "Yes," Howard had promised. "Monday evening."

* * *

The summer evening was warm, and in the storefront the back windows and front door were opened wide. Young men, several of them dressed in black denims and button-down sport shirts with broad, dull stripes, had left their worn sneakers by the front door and were now sitting on the floor. Most of them were from the Lower East Side; no one had had to go to great trouble to come here. The little room was barren. No pictures, no furniture, no rug, not even a chair. Only a few plain straw mats. A single bulb hung from the ceiling into the center of the room. It was seven o'clock, and about a dozen people had gathered, when Bhaktivedanta Swami suddenly opened a side door and entered the room.

He wasn't wearing a shirt, and the saffron cloth that draped his torso left his arms and some of his chest bare. His complexion was smooth golden brown, and as they watched him, his head shaven, his ears long-lobed, and his aspect grave, he seemed like pictures they had seen of the Buddha in meditation. He was old, yet erect in his posture, fresh and radiant. His forehead was decorated with the yellowish clay markings of the Vaiṣṇavas. Bhaktivedanta Swami recognized big, bearded Howard and smiled. "You have brought your friends?"

"Yes," Howard answered in his loud, resonant voice.

"Ah, very good."

Bhaktivedanta Swami stepped out of his white shoes, sat down on a thin mat, faced his congregation, and indicated they could all be seated. He distributed several pairs of brass cymbals and briefly demonstrated the rhythm: one . . . two . . . *three*. He began playing—a startling, ringing sound. He began singing: Hare Kṛṣṇa, Hare Kṛṣṇa, Kṛṣṇa Kṛṣṇa, Hare Hare/ Hare Rāma, Hare Rāma, Rāma Rāma, Hare Hare. Now it was the audience's turn. "Chant," he told them. Some already knew, gradually the others caught on, and after a few rounds, all were chanting together.

Most of these young men and the few young women present had at one time or another embarked on the psychedelic voyage in search of a new world of expanded consciousness. Boldly and recklessly, they had entered the turbulent, forbidden waters of LSD, peyote, and magic mushrooms. Heedless of warnings, they had risked everything and done it. Yet there was merit in their valor, their eagerness to find out the extra dimensions of the self, to get beyond ordinary existence—even if they didn't know what the beyond was or whether they would ever return to the comfort of the ordinary.

Nonetheless, whatever truth they had found, they remained unfulfilled, and whatever worlds they had reached, these young psychedelic voyagers had always returned to the Lower East Side. Now they were sampling the Hare Kṛṣṇa mantra.

When the *kīrtana* suddenly sprang up from the Swami's cymbals and sonorous voice, they immediately felt that it was going to be something far out. Here was another chance to "trip out," and willingly they began to flow with it. They would surrender their minds and explore the limits of the chanting for all it was worth. Most of them had already associated the mantra with the mystical *Upaniṣads* and *Gītā,* which had called out to them in words of mystery: "Eternal spirit . . . Negating illusion." But whatever it is, this Indian mantra, let it come, they thought. Let its waves carry us far and high. Let's take it, and let the effects come. Whatever the price, let it come. The chanting seemed simple and natural enough. It was sweet and wasn't going to harm anyone. It was, in its own way, far out.

As Bhaktivedanta Swami chanted in his own inner ecstasy, he observed his motley congregation. He was breaking ground in a new land now. As the hand cymbals rang, the lead-and-response of the Hare Kṛṣṇa mantra swelled, filling the evening. Some neighbors were annoyed. Puerto Rican children, enchanted, appeared at the door and window, looking. Twilight came.

Exotic it was, yet anyone could see that a swami was raising an ancient prayer in praise of God. This wasn't rock or jazz. He was a holy man, a swami, making a public religious demonstration. But the combination was strange: an old Indian swami chanting an ancient mantra with a storefront full of young American hippies singing along.

Bhaktivedanta Swami sang on, his shaven head held high and tilted, his body trembling slightly with emotion. Confidently, he led the mantra, absorbed in pure devotion, and they responded. More passersby were drawn to the front window and open door. Some jeered, but the chanting was too strong. Within the sound of the *kīrtana,* even the car horns were a faint staccato. The vibration of auto engines and the rumble of trucks continued, but in the distance now, unnoticed.

Gathered under the dim electric light in the bare room, the group chanted after their leader, growing gradually from a feeble, hesitant chorus to an approximate harmony of voices. They continued clapping and chanting, putting into it whatever they could, in hopes of discovering its secrets. This swami was not simply giving some five-minute sample demonstration. For the moment he was their leader, their guide in an unknown realm. Howard and Keith's little encounter with a *kīrtana* in Calcutta had left them outsiders. The chanting had never before come like this, right in the middle of the Lower East Side with a genuine swami leading them.

In their minds were psychedelic ambitions to see the face of God, fantasies and visions of Hindu teachings, and the presumption that "IT" was all impersonal light. Bhaktivedanta Swami had encountered a similar group on the Bowery, and he knew this group wasn't experiencing the mantra in the proper disciplined reverence and knowledge. But he let them chant in their own way. In time their submission to the spiritual sound, their purification, and their enlightenment and ecstasy in chanting and hearing Hare Kṛṣṇa would come.

He stopped the *kīrtana*. The chanting had swept back the world, but now the Lower East Side rushed in again. The children at the door began to chatter and laugh. Cars and trucks made their rumbling heard once more. And a voice shouted from a nearby apartment, demanding quiet. It was now past 7:30. Half an hour had elapsed.

* * *

His lecture is very basic and yet (for restless youth) heavily philosophical. Some can't take it, and they rise rudely upon hearing the Swami's first words, put on their shoes at the front door, and return to the street. Others have left as soon as they saw the singing was over. Still, this is his best group yet. A few of the Bowery congregation are present. The boys from Mott Street are here, and they're specifically looking for a guru. Many in the group have already read *Bhagavad-gītā*—and they're not too proud to hear and admit that they didn't understand it.

It's another hot and noisy July evening outside his door. Children are on summer vacation, and they stay out on the street until dark. Nearby, a big dog is barking—*"Rau! Rau! Rau!"*—the traffic creates constant rumbling, just outside the window little girls are shrieking, and all this makes lecturing difficult. Yet despite the distraction of children, traffic, and dogs, he wants the door open. If it is closed, he says, "Why is it closed? People may come in." He continues, undaunted, quoting Sanskrit, holding his audience, and developing his urgent message, while the relentless cacophony rivals his every word. . . .

"Rau! Rau! Rau!"

"Eeeeeeeek! Yaaaaaaaa!" Shrieking little girls disturb the whole block. In the distance a man shouts from his window: "Get outta here! Get outta here!"

Bhaktivedanta Swami: "Ask them not to make noise."

Roy (one of the boys in the temple): "The man is chasing the kids now."

Bhaktivedanta Swami: "Yes, yes, these children are making a disturbance. Ask them . . ."

Roy: "Yes, that's what . . . the man's chasing them right now."

Bhaktivedanta Swami: "They are making noises."

Roy: "Yes, he's chasing them now."

The man chases the children away, but they'll be back. You can't chase the children off the street—they live there. And the big dog never stops barking. And who can stop the cars? The cars are always there. Prabhupāda uses the cars to give an example: When a car momentarily comes into our vision on Second Avenue, we certainly don't think that it had no existence before we saw it or that it ceases to exist once it has passed from view; similarly, when Kṛṣṇa goes from this planet to another, it doesn't mean He no longer exists, although it may appear that way. Actually, He has only left our sight. Kṛṣṇa and His incarnations constantly appear and disappear on innumerable planets throughout the innumerable universes of the material creation.

The cars are always passing, roaring and rumbling through every word Bhaktivedanta Swami speaks. The door is open, and he is poised at the edge of a river of carbon monoxide, asphalt, rumbling tires, and constant waves of traffic. He has come a long way from the banks of his Yamunā in Vṛndāvana, where great saints and sages have gathered through the ages to discuss Kṛṣṇa consciousness. But his audience lives *here* amid this scene, so he has come here, beside Second Avenue's rushing river of traffic, to speak loudly the ageless message.

He is still stressing the same point: whatever you do in Kṛṣṇa consciousness, however little it may be, is eternally good for you. Yet now, more than uptown or on the Bowery, he is calling his hearers to take to Kṛṣṇa consciousness *fully* and become devotees. He assures them. . . .

"So, it doesn't matter what a person was doing before, what sinful activities. A person may not be perfect at first, but if he is engaged in service, then he will be purified."

Suddenly a Bowery derelict enters, whistling and drunkenly shouting. The audience remains seated, not knowing what to make of it.

Drunk: "How are ya? I'll be right back. I brought another thing."

Bhaktivedanta Swami: "Don't disturb. Sit down. We are talking seriously."

Drunk: "I'll put it up there. In a church? All right. I'll be right back."

The man is white-haired, with a short, grizzly beard and frowzy clothing. His odor reeks through the temple. But then he suddenly careens out the door and is gone.

Bhaktivedanta Swami chuckles softly and returns immediately to his lecture.

. . . But after five minutes the old derelict returns, announcing his entrance: "How are ya?" He is carrying something. He maneuvers his way through the group, straight to the back of the temple, where the Swami is sitting. He opens the toilet room door, puts two rolls of bathroom tissue inside, closes the door, and then turns to the sink, sits some paper towels on top of it and puts two more rolls of bathroom tissue and some more paper towels under the sink. He then stands and turns around toward the Swami and the audience. The Swami is looking at him and asks, "What is this?" The bum is silent now; he has done his work. The Swami begins to laugh, thanking his visitor, who is now moving toward the door: "Thank you. Thank you very much." The bum exits. "Just see," Bhaktivedanta Swami now addresses his congregation.

"It is a natural tendency to give some service. Just see, he is not in order, but he thought that 'Here is something. Let me give some service.' Just see how automatically it comes. This is natural."

The young men in the audience look at one another. This is really far out—first the chanting with the brass cymbals, the Swami looking like Buddha and talking about Kṛṣṇa and chanting, and now this crazy stuff with the bum. But the Swami stays cool, he's really cool, just sitting on the floor like he's not afraid of anything, just talking his philosophy about the soul and us becoming saints and even the old drunk becoming a saint!

After almost an hour, the dog still barks, and the kids still squeal. The Swami answers some questions and then starts another *kīrtana*. And the Lower East Side once again abates. The chanting begins: the brass cymbals, Bhaktivedanta Swami's voice carrying the melody, and the audience responding. It goes on for half an hour and then stops.

The audience sits before the Swami while a boy brings him an apple, a small wooden bowl, and a knife. As most of the audience still sits and watches, gauging the after-effects of the chanting as though it had been some new drug, the Swami cuts the apple in half, then in fourths, then in eighths, until there are many pieces. He takes one himself and asks one of the boys to pass the bowl around. The Swami holds back his head and deftly pops a slice of apple into his mouth, without touching his fingers to his lips. He chews a bit, ruminating, his lips closed.

The members of the congregation munch silently on little pieces of apple. They watch as the Swami stands, slips into his shoes, and exits through the side door.

* * *

"We shall call our society ISKCON." Bhaktivedanta Swami had laughed playfully when he had first coined the acronym.

He had initiated the legal work of incorporation that spring, while still living on the Bowery. But even before its legal beginning, he had been talking about his "International Society for Krishna Consciousness," and so it had appeared in letters to India and in *The Village Voice.* A friend had suggested a title that would sound more familiar to Westerners, "International Society for *God* Consciousness." But "God" was a vague term, whereas "Krishna" was exact and scientific; "God consciousness" was spiritually weaker, less personal. And if Westerners didn't know that Kṛṣṇa was God, then the International Society for *Krishna* Consciousness would tell them, by spreading His glories "in every town and village."

"Kṛṣṇa consciousness" was Bhaktivedanta Swami's own rendering of a phrase from Śrīla Rūpa Gosvāmī's *Padyāvalī,* written in the sixteenth century. *Kṛṣṇa-bhakti-rasa-bhāvita:* "to be absorbed in the mellow taste of executing devotional service to Kṛṣṇa."

The purposes stated within ISKCON's articles of incorporation reveal Bhaktivedanta Swami's thinking. They were seven points, similar to those given in the Prospectus for the League of Devotees he formed in Jhansi, India, in 1954. That attempt had been unsuccessful, yet his purposes remained unchanged.

Seven Purposes of the International Society for Krishna Consciousness:

(a) To systematically propagate spiritual knowledge to society at large and to educate all peoples in the techniques of spiritual life in order to check the imbalance of values in life and to achieve real unity and peace in the world.
(b) To propagate a consciousness of Krishna, as it is revealed in the *Bhagavad Gita* and *Srimad Bhagwatam.*
(c) To bring the members of the Society together with each other and nearer to Krishna, the prime entity, thus to develop the idea within the members, and humanity at large, that each soul is part and parcel of the quality of Godhead (Krishna).
(d) To teach and encourage the sankirtan movement, congregational chanting of the holy name of God as revealed in the teachings of Lord Sri Chaitanya Mahaprabhu.

(e) To erect for the members and for society at large, a holy place of transcendental pastimes, dedicated to the Personality of Krishna.
(f) To bring the members closer together for the purpose of teaching a simpler and more natural way of life.
(g) With a view towards achieving the aforementioned Purposes, to publish and distribute periodicals, magazines, books and other writings.

Regardless of what ISKCON's charter members thought of the society's purposes, Bhaktivedanta Swami saw them as imminent realities. As Mr. Ruben, the subway conductor who had met Bhaktivedanta Swami on a Manhattan park bench in 1965, had noted: "He seemed to know that he would have temples filled up with devotees. 'There are temples and books,' he said. 'They are existing, they are there, but the time is separating us from them.' "

Certainly none of his early followers who signed his articles of incorporation for ISKCON saw any immediate shape to the Swami's dream, yet these seven purposes were not simply theistic rhetoric invented to convince a few New York State government officials. Bhaktivedanta Swami meant to enact every item in the charter.

* * *

Because of the Swami's presence and the words that he spoke there and the *kīrtanas,* everyone was already referring to the storefront as "the temple." But still it was just a bare, squalid storefront. The inspiration to decorate the place came from the Mott Street boys.

Howard, Keith, and Wally devised a scheme to surprise the Swami when he came to the evening *kīrtana.* Wally removed the curtains from their apartment, took them to the laundromat (where they turned the water dark brown from filth), and then dyed them purple. The Mott Street apartment was decorated with posters, paintings, and large decorative silk hangings that Howard and Keith had brought back from India. The boys gathered up all their pictures, tapestries, incense burners, and other paraphernalia and took them, along with the purple curtains, to the storefront, where they began their day of decorating.

At the storefront the boys constructed a wooden platform for the Swami to sit on and covered it with old velvet cloth. Behind the platform, on the rear wall between the two windows to the courtyard, they hung the purple curtains, flanked by a pair of orange ones. Against one orange panel, just above the Swami's sitting place, they hung a large original painting of Rādhā and Kṛṣṇa, on a circular canvas, that a boy named James Greene had done. Bhaktivedanta Swami had commissioned James, giving him the dust jacket from his *Śrīmad-Bhāgavatam,* with its crude Indian drawing, as a model. The figures of Rādhā and Kṛṣṇa were somewhat abstract, but the Lower East Side critics who frequented the storefront hailed the work as a wonderful achievement.

Keith and Howard were less confident that the Swami would approve of their paintings and prints from India, so they hung them near the street side of the temple, away from the Swami's seat. One of these prints, well known in India, was of Hanumān carrying a mountain through the sky to Lord Rāmacandra. The boys had no idea what kind of being Hanumān was. They thought perhaps he was a cat, because of the shape of his upper lip. Then there was the picture of a male person with six arms—two arms, painted greenish, held a bow and arrow; another pair, bluish, held a flute; and the third pair, golden, held a stick and bowl.

By late afternoon they had covered the sitting platform, hung curtains, tacked up the decorative silks and prints and hung the paintings, and were decorating the dais with flowers and candlesticks. Someone brought a pillow for the Swami to sit on and a faded cushion from an overstuffed chair for a back rest.

In addition to the Mott Street cache, Robert Nelson, one of the Swami's friends from uptown, took one of his grandfather's Belgian-style Oriental rugs from his garage in the suburbs and brought it by subway to 26 Second Avenue. Even Raphael and Don, two hippies who seemed to be only interested in free food and a place to sleep, took part in the decorating.

The secret was well kept, and the boys waited to see the Swami's response. That night, when he walked in to begin the *kīrtana,* he looked at the newly decorated temple (there was even incense burning), and he raised his eyebrows in satisfaction. "You are advancing," he said as he looked around the room, smiling broadly. "Yes," he added, "this is Kṛṣṇa consciousness." His sudden, happy mood seemed almost like their reward for their earnest labors. He then stepped up onto the platform—while the boys held their breaths, hoping it would be sturdy—and he sat, looking out at the devotees and the decorations.

They had pleased him. But now he assumed a feature of extreme gravity, and though they knew he was certainly the same Swamiji, their titterings stuck in their throats, and their happy glances to each other suddenly abated in uncertainty and nervousness. As they regarded Swamiji's gravity, their joy of a few moments before suddenly seemed childish. As a cloud quickly covers the sun like a dark shade, the Swami changed his mood from jolly to grave—and they spontaneously resolved to become equally grave and sober. He picked up the *karatālas* and again smiled a ray of appreciation, and their hearts beamed back.

The temple was still a tiny storefront, with many hidden and unhidden cockroaches, tilted floor, and poor lighting. But because many of the decorations were from India, it had an authentic atmosphere, especially with Swamiji present on the dais. Now guests who entered were suddenly in a little Indian temple.

Bhaktivedanta Swami looked at his group of followers. He was moved by their offering him a seat of honor and their attempts at decorating Kṛṣṇa's storefront. To see a devotee make an offering to Kṛṣṇa was not new to him. But *this* was new. In New York, the seed of bhakti was growing, and naturally, as the gardener of that tender sprout, he was touched by Kṛṣṇa's mercy. Glancing at the pictures on the wall he said, "Tomorrow I will come look at the pictures and tell you which are good."

The next day, Bhaktivedanta Swami came down to appraise the new artwork on display. One framed watercolor painting was of a man playing a drum while a girl danced. "This one is all right," he said. But another painting of a woman was more mundane, and he said, "No, this painting is not so good." He walked to the back of the temple, followed anxiously by Howard, Keith, and Wally. When he came upon the painting of the six-armed person, he said, "Oh, this is very nice."

"Who is it?" Wally asked.

"This is Lord Caitanya," Swamiji replied.

"Why does He have six arms?"

"Because He showed Himself to be both Rāma and Kṛṣṇa. These are the arms of Rāma, and these are the arms of Kṛṣṇa."

"What are the other two arms?" Keith asked.

"Those are the arms of a sannyasi."

He went to the next picture. "This is also very nice."

"Who is it?" Howard asked.

"This is Hanumān."

"Is he a cat?"

"No," Swamiji replied. "He is a monkey."

Hanumān is glorified in the scripture *Rāmāyaṇa* as the valiant, faithful servant of Lord Rāmacandra. Millions of Indians worship the incarnation of Lord Rāma and His servitor Hanumān, whose exploits are perennially exhibited in theater, cinema, art, and temple worship. In not knowing who Hanumān was, the Mott Street boys were no less ignorant than the old ladies uptown who, when Bhaktivedanta Swami had asked whether any of them had seen a picture of Kṛṣṇa, had all stared blankly. The Lower East Side mystics didn't know Hanumān from a cat, and they had brought back from their hashish version of India a picture of Lord Caitanya Mahāprabhu without even knowing who He was. Yet there was an important difference between these boys and the ladies uptown: the boys were serving Swamiji and chanting Hare Kṛṣṇa. They were through with material life and the middle-class work-reward syndrome. Their hearts had awakened to

Swamiji's promise of expanded Kṛṣṇa consciousness, and they sensed in his personal company something exalted. Like the Bowery bum who had donated toilet paper during Bhaktivedanta Swami's lecture, the Lower East Side boys did not have their minds quite in order, and yet, as Bhaktivedanta Swami saw it, Kṛṣṇa was guiding them from within their hearts. Bhaktivedanta Swami knew they would change for the better by chanting and hearing about Kṛṣṇa.

*   *   *

The summer of 1966 moved into August, and Prabhupāda kept good health. For him these were happy days. New Yorkers complained of the summer heat waves, but this caused no inconvenience to one accustomed to the 100-degree-plus temperatures of Vṛndāvana's blazing summers. "It is like India," he said, as he went without a shirt, seeming relaxed and at home. He had thought that in America he would have to subsist on boiled potatoes (otherwise there would be nothing but meat), but here he was happily eating the same rice, *dāl*, and *capātīs*, and cooking on the same three-stacked cooker as in India. Work on the *Śrīmad-Bhāgavatam* had also gone on regularly since he had moved into the Second Avenue apartment. And now Kṛṣṇa was bringing these sincere young men who were cooking, typing, hearing him regularly, chanting Hare Kṛṣṇa, and asking for more.

Prabhupāda was still a solitary preacher, free to stay or go, writing his books in his own intimate relationship with Kṛṣṇa—quite independent of the boys in the storefront. But now he had taken the International Society for Krishna Consciousness as his spiritual child. The inquiring young men, some of whom had already been chanting steadily for over a month, were like stumbling spiritual infants, and he felt responsible for guiding them. They were beginning to consider him their spiritual master, trusting him to lead them into spiritual life. Although they were unable to immediately follow the multifarious rules that *brāhmaṇas* and Vaiṣṇavas in India followed, he was hopeful. According to Rūpa Gosvāmī the most important principle was that one should "somehow or other" become Kṛṣṇa conscious. People should chant Hare Kṛṣṇa and render devotional service. They should engage whatever they had in the service of Kṛṣṇa. And Prabhupāda was exercising this basic principle of Kṛṣṇa consciousness to the furthest limit the history of Vaiṣṇavism had ever seen.

Although he was engaging the boys in cooking and typing, Prabhupāda was not doing any less himself. Rather, for every sincere soul who came forward to ask for service, a hundred came who wanted not to serve but to challenge. Speaking to them, sometimes shouting and pounding his fists, Prabhupāda defended Kṛṣṇa against the Māyāvāda philosophy. This was also his service to Śrīla Bhaktisiddhānta Sarasvatī Ṭhākura. He had not come to America to retire. So with the passing of each new day came yet another confirmation that his work and his followers and his challengers would only increase.

How much he could do was up to Kṛṣṇa. "I am an old man," he said. "I may go away at any moment." But if he were to "go away" now, certainly Kṛṣṇa consciousness would also go away, because the Kṛṣṇa consciousness society was nothing but him: his figure leading the chanting while his head moved back and forth in small motions of ecstasy, his figure walking in and out of the temple through the courtyard or into the apartment, his person sitting down smilingly to discuss philosophy by the hour—he was the sole bearer and maintainer of the small, fragile, controlled atmosphere of Kṛṣṇa consciousness on New York's Lower East Side.

In the back room of his apartment Prabhupāda was usually alone, especially in the early morning hours—two, three, and four a.m.—when almost no one else was awake. In these early hours his room was silent, and he worked alone in the intimacy of his relationship with Kṛṣṇa. He would sit on the floor behind his suitcase-desk, worshiping Kṛṣṇa by typing the translations and purports of his *Śrīmad-Bhāgavatam*.

But this same back room was also used for meetings, and anyone who brought himself to knock on the Swami's door could enter and speak with him at any time, face to face. Prabhupāda would sit back from his typewriter and give his time to talking, listening, answering questions, sometimes arguing or joking. A visitor might sit alone with him for half an hour before someone else would knock and Swamiji would invite the newcomer to join them. New guests would come and others would go, but Swamiji stayed and sat and talked.

Generally, visits were formal—his guests would ask philosophical questions, and he would answer, much the same as after a lecture in the storefront. But occasionally some of the boys who were becoming serious followers would monopolize his time—especially on Tuesday, Thursday, Saturday, and Sunday nights, when there was no evening lecture in the temple. Often they would ask him personal questions: What was it like when he first came to New York? What about India? Did he have followers there? Were his family members devotees of Kṛṣṇa? What was his spiritual master like? And then he would talk in a different way—quieter, more intimate and humorous.

One night he told how he had met his spiritual master. He also told about his childhood in India, how he had begun his own chemical business, and how he had left home and in 1959 had taken sannyasa. The boys were interested, but so ignorant of the things the Swami was talking about that at the mention of a word like *mṛdaṅga* or sannyasa they would have to ask what it meant, and he would go on conversational tangents describing Indian spices, Indian drums, even Indian women. And whatever he spoke about, he would eventually shine upon it the light of the *śāstra*. He did not ration out such talk, but gave it out abundantly by the hour, day after day, as long as there was a real, live inquirer.

At noon the front room of Swamiji's apartment became a dining hall and in the evenings a place of intimate worship. Swamiji had kept the room, with its twelve-foot-square hardwood parquet floor, clean and bare; the solitary coffee table against the wall between the two courtyard windows was the only furniture. Daily at noon a dozen men were now taking lunch here with him. The meal was cooked by Keith, who spent the whole morning in the kitchen.

At first Keith had cooked only for the Swami. He had mastered the art of cooking *dāl,* rice, and *sabjī* in the Swami's three-tiered boiler, and usually there had been enough for one or two guests as well. But soon more guests had begun to gather, and Swamiji had told Keith to increase the quantity (abandoning the small three-tiered cooker) until he was cooking for a dozen hungry men. The boarders, Raphael and Don, though not so interested in Swamiji's talk, would arrive punctually each day for *prasādam,* usually with a friend or two who had wandered into the storefront. Steve would drop by from his job at the welfare office. The Mott Street group would come. And there were others.

The kitchen was stocked with standard Indian spices: fresh chilies, fresh ginger root, whole cumin seeds, turmeric, and asafetida. Keith mastered the basic cooking techniques and passed them on to his friend Chuck, who became his assistant. Some of the other boys would stand at the doorway of the narrow kitchenette to watch Keith, as one thick, pancakelike *capātī* after another inflated like a football over the open flame and then took its place in the steaming stack.

While the fine *bhasmatī* rice boiled to a moist, fluffy-white finish and the *sabjī* simmered, the noon cooking would climax with "the *chaunce.*" Keith prepared the *chaunce* exactly as Swamiji had shown him. Over the flame he set a metal cup, half-filled with clarified butter, and then put in cumin seeds. When the seeds turned almost black he added chilies, and as the chilies blackened, a choking smoke began to pour from the cup. Now the *chaunce* was ready. With his cook's tongs, Keith lifted the cup, its boiling, crackling mixture fuming like a sorcerer's kettle, and brought it to the edge of the pot of boiling *dāl.* He opened the tight cover slightly, dumped the boiling *chaunce* into the *dāl* with a flick of his wrist, and immediately replaced the lid. . . . POW! The meeting of the *chaunce* and *dāl* created an explosion, which was then greeted by cheers from the doorway, signifying that the cooking was now complete. This final operation was so volatile that it once blew the top of the pot to the ceiling with a loud smash, causing minor burns to Keith's hand. Some of the neighbors complained of acrid, penetrating fumes. But the devotees loved it.

When lunch was ready, Swamiji would wash his hands and mouth in the bathroom and come out into the front room, his soft, pink-bottomed feet always bare, his saffron dhoti reaching down to his ankles. He would stand by the coffee table, which held the picture of Lord Caitanya and His associates, while his own associates stood around him against the walls. Keith would bring in a big tray of *capātīs,* stacked by the dozens, and place it on the floor before the altar table along with pots of rice, *dāl,* and *sabjī.* Swamiji would then recite the Bengali prayer for offering food to the Lord, and all present would follow him by bowing down, knees and head to the floor, and approximating the Bengali prayer one word at a time. While the steam and mixed aromas drifted up like an offering of incense before the picture of Lord Caitanya, the Swami's followers bowed their heads to the wooden floor and mumbled the prayer.

Swamiji then sat with his friends, eating the same *prasādam* as they, with the addition of a banana and a metal bowl full of hot milk. He would slice the banana by pushing it downward against the edge of the bowl, letting the slices fall into the hot milk.

Bhaktivedanta Swami's open decree that everyone should eat as much *prasādam* as possible created a humorous mood and a family feeling. No one was allowed simply to sit, picking at his food, nibbling politely. They ate with a gusto Swamiji almost insisted upon. If he saw someone not eating heartily, he would call the person's name and smilingly protest, "Why are you not eating? Take *prasādam.*" And he would laugh. "When I was coming to your country on a boat," he said, "I thought, 'How will the Americans ever eat this food?' " And as the boys pushed their plates forward for more, Keith would serve seconds—more rice, *dāl, capātīs,* and *sabjī.*

After all, it was spiritual. You were supposed to eat a lot. It would purify you. It would free you from maya. Besides, it was good, delicious, spicy. This was better than American food. It was like chanting. It was far out. You got high from eating this food.

They ate with the right hand, Indian style. Keith and Howard had already learned this and had even tasted similar dishes, but as they told the Swami and a room full of believers, the food in India had never been this good.

One boy, Stanley, was quite young, and Swamiji, almost like a doting father, watched over him as he ate. Stanley's mother had personally met Swamiji and said that only if he took personal care of her son would she allow him to live in the monastery. Swamiji complied. He diligently encouraged the boy until Stanley gradually took on a voracious appetite and began consuming ten *capātīs* at a sitting (and would have taken more had Swamiji not told him to stop). But aside from Swamiji's limiting Stanley to ten *capātīs,* the word was always "More . . . take more." When Swamiji was finished, he would rise and leave the room, Keith would catch a couple of volunteers to help him clean, and the others would leave.

Occasionally, on a Sunday, Swamiji himself would cook a feast with special Indian dishes.

Steve: *Swamiji personally cooked the* prasādam *and then served it to us upstairs in his front room. We all sat in rows, and I remember him walking up and down in between the rows of boys, passing before us with his bare feet and serving us with a spoon from different pots. He would ask what did we want—did we want more of this? And he would serve us with pleasure. These dishes were not ordinary, but sweets and savories—like sweet rice and* kacaurīs—*with special tastes. Even after we had all taken a full plate, he would come back and ask us to take more.*

Once he came up to me and asked what I would like more of—would I like some more sweet rice? In my early misconception of spiritual life, I thought I should deny myself what I liked best, so I asked for some more plain rice. But even that "plain" rice was fancy yellow rice with fried cheese balls.

On off nights Swamiji's apartment was quiet. He might remain alone for the whole evening, typing and translating *Śrīmad-Bhāgavatam,* or talking in a relaxed atmosphere to just one or two guests until ten. But on meeting nights—Monday, Wednesday, and Friday—there was activity in every room of his apartment. He wasn't alone any more. His new followers were helping him, and they shared in his spirit of trying to get people to chant Hare Kṛṣṇa and hear of Kṛṣṇa consciousness.

On Monday, Wednesday, and Friday evening, there would be the evening *kīrtana*. Some of the devotees would already be downstairs greeting guests and explaining about the Swami and the chanting. But without the Swami nothing could begin. No one knew how to play the drum, and no one dared think of leading the mantra-chanting without Swamiji. Only when he entered at seven o'clock could they begin.

Freshly showered and dressed in his clean Indian handwoven cloth, his arms and body decorated with the arrowlike Vaiṣṇava markings, Swamiji would leave his apartment and go downstairs to face another ecstatic opportunity to glorify Kṛṣṇa. The tiny temple would be crowded with wild, unbrahminical, candid young Americans.

* * *

Keith was cooking lunch in the kitchen as usual, but today Swamiji was standing by the kitchen stove, watching his pupil. Keith paused and looked up from his cooking: "Swamiji, could I become your disciple?"

"Yes," Swamiji replied. "Why not? Your name will be Kṛṣṇa dāsa."

This simple exchange was the first request for discipleship and Swamiji's first granting of initiation. But there was more to it than that. Swamiji announced that he would soon hold an initiation. "What's initiation, Swamiji?" one of the boys asked, and Swamiji replied, "I will tell you later."

First they had to have beads. Keith went to Tandy's Leather Company and bought half-inch wooden beads and cord to string them on. It was much better, Swamiji said, to count on beads while chanting—a strand of 108 beads, to be exact. This employed the sense of touch, and like the Vaiṣṇavas of India one could count how many times one chanted the mantra. Some devotees in India had a string of more than a thousand beads, he had said, and they would chant through them again and again. He taught the boys how to tie a double knot between each of the 108 beads. The number 108 had a special significance: there were 108 *Upaniṣads,* as well as 108 principal *gopīs,* the chief devotees of Lord Kṛṣṇa.

The initiates would be taking vows, he said, and one vow would be to chant a prescribed number of rounds on the beads a day. About a dozen of Swamiji's boys were eligible, but there was no strict system for their selection; if they wanted to, they could do it.

Steve: *Although I was already doing whatever Swamiji recommended, I sensed that initiation was a heavy commitment. And with my last strong impulses to remain completely independent, I hesitated to take initiation.*

Swamiji's friends saw the initiation in different ways. Some saw it as very serious, and some took it to be like a party or a happening. While stringing their beads in the courtyard, Wally and Howard talked a few days before the ceremony.

Wally: "It's just a formality. You accept Swamiji as your spiritual master."

Howard: "What does that entail?"

Wally: "Nobody's very sure. In India it's a standard practice. Don't you think you want to take him as a spiritual master?"

Howard: "I don't know. He would seem to be a good spiritual master—whatever that is. I mean, I like him and his teachings a lot, so I guess in a way he's already my spiritual master. I just don't understand how it would change the situation."

Wally: "Neither do I. I guess it doesn't. It's just a formality."

* * *

September 8 was Janmāṣṭamī, the appearance day of Lord Kṛṣṇa. One year before, Bhaktivedanta Swami had observed Kṛṣṇa's birthday at sea aboard the *Jaladuta*, just out of Colombo. Now, exactly one year later, he had a small crew of Hare Kṛṣṇa chanters. He would gather them all together, have them observe a day of chanting, reading scriptures, fasting, and feasting—and the next day would be initiation.

At six o'clock, Swamiji came down and was about to give his morning class as usual, when one of the boys asked if he would read from his own manuscript. Swamiji appeared shy, yet he did not hide his pleasure at having been asked to read his own *Bhagavad-gītā* commentary. Usually he would read a verse from Dr. Radhakrishnan's Oxford edition of the *Gītā*. Although the commentary presented impersonalist philosophy, the translations, Swamiji said, were ninety-percent accurate. But this morning he sent Roy up to fetch his manuscript, and for an hour he read from its typewritten pages.

For observing Janmāṣṭamī there were special rules: there should be no eating, and the day was to be spent chanting, reading, and discussing Kṛṣṇa consciousness. If anyone became too weak, he said, there was fruit in the kitchen. But better that they fast until the feast at midnight, just like the devotees in India. He said that in India, millions of people—Hindus, Muslims, or whatever—observed the birthday of Lord Kṛṣṇa. And in every temple there were festivities and celebrations of the pastimes of Kṛṣṇa.

"And now," he said at length, "I will tell you what is meant by initiation. Initiation means that the spiritual master accepts the student and agrees to take charge, and the student accepts the spiritual master and agrees to worship him as God." He paused. No one spoke. "Any questions?" As there were none, he got up and walked out.

The devotees were stunned. What had they just heard him say? For weeks he had stressed that when anyone claims to be God he should be considered a dog.

"My mind's just been blown," said Wally.

"*Everyone's* mind is blown," said Howard. "Swamiji just dropped a bomb."

They thought of Keith. He was wise. Consult Keith. But Keith was in the hospital. Talking among themselves, they became more and more confused. Swamiji's remark had confounded their judgment. Finally, Wally decided to go to the hospital to see Keith.

Keith listened to the whole story. He heard how Swamiji had told them to fast and how he had read from his manuscript and how he had said he would explain initiation and how everybody had leaned forward all ears . . . and Swamiji had dropped a bomb: "The student accepts the spiritual master and agrees to worship him as God. Any questions?" And then Swamiji had walked out. "I don't know if I want to be initiated now," Wally confessed. "We have to worship him as God."

"Well, you're already doing that by accepting whatever he tells you," Keith replied, and he advised that they talk it over with Swamiji . . . *before* initiation.

So Wally went back to the temple and consulted Howard, and together they went up to Swamiji's apartment. "Does what you told us this morning," Howard asked, "mean we are supposed to accept the spiritual master to be God?"

"That means he is due the same respect as God, being God's representative. Therefore, he is as good as God because he can deliver God to the sincere disciple. Is that clear?" It was.

Most of the prospective initiates spent several hours that day stringing their shiny red wooden beads. Having tied one end of the string to a window bar or radiator, they would slide one bead at a time up the string and knot it tightly, chanting one mantra of Hare Kṛṣṇa for each bead. It was devotional service—chanting and stringing your beads for initiation. Every time they knotted another bead it seemed like a momentous event.

Swamiji had said that devotees in India chanted at least sixty-four rounds of beads a day. Saying the Hare Kṛṣṇa mantra once on each of the 108 beads constituted one round. His spiritual master had said that anyone who didn't chant sixty-four rounds a day was fallen.

At first some of the boys thought that they would also have to chant sixty-four rounds, and they became perplexed: that would take all day! How could you go to a job if you had to chant sixty-four rounds? How could you chant sixty-four rounds? Then someone said Swamiji had told him thirty-two rounds a day would be a sufficient minimum for the West. Wally said he had heard Swamiji say twenty-five—but even that seemed impossible. Then Swamiji offered the rock-bottom minimum: sixteen rounds a day, without fail. Whoever got initiated would have to promise.

The bead-stringing, chanting, reading, and dozing went on until eleven at night, when everyone was invited up to Swamiji's room. As they filed through the courtyard, they sensed an unusual calm in the atmosphere, and Houston Street, just over the wall, was quiet. There was no moon.

As his followers sat on the floor, contentedly eating *prasādam* from paper plates, Swamiji sat among them, telling stories about the birth of Lord Kṛṣṇa. Kṛṣṇa had appeared on this evening five thousand years ago. He was born the son of Vasudeva and Devakī in the prison of King Kaṁsa at midnight, and His father, Vasudeva, immediately took Him to Vṛndāvana, where He was raised as the son of Nanda Mahārāja, a cowherd man.

Swamiji also spoke of the necessity of purification for spiritual advancement. "It is not enough merely to chant holy words," he said. "One must be pure inside and out. Chanting in purity brings spiritual advancement. The living entity becomes impure because he wants to enjoy material pleasure. But the impure can become pure by following Kṛṣṇa, by doing all works for Kṛṣṇa. Beginners in Kṛṣṇa consciousness have a tendency to relax their efforts in a short time, but to advance spiritually you must resist this temptation and continually increase your efforts and devotion."

Michael Grant: *I first heard about the initiation just one day before it was to take place. I had been busy with my music and hadn't been attending. I was walking down Second Avenue with one of the prospective initiates, and he mentioned to me that there was going to be something called an initiation ceremony. I asked what it was about, and he said,*

"All I know is it means that you accept the spiritual master as God." This was a big surprise to me, and I hardly knew how to take it. But I didn't take it completely seriously, and the way it was mentioned to me in such an offhand way made it seem not very important. He asked me casually whether I was going to be involved, and I, also being very casual about it, said, "Well, I think I will. Why not? I'll give it a try."

Jan, Mike's girl friend, didn't think she would make an obedient disciple, and initiation sounded frightening. She liked the Swami, especially cooking with him. But it was Mike who convinced her—*he* was going, so she should come with him.

Carl Yeargens knew something about initiation from his readings in Eastern philosophy, and he, more than the others, knew what a serious commitment it was. He was surprised to hear that Swamiji was offering initiation, and he was cautious about entering into it. He knew that initiation meant no illicit sex, intoxication, or meat-eating, and an initiated disciple would have new responsibilities for spreading the teachings to others. Carl was already feeling less involved since the Swami had moved to Second Avenue, but he decided to attend the initiation anyway.

Bill Epstein had never professed to be a serious disciple. Holding initiation was just another part of the Swami's scene, and you were free to take it seriously or not. He figured it was all right to take initiation, even if you weren't serious. He would try it.

James Greene thought he wasn't pure enough to be initiated: "Who am I to be initiated?" But Swami had asked him to bring something over to the storefront. "I came, and it was just understood that I was supposed to be initiated. So, I thought, why not?"

Stanley was sticking with the Swami and his followers. He asked his mother if he could be initiated, and she said it would be all right.

Steve wanted more time to think about it.

Keith was in the hospital.

Bruce had only been attending for a week or two, and it was too soon.

Chuck was on a week's vacation from the regulated spiritual life at the temple, so he didn't know about the initiation.

No one was asked to shave his head or even cut his hair or change his dress. No one offered Swamiji the traditional *guru-dakṣiṇā,* the donation a disciple is supposed to offer as a gesture of his great obligation to his master. Hardly anyone even relieved him of his chores, so Swamiji himself had to do most of the cooking and other preparations for the initiation. He was perfectly aware of the mentality of his boys, and he didn't try to force anything on anyone. Some of the initiates didn't know until after the initiation, when they had inquired, that the four rules—no meat-eating, no illicit sex, no intoxication, and no gambling—were mandatory for all disciples. Swamiji's reply then was, "I am very glad that you are finally asking me that."

It was to be a live Vedic sacrifice, with a ceremonial fire right there in the front room of Swamiji's apartment. In the center of the room was the sacrificial arena, a platform of bricks, four inches high and two feet square, covered with a mound of dirt. The dirt was from the courtyard and the bricks were from a nearby gutted building. Around the mound were eleven bananas, clarified butter, sesame seeds, whole barley grains, five colors of powdered dyes, and a supply of kindling. The eleven initiates took up most of the remaining space in the front room as they sat on the floor knee to knee around the sacrificial arena. The guests in the hallway peered curiously through the open door. For everyone except the Swami, this was all new and strange, and every step of the ceremony took place under his direction. When some of the boys had made a mess of trying to apply Vaiṣṇava *tilaka* to their foreheads, Swamiji had patiently guided his finger up their foreheads, making a neat, narrow "V."

He sat before the mound of earth, looking out at his congregation. They appeared not much different from any other group of young hippies from the Lower East Side who might have assembled at any number of happenings—spiritual, cultural, musical, or whatever. Some were just checking out a new scene. Some were deeply devoted to the

Swami. But everyone was curious. He had requested them to chant the Hare Kṛṣṇa mantra softly throughout the ceremony, and the chanting had now become a continual drone, accompanying his mysterious movements as head priest of the Vedic rite.

He began by lighting a dozen sticks of incense. Then he performed purification with water. Taking a spoon in his left hand, he put three drops of water from a goblet into his right hand and sipped the water. He repeated the procedure three times. The fourth time he did not sip but flicked the water onto the floor behind him. He then passed the spoon and goblet around for the initiates, who tried to copy what they had seen. When some of them placed the water in the wrong hand or sipped in the wrong way, Swamiji patiently corrected them.

"Now," he said, "repeat after me." And he had them repeat, one word at a time, a Vedic mantra of purification:

oṁ apavitraḥ pavitro vā
sarvāvasthāṁ gato 'pi vā
yaḥ smaret puṇḍarīkākṣaṁ
sa bahyābhyantaraḥ śuciḥ
śrī-viṣṇuḥ śrī-viṣṇuḥ śrī-viṣṇuḥ

The initiates tried falteringly to follow his pronunciation of the words, which they had never heard before. Then he gave the translation: "Unpurified or purified, or even having passed through all situations, one who remembers the lotus-eyed Supreme Personality of Godhead is cleansed within and without." Three times he repeated the sipping of water, the drone of the Hare Kṛṣṇa mantra filling the room as the goblet passed from initiate to initiate and back again to him, and three times he led the chanting of the mantra: *oṁ apavitraḥ* . . . Then he raised a hand, and as the buzzing of the chanting trailed off into silence, he began his lecture.

After the lecture, Swamiji asked the devotees one by one to hand him their beads, and he began chanting on them—Hare Kṛṣṇa, Hare Kṛṣṇa, Kṛṣṇa Kṛṣṇa, Hare Hare/ Hare Rāma, Hare Rāma, Rāma Rāma, Hare Hare. The sound of everyone chanting filled the room. After finishing one strand, he would summon the owner of the beads and hold the beads up while demonstrating how to chant. Then he would announce the initiate's spiritual name, and the disciple would take back the beads, bow to the floor, and recite:

nama om viṣṇu-pādāya kṛṣṇa-preṣṭhāya bhū-tale
śrīmate bhaktivedānta-svamin iti nāmine

"I offer my respectful obeisances unto His Divine Grace A. C. Bhaktivedanta Swami, who is very dear to Lord Kṛṣṇa, having taken shelter at His lotus feet."

There were eleven initiates and so eleven sets of beads, and the chanting lasted for over an hour. Swamiji gave each boy a strand of neck beads, which he said were like dog collars, identifying the devotee as Kṛṣṇa's dog.

After Wally received his beads and his new name (Umāpati), he returned to his place beside Howard and said, "That was wonderful. Getting your beads is wonderful." In turn, each initiate received his beads and his spiritual name. Howard became Hayagrīva, Wally became Umāpati, Bill became Ravīndra-svarūpa, Carl became Karlāpati, James became Jagannātha, Mike became Mukunda, Jan became Jānakī, Roy became Rāya Rāma, and Stanley became Stryadhīśa. Another Stanley, a Brooklyn boy with a job, and Janis, a college student from Montreal, both of whom had rather peripheral relationships with the Swami, appeared that night and took initiation with the rest—receiving the names Satyavrata and Janārdana.

Then Swamiji began the fire sacrifice by sprinkling the colored dyes across the mound of earth before him. With fixed attention his congregation watched each mysterious move, as he picked up the twigs and wooden splinters, dipped them into clarified butter, lit them in a candle flame, and built a small fire in the center of the mound. He mixed sesame seeds, barley, and clarified butter in a bowl and then passed the mixture around. Each new disciple took a handful of the mixture to offer into the fire. He then began to recite Sanskrit prayers, asking everyone to repeat them, each prayer ending with the responsive chanting of the word *"svāhā"* three times. And with *svāhā* the initiates would toss some of the sesame-barley mixture into the fire. Swamiji kept pouring butter, piling up wood, and chanting more prayers, until the mound was blazing. The prayers kept coming and the butter kept pouring and the fire got larger and the room got hotter.

After fifteen or twenty minutes, Swamiji asked each of the initiates to place a banana in the fire. With eleven bananas heaped in the fire, the flames began to die, and the smoke thickened. A few of the initiates got up and ran coughing into the other room, and the guests retreated into the hallway. But Swamiji went on pouring the remaining butter and seeds into the fire. "This kind of smoke does not disturb," he said. "Other smoke disturbs, but this kind of smoke does not." Even though everyone's eyes were watering with irritation, he asked that the windows remain closed. So most of the smoke was contained within the apartment, and no neighbors complained.

Swamiji smiled broadly, rose from his seat before the sacrificial fire, the blazing tongue of Viṣṇu, and began clapping his hands and chanting Hare Kṛṣṇa. Placing one foot before the other and swaying from side to side, he began to dance before the fire. His disciples joined him in dancing and chanting, and the smoke abated. He had each disciple touch his beads to the feet of Lord Caitanya in the Pañca-tattva picture on the table, and finally he allowed the windows opened. As the ceremony was finished and the air in the apartment was clearing, Swamiji began to laugh: "There was so much smoke I thought they might have to call the fire brigade."

Swamiji was happy. He arranged that *prasādam* be distributed to all the devotees and guests. The fire, the prayers, the vows, and everyone chanting Hare Kṛṣṇa had all created an auspicious atmosphere. Things were going forward. Now there were initiated devotees in the Western world. Finally most of the disciples went home to their apartments, leaving their spiritual master to clean up after the initiation ceremony.

Three days later Swamiji performed his first marriage between two disciples—Mukunda and Jānakī—with a similar ceremony. He was satisfied. He was introducing some of the major elements of his Kṛṣṇa consciousness mission. He had initiated disciples, he had married them, and he had feasted the public with *kṛṣṇa-prasādam*. "If I had the means," he told his followers, "I could hold a major festival like this every day."

On Rādhāṣṭamī, the appearance day of Śrīmatī Rādhāṛāṇī, Lord Kṛṣṇa's eternal consort, Prabhupāda held his second initiation. Keith became Kīrtanānanda, Steve became Satsvarūpa, Bruce became Brahmānanda, and Chuck became Acyutānanda. It was another festive day with a fire sacrifice in Prabhupāda's front room and a big feast.

Allen Ginsberg lived nearby on East Tenth Street. One day he received a peculiar invitation in the mail:

Practice the transcendental sound vibration,
Hare Krishna, Hare Krishna, Krishna Krishna, Hare Hare
Hare Rama, Hare Rama, Rama Rama, Hare Hare.
This chanting will cleanse the dust from the mirror
of the mind.

International Society for Krishna Consciousness
Meetings at 7 a.m. daily
Mondays, Wednesdays, and Fridays at 7:00 p.m.
You are cordially invited to come and
bring your friends.

Swamiji had asked the boys to distribute the leaflet around the neighborhood.

One evening, soon after he received the invitation, Allen Ginsberg and his roommate, Peter Orlovsky, arrived at the storefront in a Volkswagen minibus. Allen had been captivated by the Hare Kṛṣṇa mantra several years before, when he had first encountered it at the Kumbha-melā festival in Allahabad, India, and he had been chanting it often ever since. The devotees were impressed to see the world-famous author of *Howl* and leading figure of the beat generation enter their humble storefront. His advocation of free sex, marijuana, and LSD, his claims of drug-induced visions of spirituality in everyday sights, his political ideas, his exploration of insanity, revolt, nakedness, and his attempts to create a harmony of likeminded souls—all were influential on the minds of American young people, especially those living on the Lower East Side. Although by middle-class standards he was scandalous and disheveled, he was, in his own right, a figure of wordly repute, more so than anyone who had ever come to the storefront before.

Allen and Peter had come for the *kīrtana,* but it wasn't quite time—Swamiji hadn't come down. They presented a new harmonium to the devotees. "It's for the *kīrtanas,*" said Allen. "A little donation." Allen stood at the entrance to the storefront, talking with Hayagrīva, telling him how he had been chanting Hare Kṛṣṇa around the world—at peace marches, poetry readings, a procession in Prague, a writers' union in Moscow. "Secular *kīrtana,*" said Allen, "but Hare Kṛṣṇa nonetheless." Then Prabhupāda entered. Allen and Peter sat with the congregation and joined in the *kīrtana.* Allen played harmonium.

Swamiji reciprocated by nodding his head and folding his palms. After the *kīrtana* they talked together briefly, and then Swamiji returned to his apartment. Allen mentioned to Hayagrīva that he would like to come by again and talk more with the Swami, so Hayagrīva invited him to come the next day and stay for lunch *prasādam.*

"Don't you think Swamiji is a little too esoteric for New York?" Allen asked.

Hayagrīva thought. "Maybe," he replied.

Hayagrīva then asked Allen to help Swamiji, since his visa would soon expire. He had entered the country with a visa for a two-month stay, and he had been extending his visa for two more months again and again. This had gone on for one year, but the last time he had applied for an extension, he had been refused. "We need an immigration lawyer," said Hayagrīva. "I'll donate to that," Allen assured him.

The next morning, Allen Ginsberg came by with a check and another harmonium. Up in Prabhupāda's apartment, he demonstrated *his* melody for chanting Hare Kṛṣṇa, and then he and Swamiji talked.

Allen: *I was a little shy with him because I didn't know where he was coming from. I had that harmonium I wanted to donate, and I had a little money. I thought it was great now that he was here to expound on the Hare Kṛṣṇa mantra—that would sort of justify my singing. I knew what I was doing, but I didn't have any theological background to satisfy further inquiries, and here was someone who did. So I thought that was absolutely great. Now I could go around singing Hare Kṛṣṇa, and if anybody wanted to know what it was, I could just send them to Swami Bhaktivedanta to find out. If anyone wanted to know the technical intricacies and the ultimate history, I could send them to him.*

He explained to me about his own teacher and about Caitanya and the lineage going back. His head was filled with so many things and what he was doing. He was already working on his translations. He always seemed to be sitting there just day after day and night after night. And I think he had one or two people helping him.

Swamiji was very cordial with Allen. Quoting a passage from *Bhagavad-gītā* where Kṛṣṇa says that whatever a great man does, others will follow, he requested Allen to continue chanting Hare Kṛṣṇa at every opportunity, so that others would follow his example. He told about Lord Caitanya's organizing the first civil disobedience movement in India, leading a *saṅkīrtana* protest march against the Muslim ruler. Allen was fascinated. He enjoyed talking with the Swami.

Allen: *The main thing, above and beyond all our differences, was an aroma of sweetness that he had, a personal, selfless sweetness like total devotion. And that was what always conquered me, whatever intellectual questions or doubts I had, or even cynical views of ego. In his presence there was a kind of personal charm, coming from dedication, that conquered all our conflicts. Even though I didn't agree with him, I always liked to be with him.*

* * *

Swamiji lived amid the drug culture, in a neighborhood where the young people were almost desperately attempting to alter their consciousness, whether by drugs or by some other means—whatever was available. Swamiji assured them that they could easily achieve the higher consciousness they desired by chanting Hare Kṛṣṇa. It was inevitable that in explaining Kṛṣṇa consciousness he would make allusions to the drug experience, even if only to show that the two were contrary paths. He was familiar already with Indian "sadhus" who took ganja and hashish on the plea of aiding their meditations. And even before he had left India, hippie tourists had become a familiar sight on the streets of Delhi.

The hippies liked India because of the cultural mystique and easy access to drugs. They would meet their Indian counterparts, who assured them that taking hashish was spiritual, and then they would return to America and perpetrate their misconceptions of Indian spiritual culture.

It was the way of life. The local head shops carried a full line of paraphernalia. Marijuana, LSD, peyote, cocaine, and hard drugs like heroin and barbiturates were easily purchased on the streets and in the parks. Underground newspapers reported important news on the drug scene, featured a cartoon character named Captain High, and ran crossword puzzles that only a seasoned "head" could answer.

Swamiji had to teach that Kṛṣṇa consciousness was beyond the revered LSD trip. "Do you think taking LSD can produce ecstasy and higher consciousness?" he once asked the storefront audience. "Then just imagine a roomful of LSD. Kṛṣṇa consciousness is like that." People would regularly come in and ask Swamiji's disciples, "Do you get high from this?" And the devotees would answer, "Oh, yes. You can get high just by chanting. Why don't you try it?"

Probably the most famous experiments with LSD in those days were by Timothy Leary and Richard Alpert, Harvard psychology instructors who studied the effects of the drug, published their findings in professional journals, and advocated the use of LSD for self-realization and fulfillment. After being fired from Harvard, Timothy Leary went on to become a national priest of LSD and for some time ran an LSD commune in Millbrook, New York.

When the members of the Millbrook commune heard about the swami on the Lower East Side who led his followers in a chant that got you high, they began visiting the storefront. One night, a group of about ten hippies from Millbrook came to Swamiji's *kīrtana*. They all chanted (not so much in worship of Kṛṣṇa as to see what kind of high the chanting could produce), and after the lecture a Millbrook leader asked about drugs. Prabhupāda replied that drugs were not necessary for spiritual life, that they could not produce spiritual consciousness, and that all drug-induced religious visions were simply hallucinations. To realize God was not so easy or cheap that one could do it just by taking a pill or smoking. Chanting Hare Kṛṣṇa, he explained, was a purifying process to uncover one's pure consciousness. Taking drugs would increase the covering and bar one from self-realization.

"But have *you* ever taken LSD?" The question now became a challenge.

"No," Swamiji replied. "I have never taken any of these things, not even cigarettes or tea."

"If you haven't taken it, then how can you say what it is?" The Millbrookers looked around, smiling. Two or three even burst out with laughter, and they snapped their fingers, thinking the Swami had been checkmated.

"I have not taken," Swamiji replied regally from his dais. "But my disciples have taken all these things—marijuana, LSD—many times, and they have given them all up. You can hear from them. Hayagrīva, you can speak." And Hayagrīva sat up a little and spoke out in his stentorian best.

"Well, no matter how high you go on LSD, you eventually reach a peak, and then you have to come back down. Just like traveling into outer space in a rocket ship. [He gave one of Swamiji's familiar examples.] Your spacecraft can travel very far away from the earth for thousands of miles, day after day, but it cannot simply go on traveling and traveling. Eventually it must land. On LSD, we experience going up, but we always have to come down again. That's not spiritual consciousness.

When you actually attain spiritual or Kṛṣṇa consciousness, you stay high. Because you go to Kṛṣṇa, you don't have to come down. You can stay high forever."

Swamiji was sitting in his back room with Hayagrīva and Umāpati and other disciples. The evening meeting had just ended, and the visitors from Millbrook had gone. "Kṛṣṇa consciousness is so nice, Swamiji," Umāpati spoke up. "You just get higher and higher, and you don't come down."

Swamiji smiled. "Yes, that's right."

"No more coming down," Umāpati said, laughing, and the others also began to laugh. Some clapped their hands, repeating, "No more coming down."

The conversation inspired Hayagrīva and Umāpati to produce a new handbill:

STAY HIGH FOREVER!
No more coming down

Practice Krishna Consciousness
Expand your consciousness by practicing the

TRANSCENDENTAL SOUND VIBRATION

HARE KRISHNA HARE KRISHNA KRISHNA KRISHNA HARE HARE
HARE RAMA HARE RAMA RAMA RAMA HARE HARE

The leaflet went on to extol Kṛṣṇa consciousness over any other high. It included phrases like "end all bringdowns" and "turn on," and it spoke against "employing artificially induced methods of self-realization and expanded consciousness." Someone objected to the flyer's "playing too much off the hippie mentality," but Swamiji said it was all right.

* * *

October 1966

Tompkins Square Park was *the* park on the Lower East Side. On the south, it was bordered by Seventh Street, with its four- and five-storied brownstone tenements. On the north side was Tenth, with more brownstones, but in better condition, and the very old, small building that housed the Tompkins Square branch of the New York Public Library. On Avenue B, the park's east border, stood St. Brigid's Church, built in 1848, when the neighborhood had been entirely Irish. The church, school, and rectory still occupied much of the block. And the west border of the park, Avenue A, was lined with tiny old candy stores selling newspapers, magazines, cigarettes, and egg-creme sodas at the counter. There were also a few bars, several grocery stores, and a couple of Slavic restaurants specializing in inexpensive vegetable broths, which brought Ukrainians and hippies side by side for bodily nourishment.

The park's ten acres held many tall trees, but at least half of the park was paved. A network of five-foot-high heavy wrought-iron fences weaved through the park, lining the walkways and protecting the grass. The fences and the many walkways and entrances to the park gave it the effect of a maze.

Since the weather was still warm and it was Sunday, the park was crowded with people. Almost all the space on the benches that lined the walkways was occupied. There were old people, mostly Ukrainians, dressed in outdated suits and sweaters, even in the warm weather, sitting together in clans, talking. There were many children in the park also, mostly Puerto Ricans and blacks but also fair-haired, hard-faced slum kids racing around on bikes or playing with balls and Frisbees. The basketball and handball courts were mostly taken by the teenagers. And as always, there were plenty of loose, running dogs.

A marble miniature gazebo (four pillars and a roof, with a drinking fountain inside) was a remnant from the old days—1891, according to the inscription. On its four sides were the words *HOPE, FAITH, CHARITY,* and *TEMPERANCE.* But someone had sprayed the whole structure with black paint, making crude designs and illegible names and initials. Today, a bench had been taken over by several conga and bongo drummers, and the whole park pulsed with their demanding rhythms.

And the hippies were there, different from the others. The bearded Bohemian men and their long-haired young girl friends dressed in old blue jeans were still an unusual sight. Even in the Lower East Side melting pot, their presence created tension. They were from middle-class families, and so they had not been driven to the slums by dire economic necessity. This created conflicts in their dealings with the underprivileged immigrants. And the hippies' well-known proclivity for psychedelic drugs, their revolt against their families and affluence, and their absorption in the avant-garde sometimes made them the jeered minority among the neighbors. But the hippies just wanted to do their own thing and create their own revolution for "love and peace," so usually they were tolerated, although not appreciated.

There were various groups among the young and hip at Tompkins Square Park. There were friends who had gone to the same school together, who took the same drug together, or who agreed on a particular philosophy of art, literature, politics, or metaphysics. There were lovers. There were groups hanging out together for reasons undecipherable, except for the common purpose of doing their own thing. And there were others, who lived like hermits—a loner would sit on a park bench, analyzing the effects of cocaine, looking up at the strangely rustling green leaves of the trees and the blue sky above the tenements and then down to the garbage at his feet, as he helplessly followed his mind from fear to illumination, to disgust, to hallucination, on and on, until the drug began to wear off and he was again a common stranger. Sometimes they would sit up all night, "spaced out" in the park, until at last, in the light of morning, they would stretch out on benches to sleep.

Hippies especially took to the park on Sundays. They at least passed through the park on their way to St. Mark's Place, Greenwich Village, or the Lexington Avenue subway at Astor Place, or the IND subway at Houston and Second, or to catch an uptown bus on First Avenue, a downtown bus on Second, or a crosstown on Ninth. Or they went to the park just to get out of their apartments and sit together in the open air—to get high again, to talk, or to walk through the park's maze of pathways.

But whatever the hippies' diverse interests and drives, the Lower East Side was an essential part of the mystique. It was not just a dirty slum; it was the best place in the world to conduct the experiment in consciousness. For all its filth and threat of violence and the confined life of its brownstone tenements, the Lower East Side was still the forefront of the revolution in mind expansion. Unless you were living there and taking psychedelics or marijuana, or at least intellectually pursuing the quest for free personal religion, you weren't enlightened, and you weren't taking part in the most progressive evolution of human existence of the ordinary, materialistic, "straight" American—that brought unity to the otherwise eclectic gathering of hippies on the Lower East Side.

Into this chaotic pageant Swamiji entered with his followers and sat down to hold a *kīrtana*. Three or four devotees who arrived ahead of him selected an open area of the park, put out the Oriental carpet Robert Nelson had donated, sat down on it, and began playing *karatālas* and chanting Hare Kṛṣṇa. Immediately some boys rode up on their bicycles, braked just short of the carpet, and stood astride their bikes, curiously and irreverently staring. Other passersby gathered to listen.

Meanwhile Swamiji, accompanied by half a dozen disciples, was walking the eight blocks from the storefront. Brahmānanda carried the harmonium and the Swami's drum. Kīrtanānanda, who was now shaven-headed at Swamiji's request and dressed in loose-flowing canary yellow robes, created an extra sensation. Drivers pulled their cars over to have a look, their passengers leaning forward, agape at the outrageous dress and shaved head. As the group passed a store, people inside would poke each other and indicate the spectacle. People came to the windows of the tenements, taking in the Swami and his group as if a parade were passing. The Puerto Rican tough guys, especially, couldn't restrain themselves from exaggerated reactions. "Hey, Buddha!" they taunted. "Hey, you forgot to change your pajamas!" They made shrill screams as if imitating Indian war whoops they had heard in Hollywood westerns.

"Hey, A-rabs!" exclaimed one heckler, who began imitating what he thought was an Eastern dance. No one on the street knew anything about Kṛṣṇa consciousness, nor even of Hindu culture and customs. To them, the Swami's entourage was just a bunch of crazy hippies showing off. But they didn't know what to make of the Swami. He was different. Nevertheless, they were suspicious. Some, however, like Irving Halpern, a veteran Lower East Side resident, felt sympathetic toward this stranger, who was "apparently a very dignified person on a peaceful mission."

Irving Halpern: *A lot of people had spectacularized notions of what a swami was. As though they were going to suddenly see people lying on little mattresses made out of nails—and all kinds of other absurd notions. Yet here came just a very graceful, peaceful, gentle, obviously well-meaning being into a lot of hostility.*

"Hippies!"

"What are they, Communists?"

While the young taunted, the middle-aged and elderly shook their heads or stared, cold and uncomprehending. The way to the park was spotted with blasphemies, ribald jokes, and tension, but no violence.

Today, the ethnic neighbors just assumed that Swamiji and his followers had come onto the streets in outlandish costumes as a joke, just to turn everything topsy-turvy and cause stares and howls. They felt that their responses were only natural for any normal, respectable American slum-dweller.

So it was quite an adventure before the group even reached the park. Swamiji, however, remained unaffected. "What are they saying?" he asked once or twice, and Brahmānanda explained. Swamiji had a way of holding his head high, his chin up, as he walked forward. It made him look aristocratic and determined. His vision was spiritual—he saw everyone as spiritual soul and Kṛṣṇa as the controller of everything. Yet aside from that, even from a worldly point of view he was unafraid of the city's pandemonium. After all, he was an experienced "Calcutta man."

The *kīrtana* had been going for about ten minutes when Swamiji arrived. Stepping out of his white rubber slippers, just as if he were home in the temple, he sat down on the rug with his followers, who had now stopped their singing and were watching him. He wore a pink sweater, and around his shoulders a *khādī* wrapper. He smiled. Looking at his group, he indicated the rhythm by counting, one . . . two . . . *three.* Then he began clapping his hands heavily as he continued counting, "One . . . two . . . *three.*" The *karatālas* followed, at first with wrong beats, but he kept the rhythm by clapping his hands, and then they got it, clapping hands, clashing cymbals artlessly to a slow, steady beat.

He began singing prayers that no one else knew. *Vande 'haṁ śrī-guroḥ śrī-yuta-pada-kamalaṁ śrī-gurūn vaiṣṇavāṁś ca.* His voice was sweet like the harmonium, rich in the nuances of Bengali melody. Sitting on the rug under a large oak tree, he sang the mysterious Sanskrit prayers. None of his followers knew any mantra but Hare Kṛṣṇa, but they knew Swamiji. And they kept the rhythm, listening closely to him while the trucks rumbled on the street and the conga drums pulsed in the distance.

As he sang—*śrī-rūpaṁ sāgrajātam*—the dogs came by, kids stared, a few mockers pointed fingers: "Hey, who is that priest, man?" But his voice was a shelter beyond the clashing dualities. His boys went on ringing cymbals while he sang alone: *śrī-rādhā-kṛṣṇa-pādān.*

Swamiji sang prayers in praise of the pure conjugal love for Kṛṣṇa of Śrīmatī Rādhārāṇī, the beloved of the *gopīs.* Each word, passed down for hundreds of years by the intimate associates of Kṛṣṇa, was saturated with deep transcendental meaning that only he understood. *Saha-gana-lalitā-śrī-viśākhānvitāṁś ca.* They waited for him to begin Hare Kṛṣṇa, although hearing him chant was exciting enough.

More people came—which was what Swamiji wanted. He wanted them chanting and dancing with him, and now his followers wanted that too. They wanted to be with him. It seemed that this would be the thing they would always do—go with Swamiji and sit and chant. He would always be with them, chanting.

Then he began the mantra—Hare Kṛṣṇa, Hare Kṛṣṇa, Kṛṣṇa Kṛṣṇa, Hare Hare/ Hare Rāma, Hare Rāma, Rāma Rāma, Hare Hare. They responded, too low and muddled at first, but he returned it to them again, singing it right and triumphant. Again they responded, gaining heart, ringing *karatālas* and clapping hands—one . . . two . . . *three,* one . . . two . . . *three.* Again he sang it alone, and they stayed hanging closely on each word, clapping, beating cymbals, and watching him looking back at them from his inner concentration—his old-age wisdom, his bhakti—and out of love for Swamiji, they broke loose from their surroundings and joined him as a chanting congregation. Swamiji played his small drum, holding its strap in his left hand, bracing the drum against his body, and with his right hand playing intricate *mṛdaṅga* rhythms.

Hare Kṛṣṇa, Hare Kṛṣṇa, Kṛṣṇa Kṛṣṇa, Hare Hare/ Hare Rāma, Hare Rāma, Rāma Rāma, Hare Hare. He was going strong after half an hour, repeating the mantra, carrying them with him as interested onlookers gathered in greater numbers. A few hippies sat down on the edge of the rug, copying the cross-legged sitting posture, listening, clapping, trying the chanting, and the small inner circle of Prabhupāda and his followers grew as gradually more people joined.

As always, his *kīrtana* attracted musicians.

Irving Halpern: *I make flutes, and I play musical instruments that I make. When the Swami came, I went up and started playing, and he welcomed me. Whenever a new musician would join and play their first note, he would extend his arms. It would be as though he had stepped up to the podium and was going to lead the New York Philharmonic. I mean, there was this gesture that every musician knows. You just know when someone else wants you to play with them and feels good that you are playing with them. And this very basic kind of musician communication was there with him, and I related to it very quickly. And I was happy about it.*

Lone musicians were almost always loitering in different parts of the park, and when they heard they could play with the Swami's chanting and that they were welcome, then they began to come by, one by one. A saxophone player came just because there was such a strong rhythm section to play with. Others, like Irving Halpern, saw it as something spiritual, with good vibrations. As the musicians joined, more passersby were drawn into the *kīrtana*. Swamiji had been singing both lead and chorus, and many who had joined now sang the lead part also, so that there was a constant chorus of chanting. During the afternoon, the crowd grew to more than a hundred, with a dozen musicians trying—with their conga and bongo drums, bamboo flutes, metal flutes, mouth organs, wood and metal "clackers," tambourines, and guitars—to stay with the Swami.

He was striking to see. His brow was furrowed in the effort of singing loud, and his visage was strong. The veins in his temples stood out visibly, and his jaw jutted forward as he sang his "Hare Kṛṣṇa! Hare Kṛṣṇa!" for all to hear. Although his demeanor was pleasant, his chanting was intensive, sometimes straining, and everything about him was concentration.

It wasn't someone else's yoga retreat or silent peace vigil, but a pure chanting be in of Bhaktivedanta Swami's own doing. It was a new wave, something everyone would take part in. The community seemed to be accepting it. It became so popular that the ice cream vendor came over to make sales. Beside Prabhupāda a group of young, blond-haired boys, five or six years old, were just sitting around. A young Polish boy stood staring. Someone began burning frankincense on a glowing coal in a metal strainer, and the sweet fumes billowed among the flutists, drummers, and chanters.

Swamiji motioned to his disciples, and they got up and began dancing. Tall, thin Stryadhīśa, his back pockets stuffed with *Stay High Forever* flyers, raised his hands and began to dance. Beside him, in black turtleneck, big chanting beads around his neck, danced Acyutānanda, his curly, almost frizzy, hair long and disarrayed. Then Brahmānanda got up. He and Acyutānanda stood facing each other, arms outstretched as in the picture of Lord Caitanya's *kīrtana.* Photographers in the crowd moved forward. The boys danced, shifting their weight from left foot to right foot, striking a series of angelic poses, their large, red chanting beads around their necks. They were doing "the Swami step."

Brahmānanda: *Once I got up, I thought I would have to remain standing for as long as Swamiji played the drum. It will be an offense, I thought, if I sit down while he's still playing. So I danced for an hour.*

Swamiji gave a gesture of acceptance by a typically Indian movement of his head, and then he raised his arms, inviting more dancers. More of his disciples began dancing, and even a few hippies got up and tried it. Swamiji wanted everyone to sing and dance in *saṅkīrtana.* The dance was a sedate swaying and a stepping of bare feet on the rug, and the dancers' arms were raised high, their fingers extended toward the sky above the branches of the autumn trees. Here and there throughout the crowd, chanters were enjoying private ecstasies: a girl with her eyes closed played finger cymbals and shook her head dreamily as she chanted. A Polish lady with a very old, worn face and a babushka around her head stared incredulously at the girl. Little groups of old women in kerchiefs, some of them wearing sunglasses, stood here and there among the crowd, talking animatedly and pointing out the interesting sights in the *kīrtana.* Kīrtanānanda was the only one in a dhoti, looking like a young version of Prabhupāda. The autumn afternoon sunlight fell softly on the group, spotlighting them in a golden glow with long, cool shadows.

The harmonium played a constant drone, and a boy wearing a military fatigue jacket improvised atonal creations on a wooden recorder. Yet the total sound of the instruments blended, and Swamiji's voice emerged above the mulling tones of each chord. And so it went for hours. Prabhupāda held his head and shoulders erect, although at the end of each line of the mantra, he would sometimes shrug his shoulders before he started the next line. His disciples stayed close to him, sitting on the same rug, religious ecstasy visible in their eyes. Finally, he stopped.

Immediately he stood up, and they knew he was going to

speak. It was four o'clock, and the warm autumn sun was still shining on the park. The atmosphere was peaceful and the audience attentive and mellow from the concentration on the mantra. He began to speak to them, thanking everyone for joining in the *kīrtana*. The chanting of Hare Kṛṣṇa, he said, had been introduced five hundred years ago in West Bengal by Caitanya Mahāprabhu. *Hare* means "O energy of the Lord," Kṛṣṇa is Lord, and Rāma is also a name of the Supreme Lord, meaning "the highest pleasure." His disciples sat at his feet, listening. Rāya Rāma squinted through his shielding hand into the sun to see Swamiji, and Kīrtanānanda's head was cocked to one side, like a bird's who is listening to the ground.

Swamiji stood erect by the stout oak, his hands folded loosely before him in a proper speaker's posture, his light saffron robes covering him gracefully. The tree behind him seemed perfectly placed, and the sunshine dappled leafy shadows against the thick trunk. Behind him, through the grove of trees, was the steeple of St. Brigid's. On his right was a dumpy, middle-aged woman wearing a dress and a hairdo that had been out of style in the United States for twenty-five years. On his left was a bold-looking hippie girl in tight denims and beside her a young black man in a black sweater, his arms folded across his chest. Next was a young father holding an infant, then a bearded young street sadhu, his hair parted in the middle, and two ordinary, short-haired middle-class men and their young female companions. Many in the crowd, although standing close by, became distracted, looking off here and there.

Swamiji explained that there are three platforms—sensual, mental, and intellectual—and above them is the spiritual platform. The chanting of Hare Kṛṣṇa is on the spiritual platform, and it is the best process for reviving our eternal, blissful consciousness. He invited everyone to attend the meetings at 26 Second Avenue and concluded his brief speech by saying, "Thank you very much. Please chant with us." Then he sat down, took the drum, and began the *kīrtana* again.

If it were risky for a seventy-one-year-old man to thump a

drum and shout so loud, then he would take that risk for Kṛṣṇa. It was too good to stop. He had come far from Vṛndāvana, survived the non-Kṛṣṇa yoga society, waited all winter in obscurity. America had waited hundreds of years with no Kṛṣṇa-chanting. No "Hare Kṛṣṇa" had come from Thoreau's or Emerson's appreciations, though they had pored over English translations of the *Gītā* and *Purāṇas*. And no *kīrtana* had come from Vivekananda's famous speech on behalf of Hinduism at the World Parliament of Religions in Chicago in 1893. So now that he finally had *kṛṣṇa-bhakti* going, flowing like the Ganges to the sea, it could not stop. In his heart he felt the infinite will of Lord Caitanya to deliver the fallen souls.

He knew this was the desire of Lord Caitanya Mahāprabhu and his own spiritual master, even though caste-conscious *brāhmaṇas* in India would disapprove of his associating with such untouchables as these drug-mad American meat-eaters and their girl friends. But Swamiji explained that he was in full accord with the scriptures. The *Bhāgavatam* had clearly stated that Kṛṣṇa consciousness should be delivered to all races. Everyone was a spiritual soul, and regardless of birth could be brought to the highest spiritual platform by chanting the holy name. Never mind whatever sinful things they were doing, these people were perfect candidates for Kṛṣṇa consciousness. Tompkins Square Park was Kṛṣṇa's plan; it was also part of the earth, and these people were members of the human race. And the chanting of Hare Kṛṣṇa was the dharma for the age.

When Swamiji returned to the storefront he found a crowd of people from the park standing on the sidewalk outside his door—young people waiting for him to arrive and unlock the door to Matchless Gifts, waiting to learn more about the dance and the chant and the elderly swami and his disciples who had created such a beautiful scene in the park. They filled the storefront. Outside on the sidewalk, the timid or uncommitted loitered near the door or window, smoking and waiting or peering in, trying to see the paintings on the wall. Swamiji entered and walked directly to his dais and sat down before the largest gathering that had ever graced his temple. He spoke further of Kṛṣṇa consciousness, the words coming as naturally as breathing as he quoted the Sanskrit authority behind what they had all been experiencing in the park. Just as they had all chanted today, he said, so everyone should chant always.

It was late when he finally returned to his apartment. One of the boys brought him a cup of hot milk, and someone remarked they should do the chanting in the park every week. "Every day," Swamiji replied. Even while half a dozen people were present, he lay down on his thin mat. He continued to speak for some minutes, and then his voice trailed off, preaching in fragmented sentences. He appeared to doze. It was ten o'clock. They tiptoed out, softly shutting the door.

* * *

Hare Kṛṣṇa was becoming popular—regular *kīrtanas* in the parks, newspaper coverage. Hayagrīva called it "the Hare Kṛṣṇa explosion." The Lower East Side hippies considered the chanting of Hare Kṛṣṇa "one of the grooviest things happening," and that the Swami's disciples didn't take LSD didn't seem to affect their popularity. The devotees were accepted as angelic people, carrying the peaceful chanting to others and offering free food and a free place to stay. You could get the most interesting vegetarian food free at their place (if you went at the right time). And in their storefront, on the shelf by the door, were books from India.

In the clubs, local musicians played the melody that they had picked up from the Swami when he chanted in the park and at the temple. The Lower East Side was a neighborhood of artists and musicians, and now it was also the neighborhood of Hare Kṛṣṇa.

Evening *kīrtanas* were always big. Every night the little storefront would fill up until there was no place left to sit. There was a lot of interest in the group chanting and music-making, but after the *kīrtana,* when the talk was to begin, people would start to leave. It was not uncommon for half the audience to leave before the talk began, and sometimes people would leave in the middle of the lecture.

One evening, Allen Ginsberg brought Ed Sanders and Tuli Kupferberg of the Fugs to the meeting. The Fugs, a local group that had made a name for themselves, specialized in obscene lyrics. Among the popular songs of Ed Sanders were "Slum Goddess of the Lower East Side," "Group Grope," and "I Can't Get High." Ed had wild red hair and an electric-red beard, and he played a guitar during the *kīrtana.* The devotees were happy to see their prestigious guests.

The night of the Fugs, however, Swamiji chose to speak on the illusion of sexual pleasure. "Sex pleasure binds us to this material world birth after birth," he said, and he quoted, as he often did, a verse of Yāmunācārya: "Since I have become Kṛṣṇa conscious, whenever I think of sex life with a woman my face at once turns from it, and I spit at the thought." The Fugs never returned.

To speak ill of sexual pleasure was certainly not a strategic move for one who wanted to create followers among the Lower East Side hippies. But Bhaktivedanta Swami never considered changing his message. In fact, when Umāpati had mentioned that Americans didn't like to hear that sex was only for conceiving children, Bhaktivedanta Swami had replied, "I cannot change the philosophy to please the Americans."

"What about sex?" asked the ISKCON attorney, Steve Goldsmith, one evening, speaking out from the rear of the crowded temple.

"Sex should only be with one's wife," Swamiji said, "and that is also restricted. Sex is for the propagation of Kṛṣṇa conscious children. My spiritual master used to say that to beget Kṛṣṇa conscious children he was prepared to have sex a hundred times. Of course, that is most difficult in this age. Therefore, he remained a *brahmacārī.*"

"But sex is a very strong force," Mr. Goldsmith challenged. "What a man feels for a woman is undeniable."

"Therefore in every culture there is the institution of marriage," Prabhupāda replied. "You can get yourself married and live peacefully with one woman, but the wife should not be used as a machine for sense gratification. Sex should be restricted to once a month and only for the propagation of children."

Hayagrīva, who was seated just to Swamiji's left, beside the large, dangling cymbal, spoke out suddenly. "Only once a month?" And with a touch of facetious humor he added loudly, "Better to forget the whole thing!"

"Yes! That's it! Very good boy." Swamiji laughed, and others joined him. "It is best not to think of it. Best just to chant Hare Kṛṣṇa." And he held up his hands as if he were chanting on a strand of beads. "That way we will be saved from so much botheration. Sex is like the itching sensation, that's all. And as when we scratch, it gets worse, so we should tolerate the itching and ask Kṛṣṇa to help us. It is not easy. Sex is the highest pleasure in the material world, and it is also the greatest bondage."

But Steve Goldsmith was shaking his head. Swamiji looked at him, smiling: "There is still a problem?"

"It's just that . . . well, it's been proved dangerous to repress the sex drive. There's a theory that we have wars because—"

"People are eating meat," Prabhupāda interrupted. "As long as people eat meat, there will be war. And if a man eats meat, he will be sure to have illicit sex also."

Steve Goldsmith was an influential friend and supporter of ISKCON. But Prabhupāda would not change the philosophy of Kṛṣṇa consciousness "to please the Americans."

* * *

It was 11:00 p.m., and only one light was on in Swamiji's apartment—in the kitchenette. Swamiji was staying up, teaching Kīrtanānanda and Brahmānanda how to cook, because the next day (Sunday) they would be holding a feast for the public. Kīrtanānanda had suggested it be advertised as a "Love Feast," and Swamiji had adopted the name, although some thought it sounded strange at first to hear him say "Love Feast." The devotees had put up posters around the neighborhood and had made a sign for the window of the storefront, and Swamiji had said he would cook enough for at least fifty people. He said the Love Feasts should become an important part of ISKCON. As he had explained many times, food offered to Kṛṣṇa becomes spiritual, and whoever eats the *prasādam* receives great spiritual benefit. *Prasādam* meant "mercy."

Swamiji saw each of the nearly one dozen dishes through its final stages, and his disciples carried them into the front room in pots, one by one, and placed them before the picture of Lord Caitanya. There was *halavā, dāl,* two *sabjīs,* fancy rice, *purīs, samosās,* sweet rice, apple chutney, and *gulāb-jāmuns,* or sweetballs—ISKCON bullets. Swamiji had spent much time slowly deep-frying the sweetballs on a low heat, until they had turned golden brown and full. Then, one by one, he had lifted them out of the ghee with a slotted spoon and put them to soak in sweet syrup. He recognized that these golden, ghee-fried milk balls were his disciples' favorite *prasādam* treat. He called them "ISKCON bullets" because they were weapons in the war against maya. He even allowed that a jar of ISKCON bullets, floating in their syrup, be always on hand in the front room, where his disciples could take them without asking permission and without observing any regulated hours. They could take as many as they liked.

The first few Love Feasts were not very well attended, but the devotees were so enthusiastic about the feast *prasādam* that they showed no disappointment over the scarcity of guests. They were prepared to eat everything.

Satsvarūpa: *There was something called* "brāhmaṇa spaghetti," *which was rice-flour noodles cooked in ghee and soaked in sugar water. And there was* halavā, puṣpānna *rice with fried cheese balls,* samosās, *split mung beans fried into crunchy pellets and mixed with salt and spices,* purīs, gulāb-jāmuns. *And everything was succulent—that was the word*

His Divine Grace
A. C. Bhaktivedanta Swami Prabhupāda
Founder-Ācārya of the International Society for Krishna Consciousness

Gour Mohan De taught his son Abhay to worship the Rādhā-Kṛṣṇa Deities.

Begining from the age of five, Abhay performed a miniature Ratha-yātrā festival. More than sixty-five years later, he enacted the same festival on a magnificent scale in many Western cities.

Abhay Charan first met his spiritual master, Bhaktisiddhānta Sarasvatī, in Calcutta in 1922.

Soon after his first meeting with Śrīla Bhaktisiddhānta Sarasvatī in Calcutta, Abhay moved his family to Allahabad, where he based his pharmaceutical business. Although ten years elapsed before their next meeting, within his heart Abhay accepted Śrīla Bhaktisiddhānta Sarasvatī as his spiritual master and thought of him always.

Bhaktisiddhānta Sarasvatī initiated Abhay in Allahabad in 1932.

It was at Rādhā-kuṇḍa Vṛndāvana, in November 1935, that Bhaktisiddhānta Sarasvatī told Abhay, "If you ever get money, print books."

In the 1940s, while living in Calcutta, Abhay tried to involve his wife and son in preaching.

In Jhansi in the early 1950s, Abhay attempted to form a worldwide organization, The League of Devotees.

Begining in 1956, Abhay distributed his *Back to Godhead* magazine in New Delhi.

In the year 1962-1965, A.C. Bhaktivedanta Swami wrote and printed the first three volumes of *Śrīmad-Bhāgavatam*.

Abhay used this picture of Bhaktisiddhānta Sarasvatī in the logo of *Back to Godhead* magazine.

An Ad for one of Abhay's pharmaceutical products.

Allahabad, circa 1924. Left to right: (sitting) Abhay and his son Prayag Raj; his father, Gour Mohan; His eldest sister, Rajesvari, with his daughter, Sulakshman; (standing) Abhay's wife, Radharani; his nephew Tulasi; his brother Krishna Charan.

Sita Kanta Banerjee Lane, Calcutta, where Abhay and his family lived in the 1940s.

September 17, 1959, the day Abhay took *sannyāsa.* Left to right: Muni Maharaja, Bhaktiprajñāna Keśava Mahārāja, and A. C. Bhaktivedanta Swami.

A. C. Bhaktivedanta Swami's room at the Rādhā-Dāmodara temple.

A. C. Bhaktivedanta Swami's kitchen at the Rādhā-Dāmodara temple in Vṛndāvana. From this room he could see the *samādhi* of Rūpa Gosvāmi.

The press that printed the first volume of *Śrīmad Bhāgavatam* in 1962.

A. C. Bhaktivedanta Swami and Prime Minister Lal Bahadur Shastri at the Parliament Buildi in New Delhi in June 1964.

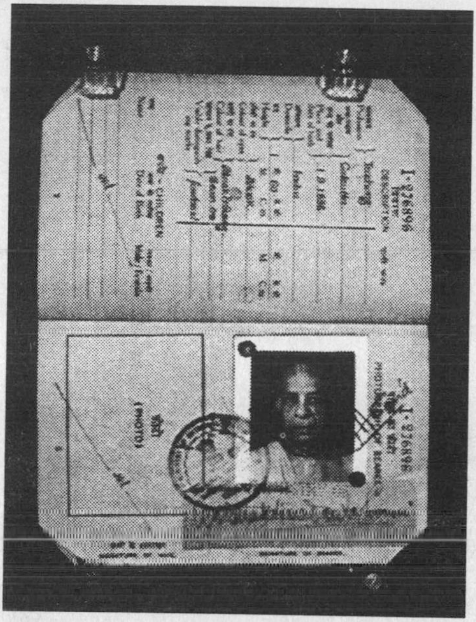

Śrīla Prabhupāda's passport.

The *Jaladuta: "If the Atlantic would have shown its usual face, perhaps I would have died. But Lord Kṛṣṇa has taken charge of the ship."*

Photo from the *Butler Eagle,* September 22, 1965. This was the first news coverage of Śrīla Prabhupāda in America.

Cooking lunch in Sally Agarwal's kitchen: *"He prepares his meals in a brass pan with separate levels for steaming rice, vegetables and making 'bread' at the same time."*

Hayagrīva used. "Yes," he would say, expressing it waggishly, "everything was very succulent."

Eating the feast was an intense experience. We were supposed to be subduing our senses all week, following strict regulations, controlling the tongue. And the feast was a kind of reward. Swamiji and Kṛṣṇa were giving us a taste of full spiritual ecstasy, even though we were still beginners and still in the material world. Before taking my plateful, I would pray, "Please let me remain in Kṛṣṇa consciousness, because it is so nice and I am so fallen. Let me serve Swamiji, and let me now enjoy this feast in transcendental bliss." And I would begin eating, going from one taste sensation to another—the good rice, the favorite vegetable, the bread, and saving the gulābjāmun *for last, thinking, "I can have seconds, and if I like, thirds." We would keep our eyes on the big pots, confident that there was as much as we wanted. It was a time of rededication. We all enjoyed with completely open relish and sense gratification. Eating was very important.*

Gradually, attendance picked up. The feasts were free, and they were reputed to be delicious. Mostly local hippies came, but occasionally a higher class of experimenting New Yorkers or even parents of one of the devotees would come. When the small temple was filled, guests would sit in the courtyard. They would take their *prasādam*-laden paper plates into the backyard garden and sit beneath the fire escape or at the picnic table or anywhere. And after eating, they would go back into the storefront for more. Devotees were stationed behind the pots of *prasādam*, and guests would come by for seconds. The other tenants were not very happy about seeing the courtyard full of festive guests, and the devotees tried to pacify them by bringing them plates of *prasādam*. Although Swamiji would not go down to the temple, he would take a plate in his room and hear with pleasure about the success of his new program.

One time the devotees were eating so ravenously that they threatened to eat everything available before the guests had all been served, and Kīrtanānanda had to admonish them for their selfish attitude. Gradually, they were understanding that the Sunday feast was not just for their fun and pleasure, but to bring people to Kṛṣṇa consciousness.

* * *

Bhaktivedanta Swami had begun *Back to Godhead* magazine in India. Although he had been writing articles since the 1930s, it was in 1944, in Calcutta, that he had single-handedly begun the magazine, in response to his spiritual master's request that he preach Kṛṣṇa consciousness in English. It had been with great difficulty that through his pharmaceutical business he had managed to gather the four hundred rupees a month for printing. And he had single-handedly written, edited, published, financed, and distributed each issue. In those early years, *Back to Godhead* had been Bhaktivedanta Swami's major literary work and preaching mission. He had envisioned widespread distribution of the magazine, and he had thought of plans for spreading the message of Lord Caitanya all over the world. He had drawn up a list of major countries and the number of copies of *Back to Godhead* he wanted to send to each. He sought donations to finance this project, but help was scarce. Then, in 1959 he had turned his energies toward writing and publishing the *Śrīmad-Bhāgavatam*. But now he wanted to revive *Back to Godhead,* and this time it would not be done single-handedly. This time he would give the responsibility to his disciples.

One of Swamiji's disciples, Gargamuni, learned that a country club in Queens was trying to sell its small A.B. Dick press. Swamiji was interested, and he rode out to Queens in a borrowed van with Gargamuni and Kīrtanānanda to see the machine. It was old, but in good condition. The manager of the country club wanted $250 for it. Swamiji looked over the machine carefully and talked with the manager, telling him of his spiritual mission. The manager mentioned a second press he had on hand and explained that neither machine was actually of any use to him. So Swamiji said he would pay $250 for both machines; the country club did not really need them, and besides, the manager should help out, since Swamiji had an important spiritual message to print for the benefit of all humanity. The man agreed. Swamiji had Gargamuni and Kīrtanānanda load both machines into the van, and ISKCON had its printing press.

Bhaktivedanta Swami gave over the editorship of *Back to Godhead* to Hayagrīva and Rāya Rāma. For so many years he had taken *Back to Godhead* as his personal service to his spiritual master, but now he would let young men like Hayagrīva, the college English teacher, and Rāya Rāma, the professional writer, take up *Back to Godhead* magazine as their service to *their* spiritual master. In a short time, Hayagrīva and Rāya Rāma had compiled the first issue and were ready to print.

It was an off night—no public *kīrtana* and lecture—and Swamiji was up in his room working on his translation of *Śrīmad-Bhāgavatam.* Downstairs, the printing of the first issue had been going on for hours. Rāya Rāma had typed the stencils, and during the printing he had stood nervously over the machine, examining the printing quality of each page, stroking his beard, and murmuring "Hmmmmm." Now it was time to collate and staple each magazine. The stencils had lasted for one hundred copies, and one hundred copies of each of the twenty-eight pages and the front and back covers were now lined up along two of the unvarnished benches Raphael had made that summer. A few devotees collated and stapled the magazine in an assembly line, walking along the stacks of pages, taking one page under another until they reached the end of the bench and gave the assembled stack of pages to Gargamuni, who stood brushing his long hair out of his eyes, stapling each magazine with the stapler and staples Brahmānanda had brought from his Board of Education office. Even Hayagrīva, who usually didn't volunteer for menial duties, was there, walking down the line, collating.

Suddenly the side door opened, and to their surprise they saw Swamiji looking in at them. Then he opened the door wide and entered the room. He had never come down like this on an off night before. They felt an unexpected flush of emotion and love for him, and they dropped down on their knees, bowing their heads to the floor. "No, no," he said, raising his hand to stop them as some were still bowing and others already rising to their feet. "Continue what you are doing." When they stood up and saw him standing with them, they weren't sure what to do. But obviously he had come down to see them producing his *Back to Godhead* magazine, so they continued working, silently and efficiently. Prabhupāda walked down the row of pages, his hand and wrist extending gracefully from the folds of his shawl as he touched a stack of pages and then a finished magazine. "ISKCON Press," he said.

Jagannātha had designed the cover, using a pen-and-ink drawing of Rādhā and Kṛṣṇa similar to his painting in the temple. It was a simple drawing set within a pattern of concentric circles. The first page opened with the same motto Prabhupāda had used for years on his *Back to Godhead:* "Godhead is light, nescience is darkness. Where there is Godhead there is no nescience."

Prabhupāda's first and main instruction to his editors had been that they should produce the magazine *regularly—every month.* Even if they didn't know how to sell the copies or even if they only turned out two pages, they had to continue bearing the standard.

He called Hayagrīva to his room and presented him a complete three-volume set of his *Śrīmad-Bhāgavatam.* On the front page of each volume he had written, "To Sriman Hayagriva das Brahmacari with my blessings, A. C. Bhaktivedanta Swami." Hayagrīva was grateful and mentioned that he had not been able to afford them. "That's all right," Prabhupāda said. "Now you compile this *Back to Godhead.* Work sincerely, and make it as big as *Time* magazine."

Prabhupāda wanted all his disciples to take part in it. "Don't be dull," he said. "Write something." He wanted to give his disciples *Back to Godhead* for their own preaching. Brahmānanda and Gargamuni took the first issues out that same night on bicycles, riding to every head shop on the Lower East Side, all the way to Fourteenth Street and as far west as the West Village, until they had distributed all one hundred issues. This was an increase in the preaching. Now all his students could take part in the work—typing, editing, writing, assembling, selling. It was *his* preaching, of course, but he wasn't alone any more.

* * *

Not long after their wedding, Mukunda and Jānakī had left for the West Coast. Mukunda had told Swamiji that he wanted to go on to India to study Indian music, but after a few weeks in southern Oregon he had ended up in San Francisco. Now he had a better idea. He wanted to rent a place and invite Swamiji to come and start his Hare Kṛṣṇa movement in the Haight-Ashbury district, just as he was doing on the Lower East Side. He said that the prospects there for Kṛṣṇa consciousness were very good.

Sometimes, during the evening gatherings in his room, Swamiji would ask whether Mukunda was ready on the West Coast. For months, Swamiji's going to the West Coast had been one of a number of alternatives. But then, during the first week of January 1967, a letter arrived from Mukunda: he had rented a storefront in the heart of the Haight-Ashbury district, on Frederick Street. "We are busy converting it into a temple now," he wrote. And Swamiji announced, "I shall go immediately."

Mukunda told of a "Gathering of the Tribes" in San Francisco's Haight-Ashbury. Thousands of hippies were migrating from all over the country to the very neighborhood where Mukunda had rented the storefront. It was a youth renaissance much bigger than what was going on in New York City. In a scheme to raise funds for the new temple, Mukunda was planning a "Mantra-Rock Dance," and famous bands were going to appear. And Swami Bhaktivedanta and the chanting of Hare Kṛṣṇa were to be the center of attraction!

Although in his letter Mukunda had enclosed a plane ticket, some of Swamiji's followers refused to accept that Swamiji would use it. Those who knew they could not leave New York began to criticize the idea of Swamiji's going to

San Francisco. They didn't think that people out on the West Coast could take care of Swamiji properly. Swamiji appearing with rock musicians? Those people out there didn't seem to have the proper respect. Anyway, there was no suitable temple there. There was no printing press, no *Back to Godhead* magazine. Why should Swamiji leave New York to attend a function like *that* with strangers in California? How could he leave them behind in New York? How could their spiritual life continue without him?

Timidly, one or two dissenters indirectly expressed some of these feelings to Swamiji, as if almost wishing to admonish him for thinking of leaving them, and even hinting that things would not go well, either in San Francisco or New York, if he departed. But they found him quite confident and determined. He did not belong to New York; he belonged to Kṛṣṇa. And he had to go wherever Kṛṣṇa desired him to preach. He was completely detached, eager to travel and expand the chanting of Hare Kṛṣṇa.

Brahmānanda: *But we were shocked that he was going to leave. I never thought that Kṛṣṇa consciousness would go beyond the Lower East Side, what to speak of New York City. I thought that this was it, and it would stay here eternally.*

In the last days of the second week of January, final plane reservations were made, and the devotees began packing Swamiji's manuscripts away in trunks. Raṇacora, a new devotee recruited from Tompkins Square Park, had collected enough money for a plane ticket, and the devotees decided that he should accompany Swamiji as his personal assistant. Swamiji explained that he would only be gone a few weeks, and that he wanted all the programs to go on in his absence.

He waited in his room while the boys arranged for a car to take him to the airport. The day was gray and cold, and steam hissed in the radiators. He would take only a suitcase—mostly clothes and some books. He checked the closet to see that his manuscripts were in order. Kīrtanānanda would take care of the things in his apartment. He sat down at his desk where, for more than six months, he had sat so many times, working for hours at the typewriter preparing his *Bhagavad-gītā* and *Śrīmad-Bhāgavatam,* and where he had sat talking to so many guests and to his followers. But today he would not be talking with friends or typing a manuscript, but waiting a last few minutes alone before his departure.

This was his second winter in New York. He had launched a movement of Kṛṣṇa consciousness. A few sincere boys and girls had joined. They were already well known on the Lower East Side—many notices in the newspapers. And it was only the beginning.

He had left Vṛndāvana for this. At first he had not been certain whether he would stay in America more than two months. In Butler he had presented his books. But then in New York he had seen how Dr. Mishra had developed things, and the Māyāvādīs had a big building. They were taking money and not even delivering the real message of the *Gītā.* But the American people were looking.

These months in America had been difficult. His Godbrothers hadn't been interested in helping, although this was what their Guru Maharaja, Śrīla Bhaktisiddhānta Sarasvatī Ṭhākura, wanted, and what Lord Caitanya wanted. Because Lord Caitanya wanted it, His blessings would come, and it would happen.

This was a nice place, 26 Second Avenue. He had started here. The boys would keep it up. Some of them were donating their salaries. It was a start.

Bhaktivedanta Swami looked at his watch. He put on his tweed winter coat and his hat and shoes, put his right hand in his bead bag, and continued chanting. He walked out of the apartment, down the stairs, and through the courtyard, which was now frozen and still, its trees starkly bare without a single leaf remaining. And he left the storefront behind.

He left, even while Brahmānanda, Rūpānuga, and Satsvarūpa were at their office jobs. There was not even a farewell scene or a farewell address.

CHAPTER THREE

Only He Could Lead Them

San Francisco
January 16, 1967

When the announcement for United Airlines Flight 21 from New York came over the public-address system, the group of about fifty hippies gathered closer together in anticipation. For a moment they appeared almost apprehensive, unsure of what to expect or what the Swami would be like.

Roger Segal: *We were quite an assorted lot, even for the San Francisco airport. Mukunda was wearing a Merlin the Magician robe with paisley squares all around, Sam was wearing a Moroccan sheep robe with a hood—he even smelled like a sheep—and I was wearing a sort of blue homemade Japanese samurai robe with small white dots. Long strings of beads were everywhere. Buckskins, boots, army fatigues, people wearing small, round sunglasses—the whole phantasmagoria of San Francisco at its height.*

Only a few people in the crowd knew Swamiji: Mukunda and his wife, Jānakī; Ravīndra-svarūpa; Rāya Rāma—all from New York. And Allen Ginsberg was there. (A few days before, Allen had been one of the leaders of the Human Be-In in Golden Gate Park, where over two hundred thousand had come together—"A Gathering of the Tribes . . . for a joyful pow-wow and Peace Dance.")

Swamiji would be pleased, Mukunda reminded everyone, if they were all chanting Hare Kṛṣṇa when he came through the gate. They were already familiar with the Hare Kṛṣṇa mantra. They had heard about the Swami's chanting in the park in New York or they had seen the article about Swamiji and the chanting in the local underground paper, *The Oracle*. Earlier today they had gathered in Golden Gate Park—most of them responding to a flyer Mukunda had distributed—and had chanted there for more than an hour before coming to the airport in a caravan of cars. Now many of them—also in response to Mukunda's flyer—stood with incense and flowers in their hands.

As the disembarking passengers entered the terminal gate and walked up the ramp, they looked in amazement at the reception party of flower-bearing chanters. The chanters, however, gazed past these ordinary, tired-looking travelers, searching for that special person who was supposed to be on the plane. Suddenly, walking toward them was Swamiji, golden-complexioned, dressed in bright saffron robes.

He had heard the chanting even before he had entered the terminal, and he had begun to smile. He was happy and surprised. Glancing over the faces, he recognized only a few. Yet here were fifty people receiving him and chanting Hare Kṛṣṇa without his having said a word!

The crowd of hippies had formed a line on either side of a narrow passage through which Swamiji would walk. As he passed among his new admirers, dozens of hands stretched out to offer him flowers and incense. He smiled, collecting the offerings in his hands while Raṇacora looked on. Allen Ginsberg stepped forward with a large bouquet of flowers, and Bhaktivedanta Swami graciously accepted it. Then he began offering the gifts back to all who reached out to receive them. He proceeded through the terminal, the crowd of young people walking beside him, chanting.

At the baggage claim he waited for a moment, his eyes taking in everyone around him. Lifting his open palms, he beckoned everyone to chant louder, and the group burst into renewed chanting, with the Swami standing in their midst, softly clapping his hands and singing Hare Kṛṣṇa. Gracefully, he then raised his arms above his head and began to dance, stepping and swaying from side to side.

To the mixed chagrin, amusement, and irresistible joy of the airport workers and passengers, the reception party stayed with the Swami until he got his luggage. Then they escorted him outside into the sunlight and into a waiting car, a black 1949 Cadillac Fleetwood. Swamiji got into the back seat with Mukunda and Allen Ginsberg. Until the moment the car pulled away from the curb, Swamiji, still smiling, continued handing flowers to all those who had come to welcome him as he brought Kṛṣṇa consciousness west.

The Cadillac belonged to Harvey Cohen, who almost a year before had allowed the Swami to stay in his Bowery loft. Harvey was driving, but because of his chauffeur's hat (picked up at a Salvation Army store) and his black suit and his beard, Swamiji didn't recognize him.

"Where is Harvey?"

"He's driving," Mukunda said.

"Oh, is that you? I didn't recognize you."

Harvey smiled. "Welcome to San Francisco, Swamiji."

Bhaktivedanta Swami was happy to be in another big Western city on behalf of his spiritual master, Bhaktisiddhānta Sarasvatī, and Lord Caitanya. The further west one goes, Lord Caitanya had said, the more materialistic the people. Yet Lord Caitanya had also said that Kṛṣṇa consciousness should spread all over the world. Swamiji's Godbrothers had often wondered about Lord Caitanya's statement that one day the name of Kṛṣṇa would be sung in every town and village. Perhaps that verse should be taken symbolically, they said; otherwise, what could it mean—Kṛṣṇa in every town? But Bhaktivedanta Swami had deep faith in that statement by Lord Caitanya and in the instruction of his spiritual master. Here he was in the far-Western city of San Francisco, and already people were chanting. They had enthusiastically received him with flowers and *kīrtana*. And all over the world there were other cities much like this one.

The temple Mukunda and his friends had obtained was on Frederick Street, in the Haight-Ashbury district. Like the temple at 26 Second Avenue in New York, it was a small storefront with a display window facing the street. A sign over the window read, SRI SRI RADHA KRISHNA TEMPLE.

Mukunda and his friends had also rented a three-room apartment for Swamiji on the third floor of the adjoining building. It was a small, bare, run-down apartment facing the street.

Followed by several carloads of devotees and curious seekers, Swamiji arrived at 518 Frederick Street and entered the storefront, which was decorated only by a few madras cloths on the wall. Taking his seat on a cushion, he led a *kīrtana* and then spoke, inviting everyone to take up Kṛṣṇa consciousness.

After his lecture he left the storefront and walked next door and up the two flights of stairs to his apartment. As he entered his apartment, number 32, he was followed not only by his devotees and admirers but also by reporters from San Francisco's main newspapers: the *Chronicle* and the *Examiner.* While some devotees cooked his lunch and Raṇacora unpacked his suitcase, Swamiji talked with the reporters, who sat on the floor, taking notes on their pads.

Reporter: "Downstairs, you said you were inviting everyone to Kṛṣṇa consciousness. Does that include the Haight-Ashbury Bohemians and beatniks?"

Swamiji: "Yes, everyone, including you or anybody else, be he or she what is called an 'acidhead' or a hippie or something else. But once he is accepted for training, he becomes something else from what he had been before."

Reporter: "What does one have to do to become a member of your movement?"

Swamiji: "There are four prerequisites. I do not allow my students to keep girl friends. I prohibit all kinds of intoxicants, including coffee, tea, and cigarettes. I prohibit meat-eating. And I prohibit my students from taking part in gambling."

Reporter: "Do these shall-not commandments extend to the use of LSD, marijuana, and other narcotics?"

Swamiji: "I consider LSD to be an intoxicant. I do not allow any one of my students to use that or any intoxicant. I train my students to rise early in the morning, to take a bath early in the day, and to attend prayer meetings three times a day. Our sect is one of austerity. It is the science of God."

Although Bhaktivedanta Swami had found that reporters generally did not report his philosophy, he took the opportunity to preach Kṛṣṇa consciousness. Even if the reporters didn't want to delve into the philosophy, his followers did. "The big mistake of modern civilization," Swamiji continued, "is to encroach upon others' property as though it were one's own. This creates an unnatural disturbance. God is the ultimate proprietor of everything in the universe. When people know that God is the ultimate proprietor, the best friend of all living entities, and the object of all offerings and sacrifices—then there will be peace."

After the reporters left, Swamiji continued speaking to the young people in his room. Mukunda, who had allowed his hair and beard to grow but who wore around his neck the strand of large red beads Swamiji had given him at initiation, introduced some of his friends and explained that they were all living together and that they wanted to help Swamiji present Kṛṣṇa consciousness to the young people of San Francisco. Mukunda's wife, Jānakī, asked Swamiji about his plane ride. He said it had been pleasant except for some pressure in his ears. "The houses looked like matchboxes," he said, and with his thumb and forefinger he indicated the size of a matchbox.

He leaned back against the wall and took off the garlands he had received that day, until only a beaded necklace—a common, inexpensive item with a small bell on it—remained hanging around his neck. He held it, inspected the workmanship, and toyed with it. "This is special," he said, looking up, "because it was made with devotion." He continued to pay attention to the necklace, as if receiving it had been one of the most important events of the day.

When Swamiji's lunch arrived, he distributed some to everyone, and then Raṇacora efficiently though tactlessly asked everyone to leave and give the Swami a little time to eat and rest.

Outside the apartment and in the storefront below, the talk was of Swamiji. No one had been disappointed. Everything Mukunda had been telling them about him was true. They particularly enjoyed how he had talked about seeing everything from Kṛṣṇa's viewpoint.

That night on television Swamiji's arrival was covered on the eleven o'clock news, and the next day it appeared in the newspapers. The *Examiner's* story was on page two—"Swami Invites the Hippies"—along with a photo of the temple, filled with followers, and some shots of Swamiji, who looked very grave. Swamiji had Mukunda read the article aloud.

San Francisco's largest paper, the *Chronicle,* also ran an article: "Swami in Hippie-Land—Holy Man Opens S.F. Temple." The article began, "A holy man from India, described by his friend and beat poet Allen Ginsberg as one of the more conservative leaders of his faith, launched a kind of evangelistic effort yesterday in the heart of San Francisco's hippie haven."

Swamiji objected to being called conservative. He was indignant: "Conservative? How is that?"

"In respect to sex and drugs," Mukunda suggested.

"Of course, we are conservative in that sense," Swamiji said. "That simply means we are following *śāstra.* We cannot depart from *Bhagavad-gītā.* But conservative we are not. Caitanya Mahāprabhu was so strict that He would not even look on a woman, but we are accepting everyone into this movement, regardless of sex, caste, position, or whatever. Everyone is invited to come chant Hare Kṛṣṇa. This is Caitanya Mahāprabhu's munificence, His liberality. No, we are not conservative."

* * *

Bhaktivedanta Swami rose from bed and turned on the light. It was one a.m. Although the alarm had not sounded and no one had come to wake him, he had risen on his own. The apartment was cold and quiet. Wrapping his *cādar* around his shoulders, he sat quietly at his makeshift desk (a trunk filled with manuscripts) and in deep concentration chanted the Hare Kṛṣṇa mantra on his beads.

After an hour of chanting, Bhaktivedanta Swami turned to his writing. Although two years had passed since he had published a book (the third and final volume of the First Canto of *Śrīmad-Bhāgavatam*), he had daily been working, sometimes on his translation and commentary of the Second Canto but mostly on *Bhagavad-gītā*. In the 1940s in India he had written an entire *Bhagavad-gītā* translation and commentary, but his only copy had mysteriously disappeared. Then in 1965, after a few months in America, he had begun again, starting with the Introduction, which he had composed in his room on Seventy-second Street in New York. Now thousands of manuscript pages filled his trunk, completing his *Bhagavad-gītā*. If his New York disciple Hayagrīva, formerly an English professor, could edit it, and if some of the other disciples could get it published, that would be an important achievement.

But publishing books in America seemed difficult—more difficult than in India. Even though in India he had been alone, he had managed to publish three volumes in three years. Here in America he had many followers; but many followers meant increased responsibilities. And none of his followers as yet seemed seriously inclined to take up typing, editing, and dealing with American businessmen. Yet despite the dim prospects for publishing his *Bhagavad-gītā*, Bhaktivedanta Swami had begun translating another book, *Caitanya-caritāmṛta*, the principal Vaiṣṇava scripture on the life and teachings of Lord Caitanya.

Putting on his reading glasses, Swamiji opened his books and turned on the dictating machine. He studied the Bengali and Sanskrit texts, then picked up the microphone, flicked the switch to *record*, flashing on a small red light, and began speaking: "While the Lord was going, chanting and dancing, . . ." (he spoke no more than a phrase at a time, flicking the switch, pausing, and then dictating again) "thousands of people were following Him, . . . and some of them were laughing, some were dancing, . . . and some singing. . . . Some of them were falling on the ground offering obeisances to the Lord." Speaking and pausing, clicking the switch on and off, he would sit straight, sometimes gently rocking and nodding his head as he urged forward his words. Or he would bend low over his books, carefully studying them through his reading glasses.

An hour passed, and Swamiji worked on. The building was dark except for Swamiji's lamp and quiet except for the sound of his voice and the click and hum of the dictating machine. He wore a faded peach turtleneck jersey beneath his gray wool *cādar,* and since he had just risen from bed, his saffron dhoti was wrinkled. Without having washed his face or gone to the bathroom, he sat absorbed in his work. At least for these few rare hours, the street and the Rādhā-Kṛṣṇa temple were quiet.

This situation—at night, with the surroundings quiet, and him at his transcendental literary work—was not much different from his early-morning hours in his room at the Rādhā-Dāmodara temple in Vṛndāvana, India. There, of course, he had had no dictating machine, but he had worked during the same hours and from the same text, *Caitanya-caritāmṛta.* Once he had begun a verse-by-verse translation with commentary, and another time he had written essays on the text. Now, having just arrived in this corner of the world, so remote from the scenes of Lord Caitanya's pastimes, he was beginning the first chapter of a new English version of *Caitanya-caritāmṛta.* He called it *Teachings of Lord Caitanya.*

He was following what had become a vital routine in his life: rising early and writing the *paramparā* message of Kṛṣṇa consciousness. Putting aside all other considerations, disregarding present circumstances, he would merge into the timeless message of transcendental knowledge. This was his most important service to Bhaktisiddhānta Sarasvatī. The thought of producing more books and distributing them widely inspired him to rise every night and translate.

Bhaktivedanta Swami worked until dawn. Then he stopped and prepared himself to go down to the temple for the morning meeting.

* * *

Though some of the New York disciples had objected, Swamiji was still scheduled for the Mantra-Rock Dance at the Avalon Ballroom. It wasn't proper, they had said, for the devotees out in San Francisco to ask their spiritual master to go to such a place. It would mean amplified guitars, pounding drums, wild light shows, and hundreds of drugged hippies. How could his pure message be heard in such a place?

But in San Francisco Mukunda and others had been working on the Mantra-Rock Dance for months. It would draw thousands of young people, and the San Francisco Rādhā-Kṛṣṇa Temple stood to make thousands of dollars. So although among his New York disciples Swamiji had expressed uncertainty, he now said nothing to deter the enthusiasm of his San Francisco followers.

Sam Speerstra, Mukunda's friend and one of the Mantra-Rock organizers, explained the idea to Hayagrīva, who had just arrived from New York: "There's a whole new school of San Francisco music opening up. The Grateful Dead have already cut their first record. Their offer to do this dance is a great publicity boost just when we need it."

"But Swamiji says that even Ravi Shankar is maya," Hayagrīva said.

"Oh, it's all been arranged," Sam assured him. "All the bands will be onstage, and Allen Ginsberg will introduce Swamiji to San Francisco. Swamiji will talk and then chant Hare Kṛṣṇa, with the bands joining in. Then he leaves. There should be around four thousand people there."

Bhaktivedanta Swami knew he would not compromise himself; he would go, chant, and then leave. The important thing was to spread the chanting of Hare Kṛṣṇa. If thousands of young people gathering to hear rock music could be engaged in hearing and chanting the names of God, then what was the harm? As a preacher, Bhaktivedanta Swami was prepared to go anywhere to spread Kṛṣṇa consciousness. Since chanting Hare Kṛṣṇa was absolute, one who heard or chanted the names of Kṛṣṇa—anyone, anywhere, in any condition—could be saved from falling to the lower species in the next life. These young hippies wanted something spiritual, but they had no direction. They were confused, accepting hallucinations as spiritual visions. But they were seeking genuine spiritual life, just like many of the young people on the Lower East Side. Bhaktivedanta Swami decided he would go; his disciples wanted him to, and he was their servant and the servant of Lord Caitanya.

Mukunda, Sam, and Harvey Cohen had already met with rock entrepreneur Chet Helms, who had agreed that they could use his Avalon Ballroom and that, if they could get the bands to come, everything above the cost for the groups, the security, and a few other basics would go as profit for the San Francisco Rādhā-Kṛṣṇa Temple. Mukunda and Sam had then gone calling on the music groups, most of whom lived in the Bay Area, and one after another the exciting new San Francisco rock bands—the Grateful Dead, Moby Grape, Big Brother and the Holding Company, Jefferson Airplane, Quicksilver Messenger Service—had agreed to appear with Swami Bhaktivedanta for the minimum wage of $250 per group. And Allen Ginsberg had agreed. The lineup was complete.

On the night of the Mantra-Rock Dance people lined up all the way down the street and around the block, waiting for tickets at $2.50 apiece. Attendance would be good, a capacity crowd, and most of the local luminaries were coming. LSD pioneer Timothy Leary arrived and was given a special seat onstage. Swami Kriyananda came, carrying a tamboura. A man wearing a top hat and a suit with a silk sash that said SAN FRANCISCO arrived, claiming to be the mayor. At the door Mukunda stopped a respectably dressed young man who didn't have a ticket. But then someone tapped Mukunda on the shoulder: "Let him in. It's all right. He's Owsley." Mukunda apologized and submitted, allowing Augustus Owsley Stanley II, folk hero and famous synthesizer of LSD, to enter without a ticket.

Almost everyone who came wore bright or unusual costumes: tribal robes, Mexican ponchos, Indian *kurtās*, "God's-eyes," feathers, and beads. Some hippies brought their own flutes, lutes, gourds, drums, rattles, horns, and guitars. The

Hell's Angels, dirty-haired, wearing jeans, boots, and denim jackets and accompanied by their women, made their entrance, carrying chains, smoking cigarettes, and displaying their regalia of German helmets, emblazoned emblems, and so on—everything but their motorcycles, which they had parked outside.

The devotees began a warm-up *kīrtana* onstage, dancing the way Swamiji had shown them. Incense poured from the stage and from the corners of the large ballroom. And although most in the audience were high on drugs, the atmosphere was calm; they had come seeking a spiritual experience. As the chanting began, very melodiously, some of the musicians took part by playing their instruments. The light show began; strobe lights flashed, colored balls bounced back and forth to the beat of the music, large blobs of pulsing color splurted across the floor, walls, and ceiling.

A little after eight o'clock, Moby Grape took the stage. With heavy electric guitars, electric bass, and two drummers, they launched into their first number. The large speakers shook the ballroom with their vibrations, and a roar of approval rose from the audience.

Around nine-thirty, Swamiji left his Frederick Street apartment and got into the back seat of Harvey's Cadillac. He was dressed in his usual saffron robes, and around his neck he wore a garland of gardenias, whose sweet aroma filled the car. On the way to the Avalon he talked about the need to open more centers.

At ten o'clock Swamiji walked up the stairs of the Avalon, followed by Kīrtanānanda and Raṇacora. As he entered the ballroom, devotees blew conchshells, someone began a drum roll, and the crowd parted down the center, all the way from the entrance to the stage, opening a path for him to walk. With his head held high, Swamiji seemed to float by as he walked through the strange milieu, making his way across the ballroom floor to the stage.

Suddenly the light show changed. Pictures of Kṛṣṇa and His pastimes flashed onto the wall: Kṛṣṇa and Arjuna riding together on Arjuna's chariot, Kṛṣṇa eating butter, Kṛṣṇa subduing the whirlwind demon, Kṛṣṇa playing the flute. As Swamiji walked through the crowd, everyone stood, applauding and cheering. He climbed the stairs and seated himself softly on a waiting cushion. The crowd quieted.

Looking over at Allen Ginsberg, Swamiji said, "You can speak something about the mantra."

Allen began to tell of his understanding and experience with the Hare Kṛṣṇa mantra. He told how Bhaktivedanta Swami had opened a storefront on Second Avenue and had chanted Hare Kṛṣṇa in Tompkins Square Park. And he invited everyone to the Frederick Street temple. "I especially recommend the early-morning *kīrtanas,*" he said, "for those who, coming down from LSD, want to stabilize their consciousness on reentry."

Swamiji spoke, giving a brief history of the mantra. Then he looked over at Allen again: "You may chant."

Allen began playing his harmonium and chanting into the microphone, singing the tune he had brought from India. Gradually more and more people in the audience caught on and began chanting. As the *kīrtana* continued and the audience got increasingly enthusiastic, musicians from the various bands came onstage to join in. Raṇacora, a fair drummer, began playing Moby Grape's drums. Some of the bass and other guitar players joined in as the devotees and a large group of hippies mounted the stage. The multicolored oil slicks pulsed, and the balls bounced back and forth to the beat of the mantra, now projected onto the wall: Hare Kṛṣṇa, Hare Kṛṣṇa, Kṛṣṇa Kṛṣṇa, Hare Hare/ Hare Rāma, Hare Rāma, Rāma Rāma, Hare Hare. As the chanting spread throughout the hall, some of the hippies got to their feet, held hands, and danced.

Allen Ginsberg: *We sang Hare Kṛṣṇa all evening. It was absolutely great—an open thing. It was the height of the Haight-Ashbury spiritual enthusiasm. It was the first time that there had been a music scene in San Francisco where everybody could be a part of it and participate. Everybody could sing and dance rather than listen to other people sing and dance.*

Jānakī: *People didn't know what they were chanting for. But to see that many people chanting—even though most of them were intoxicated—made Swamiji very happy. He loved to see the people chanting.*

Hayagrīva: *Standing in front of the bands, I could hardly hear. But above all, I could make out the chanting of Hare Kṛṣṇa, building steadily. On the wall behind, a slide projected a huge picture of Kṛṣṇa in a golden helmet with a peacock feather, a flute in His hand.*

Then Swamiji stood up, lifted his arms, and began to dance. He gestured for everyone to join him, and those who were still seated stood up and began dancing and chanting and swaying back and forth, following Swamiji's gentle dance.

Roger Segal: *The ballroom appeared as if it was a human field of wheat blowing in the wind. It produced a calm feeling in contrast to the [usual] Avalon Ballroom atmosphere of gyrating energies. The chanting of Hare Kṛṣṇa continued for over an hour, and finally everyone was jumping and yelling, even crying and shouting.*

Someone placed a microphone before Swamiji, and his voice resounded strongly over the powerful sound system. The tempo quickened. Swamiji was perspiring profusely. Kīrtanānanda insisted that the *kīrtana* stop. Swamiji was too old for this, he said; it might be harmful. But the chanting continued, faster and faster, until the words of the mantra finally became indistinguishable amidst the amplified music and the chorus of thousands of voices.

Then suddenly it ended. And all that could be heard was the loud hum of the amplifiers and Swamiji's voice, ringing out, offering obeisances to his spiritual master: "Om Viṣṇu-pāda Paramahaṁsa Parivrājakācārya Aṣṭottara-śata Śrī Śrīmad Bhaktisiddhānta Sarasvatī Gosvāmī Mahārāja *ki jaya!* . . . All glories to the assembled devotees!"

Swamiji made his way offstage, through the heavy smoke and crowds, and down the front stairs, with Kīrtanānanda and Raṇacora close behind him. Allen announced the next rock group.

As Swamiji left the ballroom and the appreciative crowd

behind, he commented, "This is no place for a *brahmacārī.*"

* * *

Some of Bhaktivedanta Swami's more thoughtful followers in San Francisco felt that certain candidates for initiation did not intend to fulfill the exclusive lifelong commitment a disciple owes to his guru. "Swamiji," they would say, "some of these people come only for their initiation. We have never seen them before, and we never see them again." Swamiji replied that that was the risk he had to take. One day in a lecture in the temple, he explained that although the reactions for a disciple's past sins are removed at initiation, the spiritual master remains responsible until the disciple is delivered from the material world. Therefore, he said, Lord Caitanya warned that a guru should not accept many disciples.

One night in the temple during the question-and-answer session, a big, bearded fellow raised his hand and asked Swamiji, "Can I become initiated?"

The brash public request annoyed some of Swamiji's followers, but Swamiji was serene. "Yes," he replied. "But first you must answer two questions. Who is Kṛṣṇa?"

The boy thought for a moment and said, "Kṛṣṇa is God."

"Yes," Swamiji replied. "And who are you?"

Again the boy thought for a few moments and then replied, "I am the servant of God."

"Very good," Swamiji said then. "Yes, you can be initiated tomorrow."

Bhaktivedanta Swami knew that it would be difficult for his Western disciples to stick to Kṛṣṇa consciousness and attain the goal of pure devotional service. All their lives they had had the worst of training, and despite their nominal Christianity and philosophical searching, most of them knew nothing of the science of God. They did not even know that illicit sex and meat-eating were wrong, although when he told them they accepted what he said. And they freely chanted Hare Kṛṣṇa. So how could he refuse them?

Of course, whether they would be able to persevere in Kṛṣṇa consciousness despite the ever-present attractions of maya would be seen in time. Some would fall—that was the human tendency. But some would not. At least those who sincerely followed his instructions to chant Hare Kṛṣṇa and avoid sinful activities would be successful. Swamiji gave the example that a person could say that today's fresh food, if not properly used, would spoil in a few days. But if it is fresh now, to say that in the future it will be misused and therefore spoil is only a surmise. Yes, in the future anyone could fall down. But Bhaktivedanta Swami took it as his responsibility to engage his disciples *now*. And he was giving them the methods which if followed would protect them from ever falling down.

Aside from Vedic standards, even by the standard of Swamiji's New York disciples the devotees in San Francisco were not very strict. Some continued going to the doughnut shop, eating food without offering it to Kṛṣṇa, and eating forbidden things like chocolate and commercial ice cream. Some even indulged in after-*kīrtana* cigarette breaks right outside the temple door. Some got initiated without knowing precisely what they had agreed to practice.

Kīrtanānanda: *The mood in San Francisco was a lot more relaxed. The devotees liked to go to the corner and have their coffee and doughnuts. But Swamiji loved the way so many people were coming. And he loved the program at the Avalon Ballroom. But there were two sides: those who strictly followed the rules and regulations and emphasized purity and then those who were not so concerned about strictness but who wanted to spread Kṛṣṇa consciousness as widely as possible. Swamiji was so great that he embraced both groups.*

* * *

The morning and evening *kīrtanas* had already made the Rādhā-Kṛṣṇa temple popular in Haight-Ashbury, but when the devotees began serving a daily free lunch, the temple became an integral part of the community. Swamiji told his disciples simply to cook and distribute *prasādam*—that would be their only activity during the day. In the morning they would cook, and at noon they would feed everyone who came—sometimes 150 to 200 hippies from the streets of Haight-Ashbury.

Before the morning *kīrtana* the girls would put oatmeal on the stove, and by breakfast there would be a roomful of hippies, most of whom had been up all night. The cereal and fruit was for some the first solid food in days.

But the main program was the lunch. Mālatī would go out and shop, getting donations whenever possible, for whole-wheat flour, garbanzo flour, split peas, rice, and whatever vegetables were cheap or free: potatoes, carrots, turnips, rutabagas, beets. Then every day the cooks would prepare spiced mashed potatoes, buttered *capātīs,* split-pea *dāl,* and a vegetable dish—for two hundred people. The lunch program was possible because many merchants were willing to donate to the recognized cause of feeding hippies.

Harṣarāṇī: *The lunch program attracted a lot of the Hippie Hill crowd, who obviously wanted food. They were really hungry. And there were other people who would come also, people who were working with the temple but weren't initiated. The record player would be playing the record Swamiji had made with his disciples in New York. It was a nice, family atmosphere.*

Haridāsa: *It was taken outside too, outside the front. But the main food was served inside. It was amazing. The people would just all huddle together, and we would really line them wall to wall. A lot of them would simply eat and leave. Other stores along Haight-Ashbury were selling everything from beads to rock records, but our store was different, because we weren't selling anything—we were giving it away.*

And we were welcoming everybody. We were providing a kind of refuge from the tumult and madness of the scene. So it was in that sense a hospital, and I think a lot of people were helped and maybe even saved. I don't mean only their souls—I mean their minds and bodies were saved, because of what was going on in the streets that they just simply couldn't handle. I'm talking about overdoses of drugs, people who were plain lost and needed comforting and who sort of wandered or staggered into the temple.

Some of them stayed and became devotees, and some just took prasādam *and left. Daily we had unusual incidents, and*

Swamiji witnessed it and took part in it. The lunch program was his idea.

Those who were more interested and had questions—the spiritual seekers—would visit Swamiji in his room. Many of them would come in complete anxiety over the war in Vietnam or whatever was going on—trouble with the law, bad experiences on drugs, a falling out with school or family.

There was much public concern about the huge influx of youth in San Francisco, a situation that was creating an almost uncontrollable social problem. Police and social welfare workers were worried about health problems and poor living conditions, especially in Haight-Ashbury. Some middle-class people feared a complete hippie takeover. The local authorities welcomed the service offered by Swami Bhaktivedanta's temple, and when civic leaders in Haight-Ashbury talked of forming a council to deal with the crisis, they requested Swami Bhaktivedanta to take part.

Michael Bowen: *Bhaktivedanta had an amazing ability through devotion to get people off drugs, especially speed, heroin, burned-out LSD cases—all of that.*

Haridāsa: *The police used to come with their paddy wagons through the park in the early hours of the morning and pick up runaway teenagers sleeping in the park. The police would round them up and try to send them back home. The hippies needed all the help they could get, and they knew it. And the Rādhā-Kṛṣṇa temple was certainly a kind of spiritual haven. Kids sensed it. They were running, living on the streets, no place where they could go, where they could rest, where people weren't going to hurt them. A lot of kids would literally fall into the temple. I think it saved a lot of lives; there might have been a lot more casualties if it hadn't been for Hare Kṛṣṇa. It was like opening a temple in a battlefield. It was the hardest place to do it, but it was the place where it was most needed. Although the Swami had no precedents for dealing with any of this, he applied the chanting with miraculous results. The chanting was wonderful. It worked.*

As Allen Ginsberg had advised five thousand hippies at the Avalon, the early-morning *kīrtana* at the temple provided a vital community service for those who were coming down from LSD and wanted to "stabilize their consciousness on reentry." Allen himself sometimes dropped by in the morning with acquaintances with whom he had stayed up all night. But on occasion, the "reentries" would come flying in out of control for crash landings in the middle of the night.

One morning at two a.m. the boys sleeping in the storefront were awakened by a pounding at the door, screaming, and police lights. When they opened the door, a young hippie with wild red hair and beard plunged in, crying, "Oh, Kṛṣṇa, Kṛṣṇa! Oh, help me! Oh, don't let them get me. Oh, for God's sake, help!"

A policeman stuck his head in the door and smiled. "We decided to bring him by here," he said, "because we thought maybe you guys could help him."

"I'm not comfortable in this body!" the boy screamed as the policeman shut the door. The boy began chanting furiously and turned white, sweating profusely in terror. Swamiji's boys spent the rest of the early morning consoling him and chanting with him until the Swami came down for *kīrtana* and class.

The devotees often sent distressed young people to Swamiji with their problems. And they allowed almost anyone to see Swamiji and take up his valuable time. While walking around San Francisco, Ravīndra-svarūpa once met a man who claimed to have seen people from Mars in his tent when he had been stationed in Vietnam. The man, who had just been discharged from an army hospital, said that the Martians had talked to him. Ravīndra-svarūpa told him about Swamiji's book *Easy Journey to Other Planets*, which verified the idea of life on other planets, and he suggested that the Swami could probably tell him more about the people from Mars. So the man visited the Swami up in his apartment. "Yes," Swamiji answered, "there are Martians."

Gradually, Swamiji's followers became more considerate of their spiritual master and began protecting him from persons they thought might be undesirable. One such undesirable was Rabbit, perhaps the dirtiest hippie in Haight-Ashbury. Rabbit's hair was always disheveled, dirty, and even filled with lice. His clothes were ragged and filthy, and his dirt-caked body stank. He wanted to meet the Swami, but the devotees refused, not wanting to defile Swamiji's room with Rabbit's nasty, stinking presence. One night, after the lecture, however, Rabbit waited outside the temple door. As Swamiji approached, Rabbit asked, "May I come up and see you?" Swamiji agreed.

As for challengers, almost every night someone would come to argue with Swamiji. One man came regularly with prepared arguments from a philosophy book, from which he would read aloud. Swamiji would defeat him, and the man would go home, prepare another argument, and come back again with his book. One night, after the man had presented his challenge, Swamiji simply looked at him without bothering to reply. Swamiji's neglect was another defeat for the man, who got up and left.

Israel, like Rabbit, was another well-known Haight-Ashbury character. He had a long ponytail and often played the trumpet during *kīrtana*. After one of Swamiji's evening lectures, Israel challenged, "This chanting may be nice, but what will it do for the world? What will it do for humanity?"

Swamiji replied, "Are you not in the world? If you like it, why will others not like it? So you chant loudly."

A mustached man standing at the back of the room asked, "Are you Allen Ginsberg's guru?" Many of the devotees knew that the question was loaded and that to answer either yes or no would be difficult.

Swamiji replied, "I am nobody's guru. I am everybody's servant." To the devotees, the whole exchange became transcendental due to Swamiji's reply. Swamiji had not simply given a clever response; he had answered out of a deep, natural humility.

One morning a couple attended the lecture, a woman carrying a child and a man wearing a backpack. During the question-and-answer period the man asked, "What about my mind?" Swamiji gave him philosophical replies, but the man kept repeating, "What about my mind? What about my mind?"

With a pleading, compassionate look, Swamiji said, "I have no other medicine. Please chant this Hare Kṛṣṇa. I have no other explanation. I have no other answer."

But the man kept talking about his mind. Finally, one of the women devotees interrupted and said, "Just do what he says. Just try it." And Swamiji picked up his *karatālas* and began *kīrtana*.

One evening a boy burst into a lecture exclaiming that a riot was gathering on Haight Street. The Swami should come immediately, address the crowd, and calm everyone down. Mukunda explained that it wasn't necessary for Swamiji to go; others could help. The boy just stared at Swamiji as if giving an ultimatum: unless Swamiji came immediately, there would be a riot, and Swamiji would be to blame. Swamiji spoke as if preparing to do what the boy wanted: "Yes, I am prepared." But nobody went, and there was no riot.

Usually during the *kīrtana* at least one dancer would carry on in a narcissistic, egoistic way, occasionally becoming lewd to the point where Swamiji would ask the person to stop. One evening, before Swamiji had come down from his apartment, a girl in a miniskirt began writhing and gyrating in the temple during *kīrtana*. When one of the devotees went upstairs and told Swamiji, he replied, "That's all right. Let her use her energy for Kṛṣṇa. I'm coming soon, and I will see for myself." When Swamiji arrived and started another *kīrtana*, the girl, who was very skinny, again began to wriggle and gyrate. Swamiji opened his eyes and saw her; he frowned and glanced at some of his disciples, indicating his displeasure. Taking the girl aside, one of the women escorted her out. A few minutes later the girl returned, wearing slacks and dancing in a more reserved style.

Swamiji was sitting on his dais, lecturing to a full house, when a fat girl who had been sitting on the window seat suddenly stood up and began hollering at him. "Are you just going to sit there?" she yelled. "What are you going to do now? Come on! Aren't you going to say something? What are you going to do? *Who are* you?" Her action was so sudden and her speech so violent that no one in the temple responded. Unangered, Swamiji sat very quietly. He appeared hurt. Only the devotees sitting closest to him heard him say softly, as if to himself, "It is the darkest of darkness."

Another night while Swamiji was lecturing, a boy came up and sat on the dais beside him. The boy faced out toward the audience and interrupted Swamiji: "I would like to say something now."

Swamiji politely said, "Wait until after the class. Then we have questions."

The boy waited for a few minutes, still sitting on the dais, and Swamiji continued to lecture. But again the boy interrupted: "I got something to say. I want to say what I have to say now." The devotees in the audience looked up, astonished, thinking that Swamiji would handle the matter and not wanting to cause a disturbance. None of them did anything; they simply sat while the boy began talking incoherently.

Then Swamiji picked up his *karatālas:* "All right, let us have *kīrtana.*" The boy sat in the same place throughout the *kīrtana,* looking crazily, sometimes menacingly, at Swamiji. After half an hour the *kīrtana* stopped.

Swamiji cut an apple into small pieces, as was his custom. He then placed the paring knife and a piece of apple in his right hand and held his hand out to the boy. The boy looked at Swamiji, then down at the apple and knife. The room became silent. Swamiji sat motionless, smiling slightly at the boy. After a long, tense moment, the boy reached out. A sigh rose from the audience as the boy chose the piece of apple from Swamiji's open hand.

Haridāsa: *I used to watch how Swamiji would handle things. It wasn't easy. To me, that was a real test of his powers and understanding—how to handle these people, not alienate or antagonize or stir them up to create more trouble. He would turn their energy so that before they knew it they were calm, like when you pat a baby and it stops crying. Swamiji had a way of doing that with words, with the intonation of his voice, with his patience to let them carry on for a certain period of time, let them work it out, act it out even. I guess he realized that the devotees just couldn't say, "Listen, when you come to the temple you can't behave this way." It was a delicate situation.*

Often someone would say, "I am God." They would get an insight or hallucination from their drugs. They would try to steal the spotlight. They wanted to be heard, and you could feel an anger against the Swami from people like that. Sometimes they would speak inspired and poetic for a while, but they couldn't sustain it, and their speech would become gibberish. And the Swami was not one to simply pacify people. He wasn't going to coddle them. He would say, "What do you mean? If you are God, then you have to be all-knowing. You have to have the attributes of God. Are you omniscient and omnipotent?" He would then name all the characteristics that one would have to have to be an avatāra, *to be God. He would rationally prove the person wrong. He had superior knowledge, and he would rationally explain to them, "If you are God, can you do this? Do you have this power?"*

Sometimes people would take it as a challenge and would try to have a verbal battle with the Swami. The audience's attention would then swing to the disturbing individual, the person who was grabbing the spotlight. Sometimes it was very difficult. I used to sit there and wonder, "How is he going to handle this guy? This one is really a problem." But Swamiji was hard to defeat. Even if he couldn't convince the person, he convinced the other people in the crowd so that the energy of the room would change and would tend to quiet the person. Swamiji would win the audience by showing them that this person didn't know what he was talking about. And the person would feel the vibrations of the room change, that the audience was no longer listening or believing his spiel, and so the person would shut up.

So Swamiji would remove the audience rather than the person. He would do it without crushing the person. He would do it by superior intelligence, but also with a lot of compassion. When I saw him do these things, then I realized he was a great teacher and a great human being. He had the sensitivity not to injure a person physically or emotionally, so that when the person sat down and shut up, he wouldn't be doing it in defeat or anger—he wouldn't be hurt. He would just be outwitted by the Swami.

* * *

"We shall go for a walk at six-thirty," Swamiji said one morning. "You can drive me to the park."

Several devotees accompanied him to Golden Gate Park's Stowe Lake. They knew the park well and led Swamiji on a scenic walk around the lake, over a bridge, through forest-enclosed paths, and across a small rivulet, hoping to please him with nature's beauty.

Whatever Swamiji saw he saw through the eyes of scripture, and his comments on the most ordinary things were full of transcendental instruction. As he walked, he reflected aloud, "Those who want to see God must first have the qualifications to see God. They must be purified. Just like the cloud is now covering the sun. They say, 'Oh, the sun is not out . . .' but the sun is there. Only our eyes are covered."

Like tour guides the boys led the Swami to the more picturesque areas. They came upon swans gliding on the lake. "*Śrīmad-Bhāgavatam,*" Swamiji said, "compares devotees to swans, and literature about Lord Kṛṣṇa to beautiful, clear lakes." The nondevotees, he said, were like crows attracted by the rubbish of mundane topics. Walking over a gravel path, he stopped and drew their attention: "Look at the pebbles. As many pebbles as there are, there are that many living entities."

The devotees delighted in bringing Swamiji to a rhododendron glen, its big bushes completely covered with white and pink flowers. And they felt privileged to see Kṛṣṇa through the Swami's eyes.

The next morning, when Swamiji again wanted to go to the park, more devotees accompanied him; they had heard from the others how Swamiji had displayed a different mood while walking. Again the boys were ready to lead him along new trails around the lake; but without announcing a change in plans, he walked up and down the macadam road beside the lake.

Swamiji stopped beneath a large tree and pointed to some bird droppings on the ground. "What does this mean?" he asked, turning to a new boy who stood beside him. Swamiji's face was serious. The boy blushed. "I . . . *uh* . . . I don't know what it means." Swamiji remained thoughtful, waiting for an explanation. The devotees gathered around him. Looking intently down at the bird droppings, the boy thought Swamiji might be expecting him to decipher some hidden meaning in the pattern of the droppings, the way people read the future in tea leaves. He felt he should say something: "It's the . . . *uh* . . . excreta, the defecations of . . . *uh* . . . birds." Swamiji smiled and turned towards the others for an answer. They were silent.

"It means," said Swamiji, "that these birds [he pronounced the word "*bards*"] have lived in the same tree for more than two weeks." He laughed. "Even the birds are attached to their apartments."

As they passed the shuffleboard courts and the old men playing checkers, Swamiji stopped and turned to the boys. "Just see," he said. "Old people in this country do not know what to do. So they play like children, wasting their last days, which should be meant for developing Kṛṣṇa consciousness. Their children are grown and gone away, so this is a natural time for spiritual cultivation. But no. They get some cat or dog, and instead of serving God, they serve dog. It is most unfortunate. But they will not listen. Their ways are set. Therefore we are speaking to the youth, who are searching."

When Swamiji and the boys passed a sloping green lawn just off Kezar Drive, the boys pointed out that this was the famous Hippie Hill. In the early morning the gently sloping hill and the big quiet meadow surrounded by eucalyptuses and oaks were silent and still. But in a few hours hundreds of hippies would gather here to lounge on the grass, meet friends, and get high. Swamiji advised the boys to come here and hold *kīrtanas*.

The chanting was popular, drawing many more people than the first *kīrtanas* in New York's Tompkins Square Park. Sometimes Swamiji himself would come to the park to join his disciples. One Sunday he walked up suddenly, and to the surprise and delight of the devotees, he sat down and began playing the *mṛdaṅga* and leading the singing in a loud voice.

Swamiji was the center of attraction. Even his age and dress made him prominent. Whereas the others in the park were mostly young people dressed in denims or various hippie costumes, Swamiji was seventy and distinctly dressed in saffron robes. And the way the devotees had all cheered and bowed before him and were now looking at him so lovingly caused onlookers to regard him with curiosity and respect. As soon as he had sat down, some young children had gathered in close to him. He had smiled at them, deftly playing the *mṛdaṅga*, enthralling and entertaining them with his playing.

Govinda dāsī: *With Swamiji's arrival there was a mastery and an authority about the whole* kīrtana *that was absent before. We were no longer kids in San Francisco chanting Hare Krsna. Now we had historical depth and meaning. Now the* kīrtana *had credentials. His presence established the ancient historical quality of the chanting. When Swamiji came, the whole disciplic succession came.*

After an hour of chanting, Swamiji stopped the *kīrtana* and addressed the crowd: "Hare Kṛṣṇa, Hare Kṛṣṇa, Kṛṣṇa Kṛṣṇa, Hare Hare/ Hare Rāma, Hare Rāma, Rāma Rāma, Hare Hare. This is the sound vibration, and it is to be understood that the sound vibration is transcendental. And because it is transcendental vibration, therefore it appeals to everyone, even without understanding the language of the sound. This is the beauty. Even children respond to it. . . ."

After speaking five minutes, Swamiji began the *kīrtana* again. Some of the young people joined hands, forming a circle, and began to dance around and around in front of Swamiji. Then they encircled him and danced around him hand in hand. As he surveyed the activities in the meadow, Swamiji seemed deeply pleased to see the ring of dancers singing all around him, chanting Hare Kṛṣṇa. Although the enthusiasm of these hippies was often wild and sensual, the gathering assumed a wholesome sweetness due to the chanting of Hare Kṛṣṇa. For Swamiji the main thing was that the chanting was going on and on. Dressed in his saffron cloth that seemed to change colors subtly in the fading afternoon sunlight, he watched in a kindly, fatherly way, not imposing any restraint but simply inviting everyone to chant Hare Kṛṣṇa.

* * *

One day Mālatī hurried into Swamiji's apartment, took a small item out of her shopping bag, and placed it on Swamiji's desk for his inspection. "What is this, Swamiji?"

Bhaktivedanta Swami looked down and beheld a three-inch wooden doll with a flat head, a black, smiling face, and big, round eyes. The figure had stubby, forward-jutting arms, and a simple green and yellow torso with no visible feet.

Immediately, Swamiji folded his palms and bowed his head, offering the little figure respects.

"You have brought Lord Jagannātha, the Lord of the universe," he said, smiling and bright-eyed. "He is Kṛṣṇa. Thank you very much." Swamiji beamed with pleasure while Mālatī and others sat, amazed at their good fortune of seeing Swamiji so pleased. Swamiji explained that this was Lord Jagannātha, a Deity of Kṛṣṇa worshiped all over India for thousands of years. Jagannātha, he said, is worshiped along with two other deities: His brother, Balarāma, and His sister, Subhadrā.

Excitedly, Mālatī confirmed that there were other, similar figures at Cost Plus, the import store where she had found the little Jagannātha, and Swamiji said she should go back and buy them. Mālatī told her husband, Śyāmasundara, and together they hurried back and bought the two other dolls in the set.

Bhaktivedanta Swami placed the black-faced, smiling Jagannātha on the right. In the center he placed the smallest figure, Subhadrā, who had a red, smiling mouth and a rectangular black and yellow torso. The third figure, Balarāma, with a white, round head, red-rimmed eyes, and a happy red smile, had the forward-jutting arms like Jagannātha and a blue and yellow base. Swamiji placed Him next to Subhadrā. As Swamiji looked at them together on his desk, he asked if anyone knew how to carve. Śyāmasundara said he was a wood sculptor, and Swamiji asked him to carve three-foot-high copies of the little Jagannātha, Balarāma, and Subhadrā.

More than two thousand years ago, Bhaktivedanta Swami told them, there was a king named Indradyumna, a devotee of Lord Kṛṣṇa. Mahārāja Indradyumna wanted a statue of the Lord as He had appeared when He and His brother and sister had traveled on chariots to the holy field of Kurukṣetra during a solar eclipse. When the king requested a famous artist from the heavenly planets, Viśvakarmā, to sculpt the forms, Viśvakarmā agreed—on the condition that no one interrupt his work. The king waited for a long time, while Viśvakarmā worked behind locked doors. One day, however, the king felt he could wait no longer, and he broke in to see the work in progress. Visvakarmā, true to his word, vanished, leaving behind the uncompleted forms of the three deities. The king was nevertheless so pleased with the wonderful forms of Kṛṣṇa, Balarāma, and Subhadrā that he decided to worship them as they were. He installed them in a temple and began worshiping them with great opulence.

Since that time, Bhaktivedanta Swami continued, Lord Jagannātha has been worshiped all over India, especially in the province of Orissa, where there is a great temple of Lord Jagannātha at Purī. Each year at Purī, during the gigantic Ratha-yātrā festival, millions of pilgrims from all over India come to worship Lord Jagannātha, Balarāma, and Subhadrā, as the deities ride in procession on three huge carts. Lord Caitanya, who spent the last eighteen years of His life at Jagannātha Purī, used to dance and chant in ecstasy before the Deity of Lord Jagannātha during the yearly Ratha-yātrā festival.

Seeing this appearance of Lord Jagannātha in San Francisco as the will of Kṛṣṇa, Swamiji said that they should be careful to receive and worship Lord Jagannātha properly. If Śyāmasundara could carve the forms, Swamiji said he would personally install them in the temple, and the devotees could then begin worshiping the deities. San Francisco, he said, could be renamed New Jagannātha Purī. He chanted, *jagannāthaḥ svāmī nayana-patha-gāmī bhavatu me.* "This is a mantra for Lord Jagannātha," he said. "*Jagannātha* means 'Lord of the universe.' 'O Lord of the universe, kindly be visible unto me.' It is very auspicious that He has chosen to appear here."

Śyāmasundara bought three large blocks of hardwood, and Swamiji made a sketch and pointed out a number of details. Using the small statues, Śyāmasundara calculated ratios and new dimensions and began carving on the balcony of his apartment. Meanwhile, the devotees bought the rest of the tiny Jagannāthas from Cost Plus, and it became a fashion to glue a little Jagannātha to a simple necklace and wear Him around the neck. Because Lord Jagannātha was very liberal and merciful to the most fallen, Swamiji explained, the devotees would soon be able to worship Him in their temple. The worship of the forms of Rādhā and Kṛṣṇa in the temple required very high, strict standards, which the devotees were not yet able to meet. But Lord Jagannātha was so merciful that He could be worshiped in a simple way (mostly by chanting Hare Kṛṣṇa), even if the devotees weren't very advanced. Gradually, as they progressed in spiritual life, Swamiji would introduce to them more and more of the detailed practices of Deity worship, along with the deep theological understanding that supports it.

The evening of the installation, devotees and hippie guests filled the room to capacity. Swamiji was present, and the mood was reverential and festive. It was a special event. The just-finished deities sat on the altar, and everyone was glancing at them as they stood on their redwood shelf beneath a yellow canopy, their features illumined by spotlights. The deities wore no clothes or ornaments, but were freshly painted in bright black, red, white, green, yellow, and blue. They were smiling. Swamiji was also glancing at them, looking up to their high altar.

Then Swamiji began the deity installation. Everything necessary for spiritual life was here: the temple, the devotees, the books, the Deity, *prasādam*. He wanted these young people to take advantage of it. Why should they remain living like animals and thinking of spiritual life as a vague groping for "something"? They should take advantage of Kṛṣṇa's mercy and be successful and happy. And for this, Swamiji was their tireless servant.

Swamiji: "So, Hayagrīva? Come here." Swamiji had had the devotees arrange for a large candle on a plate. The ceremony he had planned would be a simple one, with devotees and guests one after another coming up and offering the flame in circles before the Jagannātha deities. "This should be lighted up," Swamiji said, "and when there is *kīrtana*, one must be doing like this before the Deity. [Swamiji moved his hands around in a circle before the Deity.] You see?"

Hayagrīva: "Yes, yes."

Swamiji: "Yes, with the *kīrtana*. And then when one person is tired he should hand it over to another person, devotee. When he is tired he should give to another—as long as the *kīrtana* will go on. This should be done with the *kīrtana* just now. Do you follow? Yes. You begin, and when you are tired you hand over to another. It will go on like that."

Swamiji, from his seat, guided Hayagrīva in approaching the Deity with the lit candle. Some of the girls tittered with nervous expectation. "Before the Deity," Swamiji said. "All right. Now better begin *kīrtana*."

Swamiji began playing *karatālas* and singing the Hare Kṛṣṇa mantra to the popular melody he had introduced in America. "Just in front," he called out, gesturing to Hayagrīva to stand more directly before the deities. Devotees and guests began rising to their feet and dancing, arms raised, bodies swaying rhythmically back and forth as they faced the bright, personal forms of the deities and chanted. Colored lights within the canopy began flashing intermittently blue, red, and yellow, highlighting the extraordinary eyes of Lord Jagannātha, Subhadrā, and Balarāma. Mukunda, who had arranged the lights, smiled and looked to Swamiji, hoping for approval. Swamiji nodded and continued forcefully singing Hare Kṛṣṇa.

The young hippies were enthusiastic in singing and dancing, knowing that the *kīrtana* usually lasted an hour. Some had grasped the Swami's words when he had spoken of fixing the mind on the personal form of the Supreme Lord; and they had understood when he had looked up at the Deities and said, "Here is Kṛṣṇa." Others hadn't followed, but thought that it was just great and blissful to sing Hare Kṛṣṇa and look at the grinning, big-eyed Deities up on the altar, amid the flowers and billowing incense.

Bhaktivedanta Swami watched with pleasure as one person after another took a turn at offering the candle before Lord Jagannātha. This was a simple procedure for installing the Deity. Although in big temples in India the installation of the Deity was a complex, exact procedure, requiring several days of continuous rituals directed by highly paid priests, in San Francisco there were no *brāhmaṇa* priests to pay, and the many other standards would be impossible to maintain.

For non-Hindus to handle Lord Jagannātha and conduct His worship would be considered heresy by the caste-conscious *brāhmaṇas* of India. Except for Swamiji, none of the persons present would have been allowed even to enter the temple at Jagannātha Purī. The white man, the Westerner, was not allowed to see Lord Jagannātha except once a year as He rode in His cart during the Ratha-yātrā festival. But these restrictions were social customs, not scriptural injunctions. Śrīla Bhaktisiddhānta Sarasvatī had introduced Deity worship and initiation for anyone, regardless of caste, race, or nationality. And Bhaktivinoda Ṭhākura, Śrīla Bhaktisiddhānta Sarasvatī's father, had longed for the day when the people of the West could mingle with their Indian brothers and chant Hare Kṛṣṇa.

Bhaktivedanta Swami had come to the West to fulfill the desires and the vision of his spiritual master and of Bhaktivinoda Ṭhākura by creating Vaiṣṇavas among the Westerners. Now, if the Westerners were to become actual devotees, they would have to be given the Deity worship.

Otherwise it would be more difficult for them to become purified. Bhaktivedanta Swami was confident in his spiritual master's direction and in the scriptures. He had faith that Lord Jagannātha was especially merciful to the fallen. He prayed that the Lord of the universe would not be offended by His reception at New Jagannātha Purī.

When the *kīrtana* ended, Swamiji asked Haridāsa to bring him the candle. Swamiji passed his hands across the flame and touched them to his forehead. "Yes," he said, "show everyone. Each and everyone. Whatever they can contribute. Here, take it like this and show everyone." He indicated that Haridāsa should present the candle before each person in the room so that all present could touch their hands to the flame as he had shown and then touch their foreheads. As Haridāsa went from person to person, a few devotees dropped some coins on the plate, and others followed.

Swamiji explained further: "The *Bhāgavatam* has recommended hearing, chanting, thinking, and worshiping. This process which we just now introduced on the advent of Jagannātha Svāmī means that now this temple is now completely fixed. So this is the worshiping process. This is called *ārati*. So at the end of *kīrtana*, this *ārati* will go on. And the worshiping process is to take the heat of the light and, whatever your condition is, pay something for the worship. So this simple process, if you follow, you just see how you realize the Absolute Truth.

"Another thing I request you: All the devotees—when you come to the temple, you bring one fruit and one flower. If you can bring more fruit, more flower, it is very good. If not, it is not very expensive to bring one fruit and one flower. And offer it to the Deity. So I will request you, when you come to the temple, you bring this. Whatever fruit it may be. It does not mean that you have to bring very costly fruit. Any fruit. Whatever you can afford. One fruit and one flower."

He paused, looking around the room: "Yes, now you can distribute *prasādam.*"

The guests sat in rows on the floor, and the devotees began serving *prasādam,* offering the first plate to Swamiji. The food preparations were those Swamiji had personally taught the devotees in his kitchen: *samosās, halavā, purīs,* rice, several cooked vegetables, fruit chutney, sweets—all the Sunday specials. The guests loved the *prasādam* and ate as much as they could get. While the devotees, especially the expert women, served more and more *prasādam,* the guests relaxed and enjoyed an evening of feasting and convivial conversation. After Swamiji had tasted all the preparations, he looked up with raised eyebrows: "Very nice preparations. All glories to the cookers!"

Lord Jagannātha's presence quickly beautified the temple. Devotees made garlands for Him daily. Jadurāṇī's paintings of Lord Viṣṇu arrived from New York, and Govinda dāsī had painted a large portrait of Swamiji, which now hung beside his seat. Devotees also put Indian prints of Kṛṣṇa on the walls. The lights flashing upon Lord Jagannātha made His eyes seem to pulsate and His colors move and jump, and He became a special attraction in the psychedelic neighborhood of Haight-Ashbury.

As Swamiji had requested, devotees and guests began bringing offerings before the altar of Lord Jagannātha. Hippies would come by and leave whatever they could: a stalk of wheat, half a loaf of bread, a box of Saltines, a piece of fudge, or candles, flowers, or fruit. Hearing that before using something for yourself you should first offer it to God, some hippies began bringing their new clothes and offering them with a prayer to Lord Jagannātha before wearing them. These hippies didn't follow Lord Jagannātha's instructions, but they wanted His blessings.

Each night, the devotees performed the *ārati* ceremony just as Swamiji had taught them, taking turns offering a candle before Lord Jagannātha. When the devotees asked whether they could add anything to the ceremony, Swamiji said yes, they could also offer incense. He said there were many more details of Deity worship, numerous enough to keep the devotees busy twenty-four hours a day; but if he were to tell them everything at once, they would faint.

Speaking privately in his room to one of his disciples,

Swamiji said that during *kīrtana* in the temple he thought of Lord Caitanya dancing before Lord Jagannātha. He told how Lord Caitanya had traveled to Purī and danced before Lord Jagannātha in such ecstasy that He had been unable to say anything more than "Jag—, Jag—." Lord Caitanya had been thinking, "Kṛṣṇa, for so long I wanted to see You. And now I am seeing You." When Lord Caitanya had lived in Purī, as many as five hundred men at a time would visit Him, and every evening there would be a huge *kīrtana* with four parties, each with four *mṛdaṅga* players and eight *karatāla* players. "One party this side, one party this side," Swamiji explained. "One party back side, one party front side. And Caitanya Mahāprabhu in the middle. They would all dance, and the four parties would chant, 'Hare Kṛṣṇa, Hare Kṛṣṇa, Kṛṣṇa Kṛṣṇa . . .' That was going on every evening so long He stayed at Jagannātha Purī."

The devotees understood that there was a great difference between themselves and Swamiji. He had never been a hippie. He wasn't at home amid the illusion of Haight-Ashbury's LSD, psychedelic posters, rock musicians, hippie jargon, and street people. They knew he was different, though sometimes they forgot. He spent so much time with them every day—eating with them, joking with them, depending on them. But then sometimes they would remember his special identity. When they chanted with him in the temple before Lord Jagannātha, he, unlike them, would be thinking of Lord Caitanya's *kīrtanas* before Lord Jagannātha in Purī. When Lord Caitanya had seen Jagannātha, He had seen Kṛṣṇa, and His love for Kṛṣṇa had been so great that He had gone mad. Swamiji thought of these things to a degree far beyond what his disciples could understand—and yet he remained with them as their dear friend and spiritual instructor. He was their servant, teaching them to pray, like him, to be able to serve Kṛṣṇa: "O Lord of the universe, kindly be visible unto me."

* * *

His top cloth wrapped loosely around his shoulders, Swamiji stood a last moment by the open door of the car and looked back in farewell to the devotees and the storefront temple. It was no longer a mere storefront but had become something worthy: New Jagannātha Purī. Śrīla Bhaktisiddhānta Sarasvatī had asked him to come here. Who among his Godbrothers could imagine how crazy these American hippies were—hallucinating on drugs, crying out, "I am God!"? So many girls and boys—unhappy, mad, despite their wealth and education. But now, through Kṛṣṇa consciousness, some were finding happiness.

The first day he had arrived the reporter had asked him why he had come to Haight-Ashbury. "Because the rent is cheap," he had replied. His desire was to spread the movement of Lord Caitanya; why else would he have come to such a dilapidated little storefront to live next to a Chinese laundry and the Diggers' Free Store? The reporters had asked if he were inviting the hippies and Bohemians to take to Kṛṣṇa consciousness. "Yes," he had said, "everyone." But he had known that once joining him, his followers would become something different from what they had been before.

Now the devotees were a family. If they followed his instructions they would remain strong. If they were sincere, Kṛṣṇa would help them. Lord Jagannātha was present, and the devotees would have to worship Him faithfully. They would be purified by chanting Hare Kṛṣṇa and following their spiritual master's instructions.

Swamiji got into the car, accompanied by some of his disciples, and a devotee drove him to the airport. Several carloads of devotees followed behind.

At the airport the devotees were crying. But Swamiji assured them he would return if they would hold a Ratha-yātrā festival. "You must arrange a procession down the main street," he told them. "Do it nicely. We must attract many people. They have such a procession yearly in Jagannātha Purī. At this time the Deity may leave the temple."

He would have to return, he knew, to tend the delicate devotional plants he had placed in their hearts. Otherwise, how could he expect these neophytes to survive in the ocean of material desires known as Haight-Ashbury? Repeatedly he promised them he would return. He asked them to cooperate among themselves—Mukunda, Śyāmasundara, Guru dāsa, Jayānanda, Subala, Gaurasundara, Hayagrīva, Haridāsa, and the girls.

Only two and a half months ago he had arrived here at this very terminal, greeted by a throng of chanting young people. Many were now his disciples, although just barely assuming their spiritual identities and vows. Yet he felt no compunctions about leaving them. He knew that some of them might fall away, but he couldn't stay with them always. His time was limited.

Bhaktivedanta Swami, the father of two small bands of neophytes, tenderly left one group and headed east, where the other group waited in a different mood, a mood of joyful reception.

* * *

New York City
May 1967

There was no warning that Swamiji's health would break down; or, if there were, no one heeded it. As he moved from his devotees in San Francisco to his devotees in New York, no one passed any message that Swamiji should slow down. After the five-and-a-half-hour jet flight, he spoke of a "blockading" in his ears, but he seemed all right. He didn't rest, but went straight through the festive airport reception into three hours of strong lecturing and chanting in the storefront at 26 Second Avenue. To his New York disciples he appeared dazzling and lovable, and by his presence, his glances, and his words, he increased their Kṛṣṇa consciousness. To them his advanced age, now nearing seventy-two years, was but another of his transcendental features. He was their strength, and they never thought to consider *his* strength.

There were signs that he should be cautious about his health. He had gone through difficulty while appearing on the Allen Burke TV show, and on the way back to the temple, Swamiji had said that the TV lights had caused him so much pain in his head that at one point he had thought he wouldn't be able to continue.

Then one day Rūpānuga, sitting close to Swamiji's dais during a lecture, noticed Swamiji's hand shaking as he spoke. Kīrtanānanda had been there when months ago, the morning after they had made a record, Swamiji had slept late and complained of his heart skipping and of not being able to move. "If I ever get badly sick," he had told Kīrtanānanda, "don't call a doctor. Don't take me to a hospital. Just give me my beads and chant Hare Kṛṣṇa."

Swamiji's disciples were reluctant to restrain him. Kīrtanānanda had tried. At the Avalon, when Swamiji had been dancing and jumping and streaming with perspiration, Kīrtanānanda had insisted that the *kīrtana* stop. But the others had called him paranoid.

Besides, Swamiji didn't like to be restrained. And who were *they* to restrain *him*? He was Kṛṣṇa's empowered representative, able to surmount any difficulty. He was a pure devotee. He could do anything. Hadn't he often described how a pure devotee is transcendental to material pangs?

Swamiji had written a letter consoling a disciple's ailing grandmother. But the devotees figured that although Swamiji might give good instructions to someone's old grandmother, nothing like what had befallen her was ever going to affect him. Of course, he referred to himself as an old man, but that was mostly in lectures to show the inevitability of old age.

To the devotees, Swamiji's health appeared strong. His eyes shone brightly with spiritual emotions, his complexion was smooth and golden, and his smile was a display of health and well-being. One time, one of the boys said that Swamiji's smile was so virile that it made him think of a bull and iron nails. Swamiji was taking cold showers, going on early-morning walks around the Lower East Side, playing *mṛdaṅga,* and eating well. Even if his disciples wanted to slow him down, what could they do?

During the last week of May, however, Swamiji began to feel exhausted. He spoke of heart palpitations. Hoping that the symptoms would clear up in a day or two, Kīrtanānanda suggested he rest and see no visitors. But his condition became worse.

Kīrtanānanda: *Swamiji began to complain that his left arm wasn't functioning properly. And then he began to develop a twitching in his left side, and his left arm would twitch uncontrollably. It seemed to pain him in some mysterious way, internally or psychologically.*

Acyutānanda: *It was Sunday, two days before Memorial Day, and we had arranged a large program in the afternoon in a hall uptown. I went up to get Swamiji, since all the devotees were ready. Swamiji was lying down, and his face was pale. He said, "Feel my heart." And I felt a quivering vibration in his chest.*

I went down, but I didn't want to alert everyone and panic them. I went to Kīrtanānanda and quietly said, "The Swami is having some kind of mild heart palpitations." And immediately we both flew back up. Swamiji said, "Just massage here." So I rubbed him on the chest, and he showed me how. He said, "The others go, and Acyutānanda can stay here. If anything happens, he can call you."

So the others went and did the program, and I waited. Once or twice he called me in and had me quickly rub over his chest. Then he looked up, and his color had come back. I was staring with my mouth open, wondering what to do. He looked up at me and said, "Why are you sitting idle? Chant Hare Kṛṣṇa." During the evening, palpitations again occurred, so I slept in the room next to his. And late at night he called me in and again had me massage.

Kīrtanānanda: *It was on Tuesday afternoon, Memorial Day, and I was sitting with Swamiji in his room. While* kīrtana *was going on downstairs, the twitching began again. The Swami's face began to tighten up. His eyes started rolling. Then all of a sudden he threw himself back, and I caught him. He was gasping: "Hare Kṛṣṇa." And then everything stopped. I thought it was the last, until his breathing started again, and with it the chanting. But he didn't regain control over his body.*

Brahmānanda: *I was there along with Kīrtanānanda. It was on Memorial Day weekend. We couldn't understand what was wrong with Swamiji. He couldn't sit up, he was moaning, and nobody knew what was happening. We nursed him—myself and Kīrtanānanda—trying all different things. I had to go out and buy a bedpan for him.*

Swamiji's left side was paralyzed. He asked that a picture of his spiritual master be put on the wall in front of him. Devotees entered the front room of the apartment, and Swamiji told them to chant Hare Kṛṣṇa. Then he told them to pray to Kṛṣṇa in His form of Nṛsiṁhadeva.

Satsvarūpa: *Swamiji said we should pray to Lord Nṛsiṁha and the prayer should be "My master has not finished his work." At different times he would allow us to take turns and massage different parts of his body. Then he had us go downstairs and hold* kīrtana *through the night.*

During the night, Swamiji's heart pained him. The next day he remained in critical condition. He could speak but softly and was too exhausted to converse. Skeptical of the doctors, he diagnosed himself: a heart attack affecting part of his brain, thus paralyzing the left side of his body. Massage, he said, was the cure.

Brahmānanda: *The day after Memorial Day we had to arrange for an ambulance. Beth Israel had no ambulance, so I called a private ambulance company. It was all arranged with the hospital that Swamiji would arrive at nine o'clock that morning. But the ambulance didn't come until about noon. During this time Swamiji kept moaning. Then finally the ambulance came, and they were horrible guys. They treated Swamiji like a bundle of cloth. I thought it would have been better if we had taken Swamiji in a cab.*

At Beth Israel the doctors, or more often their aides, took blood, gave injections, and investigated. Their diagnosis wasn't conclusive; they had plans for experiments. Then suddenly a doctor came in and announced their next move: a spinal tap. Swamiji was too weak to discuss the pros and cons of a spinal tap. He had put himself in the care of his disciples and Kṛṣṇa.

The doctor didn't want to be impeded. He explained why a spinal tap was necessary, but he wasn't asking for consultation or permission. Everyone—except Kīrtanānanda, who insisted on staying—had to leave the room while the doctor performed the spinal tap. Neither Swamiji, who was too weak, nor his boys, who were uncertain how to act on his behalf, opposed the doctor. The devotees filed out of Swamiji's room while the doctor readied the largest, most frightening needle they had ever seen.

When they were allowed back, one disciple asked cautiously, "Did it hurt?" Swamiji, his golden-skinned form wrapped in white hospital garments and lying between the white sheets, turned slightly and said, "We are tolerant."

Rūpānuga: *When Swamiji was first admitted to the hospital it was very hard for me. I didn't know how I should act. I didn't have much experience with this kind of emergency. I was very uncertain as to what service to do for Swamiji. It was a frightening experience.*

Swamiji's life was at stake, yet his disciples didn't know what to do to save him. He lay on the bed as if at their mercy, but the hospital staff considered him their property—an old man with heart trouble, a subject of investigation. Should they allow the EEG? What was an EEG? Was an operation necessary? An operation! But Swamiji had said that he should never even be brought to a hospital. "Give me massage," was all he had said, and "Chant Hare Kṛṣṇa."

On June 5, Swamiji received an affectionate letter signed by all his disciples in San Francisco. After reading how they had stayed up all night chanting and praying for his recovery, he dictated a short letter.

> My dear boys and girls,
>
> I am so much obliged to you for your prayers to Krishna to save my life. Due to your sincere and ardent prayer, Krishna has saved my life. I was to die on Tuesday certainly but because you prayed sincerely I am saved. Now I am improving gradually and coming to original condition. Now I can hope to meet you again and chant with you Hare Krishna. I am so glad to receive the report of your progressive march and hope there will be no difficulty in your understanding Krishna consciousness. My blessings are always with you and with confidence you go on with your chanting Hare Krishna Hare Krishna Krishna

Krishna Hare Hare Hare Rama Hare Rama Rama Rama Hare Hare.

Swamiji was eager to leave the hospital. For several days, he had wanted to go. "They are simply sticking needles," he complained. And each day was putting his Society into further debt. The devotees had rented a small seaside house in Long Branch, New Jersey, where Swamiji could go to recuperate. Kīrtanānanda, they decided, would be Swamiji's cook, and Gaurasundara and his wife, Govinda dāsī, were arriving from San Francisco to do the housekeeping and help. But the doctor wanted Swamiji to stay for another brain wave test and more observation.

One day while Brahmānanda and Gargamuni were visiting Swamiji, the doctor entered and announced that the Swami would have to go downstairs for an X ray.

"No needle?" Swamiji asked.

"Yes," the doctor replied, "it's all right."

When the nurse brought in a bed on wheels, Swamiji said he wanted Gargamuni to push it. He then sat on it cross-legged and put his hand in his bead bag, and Gargamuni, following the nurse, wheeled him out the door, down the hall, and onto the elevator. They went down to the third floor and entered a room. The nurse left them alone. Gargamuni could sense Swamiji's uneasiness. He was also nervous. It was such an unlikely place for him to be with his spiritual master. Then a different nurse entered, with a needle: "Time to give the Swami a little injection."

"No." Swamiji shook his head.

"I'm sorry," Gargamuni said flatly. "We're not going to do it."

The nurse was exasperated but smiled: "It won't hurt."

"Take me back," Swamiji ordered Gargamuni. When the nurse insisted, Gargamuni acted rashly—his usual tendency—and stepped between the nurse and his spiritual master.

"I'm ready to fight if I have to," Gargamuni thought. "I won't let you do it," he said and wheeled the bed out of the room, leaving the nurse behind.

Gargamuni was lost. He was somewhere on the third or fourth floor, faced with corridors and doors. And Swamiji's room was on the sixth floor. Unsure where he was going, Gargamuni wheeled through the corridors with Swamiji sitting cross-legged, chanting on his beads.

Brahmānanda arrived at the X-ray lab seconds after Gargamuni's escape. The nurse and intern complained to him about what had happened.

Brahmānanda: *They considered this a theft. Swamiji was their property. As long as he was in the hospital, he was theirs to do whatever they pleased with. Gargamuni had stolen Swamiji away from them.*

Gargamuni got to the elevator. He had difficulty maneuvering the bed and in his haste bumped into the wall. He forgot what floor Swamiji was on. He only knew that he was protecting Swamiji, who wanted to be taken away.

When Gargamuni finally reached Swamiji's room, 607, an intern was there and spoke angrily. "I don't care," Gargamuni said. "He doesn't want any more needles or tests. We want to leave." Brahmānanda arrived, calmed his younger brother, and helped Swamiji back into bed.

Swamiji said he wanted to leave. When the doctor came in, Swamiji sat up and spoke decisively. "Doctor, I am all right. I can go." And he shook the doctor's hand to show him he was hale and hearty. The doctor chuckled. He said that although Swamiji was getting stronger, he would have to stay a few more days. He was by no means out of danger yet. He required careful medical surveillance. They needed to run another electroencephalogram.

Swamiji still had pains around his heart, but he told the doctors his boys had a place for him to rest by the seaside. This was very good, the doctor said, but he couldn't let his patient go just yet.

But Swamiji had made up his mind. Brahmānanda and Gargamuni arranged for a rented car. They gathered Swamiji's things and helped him dress. As they escorted him out of his room and the hospital staff saw that the boys were actually taking the old man away, some of the doctors and nurses tried to stop them. Brahmānanda told them not to worry; Swamiji was very dear to them, and they would take good care of him. He would get regular massages and plenty of rest, and they would get him whatever medicines the doctors prescribed. After a rest by the seaside he could come back for a checkup.

Brahmānanda: *Then the doctors became fed up. They threatened us: "This man is going to die." They really scared us. They said, "This man is going to die, and it is going to be your fault." Even as we left they said, "This man is condemned to death." It was horrible.*

At ten a.m. on June 8 they left the hospital. Swamiji wanted to stop briefly at the temple at 26 Second Avenue before going to the house in Long Branch. Entering the storefront, walking shakily, he came before the portraits of his spiritual master, Bhaktisiddhānta Sarasvatī, and his spiritual master's father, Bhaktivinoda Ṭhākura. For the first time, Swamiji's disciples saw him offer fully prostrated obeisances. As he prostrated himself before his Guru Mahārāja, his disciples also paid obeisances and felt their devotion increase.

The small one-story cottage was situated in a quiet suburb a short walk from the beach. The backyard was enclosed by trees and shrubs, and the neighborhood bloomed with fragrant roses. But the weather was often blustery and the sky gray, and Swamiji talked of going to India. Not only for his health, however; he told Kīrtanānanda and Gaurasundara he wanted to start in Vṛndāvana an "American House," a place where his American disciples could learn Vedic culture to help them preach all over the world. He also said he wanted to make some of his disciples—Kīrtanānanda, Brahmānanda, Hayagrīva—into sannyasis, and he would do that also in India. His real work, however, was in America—if he could just regain his health. But where was the sunshine?

In India he could get sunshine and Āyur-Vedic treatment. But his plans would vary from one day to another—San Francisco, Montreal, India, New York. He told Kīrtanānanda to inform the devotees in San Francisco that if they held a Ratha-yātrā festival he would come.

At the end of June, Swamiji returned to 26 Second Avenue and to the hospital for a checkup. The doctor was surprised at Swamiji's recovery and had no objection to his flying to San Francisco. So in search of sunny skies, and eager to guide his followers in performing the first Ratha-yātrā, Swamiji had airline tickets booked for himself and Kīrtanānanda to San Francisco, New Jagannātha Purī.

* * *

At the San Francisco airport, Swamiji smiled but said little as the devotees greeted him with flowers and *kīrtana*. It was different this time. He walked straight ahead, with the aid of a cane.

Jayānanda was waiting with his station wagon to drive Swamiji to the private house they had rented north of the city, at Stinson Beach. But first, Swamiji said, he wanted to visit the San Francisco Rādhā-Kṛṣṇa temple. Jayānanda drove to 518 Frederick Street. Swamiji got out of the car and entered the small storefront, which was filled with waiting devotees and guests. He bowed before the smiling Jagannātha deities and, without speaking a word, left the room, returned to the car, and departed for Stinson Beach.

The ride up through the seaside cliffs was so winding and climbing that Swamiji became nauseated. And even lying down in the back seat and having Jayānanda drive slower didn't help much. Kīrtanānanda realized that it would be too difficult for Swamiji to visit the San Francisco temple from Stinson Beach. But maybe that would be just as well; he could spend all of his time recuperating.

On July 8, after Swamiji had been at Stinson Beach for two days, Śyāmasundara and Mukunda drove up from San Francisco. The next day was to be Ratha-yātrā, and Śyāmasundara and Mukunda, the first devotees to visit Swamiji since his arrival at Stinson Beach, told Swamiji all about the festival preparations. Of course, the whole festival had been

Swamiji's idea, but the devotees in San Francisco were trying to do exactly as he had asked.

Swamiji had first gotten the idea for the festival while looking out the window of his room above Frederick Street. Noticing flatbed trucks passing below, he thought of putting Jagannātha deities on the back of such a truck and conducting an American-style Ratha-yātrā festival. He had even sketched a truck with a four-pillared canopy on the back and decorated with flags, bells, and flower garlands. And he had called in Śyāmasundara: "Make me this cart for Ratha-yātrā." Now, ready and sitting outside the temple on Frederick Street, was the cart—a yellow Hertz rental truck, compliments of the Diggers and complete with five-foot columns and a pyramidal cloth canopy.

Sitting with Swamiji on the beach, Mukunda told how all the devotees were working with great enthusiasm and how the hippies in Haight-Ashbury were talking about the Jagannātha parade that would take place the next day. The devotees had tried to route the parade through Golden Gate Park, but the police department would only give permission for them to go south down Frederick Street to the sea. Mukunda said the devotees planned to have Jagannātha under the canopy, facing the right side of the truck, Subhadrā facing the rear, and Balarāma facing the left side; he wanted to know if that was all right. Actually, Swamiji said, the deities should ride in separate carts, pulled with ropes by the crowd through the streets; maybe that could happen in future years.

"Do it nicely," he cautioned them. "And don't hurry it up." The devotees should drive the truck slowly through the streets down to the beach, and there should be constant *kīrtana*.

Mukunda and Śyāmasundara praised their Godbrother Jayānanda: he drove all around San Francisco getting donations of fruits and flowers, found people to help decorate the cart, installed the sound system on the truck, and distributed posters in the stores. He was tireless, and his enthusiasm was inspiring everyone else to take part. The women had been cooking *capātīs* all day, so there should be thousands to give away to the crowd. The devotees had prepared hundreds of

Hare Kṛṣṇa Ratha-yātrā festival balloons to r streets as the parade began.

When the devotees asked what else they should d miji said that this was all—a procession, *prasādam* dis tion, *kīrtana*. The people should get a chance to see L Jagannātha and chant Hare Kṛṣṇa. There should be chanting and dancing in front of the cart throughout the procession. "But do everything nicely," Swamiji said. "Do it as well as you can, and Lord Jagannātha will be satisfied."

The next day, in the quiet afternoon, Swamiji was sitting in the living room, chanting on his beads, while Kīrtanānanda was in the kitchen cooking a feast. Suddenly Swamiji heard the familiar ringing of hand-cymbals, and he became very happy, his eyes widening. Looking outside, he saw the Ratha-yātrā truck, with Lord Jagannātha, Subhadrā, and Balarāma and dozens of devotees and hippies eager to see him. He went out to greet them and had them bring the deities inside and set them up on top of the upright piano. Devotees and guests followed, filling the large living room. Smiling, Swamiji embraced some of the men while others made obeisances at his feet. Some devotees helped Kīrtanānanda in the kitchen get ready to distribute the large feast he had prepared. Others reported on the success of the Ratha-yātrā festival.

It was great! It was wonderful! It was a beautiful day, they said. And Swamiji listened, moved by his disciples' descriptions of the celebration. Many hippies had joined the large procession. Mukunda, Haridāsa, Hayagrīva, and some of the women had been on the cart, and the instruments, including Yamunā's playing on the harmonium, had all been amplified. Everyone in the streets had liked it. The police motor escorts had tried to hurry the devotees, but so many people had crowded in front that the parade had been obliged to go slowly, just as Swamiji had asked. Subala had danced wildly the whole time, and Jayānanda had been jumping up and down, playing *karatālas*. From the truck some of the women had handed out cut oranges, apples, and bananas, and others ad thrown flowers. The crowds had loved it.

Subala related how, after the festival, they had traveled out on the freeway in their flower-bedecked, canopy-covered truck carrying thirty devotees and the deities of Jagannātha, Subhadrā, and Balarāma. They had driven up through the mountains in what must have been one of the most unusual vehicles ever seen.

After all the visitors had departed, the deities remained in the house with Swamiji and his servants. Swamiji felt satisfied that his disciples had successfully held a Ratha-yātrā festival. Although untrained, they were sincere. Bhaktisiddhānta Sarasvatī and Bhaktivinoda Ṭhākura would have been pleased to see the first American Ratha-yātrā.

The whole world was in anxiety, Swamiji explained to the devotees gathered in his room that evening. Only in the spiritual world was there freedom from anxiety. Becoming free from all anxiety and returning to the spiritual world was the purpose of Kṛṣṇa consciousness. And festivals like Ratha-yātrā made people Kṛṣṇa conscious. Swamiji had many, many ideas for festivals. If he had the money and the manpower, he said, he could have a festival every day. Kṛṣṇa consciousness was unlimited. This Ratha-yātrā festival was another sign of the good reception for Kṛṣṇa consciousness in the West.

*　　*　　*

Swamiji still talked of going to India. He had virtually made up his mind to go; the question now was when, and whether by the western route, via Japan, or the eastern route, via New York. The gray skies and unseasonably cool temperatures of Stinson Beach were a disappointment. His health was still poor. He even spoke of dying. It didn't matter whether he died in America or Vṛndāvana, he said. If a Vaiṣṇava dies in Vṛndāvana, the land where Kṛṣṇa appeared, he is assured of joining Kṛṣṇa in the spiritual world. Yet when Lord Caitanya had traveled outside Vṛndāvana, His devotee Advaita had assured Him, "Wherever You are is Vṛndāvana." To be always absorbed in thinking of Kṛṣṇa was also Vṛndāvana. So if he were to pass away while preaching Kṛṣṇa consciousness—anywhere in the world—certainly he would still attain to the eternal Vṛndāvana in the spiritual sky.

Nevertheless, Swamiji wanted to go to Vṛndāvana. It was the best place—to die or to recuperate. Besides, he had a plan for bringing his disciples to Vṛndāvana for training. Swamiji told Kīrtanānanda, Hayagrīva, and others that he would take them with him and show them the sacred places of Kṛṣṇa's pastimes. With the New York temple's building fund, he would start his American House in Vṛndāvana.

Most of the devotees had to remain in San Francisco, hoping for a chance to visit Swamiji. From the few who knew firsthand, they heard about Swamiji's plans to leave for India, perhaps never to return. It was painful to hear. His going almost to death but then returning by Kṛṣṇa's grace and rejoining them in San Francisco, yet being unable to stay with them as before, and now his plans of going to India, maybe forever—these activities intensified their concern and love for him.

Devotees worried, speculating on whether they could carry on without Swamiji. One devotee suggested that perhaps one of Swamiji's Godbrothers should come to America and fill in for Swamiji and, if the worst happened, take over the leadership of the International Society for Krishna Consciousness. When the suggestion reached Swamiji, he considered it without immediately replying.

Mukunda: *I was sitting alone with Swamiji in his room, and he was very grave and silent. His eyes were closed. Then, suddenly, tears began flowing from his eyes. And he said in a choked voice, "My spiritual master was no ordinary spiritual master." Then he paused for some time, and wiping the tears from his cheeks, he said in an even more choked voice, "He saved me." At that point I began to understand the meaning of "spiritual master" and dropped all consideration of ever replacing Swamiji.*

After two days Swamiji said he would not call any of his Godbrothers to come and take care of his disciples. He said, "If this person speaks just one word different from what I am speaking, there will be great confusion among you." Actually, he said, the idea was an insult to the spiritual master.

* * *

Swamiji told Kīrtanānanda he had definitely decided to go to India, via New York, as soon as possible. Kīrtanānanda packed Swamiji's things and drove him down to San Francisco to spend the night at the temple. They would leave the next morning.

The temple and even Swamiji's apartment were very hectic that night, with many devotees and guests wanting to see Swamiji and dozens of people wanting initiation. When Kīrtanānanda advised Swamiji not to exert himself by going down for the evening program, he insisted on at least going and sitting during the *kīrtana.*

When he entered the storefront, the devotees immediately stopped their *kīrtana,* dropping down to offer obeisances. There was a hush. He commanded a new reverence. This might be the last time they would see him. They watched him during the *kīrtana* as he played his *karatālas,* singing with them for the last time. The uninitiated wanted to accept him as their spiritual master—tonight, before it was too late. Swamiji asked for the microphone. No one had expected him to speak. Kīrtanānanda, the only person in a position to restrain him, said nothing and sat before him like the others, submissive and expectant. Swamiji spoke quietly about his mission; under the order of his spiritual master he was bringing Lord Caitanya's movement to America, and Kṛṣṇa had kindly sent him so many sincere souls. "I have a few children in India from my family days," he said, "but you are my real children. Now I am going to India for a little while."

"I am an old man," he said. "I may die at any moment. But please, you all carry on this *saṅkīrtana* movement. You have to become humble and tolerant. Lord Caitanya says, be as humble as a blade of grass and more tolerant than a tree. You must have enthusiasm and patience to push on this Kṛṣṇa conscious philosophy."

He sat still and continued speaking to them gravely, asking them to stick together and push on the movement, for their own benefit and for others. Whatever they had learned, he said, they should repeat.

They realized, perhaps for the first time, that they were part of a preaching mission, a movement. They were together not just for good times and good vibrations; they had a loving obligation to Swamiji and Kṛṣṇa.

* * *

In New York the devotees didn't have much time for sadness. Kīrtanānanda telegraphed Sri Krishna Pandit that Bhaktivedanta Swami's arrival in Delhi would be on July 24 at 7:30 a.m. and that Sri Krishna Pandit should prepare the Swami's quarters at the Chippiwada temple. The telegram mentioned Swamiji's intention to consult a physician in Delhi and then go to Vṛndāvana. He was anxious to return to Vṛndāvana.

Devotees had been asking Satsvarūpa to transfer his civil service job to Boston and open a Kṛṣṇa conscious center there. They had also asked Rūpānuga to do the same in Buffalo. When Satsvarūpa and Rūpānuga approached Swamiji to find out what he wanted, he became very pleased. Subala was going to open a center in Santa Fe, he said, and Dayānanda was going to Los Angeles. "Hare Kṛṣṇa mantra is like a big cannon," he told them. "Go and sound this cannon so everyone can hear it, and it will drive away maya."

The devotees wanted to ask, "But what if you don't return?" They were fearful. What if Kṛṣṇa kept Swamiji in Vṛndāvana? What if Swamiji never returned? How could they survive against maya? But Swamiji had already assured them that whatever Kṛṣṇa consciousness he had given them would be enough, even if he never returned.

Just thirty minutes before he had to leave for the airport,

Swamiji sat in his room chanting on the beads of a girl who had asked to be initiated. Then, as he had done many times before, he left his apartment, went downstairs, crossed the courtyard, and entered the storefront.

Sitting on the old carpet, he spoke quietly and personally. "I am going, but my Guru Mahārāja and Bhaktivinoda are here." He looked toward the paintings of his spiritual master and Bhaktivinoda Ṭhākura. "I have asked them to kindly take care of all of you, my spiritual children. The grandfather always takes care of the children much better than the father. So do not fear. There is no question of separation. The sound vibration fixes us up together, even though the material body may not be there. What do we care for this material body? Just go on chanting Hare Kṛṣṇa, and we will be packed up together. You will be chanting here, and I will be chanting there, and this vibration will circulate around this planet."

Several devotees rode with Swamiji in the taxi—Brahmānanda in the front with the driver, Rāya Rāma and Kīrtanānanda in the back beside their spiritual master. "When Kīrtanānanda sees Vṛndāvana," Swamiji said, "he will not be able to understand how I could have left that place and come to this place. It is so nice. There are no motorcars there like here, rushing whoosh! whoosh! and smelling. Only there is Hare Kṛṣṇa. Everybody always chanting. Thousands and thousands of temples. I will show you, Kīrtanānanda. We will walk all about there, and I will show you."

Brahmānanda began to cry, and Swamiji patted him on the back. "I can understand that you are feeling separation," he said. "I am feeling for my Guru Mahārāja. I think this is what Kṛṣṇa desires. You may be coming there to me and be training up, and we will spread this movement all over the world. Rāya Rāma—you will go to England. Brahmānanda—you want to go to Japan or Russia? That's all right."

The devotees converged on the Air-India waiting room, near a crowded cocktail lounge. Wearing a sweater, his *cādar* folded neatly over one shoulder, Swamiji sat in a chair, while his disciples sat as closely as possible around his feet. He held an umbrella, just as when he had first come alone to New

York, almost two years ago. Although exhausted, he was smiling.

Swamiji noted a mural of Indian women carrying large jars on their heads, and he called the name of a young girl who had recently gone with her husband, Haṁsadūta, to join the ISKCON center in Montreal. "Himavatī, would you like to go to India and learn to carry this waterpot like the Indian women?"

"Yes, yes," she said. "I'll go."

"Yes," Swamiji said, "some day we will all go."

Kīrtanānanda was carrying a portable battery-operated phonograph and two copies of the Hare Kṛṣṇa mantra record. "Kīrtanānanda," Swamiji asked, "why not play the record? They will enjoy." Kīrtanānanda played the record very softly, its sound catching the attention of people in the cocktail lounge. "Make it a little louder," Swamiji asked, and Kīrtanānanda increased the volume, while Swamiji nodded his head, keeping time.

Soon the devotees began humming along with the record, and then quietly singing, until gradually they were singing loudly. Some of the devotees began to cry.

When the time came to board the plane, Swamiji embraced each of his men. They stood in a line, and one after another approached him and embraced him. He patted a few of the women on the head.

Accompanied by Kīrtanānanda, whose head was shaven and who wore an incongruous black woolen suit, Swamiji walked slowly toward the gate. As he disappeared from view, the devotees ran for the observation deck to get a last look at his departing plane.

A gentle rain was washing the airfield as the devotees raced across the wet observation deck. There below were Swamiji and Kīrtanānanda, walking towards their plane. Abandoning decorum, the devotees began to shout. Swamiji turned and waved. He climbed the movable stairway, turning again at the top and raising his arms, and then entered the plane. The devotees chanted wildly while the boarding steps moved away, the door closed, and the plane began to turn. The devotees had pressed close to the rail, but they pulled back as the jet exhaust blasted them with the heat. With a great roar the Air-India jet, lights blinking, taxied out to the runway. The devotees continued to chant Hare Kṛṣṇa until the plane left the ground, became a speck in the sky, and then disappeared.

* * *

New Delhi
July 25, 1967

The wall of heat that greeted them felt good to Swamiji. He had come for this. Inside the airport terminal, overhead fans stirred the muggy air as Swamiji and Kīrtanānanda stood in slow-moving lines while uniformed clerks checked passports and customs forms, without Western-style computers or efficiency. Just beyond the areas for immigration and customs, people waiting for arriving passengers were waving, calling, and coming together with friends and family members.

After Swamiji and Kīrtanānanda claimed their luggage and cleared customs, they stood on the sidewalk outside the terminal. Although Swamiji had removed his sweater, Kīrtanānanda stood sweltering in his black wool suit. It was two a.m. All around, passengers were meeting loved ones, who embraced them—sometimes even garlanded them—and helped them into cars or taxis. But no one was there for Swamiji. It was certainly different from the recent tearful airport scenes, where Swamiji had been with *his* loved ones. Now, instead of being surrounded by loving disciples, he was besieged by taxi drivers and porters wanting to carry his luggage for a fee. In Hindi Swamiji asked one of the drivers to take them to Chippiwada, in Old Delhi. The driver put their luggage in the trunk, and Swamiji and his disciple climbed into the back seat.

The small Ambassador taxi drove through streets well known to Swamiji. Nighttime traffic was light—an occasional taxi or motor ricksha. Mostly the streets were empty and quiet, the shops closed, an occasional person or cow sleeping outdoors.

Just a few years before, Bhaktivedanta Swami had sold *Back to Godhead* magazines, solicited donations, and printed his *Śrīmad-Bhāgavatams* here. In those days he had been alone, practically without money or residence. Yet he had been happy, completely dependent on Kṛṣṇa.

But India's leaders were rejecting Vedic culture and imitating the West. Although some Indians still professed to follow Vedic culture, mostly they were victims of hodgepodge teachers who didn't accept Kṛṣṇa as the Supreme Personality of Godhead. So Bhaktivedanta Swami had felt obliged to leave—to go and transplant the Vedic culture in the West. He had held strictly to the vision of his predecessor spiritual master, and he had been proven right: the West was a very good field for Kṛṣṇa consciousness.

As the taxi drove through Old Delhi and approached Chawri Bazaar, Bhaktivedanta Swami saw the printing and paper shops, now closed for the night. And the usual dense traffic of human-hauled carts was now absent, though some laborers were sleeping on their carts till the morning, when they would bathe in an outdoor well and begin another day's hauling. When Bhaktivedanta Swami had been overseeing the publishing of his first volumes of *Śrīmad-Bhāgavatam*, he had daily walked these streets, buying paper, picking up proofs from the printer, returning with the corrected proofs. His First Canto had been a triumph.

Chawri Bazaar led to side streets that led to the narrow lanes of Chippiwada, where upright metal posts blocked autos and rickshas from entering. The driver stopped the taxi on an empty road and turned for his payment. Swamiji took from his billfold forty rupees (the same forty rupees he had carried with him on the boat to America in 1965). But the driver took the entire forty rupees and said he would keep it all as the just fare. Swamiji protested; the fare should not be even half that! Loudly they argued back and forth in Hindi. The driver had pocketed the money and would give no change. Swamiji knew that to get a policeman at this hour would be very difficult. Finally, although this had been nothing less than a robbery, Swamiji let the man go. Swamiji and Kīrtanānanda took their luggage and walked the last block, up to the door of the Chippiwada Rādhā-Kṛṣṇa temple.

It was locked. As they pounded loudly, Swamiji called out for Sri Krishna Pandit until a man came to the door, recognized Bhaktivedanta Swami, and let them in. The man showed them upstairs and unlocked the door to Swamiji's room. Swamiji turned on the light.

The room was bare and dusty, and the bulb hanging from the ceiling created stark light and shadow. On the floor was the three-foot-high cement dome indicating that directly below were the altar and the Deities of Rādhā and Kṛṣṇa. (The dome prevented anyone from accidentally committing the offense of walking directly above the Deities.) The closet was stacked with printed *Śrīmad-Bhāgavatam* pages, *Śrīmad-Bhāgavatam* dust jackets, and form letters to prospective members of the League of Devotees. Everything was just as Bhaktivedanta Swami had left it.

"This is the room where I compiled *Śrīmad-Bhāgavatam,*" Swamiji told Kīrtanānanda. "I slept here. And over here was my cooker and my typewriter. I would sleep and type and cook and type and sleep and type." Kīrtanānanda was shocked to think of Swamiji living here in such a poor, humble place. It wasn't even clean.

Although Kīrtanānanda was uncomfortable in his suit and wondered when he would be able to get rid of it, he managed to get a thin mattress for Swamiji. Two Āyur-Vedic doctors came. They both agreed that the trouble was Swamiji's heart but that the danger was now past. They gave him medicines and advised him to keep to a regulated schedule of eating, resting, and working. Sri Krishna Pandit came by to sit and converse, and Swamiji told him of his success in America and of all the young devotees in New York and San Francisco. He played his record for Sri Krishna Pandit, and this drew a crowd of curious persons from other rooms in the temple.

* * *

On August 1, after six days in Delhi, Swamiji went to Vṛndāvana, where he occupied his old rooms at the Rādhā-Dāmodara temple. After he had been there only one day and his health had only slightly improved, he began planning his return to America. "I am always thinking of you," he wrote to the devotees, whom he addressed as his "dear students."

In Delhi Swamiji had received a letter from Brahmānanda saying that the Macmillan Company was definitely interested in publishing his *Bhagavad-gītā*. Now, from Vṛndāvana, Swamiji wrote Brahmānanda to sign a contract at once on his behalf. Swamiji had been considering whether to print privately in Japan or India or to wait for Macmillan. He was less concerned with the prestige and financial advantages of publishing through Macmillan, however, than he was with printing as quickly as possible.

Although Swamiji was still very weak and was being massaged and cared for by Kīrtanānanda, who himself was listless and tired from the heat, he continued to range from one active and ambitious vision for his youthful Kṛṣṇa consciousness movement to another. He would think aloud about the volumes of *Śrīmad-Bhāgavatam* ready to be published—if Macmillan would take them and the boys could act on his behalf. There was so much to do. He wanted to return by October and oversee things personally.

Temperatures rose to more than 110 degrees, and Swamiji and Kīrtanānanda had to stay inside with the doors shut and the overhead fan on. Although Kīrtanānanda could barely perform his duties, Swamiji found the heat bracing and said that it was restoring his health. Then, after the first week, the monsoon rains began, and the heat broke.

On Janmāṣṭamī day, August 28, Swamiji awarded the order of sannyasa to Kīrtanānanda in a ceremony at the Rādhā-Dāmodara temple. Kīrtanānanda thus became Swamiji's first disciple to become a sannyasi: Kīrtanānanda Swami. In most cases, sannyasa is offered to men past fifty years of age. But Swamiji was willing to offer it to his young disciple because he very much wanted men who were prepared to devote all their energies to traveling and preaching, the traditional duties of a sannyasi. Such sannyasis would be needed to strengthen and spread the Kṛṣṇa consciousness movement. During Kīrtanānanda's initiation hundreds of visitors were present, observing the birthday of Lord Kṛṣṇa, and many of them came by to congratulate the new sannyasi. Someone said he looked like Lord Caitanya. Swamiji wrote,

> He will go back to the States very soon to begin preaching work with greater vigor and success. In the meantime, I shall try to utilize this "white sannyasi" for recruiting some members in India.

Early in September, Acyutānanda arrived in Vṛndāvana to be with Swamiji. For Acyutānanda, the most wonderful thing about Swamiji in Vṛndāvana was the simplicity of his life. Although in New York Swamiji had worn simple robes, he had always been regal, the guru. But here he lived very simply and humbly. Once when he sat down on the veranda outside his room to wash his hands, his body instantly became covered with flies. Kīrtanānanda and Acyutānanda were always being bothered by the flies—this was the rainy season—but Swamiji scarcely noticed them and sat quietly washing his hands.

Kīrtanānanda and Acyutānanda agreed that Swamiji wasn't just another Vṛndāvana *bābājī.* No one else was like him. Certainly Gaurachand Goswami, proprietor of the Rādhā-Dāmodara temple, wasn't like Swamiji. He wore thick glasses and could barely see, and when Kīrtanānanda and Acyutānanda went before the Deities in the temple, Gaurachand Goswami asked them loudly, "So how do you like 'em? Which one do you like the best?"

"I like them all," said Acyutānanda.

"I like that big one on the end there," said the priest, pointing in an offhand manner at the Deity of Kṛṣṇa. "It looks a bit like General Choudry." The Swami's boys exchanged looks—what kind of guys are these?—and went back to Swamiji for an explanation.

"They are caste *gosvāmīs,"* Swamiji explained. The original *gosvāmīs,* such as Jīva Gosvāmī, who established the Rādhā-Dāmodara temple, had engaged householders to worship the Deities. And these caste *gosvāmīs* were descendants of those first householder *pūjārīs*. Swamiji explained that the caste *gosvāmīs* were the proprietors of the temples and that they maintained the temples and ran the Deity worship as a business to support their families. Several years ago each of the Deities now on the altar had had His own temple, land, income, and priests. But for economy the *gosvāmīs* had sold the property, reduced the opulence of the worship, and amalgamated the Deities.

There were many other interesting characters: the old widow Sarajini, with bald head and *śikhā* and callused bare feet, who slept in a room by the gate of the temple and swept Swamiji's kitchen and washed his clothes; Pancudas Goswami, the temple proprietor's son, who always chewed pan and went around sleepy-eyed in a silk dhoti with a red-embroidered border; the dark, old *bābājī* who came at night, who was constantly laughing, and who made sandalwood paste for Swamiji; the local herbal doctor, Vanamali Kaviraja, who presided, brightly smiling, from behind a desk in a tiny chamber filled from ceiling to floor with little bottles; and a famous pandit who visited Swamiji and wore a gold-linked *tulasī* necklace and diamond rings. All of these persons were devotees, residents of holy Vṛndāvana. But no one was like Swamiji.

Kīrtanānanda Swami even became disappointed that no one else in Vṛndāvana was like Swamiji. In the land where everyone was an Indian and everyone was a devotee, Swamiji was still unique. No one else was so simple, so grave, so able to penetrate through falsity, so attractive to the heart, or so absolutely attached to Kṛṣṇa. No one else could lead them.

* * *

With regular medication, massages, rest, and the heat of Vṛndāvana, Swamiji felt himself recovering. By mid-September he declared himself ninety-percent fit to return to the United States. He predicted that he would be back there by the end of October. Accompanied by Kīrtanānanda and Acyutānanda, he left Vṛndāvana and returned to the Chippiwada temple in Delhi.

On October 11, he wrote to Brahmānanda,

> We must have our books printed; we have wasted much time in the matter of editing and finding out a suitable publisher. When I was alone there were three volumes published but during the last two years I could not publish a single volume more. It is a great defeat. If I have one or two sincere souls like you and if we can make more publications, then our mission will be a great success. I am prepared to sit down underneath a tree with one sincere soul and in such activity I shall be freed of all diseases.

* * *

Knowing that Swamiji would soon be returning, the devotees in America began to increase their entreaties, each group asking him to come to their particular city. On November 4, Swamiji wrote Mukunda, "As you say that my absence is being felt now surely more deeply than ever, so I also feel to start immediately without waiting." And to Mukunda's wife, Jānakī, he wrote, "Every minute I think of you, and as you asked me to go to San Francisco while returning from India, I am trying to fulfill my promise. I am thinking of going directly to San Francisco." At the bottom of the same letter to Mukunda and Jānakī, Acyutānanda added a health report: "Swamiji is looking healthy and living and working regularly, but his pulse rate is generally too fast. Last night it was 95—unusually fast even for him as it generally hovers between 83 and 86."

Swamiji decided not to wait any longer, even though by waiting he might be able to secure permanent U.S. residency. "I want to return to your country, where there is good air and good water," he told Acyutānanda one day. "Every day we are receiving letters that the devotees want me there. I thought that in my absence they might deteriorate, and I was reluctant to even come to India. But now I see that it is growing. There is need for me to go and supervise the expansion. So I want to go back."

Just to make certain that Swamiji would come first to San Francisco, Mukunda sent a telegram: "SWAMIJI, BRAH-

MANANDA AND I AGREE YOU START IMMEDIATELY. ADVISE EXACT ARRIVAL DATE. MUKUNDA."

Swamiji had planned his route through Tokyo, intending to stop for a day "to probe if there is any possibility of starting a center." In Tokyo he would let Mukunda know by telephone his arrival time in San Francisco. But three weeks passed while Swamiji waited for his P-form, a clearance from the Bank of India required for an Indian citizen traveling abroad.

Meanwhile, he received good news from New York. The Macmillan Company's interest in *Bhagavad-gītā* was real; the contract was being drawn. Pleased with Brahmānanda, he wrote to him on November 11 explaining his visions for distributing Kṛṣṇa conscious literature.

> If publications are there we can work from one center only like New York or San Francisco for propagating our cult all over the world. Let us stick to the publication of BTG more and more nicely and publish some Vedic literatures like Srimad Bhagavatam, Chaitanya Charitamrita, etc. . . .

As Swamiji's thoughts turned more to the preaching that awaited him in America, he assessed what he had done so far, what he would do, and the process by which he would do it. When the day for his departure finally arrived he gave last instructions to Acyutānanda, who would be remaining to preach Kṛṣṇa consciousness in India.

"Just pray to Lord Kṛṣṇa that I can go to America," he requested Acyutānanda.

"How can I? You'll be leaving me."

"No, we'll always remain packed up together if you remember my teachings. If you preach you will become strong, and all these teachings will be in the proper perspective. When we stop our preaching, then everything becomes stagnated, and we lose our life. Even here in India people think that they know everything, but they are wrong. There is no end to hearing about Kṛṣṇa. God is unlimited. So no one can say, 'I know everything about God.' Those who say they know everything about God do not know. So everyone will appreciate you. Do not fear."

* * *

The passengers and flight crew saw Swamiji as an elderly Indian man dressed in saffron robes. The stewardesses weren't sure at first whether he spoke English, but when he asked them for fruits, they saw that he could and that he was a kind gentleman. He was quiet, putting on his glasses and reading from an old book of Indian scripture for hours at a time, or moving his lips in prayer while fingering Indian prayer beads in a cloth pouch, or sometimes resting beneath a blanket, his eyes shut.

No one knew or bothered to inquire into what he was doing. They didn't know that anxious young hearts were awaiting him in San Francisco, or that the Macmillan Company in New York wanted to publish his English translation of *Bhagavad-gītā*, or that he had spiritual centers in two countries, with plans for expansion all over the world. He sat patiently, chanting often, his hand in his bead bag, depending on Kṛṣṇa as the hours passed.

The plane landed in San Francisco. Standing with hundreds of other passengers, Swamiji gradually made his way to the exit. Down the long attached tunnel, even before he reached the terminal building, he could see a few disciples smiling and waving on the other side of a glass partition. As he entered the terminal building he moved toward the glass, and his disciples dropped to their knees, offering obeisances. As they raised their heads he smiled and continued walking down the corridor while they walked alongside, only the glass partition separating them. Then they disappeared from his view as he walked down the stairway toward immigration and customs.

The downstairs area was also glassed in, and Swamiji could see more than fifty devotees and friends waiting eagerly. As they again caught sight of him, they cried out as a group, "Hare Kṛṣṇa!"

Swamiji looked wonderful to them, tanned from his five months in India, younger, and more spritely. He smiled and triumphantly held up his hands in greeting. Devotees were crying in happiness.

As Swamiji stood in line at the customs inspection point, he could hear the devotees' *kīrtana,* the glass walls only partially masking the sound. The customs officials ignored the chanting, although the connection between the saffron-robed passenger and the joyful chanters was not hard to see.

Swamiji waited in line, glancing now and then at his chanting disciples. He had only one suitcase to place on the table before the inspector. Methodically, the inspector went through the contents: cotton saris for the girls, silk garlands for the Jagannātha deities, *karatālas,* saffron dhotis and *kurtās,* a coconut grater, and little bottles of Ayur-Vedic medicine.

"What are these?" the inspector probed. The little bottles looked strange, and he called for another inspector. A delay. Swamiji's disciples became perturbed by the petty-minded customs inspectors' poking through Swamiji's things, now opening the tightly corked bottles, sniffing and checking the contents.

The inspectors seemed satisfied. Swamiji tried to close his suitcase, but he couldn't work the zipper. Another delay. The devotees, still anxiously chanting, watched as he managed to zip his suitcase closed, with the help of the gentleman behind him.

He walked towards the glass doors. The devotees began chanting madly. As he stepped through the door a devotee blew a conchshell that resounded loudly throughout the hall. Devotees garlanded him, and everyone pressed in, handing him flowers. He entered their midst as a beloved father enters and reciprocates the embrace of his loving children.

CHAPTER FOUR

In Every Town and Village

After a few weeks in San Francisco, Swamiji went to Los Angeles, where a small group of his disciples had opened a storefront temple in a middle-class black and Hispanic neighborhood. The storefront was bare and the location secluded. Swamiji stayed there two months, delivering lectures, holding *kīrtanas,* and giving strength and inspiration to his disciples. Although a buzzing in his head made working difficult, he found the warm climate and sunshine agreeable, and he continued to translate *Śrīmad-Bhāgavatam.*

In May, a few months after leaving Los Angeles, Swamiji paid a first visit to his ISKCON center in Boston. There also he found a few disciples based in a small storefront. It was in Swamiji's room one day in Boston that he accepted the name "Prabhupāda." While his secretary was taking dictation, Prabhupāda mentioned that the affix "ji" was a third-class address.

"Then why do we call you Swami-ji? What should we call you?"

"A spiritual master," Swamiji replied, "is usually addressed by names like Gurudeva, Viṣṇupāda, or Prabhupāda."

"May we call you Prabhupāda?"

"Yes."

At first some of the devotees were reluctant to give up the long-cherished "Swamiji," which for them was a name of affection.

"I heard we shouldn't use the name 'Swamiji' anymore," one of the boys asked one morning on a walk.

"Who said?" Prabhupāda replied quickly.

"They said you said it was third class, and we shouldn't say it."

"I never said that."

"Then can we use it?"

"Yes, that is all right."

But "Swamiji" soon disappeared. The devotees even printed an explanation in *Back to Godhead.*

PRABHUPADA

The word Prabhupada is a term of utmost reverence in Vedic religious circles, and it signifies a great saint even amongst saints. The word actually has two meanings: first, one at whose feet (pada) there are many Prabhus (a term meaning "master" which the disciples of a guru use in addressing each other). The second meaning is one who is always found at the lotus feet of Krishna (the supreme master). In the line of disciplic succession through which Krishna consciousness is conveyed to mankind there have been a number of figures of such spiritual importance as to be called Prabhupada.

Srila Rupa Goswami Prabhupada executed the will of his master, Sri Caitanya Mahaprabhu, and therefore he and his associate Gosvamis are called Prabhupada. Srila Bhaktisiddhanta Sarasvati Goswami Thakura executed the will of Srila Bhaktivinoda Thakura, and therefore he is also addressed as Prabhupāda. Our spiritual master, Om Visnupada 108 Sri Srimad Bhaktivedanta Swami Maharaja, has in the same way executed the will of Srila Bhaktisiddhanta Saraswati Goswami Prabhupada in carrying the message of love of Krishna to the Western world, and therefore the humble servants of His Divine Grace, from all the different centers of the sankirtana movement, are following in the footsteps of Srila Rupa Goswami Prabhupāda and prefer to address his grace our spiritual master as Prabhupāda. And he has kindly said, "Yes."

Montreal
August 1968

Śrīla Prabhupāda was in his room, speaking with several disciples. "So, Annapūrṇā, you have got some news?" he asked. Annapūrṇā was a young British girl. A few months ago her father had written from England that he might be able to provide a house if some devotees came there.

"Yes," she replied.

"So, what is our next program?" She was reticent. "That letter from your father is encouraging?"

"Yes, he encourages me. But he says he can't provide any place if we come there."

Prabhupāda looked disappointed. "That's all right. It is up to Kṛṣṇa. When we go to someone to preach, we have to stand before them with folded hands, with all humility. 'My dear sir, please take to Kṛṣṇa consciousness.' "

"Prabhupāda?" Pradyumna spoke up. "I was reading a book by this big atheist swami."

"Hmm?"

"There are some letters in the back of the book, and I was looking at them . . ."

"Atheist swami's book," Prabhupāda said, "we have nothing to do with."

"I wasn't looking at his philosophy," Pradyumna explained. "I was just looking at the techniques he used when he was in America. He wanted to go to Europe, so he had a man, a rich benefactor, who went on a six-week tour of France, England, Germany, Switzerland, Holland, and then back, arranging lectures. That's how he did most of his tour. He had one or two influential people, and they arranged everything. And the lectures were arranged, and the society . . ."

"So, you can arrange like that?" Prabhupāda asked.

"I was thinking that there would be a Royal Asiatic Society in London. I think Ṭhākura Bhaktivinoda was a member of that."

"But where is Ṭhākura Bhaktivinoda's *saṅga* [association]?" Prabhupāda asked.

"Well," Pradyumna continued, "still there may be some people you could open correspondence with. They might be interested in sponsoring you."

"Is there anything about Kṛṣṇa in that swami's speech?" Prabhupāda asked.

"No."

Prabhupāda sat thoughtfully. In England he would have no place to stay. Pradyumna might talk of influential persons traveling ahead and making all the arrangements, but where were such persons? Here was a shy girl who could barely speak up, whose father would not help, and Pradyumna reading an atheist swami and talking of a Royal Asiatic Society—but nothing practical. Prabhupāda had plans, though. He had asked Mukunda and Śyāmasundara to go to London and try to establish an ISKCON center. They had agreed and would be arriving in Montreal from San Francisco in a few days.

Śrīla Bhaktisiddhānta Sarasvatī, Prabhupāda's own spiritual master, had wanted Kṛṣṇa consciousness in Europe. During the 1930s he had sent his most experienced sannyasis to London, but they had returned, nothing accomplished. It wasn't possible to teach Kṛṣṇa consciousness to the *mlecchas,* they had complained. Europeans couldn't sit long enough to hear the Vaiṣṇava philosophy.

Still, Prabhupāda had faith that his disciples would succeed; they would help him establish ISKCON centers in Europe, just as they had in North America. Certainly such success would greatly please Śrīla Bhaktisiddhānta Sarasvatī. Prabhupāda told of a man who found a gourd lying on the road and picked it up and then found a stick and a wire and picked them up. In themselves, the three parts were useless. But by putting the gourd, the stick, and the wire together, the man made a *vīṇā* and began to play beautiful music. Similarly, Prabhupāda had come to the West and found some rejected youths lying here and there, and he himself had been rejected by the people of New York City; but by Kṛṣṇa's grace the combination had become successful. If his disciples remained sincere and followed his orders, they would succeed in Europe.

Three married couples—Mukunda and Jānakī, Śyāmasundara and Mālatī (with their infant daughter, Sarasvatī), and Guru dāsa and Yamunā—arrived in Montreal, eager to travel to London. These three couples had begun the temple in San Francisco, where they had had close association with Śrīla Prabhupāda. They had helped Prabhupāda introduce *kīrtana, prasādam,* and Ratha-yātrā among the hippies of Haight-Ashbury. Now they were eager to help him introduce Kṛṣṇa consciousness in London.

Prabhupāda asked the three couples to remain with him in Montreal for a week or two, so that he could train them to perform *kīrtana* expertly. Chanting Hare Kṛṣṇa was not a theatrical performance but an act of devotion, properly conducted only by pure devotees—not by professional musicians. Yet if Prabhupāda's disciples became proficient in their singing, Londoners would better appreciate Kṛṣṇa consciousness.

* * *

Even while recuperating in India, Prabhupada had always thought of returning to America to continue his movement. The Indians had seemed interested only in sense gratification, like that of the Americans. But many American youths, disillusioned with their fathers' wealth, were not going to the skyscrapers or to their fathers' businesses. As Prabhupāda had seen from his stays in New York City and San Francisco, thousands of youths were seeking an alternative to materialism. Frustrated, they were ripe for spiritual knowledge.

The devotees, still neophytes, knew nothing of spiritual life and in most cases very little of material life. But because they were sincerely taking to Kṛṣṇa consciousness, Prabhupāda was confident that their shortcomings would not prevent their spiritual progress. Although naturally beautiful, these Western youths were now dirty and morose; their beauty had become covered. But the chanting of Hare Kṛṣṇa was reviving them, Prabhupāda said, just as the monsoon revives the land of Vṛndāvana, making it fresh and verdant. And as the Vṛndāvana peacocks sometimes dance jubilantly, so the devotees, having shed their material bonds, were now ecstatically dancing and chanting the holy names. When a reporter asked Prabhupāda if his disciples were hippies, Prabhupāda replied, "No, we are not hippies. We are happies."

More than being a visiting lecturer or a formal guide, Śrīla Prabhupāda was the spiritual father of his disciples. They accepted him as their real father, and he found them devoted and affectionate, far more than his own family had been. These young American boys and girls—"the flower of your country," Prabhupāda called them—had received the blessing of Lord Caitanya and were delivering that blessing to their countrymen. Prabhupāda said it was up to his American disciples to save their country. He was giving them the method, but they would have to implement it.

Śrīla Prabhupāda loved his disciples, and they loved him. Out of love, he was giving them the greatest treasure, and out of love they were following his instructions. This was the essence of spiritual life. On the basis of this love, the Kṛṣṇa consciousness movement would grow. Not surprisingly, some disciples had fallen away to their former, materialistic ways of living. But Prabhupāda sought those sincere souls who would stay. That was the important thing, he said. One moon is more valuable than many stars; so even a few sincere workers would accomplish wonderful things. The sincere and intelligent would stay, and Lord Caitanya Mahāprabhu would empower them to carry out His desires for distributing love of Kṛṣṇa. In this way, the devotees' lives would become perfect. Many disciples, in fact, already felt this happening. Kṛṣṇa consciousness worked because they sincerely practiced it and because Śrīla Prabhupāda carefully and patiently tended the growing plants of transcendental loving service he had planted in their hearts.

New York City
April 9, 1969

Prabhupāda traveled to New York City, the birthplace of his Kṛṣṇa consciousness society, where his movement had been growing for nearly three years. Although the center was established and his books were being distributed, he still had to visit to strengthen the devotees. His presence gave them determination and courage. For seven months they had carried on without his personal touch, but his visits—when he would sit in his room and reciprocate warmly with them—were vital. Nothing could equal these intimate meetings.

Many devotees, new and old, crowded into Prabhupāda's apartment at 26 Second Avenue. "There was one reporter," Prabhupāda said, "—he was putting questions to me. And then he wrote an article: 'The swami is a small man, but he is delivering a great message.' That is true. I am small. But the message—that is not small."

Brahmānanda showed Prabhupāda a globe with markers representing ISKCON centers. "Now there is one in North Carolina," Brahmānanda said.

"Then it becomes fifteen?" Prabhupāda asked. He was smiling and looking directly from one devotee to another. "I want each of you to go and start a center. What is the difficulty? Take one *mṛdaṅga*. Then another person will come and join you—he will take *karatālas*. When I came here, Brahmānanda and Acyutānanda were dancing. And after chanting, hundreds of men will come to your storefront and enjoy chanting and dancing."

"The girls also?" Rukmiṇī asked.

"There is no harm," Prabhupāda said. "Kṛṣṇa does not make distinction—female dress or male dress. I mean to say, the female body is weaker, but spiritually the body does not matter. In the absence of Lord Nityānanda, His wife, Jāhnavī devī, was preaching. First you must understand the philosophy. You must be prepared to answer questions. Kṛṣṇa will give you intelligence. Just like I was not prepared to answer all these questions, but Kṛṣṇa gives intelligence."

After eight days in his New York City home, Prabhupāda went to Buffalo. At State University of New York at Buffalo, Rūpānuga was teaching an accredited course in Kṛṣṇa yoga with some sixty students enrolled, regularly chanting the Hare Kṛṣṇa *mantra* on beads. Prabhupāda stayed for a few days, lecturing and initiating disciples. Then he went to Boston for more initiations and several marriages.

* * *

New Vrindaban
May 21, 1969

Accompanied by Kīrtanānanda Swami and Hayagrīva, Prabhupāda traveled to the New Vrindaban farm project in the hills of West Virginia. When their car got stuck in a neighbor's garden near the entrance to the property, Prabhupāda decided to walk the final two miles along the muddy access road that led to the farm. The road soon ended, however, and Prabhupāda and his two guides picked a footpath, entering the dense forest.

The mid-May trees were still coming into foliage, and the sunlight broke through the branches to a carpet of brilliant purple phlox. Prabhupāda walked quickly ahead of Kīrtanānanda Swami and Hayagrīva, who hurried to keep up. A winding creek repeatedly crossed the path, and Prabhupāda would cross by stepping from stone to stone. The road, he said, would not be difficult to travel by oxcart; the forest was like a jungle, just as he had expected and wanted.

For the past year, Prabhupāda had corresponded with Kīrtanānanda Swami and Hayagrīva concerning New Vrindaban, and this correspondence had established the direction for Kṛṣṇa conscious country living. Prabhupāda had said he wanted the community based on Vedic ideals, everyone living simply, keeping cows, and working the land. The devotees would have to develop these ideas gradually; it would take time. But even in the beginning the keynote should be "simple living and high thinking." Because the community would remain completely aloof from the city, it would at first appear inconvenient and austere. But life would be peaceful, free from the anxieties of the artificial urban society based on hard work for sense gratification. And most important, the members of such a community would be serving Kṛṣṇa and chanting His name.

Prabhupāda spoke little, making his way along the path as if at his own home. They stopped beside the creek, and Prabhupāda sat down on a blanket Kīrtanānanda Swami and Hayagrīva spread for him on the grass. "We are stopping for Kīrtanānanda," Prabhupāda said. "He is tired." Prabhupāda and his party drank water from the creek, rested briefly, and then continued.

As they rounded a curve in the road, Prabhupāda could see a clearing on the ridge ahead. A small frame house and a barn stood at the lower end of the ridge. These two ancient structures, Hayagrīva explained, were the only buildings on New Vrindaban's 120 acres. As no vehicles traveled here, the paths were overrun with high grass. A willow spread its branches close by the old house. The settlement was the picture of undisturbed primitive life.

Prabhupāda liked the simple life at New Vrindaban, and whatever simple thing the devotees offered him he accepted with satisfaction. They served him freshly-ground-wheat cereal cooked in milk, and he said it was wonderful. When he saw the kitchen's dirt floor covered with cow dung, he approved, saying it was just like in an Indian village.

Prabhupāda also liked his room in the attic, directly above the temple room. He brought out the small Rādhā-Kṛṣṇa Deities he had been traveling with for the last month and a half and had his servant, Devānanda, improvise an altar on a small table to one side of the room. Arranging his two trunks as a desk and placing a picture of his spiritual master on one of the trunks, Prabhupāda immediately resumed his usual schedule.

He would take his late-morning massage sitting outside and then bathe with warm water in an improvised outdoor shower stall. Kīrtanānanda Swami prepared Prabhupāda's usual lunch of *dāl,* rice, and *capātīs*—plus some local pokeweed. The previous summer, Kīrtanānanda Swami and Hayagrīva had picked and canned blackberries, which they now served Prabhupāda as blackberry chutney. The *capātīs* were from freshly milled whole wheat, and everything was cooked over a wood fire. The best fuel for cooking, Prabhupāda said, was cow dung; wood was second, gas third, and electricity last.

Prabhupāda spent much of the day out of doors, under a persimmon tree about a hundred feet from the house. There he would sit and read at a low table one of the men had built.

Often he would look up from his reading and gaze across the deep valley to the distant ridge, where the forest met the sky.

In the late afternoon, devotees would gather under the persimmon tree with Prabhupāda, sitting and talking with him until after sunset. They saw Prabhupāda's living with them as a practical demonstration of New Vrindaban's importance; if he, the greatest devotee, could be satisfied living simply and chanting Hare Kṛṣṇa in this backwoods setting, then they should follow his example.

Comparing New Vrindaban to the Vṛndāvana in India, Prabhupāda said that New Vrindaban was in some ways better, since Vṛndāvana, India, was now congested with worldly men. Five hundred years ago the Gosvāmī followers of Lord Caitanya had excavated the sites of Kṛṣṇa's pastimes in Vṛndāvana, and only pure devotees had lived there. But in recent years Vṛndāvana had become a place for materialists and impersonalists. New Vrindaban, however, should admit only the spiritually inclined. In Vedic society, Prabhupāda said, everyone had been satisfied to live like this, in a small village beside a river. Factories were unnecessary. Prabhupāda wanted this Vedic way of life for the entire world, and New Vrindaban could serve as a model for the benefit of the masses.

New Vrindaban had no phone, and mail had to be fetched by a two-mile walk. In this, Prabhupāda said, New Vrindaban was like Vṛndāvana, India—both Vṛndāvanas lacked in modern amenities. This "difficulty," however, coupled well with the Vaiṣṇava philosophy that modern amenities were not worth the trouble required to get them. A devotee, accepting whatever nature provides, spends his time and energy in spiritual life.

New Vrindaban's only cow was a black-and-white crossbreed named Kāliya, and Prabhupāda would drink a little of her milk morning, noon, and night. "I haven't tasted milk like this in sixty-five years," he said. One day, he predicted, New Vrindaban would have many cows, and their udders would be so full that the dripping milk would muddy the pastures. Although people in the West were blind to their great sin of cow slaughter and its grievous karmic reactions, he said, New

Vrindaban would demonstrate to the world the social, moral, and economic advantages of protecting the cow and utilizing her milk rather than killing her and eating her flesh.

Prabhupāda wanted the New Vrindaban devotees to build cottages. He wanted many buildings, even if at first they were primitive, and he gave a plan for a simple structure of baked mud. He also wanted a Kṛṣṇa conscious school, and the country, he said, would be the best place for it. "The city is made by man, and the country is made by God," Prabhupāda said, paraphrasing the British poet Cowper. The young students should learn reading, writing, and arithmetic, and at the same time they should become pure devotees. In their play they could imitate the pastimes of Kṛṣṇa and His cowherd boyfriends, with one child massaging Kṛṣṇa, another wrestling with Kṛṣṇa just as in the spiritual world. The women in New Vrindaban, Prabhupāda said, should care for the children, clean the temple, cook for the Deities, and churn butter.

He had many plans for New Vrindaban, and he was giving only idea seeds, with few details. "You develop it to your heart's content," he told Kīrtanānanda Swami. An ideal Vedic community with the members producing all their own food and necessities was what Prabhupāda wanted. Unless the devotees at New Vrindaban could become self-sufficient, he said, there was no use in their occupying such a big piece of land.

Even before Prabhupāda's visit to New Vrindaban, he had requested Kīrtanānanda Swami and Hayagrīva to plan for seven temples on the property. These seven temples should be named after the major temples of old Vṛndāvana: Madana-mohana, Govindajī, Gopīnātha, Rādhā-Dāmodara, Rādhā-ramaṇa, Śyāmasundara, and Rādhā-Gokulānanda. Prabhupāda said he would personally secure Rādhā-Kṛṣṇa Deities for each temple.

It was inevitable that Prabhupāda leave New Vrindaban; letters from London, Los Angeles, and San Francisco compelled him to travel. On the day of his departure, the New

Vrindaban devotees teased him, saying he couldn't go. Kīrtanānanda Swami went so far as to say they would block his way on the road. But Prabhupāda corrected him, "You can't do that to the spiritual master."

Accompanied by Kīrtanānanda Swami and the New Vrindaban devotees, Prabhupāda walked along the forest path. The New Vrindaban countryside was verdant, the summer air hot and moist. Prabhupāda was silent. He had come here to encourage his disciples, and he himself had also become encouraged. Here was simple village life as Kṛṣṇa Himself had lived it, depending on the land and the cow. So far only a few devotees were here, but by Kṛṣṇa's grace more would come.

Prabhupāda and Kīrtanānanda Swami walked together along the forest path, saying little, but their mutual understanding was deep. Prabhupāda hadn't given him many specific instructions: a few words while sitting or walking together outdoors, a gesture, a facial expression of pleasure or concern. Kīrtanānanda Swami could understand, however, that New Vrindaban was very dear to his spiritual master and should become dear to him also. Prabhupāda assured him that because the devotees of New Vrindaban were centered on chanting Hare Kṛṣṇa, serving the Deities, and protecting the cows, Kṛṣṇa would bless them with success. The community was already successful, and Kṛṣṇa would continue to protect the devotees against all impediments and difficulties.

At the end of the two-mile walk, Prabhupāda, surrounded by his followers, stood beside the car that was to take him to the airport in Pittsburgh, from where he would fly to Los Angeles. His suitcases, which had come out on a horse-drawn cart, were loaded into the car's luggage compartment, and Prabhupāda got in the back seat. Amid the cries of "Hare Kṛṣṇa!" and "Prabhupāda!" the car pulled out onto the country highway, and Prabhupāda continued chanting Hare Kṛṣṇa on his beads.

Prabhupāda had been hearing regularly from his six disciples in London. Having little money and living as separate couples in different parts of the city, they found their greatest inspiration in Prabhupāda's letters. They would repeatedly read his instructions and dream of when he would one day visit them in London. Although in San Francisco Kṛṣṇa consciousness had been fun for the three couples, in England it was becoming more and more difficult. The devotees, being foreigners, were not allowed to earn a salary, and except for a few contacts, they knew no one. Although unable to live together, they were trying to maintain their morale and Kṛṣṇa consciousness.

Then in the middle of a winter of struggle came a fortunate break for the London devotees: a meeting with George Harrison of the Beatles. For a long time the devotees had been thinking of ways to get the Beatles to chant Hare Kṛṣṇa. To the Beatles' Apple Records Studio they had once sent an apple pie with *Hare Krishna* lettered on it. Another time they had sent a wind-up walking apple with the Hare Kṛṣṇa mantra printed on it. They had even sent a tape of one of their *kīrtanas* and had received a standard rejection letter from Apple Records. So it seemed to be Kṛṣṇa's special arrangement when Śyāmasundara suddenly met one of the most sought-after celebrities in the world, George Harrison.

In a crowded room at Apple Records, Śyāmasundara, shaven-headed and wearing robes, sat hoping for a chance to have a few words with someone connected with the Beatles. Then George came down the stairs from a conference. As he entered the room, he saw Śyāmasundara. Walking over and sitting down beside Śyāmasundara, he asked, "Where have you been? I've been trying to meet the Hare Kṛṣṇa people for the last couple of years." Śyāmasundara and George talked together for an hour, while everyone hovered around. "I've really been trying to meet you people," George said. "Why don't you come to my place tomorrow?"

The next day Śyāmasundara went to George's for lunch, where he met the other Beatles: Ringo Starr, John Lennon, and Paul McCartney. They all had questions, but George was especially interested.

George: *I had a copy of the Hare Kṛṣṇa album with Śrīla Prabhupāda singing Hare Kṛṣṇa with the devotees. I'd had the record at least two years. But I got it the week it was pressed. I was open to it. You attract those things. So I used to play that a lot of the time. John and I listened to it. I remember we sang it for days, John and I, with ukulele banjos, sailing through the Greek Islands, chanting Hare Kṛṣṇa. So I was chanting the Hare Kṛṣṇa mantra long before I met Śyāmasundara, Guru dāsa, and Mukunda. I was just pleased to hear the Hare Kṛṣṇa mantra and have a copy of the record.*

And I knew about Prabhupāda because I had read all the liner notes on that album. Having been to India I could tell where the devotees were all coming from, with the style of dress and shaved heads. I had seen them on the streets of Los Angeles and New York. Having read so many books and looking for yogis, my concept of the devotees wasn't like the other people. No, I was aware of the thing and that it was a pretty heavy one, much more austerities than other groups—like no coffee, chocolate, or tea.

Śyāmasundara continued to see George regularly, and they soon became friends. George, who had been practicing a mantra given him by Maharishi Mahesh Yogi, began to hear for the first time about bhakti yoga and the Vedic philosophy. He talked openly to Śyāmasundara, Guru dāsa, and Mukunda of his spiritual quest and his realizations of karma.

George: *A yogi I met in India said, "You are really lucky. You have youth, fame, fortune, health, but at the same time that's not enough for you. You want to know about something else." Most people don't even get to the point where they realize there's something beyond that wall. They are just trying to get up on top of that wall, to be able to eat and have a nice house and be comfortable and all that. But I was fortunate enough to get all that in time to realize there's something else to life, whereas most people get worn out just trying to attain material things.*

After a visit to Haight-Ashbury in 1967 George had begun to feel guilty for his role in promulgating the LSD culture. He had had the impression that the hippies of Haight-Ashbury were creative craftsmen, but when he saw them drugged, dirty, and hopeless—"A West Coast extension of the Bowery"—he felt partly responsible. He decided to use his influential position by writing and singing songs about something more than psychedelics and sex. He was also feeling an increasing interest in Indian spirituality, due, he felt, to karma from his previous lives.

George: *I feel at home with Kṛṣṇa. I think that's something that has been there from a previous birth. So it was like the door was opening to me at that time, but it was like a jigsaw puzzle, and I needed all these little pieces to make a complete picture. And that is what has been happening by the devotees and Swami Bhaktivedanta coming along, or some devotee giving me a book or my hearing that album. It's all been slowly fitting together.*

And these are some of the reasons why I responded to Śyāmasundara and Guru dāsa when they first came to London. Let's face it, if I'm going to have to stand up and be counted, then I'll be with these guys rather than with those over there. It's like that. I'll be with the devotees rather than with the straight people who are the so-called saints.

George offered to help the devotees get a building in London, and he and Śyāmasundara spoke of making a Hare Kṛṣṇa record. But Śyāmasundara never pressed him.

When Prabhupāda heard about George, he took seriously the possibility that George might fully take up Kṛṣṇa consciousness. Carrying this to its logical conclusion, Prabhupāda envisioned a world revolution in consciousness—spearheaded by the Kṛṣṇa conscious Beatles.

> It is understood from your letter that Mr. George Harrison has a little sympathy for our movement, and if Krishna is actually satisfied on him surely he will be able to join with us in pushing on the Samkirtan movement throughout the world. Somehow or other the Beatles have become the cynosure of the neighboring European countries and America also. He is attracted by our Samkirtan Party and if Mr. George Harrison takes the leading part in organizing a huge Samkirtan Party consisting of the Beatles and our ISKCON boys, surely we shall change the face of the world so much politically harassed by the maneuvers of the politicians.

For the London devotees, George's friendship heightened the excitement of Prabhupāda's coming to London. Now that a world-famous personality was waiting to meet Prabhupāda, they felt perhaps they had another way to please him and to make preaching in London a success.

George, by his association with Kṛṣṇa consciousness and by dint of his own spiritual evolution, began to express his devotion to Lord Kṛṣṇa in his songs. Reading Prabhupāda's *Bhagavad-gītā As It Is,* he could appreciate the superiority of the personal conception of God over the impersonal. Guru dāsa showed George the verse in the *Gītā* where Kṛṣṇa says that He is the basis of the impersonal Brahman. George liked the concepts of Kṛṣṇa consciousness, but he was wary of showing exclusive devotion to Prabhupāda and Kṛṣṇa. The devotees, therefore, dealt with him accordingly, so as not to disturb him.

On January 11 Śrīla Prabhupāda wrote another letter to the devotees in London, expressing more ideas of how George could best serve Kṛṣṇa.

> I am so glad that Mr. Harrison is composing songs like "Lord whom we so long ignored." He is very thoughtful. When we actually meet, I shall be able to give him thoughts about separation from Krishna, and they will be able to compose very attractive songs for public reception. The public is in need of such songs, and if they are administered through nice agents like the Beatles, it will surely be a great success.

Later George would record some of these songs. His "My Sweet Lord" was the number-one single in America for two months, and his million-selling album *Living in the Material World* was number one on *Billboard* for five weeks.

Prabhupāda cautioned the devotees not to simply depend on George for help but to try to find a building themselves and rent it. George did want to help, however, and again he suggested the devotees make a record on the Apple label. An old favorite idea of the London devotees had been to get the Beatles to make a record chanting Hare Kṛṣṇa; if the Beatles did it, the mantra would certainly become world famous.

George liked the idea, but he preferred that the devotees sing it and he produce it on the Apple label. "You guys make the money, rather than we get it," he said. "Let's make a record."

So the devotees went over to George's house for a chanting session. George dubbed in his guitar, and a few weeks later the devotees returned and heard their tape. George was ready to try a session at the studio, so the devotees agreed to meet him and his musician friend Billy Preston at Trident Studios on St. Anne's Alley. They recorded for a few hours; the tape sounded good. George and Śyāmasundara agreed on a date for the actual recording.

On the day of the recording about a dozen devotees, including some newly recruited Britishers, assembled at E.M.I. recording studios on Abbey Road. When the first group of devotees arrived in George's Mercedes, a crowd of teenagers began singing Hare Kṛṣṇa to the tune popularized by the rock musical *Hair*. While Yamunā applied Vaiṣṇava *tilaka* to the foreheads of the recording technicians, Mālatī began unpacking the picnic baskets of *prasādam* she had brought, and some of the other devotees put up pictures of Kṛṣṇa and lit incense. The studio was Kṛṣṇa-ized.

With Paul McCartney and his wife, Linda, operating the control console, the recording session began. Everyone worked quickly, making Side One of the 45 rpm record in about an hour. George played organ, and Mukunda played *mṛdaṅga*. Yamunā sang the lead with Śyāmasundara backing her, and the other voices blended in a chorus. And to make it come out exactly right, everyone concentrated on Prabhupāda and prayed for spiritual strength.

On the fourth take, everything went smoothly, with Mālatī spontaneously hitting a brass gong at the end. Then they recorded the flip side of the record: prayers to Śrīla Prabhupāda, Lord Caitanya and His associates, and the six Gosvāmīs. Afterward, George dubbed in the bass guitar and other voices. The devotees, engineers—everyone—felt good about it. "This is going to be big," George promised.

As the record went into production the devotees returned to their regular work, still living separately. Prabhupāda set the time of his arrival for early September. He would go to Hamburg and then come to London, he said—even if there was no temple. Miraculously, only two months before Prabhupāda's arrival, things began to come together.

Guru dāsa met a real estate agent with a building on Bury Place, near the British Museum; the devotees could move in immediately. An ideal location, forty-one pounds a week, and immediate occupancy—it was wonderful. Mukunda wrote Prabhupāda asking him for money for the down payment. Prabhupāda agreed. Śyāmasundara got a letter from George on Apple Corporation, Ltd., stationery stating that Apple would guarantee payments if the devotees defaulted. Within a week, the devotees had a five-story building in central London.

But when the devotees went to live at their new center on Bury Place, city officials said they did not have the proper housing permits. The red tape could take weeks, even months. Again the devotees were without a place to live and worship together. Śyāmasundara, however, on faith that everything would work out, began constructing a temple room of California redwood in the building.

John Lennon then suggested to Śyāmasundara that the devotees come and live with him at Tittenhurst, a large estate he had recently purchased near Ascot. He needed some renovation done, and if the devotees would help he would give them a place to live. "Can our guru also stay there?" Śyāmasundara asked. John agreed, and the devotees moved into the former servants' quarters at John's estate.

Only a few weeks before Prabhupāda's arrival, the record, "Hare Krishna Mantra," was released. Apple Records staged a promotion and brought press reporters and photographers in a multicolored bus to a blue-and-white pavilion where the devotees had gathered with George.

The first day the record sold seventy thousand copies. Within a few weeks the devotees appeared on the popular TV show *Top of the Pops,* singing "their song."

John Lennon's estate, formerly owned by the Cadbury family, consisted of seventy-six acres of lawn and forest, with a large manor and many smaller buildings. John and his wife, Yoko, lived in the manor. The servants' quarters, where Prabhupāda and the devotees were to live, were four separate apartments in a single narrow building near the manor. About fifteen devotees moved in, reserving one apartment for Prabhupāda and his servant. But this was not the first time the Lennons had had devotees as guests. A few months before, in May, several devotees had chanted Hare Kṛṣṇa with John and Yoko in their suite at Montreal's Queen Elizabeth Hotel.

John wanted the devotees to tear out the hardwood walls and floors in the main house and replace them with new walls and black-and-white marble tile floors. While this renovation was beginning, Īśāna, who had recently arrived from Canada, began with a few helpers to convert the old music recital hall into a temple, complete with a *vyāsāsana* for Prabhupāda. The devotees worked day and night on Prabhupāda's quarters, the temple room, and Prabhupāda's *vyāsāsana*. With such energy did they work that John and Yoko could see that the devotees were obviously in love with their spiritual master. When the devotees were making a tape to send to Prabhupāda in Germany, Īśāna asked John if he had anything he wanted to say to their guru. John smiled and said he would like to know Prabhupāda's secret that made his followers so devoted.

The stage was set. The time had come for the principal character to enter. Lord Kṛṣṇa's pure devotee was at last coming to England. For the six devotees who had pioneered Kṛṣṇa consciousness in London, it had been a long struggle. But now it seemed that all their once-impossible dreams were coming true. They had found a place for Prabhupāda to live, and they had obtained a temple in the center of London. This was Kṛṣṇa's blessing.

* * *

September 11, 1969

With the cooperation of Apple Records and Lufthansa German Airlines, the devotees arranged a reception for Prabhupāda at London's Heathrow Airport. As soon as Prabhupāda descended the stairs of the airplane, he was escorted to a car and driven to a V.I.P. lounge, bypassing the formalities of immigration and customs. As Prabhupāda stepped from the car, the devotees ran out of the terminal and offered obeisances on the wet pavement, while Śrīla Prabhupāda looked down on them, smiling. The devotees rose, brushing wet macadam from their dhotis and saris, and joyfully surrounded Prabhupāda as he entered the lounge.

The reporters, moving in: "What do you think of this reception?"

Prabhupāda: "I am not very much fond of reception. I want to know how people give reception to this movement. That is my concern."

Devotees in unison: "Haribol!"

Reporter: "Is this a very special welcome for you, or is this a performance you go through each day?"

Prabhupāda: "No, wherever I go, I have got my disciples. In Western countries I have got now about twenty centers, especially in America. So the American boys are very enthusiastic. I think in Los Angeles and San Francisco I got a very great reception. In the Ratha-yātrā festival about ten thousand boys and girls followed me for seven miles."

Devotees: "Haribol!"

Sun reporter: "What do you try to teach, sir?"

Prabhupāda: "I am trying to teach what you have forgotten."

Devotees (laughing): "Haribol! Hare Kṛṣṇa!"

Sun reporter: "Which is what?"

Prabhupāda: "That is God. Some of you are saying there is no God. Some of you are saying God is dead. And some of you are saying God is impersonal or void. These are all nonsense. I want to teach all the nonsense people that there is God. That is my mission. Any nonsense can come to me—I shall prove that there is God. That is my Kṛṣṇa consciousness movement. It is a challenge to the atheistic people: This is

God. As we are sitting here face to face, you can see God face to face, if you are sincere and if you are serious. That is possible. Unfortunately, you are trying to forget God. Therefore you are embracing so many miseries of life. So I am simply preaching that you become Kṛṣṇa conscious and be happy. Don't be swayed by these nonsense waves of maya, or illusion."

The reporters asked about Billy Graham, the moon landing, the war in Ireland, and the whereabouts of Prabhupāda's wife and children. They asked him to turn his head toward them, and they clicked away with their cameras. They thanked him, and the reception dispersed.

Prabhupāda went from the building to the gleaming white Rolls Royce awaiting him outside, courtesy of John Lennon. Prabhupāda entered the back seat and sat crosslegged. The limousine was equipped with darkened windows and a lavish interior, including a television. The devotees had become so confused in their excitement that none of them had thought to join Prabhupāda, and the chauffeur whisked him away to Tittenhurst. Prabhupāda sat silently, except for his occasionally audible chanting, as the chauffeur headed through the winding roads leading away from the airport.

He was in England. His father, Gour Mohan, had never wanted him to come to England. Once an uncle had told Gour Mohan that his son should go to England to become a barrister. But Gour Mohan had said no; if his son went there the meat-eaters, drinkers, and sex-mongers might influence him. But now, seventy years later, Prabhupāda had indeed come to London—not to be influenced by the Englishmen but to influence them. He had come to teach them what they had forgotten.

And he was off to a good start, under Kṛṣṇa's special care. When he had had to live alone in New York City without any money, that had been Kṛṣṇa's mercy. And now he was entering England in a chauffeured limousine, also Kṛṣṇa's mercy. Accepting the ride as part of Kṛṣṇa's plan, Prabhupāda remained deeply fixed in his purpose of carrying out the order of his spiritual master, whatever circumstances awaited.

Prabhupāda arrived before his disciples. But those who

had remained at the manor excitedly received him and showed him to his room on the second floor of the servants' quarters. The small room was chilly and damp, with a low table for a desk and wall-to-wall carpeting made from pieces of rug taken from the other rooms. The adjoining room was bare and even smaller. Prabhupāda sat down at his low desk. "Where is everyone?" he asked. As he leaned back and gazed out the window he saw rain just beginning to fall.

When George, John, and Yoko dropped by after Prabhupāda's lunch, Śyāmasundara invited them to come up and meet Prabhupāda. George turned to John and asked, "Do you want to go up?" The bearded, bespectacled master of Tittenhurst, hair down to his shoulders, assented. Yoko was also curious. So they all went to Prabhupāda's little room.

Smiling graciously from behind his desk, Prabhupāda asked his guests to enter and be seated. Here were two of the most famous people in England, and Kṛṣṇa wanted him to speak to them. Prabhupāda removed his garland and handed it to Śyāmasundara, indicating that he should put it around George's neck.

"Thank you," said George. "Hare Kṛṣṇa."

Prabhupāda smiled. "This is Kṛṣṇa's blessing."

"Hare Kṛṣṇa," George replied again.

"Yes," Prabhupāda said, "there is a verse in *Bhagavad-gītā: yad yad ācarati śreṣṭhas tat tad evetaro janaḥ/ sa yat pramāṇaṁ kurute lokas tad anuvartate.* The idea is that anything which is accepted by the leading persons, ordinary persons follow. *Yad yad ācarati śreṣṭhaḥ. Śreṣṭhaḥ* means 'leading persons.' *Ācarati* means 'act.' Whatever leading persons act, people in general follow them. If the leading person says it is nice, then it is all right—the others also accept it. So by the grace of God, Kṛṣṇa, you are leaders. Thousands of young men follow you. They like you. So if you give them something actually nice, the face of the world will change."

Although George and John were about the same age as most of Prabhupāda's disciples, Prabhupāda considered them *śreṣṭhas,* respected leaders. "You are also anxious to bring some peace in the world," Prabhupāda continued. "I have read sometimes your statement. You are anxious also. Everyone is. Every saintly person should be anxious to bring in peace in the world. But we must know the process." He explained the "peace formula" according to *Bhagavad-gītā:* only those who recognize the Supreme Personality of Godhead as the proprietor of everything, the object of all sacrifices, and the friend of everyone can find real peace.

Prabhupāda then told the two Beatles even more directly what he had already hinted at: they should learn Kṛṣṇa consciousness and help teach it to the world. "I request you to at least understand this philosophy to your best knowledge," he said. "If you think it is nice, pick it up. You are also willing to give something to the world. So try this. You have read our books, this *Bhagavad-gītā As It Is?*"

John: "I've read bits of the *Bhagavad-gītā*. I don't know which version it was. There's so many different translations."

Prabhupāda: "There are different translations. Therefore I have given this edition, *Bhagavad-gītā As It Is.*"

Prabhupāda explained that the material world is a place of misery. Nature is cruel. In America President Kennedy was thought to be the most fortunate, happy man, honored throughout the world. "But within a second"—Prabhupāda loudly snapped his fingers—"he was finished. Temporary. Now what is his position? Where is he? If life is eternal, if the living entity is eternal, where he has gone? What is he doing? Is he happy, or is he distressed? He is born in America, or China? Nobody can say. But it is a fact that, as living entity, he is eternal. He is existing."

Prabhupāda explained the transmigration of the soul. Then again he requested, "Try to understand it, and if it is nice you take it up. You are after something very nice. Is my proposal unreasonable?" The two Beatles glanced at one another but didn't answer. Prabhupāda gave a soft, amused laugh. "You are all intelligent boys. Try to understand it."

Prabhupāda asked his guests what philosophy they were following.

"Following?" John asked.

"We don't follow anything," Yoko said. "We are just

living."

"We've done meditation," said George. "Or I do my meditation, mantra meditation."

They began to ask questions—the same questions Prabhupāda had heard so many times before. After hearing Prabhupāda's explanation of Brahman, the all-pervading spiritual energy of the Supreme Personality of Godhead, Yoko doubted whether Brahman could remain pure and not deteriorate in time. Prabhupāda advised that she would have to become a serious student before she could actually understand spiritual philosophy.

John and Yoko, being devoted eclectics, had difficulty accepting Prabhupāda's concept of Vedic authority.

John: "We still have to keep sifting through, like through sand, to see who's got the best."

Prabhupāda: "No. One thing you try to understand. Why these people—if Kṛṣṇa is not the supreme authority—why they are taking Kṛṣṇa's book and translating? Why don't you try to understand?"

George: "I'm not saying Kṛṣṇa isn't the Supreme. I believe that. There is a misunderstanding about the translation of the Sanskrit *Gītā* into English. And I was saying that there are many versions, and I think we thought you were trying to say your version, your translation, was the authority and that the other translations were not. But we didn't really have misunderstanding as to the identity of Kṛṣṇa."

Prabhupāda: "That's all right. If you believe Kṛṣṇa is the Supreme Lord, if that is your version, then you have to see who is most addicted to Kṛṣṇa. These people are twenty-four hours chanting *Kṛṣṇa*. And another person, who has not a single word *Kṛṣṇa*—how can he become a devotee of Kṛṣṇa? How can he, who does not utter even the name of Kṛṣṇa, become a representative of Kṛṣṇa? If Kṛṣṇa is authority—and that is accepted—therefore those who are directly addicted to Kṛṣṇa, they are authorities."

After more than an hour of conversation, Prabhupāda distributed some *prasādam* to John, George, Yoko, and the few disciples in his room. If these *śreṣṭhas* were to take up Kṛṣṇa consciousness, that would be good for them and many others also. He had done his duty and provided them the opportunity. It was Kṛṣṇa's message, and to accept it or not was now up to them.

John said he had something to do, and he excused himself. As everyone was leaving, Yoko, walking down the stairs, turned to John and said, "Look at how simply he's living. Could you live like that?"

* * *

The devotees regularly encountered John and Yoko. Although originally interested in a business relationship, John was inclined toward the devotees, but his friends advised him not to get involved with the Swami and his group. So he remained aloof.

Īśāna dāsa: *I was in the kitchen working, and John was sitting at the piano. He had a piano in the kitchen, a great upright piano with all the varnish removed—bare wood. And in this way he was sitting at the piano, playing Hare Kṛṣṇa. The man was actually a great musician, and he played Hare Kṛṣṇa in every musical idiom you could think of—bluegrass music or classical music or rock-and-roll or whatever. He would go at will from one idiom to another, always singing Hare Kṛṣṇa. It was so natural for him, and one could see he was a musical genius. And in this way he was entertaining me, and he was obviously really enjoying it. So anyway, while this piano-playing was going on with great vigor and enthusiasm, this chanting Hare Kṛṣṇa, his wife, Yoko Ono, appeared in a nightgown or what have you and said, in a very distressed tone, "Please, John, I have a* terrible *headache. Can't you stop that sort of thing and come upstairs with me?"*

George was different. He was drawn to Prabhupāda. When one of the devotees had asked, "Why out of all the Beatles are only you interested?" George replied, "It's my karma. One of the things in my sign is the spiritual side."

George Harrison: *Prabhupāda just looked like I thought he would. I had like a mixed feeling of fear and awe about meeting him. That's what I liked about later on after meeting him more—I felt that he was just more like a friend. I felt relaxed. It was much better than at first, because I hadn't been able to tell what he was saying and I wasn't sure if I was too worldly to even be there. But later I relaxed and felt much more at ease with him, and he was very warm towards me. He wouldn't talk differently to me than to anybody else. He was always just speaking about Kṛṣṇa, and it was coincidental who happened to be there. Whenever you saw him he would always be the same. It wasn't like one time he would tell you to chant the Hare Kṛṣṇa mantra and then the next time say, "Oh, no, I made a mistake." He was always the same.*

Seeing him was always a pleasure. Sometimes I would drop by, thinking I wasn't planning to go but I better go because I ought to, and I would always come away just feeling so good. I was conscious that he was taking a personal interest in me. It was always a pleasure.

George was attracted to Kṛṣṇa, and he liked to chant. Even before meeting Prabhupāda, he had learned something of Kṛṣṇa from Maharishi Mahesh Yogi, from the autobiography of Paramahansa Yogananda, and from traveling to India. But Prabhupāda's instructions in particular impressed upon him that Lord Kṛṣṇa was the Absolute Truth, the origin of everything.

George: *Prabhupāda helped me to realize the multifaceted way to approach Kṛṣṇa. Like the* prasādam, *for example. I think it is a very important thing,* prasādam, *even if it's only a trick. Like they say, the way to a man's heart is through his stomach. Well, even if it's a way to a man's spirit soul, it works. Because there is nothing better than having been dancing and singing or just sitting and talking and then suddenly they give you some food. It's like it's a blessing. And then when you learn to touch Him or taste Him, it's important.*

Kṛṣṇa is not limited. And just by Prabhupāda's being there and pouring out all this information, I was moved. It's like the mind is stubborn, but it's all Kṛṣṇa. That's all you need to know—it's all Kṛṣṇa. This world is His material energy too—the universal form. And in Prabhupāda's books there are these pictures showing Kṛṣṇa in the heart of a dog and a cow and a human being. It helps you to realize that Kṛṣṇa is within everybody.

Although Prabhupāda might have been teaching some higher aspect, what came through to me a lot was a greater understanding of how Kṛṣṇa is everywhere and in everything. Prabhupāda explained about the different aspects of Kṛṣṇa, and he provided a meditation where you could see Kṛṣṇa as a person everywhere. I mean, there isn't anything that isn't Kṛṣṇa.

Prabhupāda saw George as a "nice young boy" and a devotee of Kṛṣṇa. According to the *Bhāgavatam* no matter what a person may be materially, if he is a nondevotee and never utters the holy name of God he cannot possess *any* good qualities. Many swamis and yogis in India, even some who considered themselves Vaiṣṇavas, had no faith in or understanding of the holy names of Kṛṣṇa. But George liked to chant Hare Kṛṣṇa, and he had put the holy name of Kṛṣṇa in his songs, which were tremendously popular all over the world. So he was serving Kṛṣṇa through his music, and that made all the difference.

> Mr. George Harrison appears to be a very intelligent boy, and he is, by the Grace of Krishna, fortunate also. On the first day, he came to see me along with John Lennon, and we had talks about 2 hours. He wanted to talk with me more, but he has now gone to his sick mother in Liverpool.

Prabhupāda also saw George as a rich man, and Lord Caitanya had strictly instructed devotees in the renounced order not to mix with worldly men. But Lord Caitanya had also taught that a devotee should accept any favorable opportunity for propagating Kṛṣṇa consciousness.

> If this boy cooperates with our movement, it will be very nice impetus for after all, he is a monied man. These monied men have to be very cautiously dealt with in spiritual life. We have to sometimes deal with them on account of preaching work; otherwise, Lord Chaitanya Mahaprabhu has strictly restricted to mix with them for Krishna Conscious people. But we get instruction

from Rupa Goswami that whatever opportunity is favorable for pushing on Krishna Consciousness we should accept.

Prabhupāda dealt with George cautiously, but encouraged him to chant the Lord's name, take His *prasādam*, and surrender all his works to Him.

George: *Prabhupāda never really suggested that I shouldn't do what I was doing. I heard that at different times he would say to the devotees that I was a better devotee because of my songs and the other things I was doing. He never actually said that to me, but I always heard that. And the good thing for me was that I didn't have a feeling that I needed to join full-time. I think it would have spoiled it if he had always been on at me, saying, "Why don't you pack in doing what you are doing and go live in a temple somewhere?" He never made me feel any different, like I wasn't quite in the club. He was never like that.*

I'm a plainclothes devotee. It's like that. I saw my relationship—that I should help when and where I could, because I know people in society. It's like any half-decent person; you just try and help each other a little bit.

He was always pleased with me, because anything I did was a help. I mean not just to the Kṛṣṇa temple as such, but just to anything spiritual that I did, either through songs or whatever—it pleased him. He was just always friendly. He was always chanting, and at times he said that to me—just to keep chanting all the time, or as much as possible. I think once you do that, you realize the chanting is of benefit.

There are some gurus who go around making out that they are "it," but Prabhupāda was saying, "I am the servant of the servant of the servant of Kṛṣṇa," which is really what it is, you know. He wasn't saying, "I am the greatest," and "I am God," and all that. With him it was only in the context of being a servant, and I liked that a lot. I think it's part of the spiritual thing. The more they know, then the more they actually know that they are the servant. And the less they know, the more they think they are actually God's gift to mankind.

So although he was obviously a very powerful individual, very spiritually advanced, he always retained that humble-

ness. And I think that is one of the most important things, because you learn—more than all the words he says—you learn really from the example of how he lives and what he does.

Prabhupāda and his people and John and Yoko and theirs made an odd combination. Two days after Prabhupāda's arrival at Tittenhurst, John and Yoko had flown to Canada to perform with the Plastic Ono Band at Toronto's Rock-N-Roll Revival at Varsity Stadium. In October John and Yoko had recorded *Wedding Album* and begun work on a film, *Rock-and-Roll Circus,* and John had recorded "Cold Turkey." Although John was usually shy, the devotees working at the main house found him openhearted and generous with his possessions. He invited the devotees to stay permanently at Tittenhurst and farm. Whatever he had, he said, he would share with them. Eventually Prabhupāda and his disciples departed, but their talks with John at Tittenhurst were reflected in a song John wrote around that time—"Instant Karma."

* * *

Even though Prabhupāda's quarters were incomplete and temple renovation made 7 Bury Place noisy and hectic, Prabhupāda decided to move in. "I am not attached to a comfortable apartment," he said. "My attachment is to living in the association of devotees." He was moving into the temple at a time when the record sales were low and the devotees were having to purchase supplies piecemeal, whenever they got money. Yet with Prabhupāda living with them and supervising their work, they were satisfied.

One day a Mr. Doyal phoned, representing a large London Hindu society. He had heard the devotees wanted Rādhā-Kṛṣṇa Deities, and he had a pair he would donate. When Prabhupāda heard the news, he sent Tamāla Kṛṣṇa, Mukunda, and Śyāmasundara to Mr. Doyal's home to see the Deities.

Rādhā and Kṛṣṇa were white marble and stood about three feet high. Never before had the devotees seen such large Deities, and they offered obeisances. When they returned to the temple and told Prabhupāda, he said, "Take me there at once!"

Śrīla Prabhupāda, accompanied by Śyāmasundara, Mukunda, and Tamāla Kṛṣṇa, arrived by van at Mr. Doyal's home. Prabhupāda entered the living room and sat down. The Deities, covered by a cloth, stood on a table in the corner. Tamāla Kṛṣṇa was about to unveil Them when Prabhupāda checked him: "No. That's all right." Prabhupāda sat and spoke with Mr. Doyal, asking him about his work and where he had come from in India, and he met Mr. Doyal's family. Prabhupāda and his host chatted while the devotees listened.

"Swamiji," Mr. Doyal said at length, "I want to show you my Deities."

"Yes," Prabhupāda replied, "I will see Them after some time."

Prabhupāda began to speak about his Kṛṣṇa consciousness mission, and after a while Mr. Doyal again requested, "Please take a look at these Deities." And with that he walked over and unveiled Rādhā and Kṛṣṇa.

"Oh, yes," Prabhupāda said, folding his hands respectfully. Mr. Doyal explained that he had ordered the Deities from India for his own use, but in transit a tiny piece of Rādhārāṇī's finger had chipped off; therefore, according to Hindu tradition, the Deities could not be installed.

"Tamāla Kṛṣṇa," Prabhupāda said. "See how heavy these Deities are."

Tamāla Kṛṣṇa, placing one hand at Rādhārāṇī's base and the other around Her shoulder, lifted Her. "Not so heavy," he said.

"Śyāmasundara," Prabhupāda said. "See how heavy is Kṛṣṇa." The Deities were actually heavy for one man to carry, but the devotees understood Prabhupāda's intention.

"Not bad," Śyāmasundara said, holding Kṛṣṇa a few inches off the table.

"Yes," Prabhupāda said conclusively, "I think They're all right. Let us take Them. We have our van." And suddenly

Prabhupāda was leaving, with his disciples following, carefully carrying Rādhā and Kṛṣṇa. Prabhupāda thanked Mr. Doyal.

"But Swamiji! Swamiji!" protested Mr. Doyal, who was not prepared for this sudden exit. "Please, we will arrange to bring Them. Our society will bring Them." But Prabhupāda was already out the door and leading his men to the van.

"Please wait," Mr. Doyal persisted. "We have to fix Them first, then you can take Them."

"We have an expert man," Prabhupāda said. "He can fix these things." Prabhupāda was assuring Mr. Doyal and at the same time directing his disciples. He opened the door of the van, and Śyāmasundara and Tamāla Kṛṣṇa slowly entered, cautiously setting Rādhā and Kṛṣṇa within. Tamāla Kṛṣṇa knelt in the back to hold the Deities secure, while Śyāmasundara got into the driver's seat.

"Now drive," Prabhupāda said. And off they went, with Prabhupāda smiling from the window to Mr. Doyal and his family, who stood together on the curb.

Śyāmasundara had driven but a few blocks when Prabhupāda asked him to stop the van. Turning around in his seat, Prabhupāda began offering prayers: *Govindam ādi-puruṣaṁ tam ahaṁ bhajāmi* . . . He looked long at Kṛṣṇa, who was white with a slight bluish cast, and at the exquisite white Rādhārāṇī by His side. "Kṛṣṇa is so kind," he said. "He has come like this." Then he had Śyāmasundara continue driving slowly back to the temple.

Carefully, Prabhupāda supervised his disciples' carrying the Deities up to the second floor. The devotees were astounded and delighted to see Prabhupāda in such an animated and intense state, bringing Rādhā and Kṛṣṇa into Their temple. He had the Deities placed in a curtained-off section of his own room, and then he sat at his desk.

Śyāmasundara had completed most of the altar, except for Lord Jagannātha's altar and the canopy over Rādhā and Kṛṣṇa's throne. Both the canopy and Lord Jagannātha's altar would be supported by four heavy, wooden columns more than six feet high. Two rear columns would hold a marble slab for the Jagannātha deities to stand on, and two front columns were now supporting Rādhā and Kṛṣṇa's large velvet canopy. The columns were big and heavy; Śyāmasundara called them "elephant-leg columns." The columns now stood in place on the altar, although Śyāmasundara hadn't had a chance to secure them. The day before the installation Śyāmasundara collapsed upstairs in exhaustion.

On opening day many guests, Indians especially, crowded the temple, responding to flyers and advertisements. Apple Records had supplied a professional florist, who had decorated the room with floral arrangements. A BBC television crew was on hand to videotape the ceremony. While most of the devotees held *kīrtana,* Prabhupāda, behind a curtain at the other end of the temple, bathed Rādhā and Kṛṣṇa.

The plan was that after the bathing ceremony the Deities would be placed on the altar and Yamunā would dress Them. Once They were dressed and enthroned, the curtain would open for all the guests to behold Śrī Śrī Rādhā and Kṛṣṇa. Prabhupāda would lecture, and then everyone would feast. But because of Śyāmasundara's oversight, the installation almost became a disaster.

Prabhupāda had finished bathing the Deities and They had been placed on the marble altar, when suddenly the "elephant-leg columns" tottered. The canopy above the Deities began to collapse. Prabhupāda, seeing the danger, jumped onto the altar and seized the heavy columns in a split second. With great strength he held the two front pillars in place. "Get this out of here!" he shouted. While Prabhupāda's arms protected the Deities, the men removed the canopy, and then two men at a time carried each of the pillars away. The Deities remained unharmed.

While Prabhupāda was behind the curtain rescuing Rādhā and Kṛṣṇa, on the other side of the curtain guests and reporters awaited the unveiling of the Deities. Unaware of the mishap, the guests saw only men emerging from behind the curtain carrying large pillars and a canopy. The BBC camera crew began filming the canopy and pillars as they appeared from behind the curtain, taking them to be part of a ceremonial procession.

The few devotees behind the curtain with Prabhupāda were amazed. But there was no time now for apologies or appreciations. Yamunā dressed the Deities, Prabhupāda hurrying her. When at last everything was ready, Prabhupāda opened the main curtain, revealing the graceful forms of Lord Kṛṣṇa and Rādhārāṇī to the temple full of guests. A devotee began to offer *ārati,* while Prabhupāda, wearing a saffron *cādar* and a garland of carnations, stood to one side, reverentially looking upon Rādhā and Kṛṣṇa as Their worshiper and protector.

This was the culmination of months of effort. Actually, years of planning had preceded this auspicious occasion. One hundred years before, Bhaktivinoda Ṭhākura had hoped for the day when Kṛṣṇa consciousness would come to England, and Śrīla Bhaktisiddhānta Sarasvatī had also desired it. Now that an authorized temple of Rādhā and Kṛṣṇa was preaching Kṛṣṇa consciousness in London, it was a historic occasion for Gauḍīya Vaiṣṇavism; a long-standing order of the previous *ācāryas* had been fulfilled. Prabhupāda had sent invitations to several of his Godbrothers in India. None of them had been able to come, of course, but at least they should have been pleased to learn that this dream of Śrīla Bhaktisiddhānta Sarasvatī's had been fulfilled.

Prabhupāda was seventy-three. He had now opened twenty-one temples in three years. Recently he had told some of his disciples that they should try to form a governing body for ISKCON, to relieve him of the management and allow him to concentrate fully on presenting Kṛṣṇa conscious literature. This literature could be introduced all over the world into homes, schools, and colleges for the benefit of everyone. It would be in such literature that he would live on. How much time he had left in this world he didn't know, he said, but he wanted to go on serving and trying to please his Guru Mahārāja, life after life.

Nevertheless, despite Prabhupāda's desire to retire from active work and absorb himself in writing books, here he was installing Deities in a new temple and protecting Them from his disciples' carelessness. Had he not been present, the celebration would have been a disaster. So many hardworking disciples, and they still needed his personal guidance.

ISKCON was just beginning to grow. Prabhupāda wanted to open not just a few temples, but at least 108. His world traveling and book printing were just beginning, and, like everything else, the number of disciples would increase. The prestige of his movement would increase, and with it opposition from the atheists. Kṛṣṇa consciousness was growing, and Prabhupāda was in the forefront. "All around I see bright," he said. "That is the glory of Kṛṣṇa." He saw himself as a servant of his spiritual master; the bright future was in Kṛṣṇa's hands.

On the day of Prabhupāda's departure from London, he distributed some of his personal effects, such as sweaters and scarves, to his disciples. He then went downstairs alone into the temple to see the Deities. He offered fully prostrated obeisances on the floor for a long time and then stood, looking at Rādhā and Kṛṣṇa.

Yamunā: *Prabhupāda was looking at the Deities with complete devotion. He loved those Deities. He commented about Their exquisite beauty and how They complemented each other—how sometimes Rādhārāṇī looked more beautiful but how Kṛṣṇa's moonlike face and eyes were shining. Prabhupāda saw me and matter-of-factly said, "If you practice what I have taught you and follow the instructions of how I have taught you to worship the Deity, and if you read the books that we have printed, it is sufficient for you to go back to Godhead. You need not learn anything new. Simply practice what I have taught you, and your life will be perfect." Then he left—just left.*

* * *

After London, Śrīla Prabhupāda returned to America, where he spent some seven months at his U.S. centers—especially Los Angeles. During late July in Los Angeles, he revealed his plans for establishing a governing body commission to manage ISKCON. To this end he dictated the following on July 28, 1970:

> I, the undersigned, A. C. Bhaktivedanta Swami, disciple of Om Visnupad Paramahamsa 108 Sri Srimad Bhaktisiddhanta Sarasvati Goswami Maharaj Prabhupada, came in the United States in 1965 on September 18th for the purpose of starting Krishna Consciousness Movement. For one year I had no shelter. I was traveling in many parts of this country. Then in 1966, July, I incorporated this Society under the name and style The International Society for Krishna Consciousness, briefly ISKCON. . . . Gradually the Society increased, and one after another branches were opened. Now we have got thirty-four (34) branches enlisted herewith. As we have increased our volume of activities, now I think a Governing Body Commission (hereinafter referred to as the GBC) should be established. I am getting old, 75 years old, therefore at any time I may be out of the scene, therefore I think it is necessary to give instruction to my disciples how they shall manage the whole institution. They are already managing individual centers represented by one president, one secretary and one treasurer, and in my opinion they are doing nice. But we want still more improvement in the standard of Temple management, propaganda for Krishna consciousness, distribution of books and literatures, opening of new centers and educating devotees to the right standard.

Prabhupāda then listed the names of the twelve persons who would form the G.B.C., and he noted:

> These personalities are now considered as my direct representatives. While I am living they will act as my zonal secretaries and after my demise they will be known as Executors.

The next day Prabhupāda drafted another significant statement naming several of his disciples as trustees of his Bhaktivedanta Book Trust.

> The Bhaktivedanta Book Trust account will be used to publish my books and literature and to establish Temples throughout the world, specifically three temples are to be established, one each in Mayapur, Vrindaban, and Jagannatha Puri.

Although Śrīla Prabhupāda intended the G.B.C. to oversee the activities of ISKCON, he was not creating a monolithic structure. He wrote to Karandhara, a G.B.C. member,

> Each temple must remain independent and self-sufficient. That was my plan from the very beginning. . . . Once there is bureaucracy the whole thing will be spoiled. There must always be individual striving and work and responsibility, competitive spirit; not that one shall dominate and distribute benefits to the others, and they do nothing but beg from you, and you provide. No. Never mind there may be botheration to register each center, take tax certificate each, become separate corporations in each state. That will train men how to do these things, and they shall develop reliability and responsibility.

* * *

Calcutta
August 1970

For the first time in almost three years, Prabhupāda returned to India—to Calcutta, his hometown. Although it was late and the journey had been long, Prabhupāda felt happy as he descended the stairway from the airplane. Acyutānanda and Jayapatāka, his only American disciples in India, were standing on the airfield, and as they saw him approaching in his saffron silk robes, they bowed down. Prabhupāda smiled and embraced them.

Calcutta was in political turmoil. A group of Communist terrorists, the Naxalites, had been rioting, murdering prominent businessmen and threatening the lives of many others. Many wealthy Marwari industrialists were leaving the city for Delhi and Bombay. Aside from the terrorists, Bengali college students were growing unruly. But the older people of West Bengal, comprising most of Prabhupāda's visitors, were alarmed by the violence and unrest. The only shelter, Prabhupāda told them, was Kṛṣṇa.

> People are in very much perturbed condition. All of them are expecting me to do something for ameliorating the situation, but I am simply advising them to chant Hare Kṛṣṇa, because this transcendental sound is the only panacea for all material diseases.

Prabhupāda saw no need to fabricate a special program for the social problems of Calcutta. Chanting Hare Kṛṣṇa was "the only panacea for all material diseases." The question was how best to use his American disciples to give this panacea to the Indians. Prabhupāda had come with a party of ten devotees, and he had asked his leaders in the West for twenty more within the month. He had ordered $60,000 worth of books and magazines from Dai Nippon Printing Company in Japan, and his sannyasis were going daily into the streets to perform *kīrtana.*

The *saṅkīrtana* party was getting a good response. Shaven-headed Westerners, wearing *śikhās,* Vaiṣṇava *tilaka,* and saffron robes, playing *karatālas* and *mṛdaṅgas,* chanting Hare Kṛṣṇa with heart and soul, quoting Sanskrit verses from *Bhagavad-gītā,* affirming Lord Kṛṣṇa to be the Supreme Personality of Godhead—for the Bengalis this was sensational, and hundreds would gather to watch. Prabhupāda knew the great appeal his disciples would have; everyone would want to see them. He therefore affectionately called them his "dancing white elephants."

These same devotees, who had grown to love chanting Hare Kṛṣṇa in the streets of San Francisco, Los Angeles, and New York, were now going into an exhausting heat never encountered in America and chanting on Dalhousie Square for several hours daily. Crowds would press in closely, sometimes teasing, laughing, or scoffing, but more often looking on with deep amazement.

Prabhupāda's idea was that when Indians saw young Western people adopting the principles of Kṛṣṇa consciousness, the faith of the Indians in their own culture would increase. Prabhupāda explained to his disciples how formerly, during the time of Mahārāja Yudhiṣṭhira, India had been a Kṛṣṇa conscious state. For the last thousand years, however, India had been under foreign subjugation, first under the Moguls and then under the British. As a result, the intelligentsia and, to a lesser degree, the masses of India had lost respect for their own culture. They were now pursuing the materialistic goals of the West, and they saw this as more productive and more practical than religion, which was only sentimental.

Westerners living as renounced Vaiṣṇavas could, as Prabhupāda was well aware, turn the heads and hearts of the Indians and help them regain faith in their own lost culture. It was not a material tactic, however, but a spiritual strength. Prabhupāda stressed that the devotees must be pure in their actions; this purity would be their force.

The chanting in Dalhousie Square and along Chowringee had gone on for about ten days when Prabhupāda decided to stop it. The street *kīrtana,* although an excellent method of preaching, was not the most effective method for India, he said. There were many professional *kīrtana* groups in Bengal, and Prabhupāda didn't want his disciples to be seen like that—as professional performers or beggars. He wanted them to preach in a way that would bring them closer to the more intelligent, respectable Indians, and he unfolded his new plans.

He called it "Life Membership." His disciples would invite Indians interested in supporting and associating with ISKCON to become members. A membership fee of 1,111 rupees would entitle the member to many benefits, such as copies of Śrīla Prabhupāda's books and free accommodation in ISKCON centers around the world.

Speaking one evening in a private home before a group of wealthy businessmen, Prabhupāda initiated his life membership program. After lecturing, he invited his audience to become ISKCON life members, and several Calcutta merchants immediately signed.

B. L. Jaju: *I was really overwhelmed by the simplicity of Prabhupāda's nature. He told me how he had been carrying on his regular business when his guru had told him that four hundred years back Caitanya Mahāprabhu had said that Hare Rāma, Hare Kṛṣṇa would be chanted all throughout the world. He said that was the job given to him by his spiritual master and that he would have to go to America and do it.*

I found no snobbery in him. He was very simple. And he was telling, as if my brother was telling me, simply how he went to the U.S.A., how he started, and how gradually he planned to have this Kṛṣṇa consciousness throughout the world.

Seeing his disciples who had changed their lives, I began to think, "Why not I? In my humble way, I should do something, without worrying what other people are doing." I found that imperceptibly he was affecting my life. My wife and even my son were really surprised when they found that these white people, whom we thought could never turn to Kṛṣṇa consciousness, had changed so much. So we thought we also must try to follow better the teaching of the Gītā.

Prabhupāda continued holding programs in people's homes and talking with guests in his room. One day a Mr. Dandharia visited Prabhupāda and mentioned Bombay's upcoming Sadhu Samaj, a gathering of the most important sadhus in India. It was to be held at Chowpatti Beach and promised to be a big affair. Mr. Dandharia requested Prabhupāda to attend, and Prabhupāda accepted.

* * *

Bombay
October 1970

The sand of Chowpatti Beach was fine and clean. The audience numbered in the thousands. Sadhus sat onstage, Prabhupāda and his followers among them. It was twilight. The sky above the Arabian Sea was cloudy, and a pleasant breeze was stirring.

There had already been two lectures expounding the Māyāvāda philosophy, and now it was time for Prabhupāda to speak—the last scheduled speaker of the evening. The audience was eager to hear him; his accomplishments in the West had caused great curiosity, especially now that he had arrived in Bombay and his devotees were chanting daily in public. Prabhupāda's disciples, bored and exasperated by the preceding two hours of Hindi oratory, could scarcely wait any longer for Prabhupāda to speak. But Prabhupāda, instead of addressing the audience, turned to his disciples and said, "Begin chanting."

As soon as the devotees began the *kīrtana,* little Sarasvatī, Śyāmasundara's daughter, stood and began to dance. Following her, the other devotees rose and began to dance. As the *kīrtana* came alive with *mṛdaṅgas* and *karatālas*, the dancing and chanting of the devotees seemed to disturb some of the sadhus onstage, who rose one by one and left. The audience, however, responded enthusiastically, many of them standing and clapping. After five minutes of ecstatic *kīrtana*, the devotees spontaneously jumped down onto the sand and headed toward the audience. Thousands in the crowd rose to their feet and began to move along with the devotees in a dance, backward and forward.

Indians began crying in uncontrolled happiness, overwhelmed by the genuine *kṛṣṇa-bhakti* of these foreigners. Never before had such a thing happened. Policemen and press reporters joined in the chanting and dancing. Chowpatti Beach was in an uproar of Hare Kṛṣṇa *kīrtana*, as Prabhupāda and his disciples showed the potency of Lord Caitanya's *saṅkīrtana* movement.

After about ten minutes the *kīrtana* ended, though a tumultuous unrest pervaded the talkative crowd. Fifteen minutes elapsed before all the people returned to their seats and the program could continue. The devotees had left the stage and taken their seats on the ground level, leaving Prabhupāda alone onstage. Prabhupāda's voice echoed over the public-address system.

"Ladies and gentlemen, I was requested to speak in Hindi, but I am not very much accustomed to speak in Hindi. Therefore, the authorities in this meeting have allowed me to speak in English. I hope you will follow me, because it is Bombay and most people will be speaking English. The problem is, as this evening's speaker, His Holiness Swami Akhandanandaji spoke to you, how we can make everyone accustomed to take up good habits—*sad-ācāra*? I think in this age, Kali-yuga, there are many faults."

Prabhupāda went on to explain the power of Lord Caitanya's movement to clean the hearts of everyone. He referred to the two great rogues whom Lord Caitanya had delivered, Jagāi and Mādhāi.

"Now we are saving, wholesale, Jagāis and Mādhāis. Therefore, if we want peace, if we want to be situated on the *sad-ācāra* platform, then we must spread the *hari-nāma mahā-mantra* all over the world. And it has been practically proven. The American and European Vaiṣṇavas who have come here, who have chanted Hare Kṛṣṇa mantra— they were cow-flesh eaters, they were drunkards, they were illicit-sex–mongers, they were all kinds of gamblers. But having taken to this Kṛṣṇa consciousness movement, they have given up everything abominable. *Sad-ācāra* has come automatically. They do not even take tea, they do not even take coffee, they do not even smoke, which I think is very rare to be found in India. But they have given up. Why? Because they have taken to this Kṛṣṇa consciousness."

Prabhupāda ended his talk after about five minutes: "I do not feel that I have to say very much. You can see what is the result of Kṛṣṇa consciousness. It is not something artificial. It is there in everyone. I have not done anything magical. But this Kṛṣṇa consciousness is present in all of us. We simply have to revive it."

The audience responded with cheers and a great round of applause. Prabhupāda, with greater force and eloquence than the long-winded Māyāvādīs, had shown the essence of spiritual life—ecstatic chanting of the holy names. And he offered the living testimony of his American disciples.

For the next week, Prabhupāda and his disciples were the talk of Bombay, and they began receiving many invitations to speak and perform *kīrtana* throughout the city. The *Times Weekly's* coverage of the Sadhu Samaj spotlighted the memorable presence of Śrīla Prabhupāda and his disciples.

> A group of twenty Americans, members of the Hare Krishna delegation, took over the dais. The air was filled with the beating of mridangas, the clash of cymbals and the music of the maha-mantra. Swaying from side to side, their tufts of hair tossing in the breeze they chanted: Hare Krishna . . .
>
> One greying reporter whom I had always regarded as a particularly unsentimental person said to me in an emotion-choked voice: "Do you realize what is happening? Very soon Hinduism is going to sweep the West. The Hare Krishna movement will compensate for all our loss at the hands of padres through the centuries."

Surat
December 17, 1970

It was like a dream come true. Thousands lined the street for many blocks, while the devotees, playing *karatālas* and *mṛdaṅgas* and chanting Hare Kṛṣṇa, made their way along. Spectators stood on rooftops or clustered at windows and doorways, while others joined the procession. The police stopped traffic at the intersections, allowing only the *kīrtana* procession to pass. The earthen road, freshly swept and sprinkled with water, had been decorated with rice-flour designs of auspicious Vedic symbols. Green, freshly cut banana trees adorned either side of the way. Overhead, women's saris strung like bunting across the narrow roadway formed a brightly colored canopy over the *kīrtana* party.

Mr. Bhagubhai Jariwala, Prabhupāda's host in Surat, had advertised the daily parade routes in the local newspapers, and now, day after day, the devotees were holding a *kīrtana* procession through various sections of the city. While more than twenty of Prabhupāda's disciples led the daily procession, thousands of Indians chanted, cheered, and clamored to see, and women threw flower petals from the rooftops.

Often the procession would have to stop as families came forward to garland the devotees. Sometimes the devotees would receive so many garlands that their blissful faces would be scarcely visible, and they would distribute the garlands to the people in the crowd. Never before had the devotees met with such a reception.

"It is a city of devotees," Prabhupāda said. He compared the people of Surat to dry grass catching fire. By nature they were Kṛṣṇa conscious, but the arrival of Śrīla Prabhupāda and his *saṅkīrtana* party had been like a torch, setting the city spiritually ablaze.

The entire population of Surat seemed to turn out every morning, as tens of thousands flocked at seven a.m. to the designated neighborhood. Men, women, laborers, merchants, professionals, the young, the old, and all the children—everyone seemed to be taking part. Cramming the streets and buildings, they would wait for the *kīrtana* party, and when the devotees arrived, everyone became joyous.

Prabhupāda attended only a couple of the morning processions, preferring to stay in his quarters at Mr. Jariwala's home. Each morning Prabhupāda would come out onto his second-floor balcony, just as the devotees were leaving. Although the mornings were cold and many of the devotees sick, seeing Prabhupāda on the balcony offering them his blessings eased their troubles. Prabhupāda would wave, and the devotees would set off down the street, chanting.

The devotees had no special paraphernalia other than *mṛdaṅgas* and *karatālas*—no flags, no marching band, no *ratha* (cart)—just an enthusiastic *kīrtana* party. And there was no official *paṇḍāl,* no Sadhu Samaj, no Vedanta Sammelan, no Gita Jayanti Mahotsava—just an entire city of *kṛṣṇa-bhaktas* waiting eagerly for the American Hare Kṛṣṇa chanters.

To be worshiped for chanting Hare Kṛṣṇa was just the opposite of what the devotees had experienced in the West. In Hamburg, Chicago, New York, London, Los Angeles, the devotees had been insulted, threatened with arrests, assaulted, and ignored. Of course, sometimes they had been tolerated and even appreciated, but never honored.

After several days of *kīrtana* processions, the mayor of Surat, Mr. Vaikuntha Sastri, closed all schools and proclaimed a holiday throughout the city. Everyone was now free to celebrate the mercy of Lord Caitanya and chant Hare Kṛṣṇa. Signs throughout the city read, in Gujarati, "Welcome to the American and European Devotees of Krishna," and "Welcome to Members of the Hare Krishna Movement."

Prabhupāda had accomplished in Surat what he had intended. He had given the holy name, and the people had embraced it. The people of Surat, though not prepared to alter their lives radically and live as ISKCON devotees, appreciated that Prabhupāda had turned Westerners into devotees of Lord Kṛṣṇa and that he was teaching the pure message of the scriptures and chanting Hare Kṛṣṇa. They had responded to Prabhupāda not out of dogma or ritual but out of an appreciation of the importance of spiritual life and a recognition that Prabhupāda and ISKCON were genuine.

For Prabhupāda's disciples, the visit to Surat had given them a glimpse of what the world would be like if everyone were a devotee.

* * *

ISKCON's new Bombay headquarters was a four-room flat on the seventh floor of the Akash-Ganga Building. Rent was nearly three thousand rupees a month, and the devotees had no guaranteed monthly income. Yet because the building was in a vital, prestigious location, Prabhupāda had taken the risk. Such a headquarters would be a necessary base for the preaching he wanted to do in Bombay, and his next preaching would be a grand eleven-day *paṇḍāl* program. "If you are going to hunt," Prabhupāda said, "then you should hunt for a rhinoceros. In that way, if you don't succeed, everyone will simply say, 'Oh, it couldn't be done anyway.' But if you do succeed, then everyone will be surprised. Everyone will be amazed."

As Prabhupāda revealed his plans for a gigantic *paṇḍāl* festival, the devotees became keenly aware that Prabhupāda's inspiration was motivating all their preaching; without him they could never attempt anything so bold and ambitious as a giant *paṇḍāl* festival in Bombay. Often "the American and European disciples" had been billed along with him, as if of equal importance, but the devotees saw themselves as only foolish servants trying to help the genuine pure devotee of the Lord. Although Prabhupāda credited his disciples, his disciples knew that Prabhupāda was Kṛṣṇa's empowered representative. He was their authority and personal link with Kṛṣṇa; his words and actions evinced full transcendental potency. As Kṛṣṇa was unlimited, Śrīla Prabhupāda, Kṛṣṇa's dearmost friend, was entitled to demand unlimited service on Kṛṣṇa's behalf. In the service of Kṛṣṇa, no project was impossible. *Impossible,* Prabhupāda said, was a word in a fool's dictionary.

But as Prabhupāda unfolded his plans for the *paṇḍāl* festival, the devotees doubted: How could they ever raise the money? How could they erect such a huge tent? Where would they get so much food? And who would cook it? Prabhupāda seemed amused at their doubts. "You are all Americans," he said. "So what is the use of being American unless you do something wonderful?"

A Bombay *paṇḍāl,* Prabhupāda said, would be the perfect way to link America's ingenuity with India's spirituality. He gave the example of a blind man and a lame man. Although separately they are helpless, by cooperating—the blind man carrying the lame on his shoulders, and the lame man giving directions—the two can work successfully. America, because of materialism and ignorance of God, was blind. And India, because of foreign invasions, poverty, and misinterpretations of Vedic knowledge, was lame. America had technological advancement and wealth, and India had spiritual knowledge. The job of the Kṛṣṇa consciousness movement was to combine the two strengths and uplift the world. And one practical application would be the Bombay *paṇḍāl* festival.

Prabhupāda divided the work, assigning Śyāmasundara to publicity, Tamāla Kṛṣṇa to the *paṇḍāl* arrangements, Girirāja to fund-raising, and Madhudviṣa to the scheduled programs onstage. Catching Prabhupāda's spirit of "shooting the rhinoceros," Śyāmasundara organized a massive publicity campaign, with giant posters and banners strung across the streets, announcing, "His Divine Grace A. C. Bhaktivedanta Swami Prabhupāda will speak in English language about the science of God. Prasadam distribution and bhajan singing will be led by his American and European bhaktas—Hare Krishna Festival at Cross Maidan—March 25 to April 4."

Girirāja: *Śrīla Prabhupāda took Bombay by storm. The whole city was alive with excitement about the Hare Kṛṣṇa Festival. We had banners at all the major intersections in Bombay. We had posters up on all the walls, many posters on every wall, and we had very big advertisements in the newspaper, with a beautiful picture of Śrīla Prabhupāda superimposed over a globe, and the words* Bhagavat Dharma Discourses: A Hare Krishna Festival. World Preacher of Bhakti Cult, His Divine Grace A. C. Bhaktivedanta Swami.

Day by day the momentum grew more and more, and every

day something new was happening. Finally, in the last two days, we got a huge billboard at Victoria Train Station, the busiest intersection of downtown Bombay. By then everyone knew so much about the festival and where it was going to be and everything that all this billboard said was Hare Krishna *in huge letters. By then everyone knew, so just these two huge words* Hare Krishna *was enough.*

Then Śyāmasundara had arranged for a big helium-filled balloon that was attached to a very long rope at the Cross Maidan site. That balloon just hovered over the city, and there was a streamer attached to the balloon, saying Hare Krishna Festival. *It was real American ingenuity, flair, and dynamism.*

Prabhupāda's appearance at the *paṇḍāl* in the evening was always the high point. He would sit on his *vyāsāsana*, little Sarasvatī would walk out and garland him, and the crowd would cheer. He would just wait for the crowd to quieten, which never happened. So he would just begin speaking, his voice ringing over the powerful sound system. He titled his first lecture "Modern Civilization Is a Failure, and the Only Hope Is Krishna Consciousness."

Girirāja: *Prabhupāda was preaching forcefully to the people of Bombay, and every evening the* paṇḍāl *was packed with at least twenty thousand people. Śrīla Prabhupāda would preach so strongly, emphasizing following religious principles. He knew that these people are Hindus but they are not following these principles. Prabhupāda was speaking so powerfully that I knew that what he was saying would be hard for many of the audience to accept.*

At that time I was thinking that if Prabhupāda had wanted to flatter the audience or compromise his philosophy, he could have attracted millions of followers. But because he was preaching so boldly and forcefully without compromise, many of the audience did not like it, because it was a challenge to their sense gratification and to their sentiment.

The fact is that people were wild about Prabhupāda and ISKCON. One night we showed slides of the Ratha-yātrā in San Francisco, and the audience was going wild. In front of ten thousand people Prabhupāda announced that we will hold Jagannātha Ratha-yātrā in Bombay, and everyone started to cheer and applaud.

Day after day, the *paṇḍāl* festival was a success. Bombay's most important citizens came and were impressed. White-shirted businessmen and their well-groomed wives joined in the chanting. For hundreds of thousands of Bombay citizens, coming to the Cross Maidan to attend an evening *paṇḍāl* program was easy enough. Some were intent on listening to the lecture and inquiring deeply into devotional service; others came mostly to see the Deity, take *prasādam,* or appreciate the *kīrtana.* In any case, A. C. Bhaktivedanta Swami Prabhupāda and the Hare Kṛṣṇa devotees were a refreshing addition to the life of the city. It was the biggest public event in Bombay.

One evening Prabhupāda conducted a Vedic marriage ceremony and an initiation before thousands of people. The marriage was arranged between Vegavān, who was Swedish, and Padmavatī dāsī, who was Australian. They completely enchanted the whole audience—she with her ornate red sari and Indian jewelry, including a nose ring, and he with his white dhoti and *kurtā* and clean-shaven head. Six *brahmacārīs* were initiated at that time also.

Girirāja: *The audience was impressed. First of all they were amazed just to see foreign devotees, foreign sadhus. Then, on top of that, to see them being initiated, and even more than that, being married in front of ten thousand people—it was overwhelming. So during the ceremony, as Śrīla Prabhupāda made the boy and girl husband and wife, he mentioned that she was from Australia and he was from Sweden. Then Śrīla Prabhupāda said, "This is the real United Nations," and everyone burst into applause.*

* * *

May 1971

Śrīla Prabhupāda prepared for extensive world travel. Although his itinerary was indefinite, his general plan was to travel widely for a few months, then tour the U.S., visit London, and then return to India. He had sent disciples to

Australia and Malaysia, and he wanted to visit them. He also wanted to go to Moscow and was awaiting a letter of permission from the Soviet government. As he had spread his movement in America, visiting major cities and preaching and then stationing a few faithful disciples there to carry on, he now expanded his field to include the whole world.

Sydney
May 9, 1971

The Sydney devotees weren't ready for Prabhupāda. An early telegram had informed them he was coming, but a later telegram had said, "Prabhupāda not coming now." A third telegram had come, announcing that Bali-mardana, the Australian G.B.C. secretary, was coming. When a fourth telegram had stated only "Arriving" and the date and flight number, the devotees had presumed this referred to Bali-mardana, not to Prabhupāda. The devotees had taken a small garland and had gone to meet the plane, and when the doors to the customs area opened and Prabhupāda himself walked out, they were flabbergasted.

A white attache case in his left hand, a cane in his right, a lightweight *cādar* around his shoulders, Śrīla Prabhupāda entered the airport. Reporters, on hand to interview Bali-mardana, came eagerly forward, one of them inquiring why Prabhupāda had come to Australia.

Replying softly, Prabhupāda said he traveled everywhere, just as a salesman travels everywhere. A salesman looks for customers wherever he can find them, and Prabhupāda was traveling, searching for anyone intelligent enough to accept his message. "There is no difference in coming to Australia," he said. "The governments have made a demarcation—'This is Australia'—but we see everywhere as the land of Kṛṣṇa."

These devotees, Prabhupāda saw, knew little of Kṛṣṇa consciousness. The devotees who had come to Australia originally, Upendra and Bali-mardana, had opened the center and left, returning but rarely. Thus an entire temple of inexperienced devotees had virtually been left on its own. Since none of the Sydney devotees could lecture well, the daily classes had consisted of readings from Prabhupāda's abridged *Bhagavad-gītā As It Is,* the only book they had. Yet their firm faith in Prabhupāda compensated for their lack of training. They accepted him as a pure devotee directly in touch with God, and they accepted his books as truth and Kṛṣṇa as the Supreme Personality of Godhead. But many practical things they didn't know, such as how to cook, lecture, and worship the Deities. They knew Prabhupāda wanted them to chant Hare Kṛṣṇa publicly and distribute *Back to Godhead* magazines to the people of Sydney, and this they did daily. Despite frequent arrests, they continued with their *saṅkīrtana.* Sincerity they had. They only lacked training.

Vaibhavī-devī dāsī: *Prabhupāda installed the Deities of Rādhā and Kṛṣṇa and initiated disciples on the same day. The initiations came first. He initiated everyone in the temple, anyone who was there—even one boy who had just joined that week and had only come across Kṛṣṇa consciousness the week before, and people who weren't living in the temple, just anyone who was there and somehow serving. He wanted Kṛṣṇa consciousness to be established in Australia, so he just initiated everybody. He gave first and second initiations at the same time, because, having installed the Deities, there had to be some* brāhmaṇas.

But we didn't know anything. We weren't even ready. The altar wasn't finished. Prabhupāda explained to me that we had to string flowers for a garland—the Deity was supposed to wear one. I was running up and down the street trying to find some flowers and get some thread and make a garland.

Same with the sacred thread. There were no sacred threads. Prabhupāda gave the men a sacred thread at brāhmaṇa *initiation, but no one really knew what it was. So I had to run and buy some string. And while Prabhupāda was initiating people, I was sitting there in the arena making sacred threads, copying the one that Bali-mardana had taken off himself.*

I made five of them, and I was next. After the sacrifice, and after I came out of Prabhupāda's room, where he'd given me the Gāyatrī mantra, the other devotees said, "You're a brāhmaṇa *now. So you have to have a sacred thread, too." They told me to make one for myself, which I didn't because someone told me later a woman wasn't supposed to wear one. We just didn't know much.*

Prabhupāda stood with folded hands before the Deities of Rādhā and Kṛṣṇa he had just installed. After less than a week in Sydney, he was leaving. He knew that the devotees here were not up to the standard required for worshiping Rādhā and Kṛṣṇa. And he knew he was taking a risk, entrusting Their worship to neophyte disciples. Yet as an empowered *ācārya* and as the representative of Lord Caitanya, he had to implant Kṛṣṇa consciousness anywhere it might take root. The world was in desperate need. If his disciples followed the process he had given them—chanting, hearing, observing regulative principles—he knew they would quickly become purified.

He had given an analogy: Although in material life a man must first become a highly qualified lawyer before sitting on the judge's bench, in Kṛṣṇa consciousness a sincere devotee is first allowed to "sit on the bench," to become a *brāhmaṇa,* and later, by the mercy of the holy name and the spiritual master, he becomes qualified. The devotees in Sydney, however, were particularly immature, and Prabhupāda made an extraordinary request of Rādhā-Gopīnātha: "Now I am leaving You in the hands of the *mlecchas.* I cannot take the responsibility. You please guide these boys and girls and give them intelligence to worship You very nicely."

* * *

Moscow
June 1971

Prabhupāda, his secretary, and his servant cleared Soviet customs and immigration quickly and smoothly, and a government tourist guide escorted them by limousine to the

Hotel National. The hotel, near Red Square, Lenin's Tomb, and the Kremlin, was expensive but plain. Prabhupāda found his room dingy and cramped, with barely space for a bed and two chairs. The room for Śyāmasundara and Aravinda was far away, and Prabhupāda decided that Aravinda should share the room with him instead, crowding Prabhupāda's room all the more.

Aravinda told the hotel manager that they would not eat the hotel fare, but would have to cook their own meals. The manager refused at first, but finally allowed them use of the maid's kitchen.

That problem solved, the next was getting food. Prabhupāda sent Śyāmasundara out. Across the street, Śyāmasundara found a milk and yogurt store, but he returned to Prabhupāda's room without any fruit, vegetables, or rice. Prabhupāda sent him out again, and this time Śyāmasundara was gone practically all day, returning with only a couple of cabbages. Prabhupāda sent him out the next day for rice. When Śyāmasundara returned with rice after several hours, Prabhupāda saw that it was a poor North Korean variety, very hard. Prabhupāda asked for fruit, but Śyāmasundara had to hike for miles through the city to find anything fresh—a few red cherries. Wherever Śyāmasundara went, he would have to stand in long queues to purchase anything. Usually, however, someone in the queue would notice that he was a tourist and bring him to the front of the line. Everything Śyāmasundara purchased was with coupons.

Prabhupāda remained peaceful and regulated, keeping to his daily schedule. He would rise early and translate, and in the cool of early morning he would go out for a walk through the all-but-deserted streets. Prabhupāda, wearing a saffron *cādar,* strode quickly, Śyāmasundara sometimes running ahead to photograph him.

As they would pass Lenin's Tomb a queue would already be forming. "Just see," Prabhupāda commented one morning, "that is their God. The people don't understand the difference between the body and the spirit. They accept the body as the real person."

Prabhupāda appreciated the sparseness of the traffic—some trolleys and bicycles, but mostly pedestrians. As he walked among the old, ornate buildings, he saw elderly women hosing the wide streets—a good practice, he said. The Russian people appeared to live structured, regulated lives, much more so than the Americans. These simple, austere people, unspoiled by the rampant hedonism so common in America, were fertile for Kṛṣṇa consciousness. But devoid of spiritual sustenance, they appeared morose.

For months Prabhupāda had been planning to visit Moscow. Aside from his desire to preach to the Russian people, he had a specific meeting in mind with a Russian Indology professor, G. G. Kotovsky. Professor Kotovsky headed the department of Indian and South Asian studies at Moscow's U.S.S.R. Academy of Sciences, and Prabhupāda had been corresponding with him for a year.

Prabhupāda had Śyāmasundara arrange a meeting with Professor Kotovsky. The tourist bureau provided a car and guide, and Prabhupāda and his party rode outside the city to Professor Kotovsky's office in an old, white brick building at the Academy of Sciences.

When Prabhupāda arrived, the middle-aged Russian professor, dressed in a gray suit, got up from his cluttered desk and welcomed Prabhupāda into his small office. Professor Kotovsky appeared a bit hesitant, however, more cautious than in his letters. When Śyāmasundara mentioned Prabhupāda's eagerness to lecture before interested scholars at the Academy, Professor Kotovsky flatly refused—it would never be allowed. Prabhupāda was disappointed.

The next moment, however, Prabhupāda seemed unaffected and began speaking in his humble, genteel manner, sitting in a straight-backed office chair beside Professor Kotovsky, who sat at his desk. Śyāmasundara turned on the tape recorder, which the professor eyed cautiously but didn't object to.

Prabhupāda: "The other day I was reading in the paper, *Moscow News*. There was a Communist congress, and the president declared that, 'We are ready to get others' experiences to improve.' So I think the Vedic concept of socialism or communism will much improve the idea of communism."

Professor Kotovsky listened intently and politely as his foreign visitor explained how the *gṛhastha* in Vedic culture provides for everyone living in his house—even for the lizards—and how, before taking his meal, he calls in the road to invite any hungry person to come and eat. "In this way," Prabhupāda explained, "there are so many good concepts about the socialist idea of communism. So I thought that these ideas might have been distributed to some of your thoughtful men. Therefore I was anxious to speak."

Professor Kotovsky responded with several questions, which Prabhupāda welcomed, although they were grounded in Soviet socialist vested interests. He considered the professor not so much an academician as a pawn of the Soviet university system; much as one political power tries to understand its adversary, the professor was inquiring into Indian culture so that his government might penetrate it with their own ideology. Behind Professor Kotovsky's apparent interest in Vedic culture, Prabhupāda could see the view of the Communist party, a view diametrically opposed to Vedic philosophy. Nevertheless, Prabhupāda tactfully continued to present Kṛṣṇa consciousness in accord with *paramparā,* and he tried to convince Professor Kotovsky through scripture and logic. Modern society's missing point, Prabhupāda said, was an understanding of the purpose of human life. "They do not know what is the next life," he said. "There is no department of knowledge or scientific department to study what is there after finishing this body."

Professor Kotovsky objected—politely, completely. "Swamiji," he said, "when the body dies, the owner also dies." Prabhupāda marked his reply. The learned professor, head of the department of Indian studies in the Soviet Academy, was caught in a classic moment of ignorance. His concept of who he was was no more advanced than an animal's.

After only three days, Prabhupāda's mission in Moscow

seemed finished. The meeting with Professor Kotovsky over, what was left? The government would allow nothing else. It had not allowed him to bring in books, and now he had been refused the opportunity to speak publicly. Foreigners were not to talk with the Russians. He could go nowhere, unless on an accompanied tour. So with no preaching and no prospects, he stayed in his cramped room, taking his massage, bathing, accepting whatever food Śyāmasundara could gather and cook, dictating a few letters, chanting Hare Kṛṣṇa, and translating *Śrīmad-Bhāgavatam.*

Prabhupāda took a guided tour of Moscow, riding with other tourists on a crowded bus. He saw elderly Russians going to church, armed guards stationed at the door; and he surmised that the guards were to prevent the younger generation from entering to worship. He soon tired of the tour, however, and the tour guide got him a taxi and instructed the driver to return him to the Hotel National.

Śyāmasundara continued to spend most of his day looking for fresh food. Hearing that oranges were available at a certain market across town, he set out across the city. With his shaved head and his white dhoti and *kurtā* he drew stares from everyone he passed, and as he was returning, after dark, uniformed men wearing red armbands accosted him, taking him to be a local deviant. Grabbing him, they pinned his arms behind his back and shouted at him in Russian. Śyāmasundara caught the word *dakumyent* ("document, identification"). He replied, "*Dakumyent,* hotel! hotel!" Realizing Śyāmasundara was a tourist, the officers released him, and he returned to the hotel and informed Prabhupāda of what had taken place.

"There is no hope in Russia without Kṛṣṇa consciousness," Prabhupāda said.

Once Śyāmasundara was standing in line at the yogurt store when a man behind him asked him about yoga. "I really want to talk with you," the man said, and he gave Śyāmasundara his name and address and a time they could safely meet. When Śyāmasundara told Prabhupāda, Prabhupāda said, "No, he is a policeman. Don't go."

Standing at his window, Prabhupāda glimpsed a parade in

nearby Red Square—tanks, artillery, missiles, and troops parading through the streets. By always preparing for war, he said, the Russian leaders kept the people motivated and thus avoided a revolt. He compared warlike Russia to the *asuras* (demons) in the ancient Vedic histories like *Śrīmad-Bhāgavatam.*

One day two young men, one the son of an Indian diplomat stationed in Moscow, the other a young Muscovite, were loitering near Red Square when they saw an amazing sight. Out of the usual regimented routine of city traffic, a tall young man with a shaved head, a long, reddish ponytail, and flowing white robes approached. It was Śyāmasundara. Familiar with Śyāmasundara's dress, the son of the Indian diplomat stopped him. Śyāmasundara smiled and said, "Hare Kṛṣṇa, brother." And he began talking with the Indian, whose name was Narayana. The Russian, Ivan, knew a little English and followed the conversation as closely as he could. The talk grew serious.

"Why don't you come up and meet my spiritual master?" Śyāmasundara asked. Honored, the boys immediately accompanied Śyāmasundara to the Hotel National. When they arrived, they found Prabhupāda seated on his bed, aglow and smiling, Aravinda massaging his feet. Śyāmasundara entered, offering obeisances before Prabhupāda. Ivan was completely fascinated.

"Come on," Prabhupāda said, and the three of them sat at Prabhupāda's feet. Turning first to Narayána, Prabhupāda asked his name and his father's occupation. Narayana liked Prabhupāda and offered to bring him green vegetables; his father, being highly placed at the Indian Embassy, had produce flown in from India.

Ivan was interested even more than his Indian friend, and Prabhupāda began explaining to him the philosophy of Kṛṣṇa consciousness, while Narayana helped by translating. Ivan inquired with respect and awe, and Prabhupāda answered his questions, teaching as much basic information about Kṛṣṇa consciousness as was possible in one sitting.

Prabhupāda explained the difference between the spirit soul and the body and described the soul's eternal relationship with Kṛṣṇa, the Supreme Personality of Godhead. He spoke of *Bhagavad-gītā,* of his network of temples around the world, and of his young men and women disciples all practicing bhakti yoga.

Prabhupāda mentioned his desire to preach in Russia, which was a great field for Kṛṣṇa consciousness because the people were openminded and hadn't been polluted by sense gratification. He wanted to introduce Kṛṣṇa conscious literature in Russia through a library or a reading room or in whatever way possible. Kṛṣṇa conscious philosophy, he said, should be taught to Russia's most intelligent people, but because of government restrictions it would have to be done discreetly. Devotees would not be able to sing and dance in the streets, but they could chant quietly together in someone's home. Prabhupāda then began singing very quietly, leading the boys in *kīrtana.*

Ivan's taking to Kṛṣṇa was like a hungry man's eating a meal. After several hours, however, he and his friend had to go. They would return the next day.

Śyāmasundara began spending time with Ivan and Narayana. Ivan, a student of Oriental philosophies, was very intelligent and eager to know what was going on in the outside world. He was fond of the Beatles, and Prabhupāda told him of his association with George Harrison and John Lennon. Ivan and Śyāmasundara had long talks about the ambitions and hopes of young people outside Russia, and Śyāmasundara explained to him how Kṛṣṇa consciousness was the basic principle of all spiritual paths. Śyāmasundara also taught him basic principles of bhakti yoga, such as chanting the prescribed sixteen rounds of *japa* daily, and gave him his own copy of *Bhagavad-gītā As It Is.*

Prabhupāda showed Ivan how to prepare *capātīs* and rice and asked him to give up eating meat. Joyfully, Ivan accepted the chanting, the new way of eating—everything. Ivan was being trained so that after Prabhupāda left, Ivan could continue on his own. Ivan would be able to feel himself changing and advancing in spiritual life, and after practicing for some time he could be initiated. Ivan said he would tell his friends about Kṛṣṇa consciousness. With only two days left in Moscow, Prabhupāda taught Ivan as much as he could. In this young Russian's eagerness and intelligence, Prabhupāda found the real purpose of his visit to Russia.

Prabhupāda gave the analogy that when cooking rice the cook need test only one grain to determine whether the whole pot of rice is done. Similarly, by talking with this one Russian youth, Prabhupāda could tell that the Russian people were not satisfied in their so-called ideal land of Marxism. Just as Ivan was keenly receptive to Kṛṣṇa consciousness, millions of other Russians would be also.

Cāṇakya Paṇḍita, the Vedic philosopher, says that one blooming flower can refresh a whole forest and that a fire in a single tree can burn the whole forest. From the Marxist point of view, Ivan was the fire that would spread Kṛṣṇa consciousness to others, thus defeating the Communist ideology. And from Prabhupāda's point of view, he was the aromatic flower that would lend its fragrance to many others. Prabhupāda's visit to Russia was no obscure interlude, but had become an occasion for planting the seed of Kṛṣṇa consciousness in a destitute land.

Śrīla Prabhupāda had brought the movement of Lord Caitanya to yet another country. Caitanya Mahāprabhu Himself had predicted that the *saṅkīrtana* movement would go to every town and village, yet for hundreds of years that prediction had remained unfulfilled. Prabhupāda, however, in the few years since his first trip to America in 1965, had again and again planted Lord Caitanya's message in one unlikely place after another. And of all these places, this was perhaps the most unlikely; during a brief, government-supervised visit to Moscow, he had planted the seed of Kṛṣṇa consciousness within the Soviet Union. He was like the needle, and everyone and everything connected with him was like the thread that would follow.

Professor Kotovsky had remarked that Prabhupāda's stay in an old-fashioned hotel would not prove very interesting. But Prabhupāda, unknown to Professor Kotovsky, was transcendental to Moscow or any other place in the material world. He had come to this place, and Kṛṣṇa had sent a sincere soul to him to receive the gift of Kṛṣṇa consciousness. This had happened not by devious espionage against the Soviet government but by the presence of Kṛṣṇa's pure devotee and his natural desire to satisfy Kṛṣṇa by preaching. In response to Prabhupāda's pure desire, Kṛṣṇa had sent one boy, and from that one boy the desire would spread to others. Nothing, not even an Iron Curtain, could stop Kṛṣṇa consciousness. The soul's natural function was to serve Kṛṣṇa. And Kṛṣṇa's natural will was to satisfy the pure desires of His devotee.

* * *

Nairobi
September 1971

Prabhupāda wanted to preach to the Africans. In Kenya, Indians and Africans were completely segregated. But since a Kṛṣṇa conscious person does not make distinctions based on the body, Prabhupāda said the Indians had a duty to share their spiritual culture with the Africans.

Prabhupāda's G.B.C. representative in Africa was Brahmānanda Swami. Carefully he impressed on Brahmānanda that his first duty in Africa was to give Kṛṣṇa consciousness to the Africans. Because of bad experience in Turkey and Pakistan, Brahmānanda had been reluctant to hold public *kīrtanas* in Nairobi. Besides, the Africans spoke mostly Swahili; they were culturally different and usually too poor to buy books, so Brahmānanda didn't know how to preach to them effectively. Going to the Indians had been easy and natural.

But Prabhupāda wanted the Africans. "It is an African country," he said simply. "They are the proprietors. We should be preaching to them."

As with everything else in Kṛṣṇa consciousness, Prabhupāda demonstrated how to do this also. He got the use of a Rādhā-Kṛṣṇa temple in a predominantly African downtown area. The temple had a hall with doors opening onto the busy street, and Prabhupāda instructed the devotees to hold *kīr-*

tana in the hall, keeping the doors open. The devotees did as he asked, and in five minutes the hall began filling up with people. It was a shabby area of town, and the people who entered were illiterate and dirty. But they were curious, and they happily joined in the *kīrtana,* smiling, clapping, and dancing.

Brahmānanda Swami left the hall and went to the nearby house where Prabhupāda was staying. "The place is filled with people," Brahmānanda said, "but it's not necessary for you to come. We can carry on and do the program ourselves."

"No," Prabhupāda said, "I must go."

Brahmānanda tried to discourage him.

"No, I must go," Prabhupāda repeated. "Are you going to take me?"

When Brahmānanda arrived with Śrīla Prabhupāda, the hall was even more crowded than it had been a few minutes before. Prabhupāda, in his silken saffron robes, appeared effulgent as he entered the dingy, poorly lit auditorium. As he walked, the crowd parted, leaving an aisle for him to pass among them, and they watched him curiously. Onstage Prabhupāda led a *kīrtana* and lectured. Although the Swahili-speaking audience was unable to understand Prabhupāda's lecture, the people were respectful. And the *kīrtana* they loved.

Members of the Indian community had been apprehensive of Prabhupāda's opening their hall to the Africans, and some of them had attended to see what would happen. Observing Prabhupāda's compassionate program, however, the Indians were impressed. Such an apparently simple program had the spiritual potency to erase cultural boundaries.

This should be Brahmānanda Swami's mission in Africa, Prabhupāda insisted—offering Kṛṣṇa consciousness to the Africans. And the program should be simple: distributing *prasādam,* distributing free books, and chanting Hare Kṛṣṇa with drums and *karatālas.* Kṛṣṇa consciousness should not be just another Nairobi Hindu religious society. The Hindus should take part by donating money, but Brahmānanda Swami's preaching and recruiting should be among the

Africans.

When several black American disciples joined Prabhupāda in Nairobi, Prabhupāda told them, "Four hundred years ago your ancestors were taken away from here as slaves. But ah, just see how you have returned as masters!"

Prabhupāda also organized Nairobi's first outdoor *kīrtana* performance. The devotees went to Kamakunji Park's largest tree, a historical landmark connected with Kenyan independence. As they stood chanting beneath the tree, a large crowd gathered and many began chanting. Some even danced in a sort of tribal shuffle. One young man stepped forward and offered to translate Brahmānanda's speech into Swahili. The devotees distributed sweet *bundi,* and the people in the crowd really enjoyed themselves. The whole affair was a great success.

Rushing back to Prabhupāda, Brahmānanda reported on the wonderful *kīrtana* in the park. Brahmānanda felt the same emotion as in 1966 when he had reported to Prabhupāda the success of the first *kīrtana* at Washington Square Park in New York City. Now, as then, results had been successful. Prabhupāda, by his personal example and by his pushing Brahmānanda Swami, had within a few days changed the emphasis of preaching in Africa—from Indians to Africans.

The night of Śrīla Prabhupāda's lecture at the University of Nairobi, two thousand African students filled the auditorium, with hundreds more standing outside to look in through the doors and windows. First Prabhupāda had Bhūta-bhāvana, a black American disciple, deliver a short introduction, using some borrowed Swahili phrases. *"Harambay,"* he began—which means, "Welcome, brothers. Let us work together."

Then Prabhupāda spoke. "The whole world is simply hankering and lamenting. You African people are now hankering to be like the Europeans and Americans. But the Europeans have lost their empire. They are now lamenting. So one party is hankering, and one party is lamenting . . .

"We have come to these African countries to invite all intelligent Africans to come and understand this philosophy and distribute it. You are trying to develop yourselves; so develop very soundly. But don't imitate the Americans and Europeans, who are living like cats and dogs. Such civilization will not stand. The atom bomb is already there. As soon as the next war breaks out, all the skyscraper buildings and everything else will be finished. Try to understand from the real standpoint, the real view of human life. That is the Kṛṣṇa consciousness movement, and we request you to come and try to understand this philosophy. Thank you very much."

The audience burst into applause, giving Prabhupāda a standing ovation. This response proved once again that Kṛṣṇa's message spoke to the heart; it was for all people, regardless of their political, geographic, or social predicament. When Prabhupāda had first landed at the Nairobi airport, he had assured a reporter that he would be preaching to the Africans. And now he was. He was delivering to the Africans the same message and the same process of devotional service he had delivered to the Americans. What the Americans wanted and what the Africans wanted could be realized only in Kṛṣṇa consciousness. Kṛṣṇa consciousness would work anywhere, if sincere and intelligent persons would only come forward and help distribute it.

Prabhupāda's preaching in Nairobi had been especially active. He had established Kṛṣṇa consciousness in a new city, setting the example for Brahmānanda Swami to emulate, showing the standard for spreading Kṛṣṇa consciousness throughout the continent. And Śyāmasundara was keeping his G.B.C. Godbrothers informed of Prabhupāda's amazing activities.

> The pace has been lightning fast, and His Divine Grace is opening up yet another vast theater of operations. The people are thronging with curiosity and serious questions. . . .
>
> Prabhupada, after finishing one late-night preaching marathon, asked for food and remarked, "You see, I am hungry. Keep me talking—that is my life. Don't let me stop talking. . . ."

CHAPTER FIVE

Let There Be a Temple: Part I

Calcutta
March 1971

It was midnight. Śrīla Prabhupāda sat on a pillow behind his low desk, his light the only one on in the building. All the other devotees were in bed. On the desk before him rested the dictating machine and a volume of *Śrīmad-Bhāgavatam* with Bengali commentary. A small framed picture of his spiritual master, Bhaktisiddhānta Sarasvatī, sat between two small vases of roses and asters. On the floor beyond the desk was the broad mat covered with white cotton fabric, where a few hours before, devotees and guests had sat.

But now he was alone. Although usually he retired at ten, rising three or four hours later to translate, tonight he had not rested, and his *Bhāgavatam* lay closed, his dictating machine covered.

He had sent two of his disciples, Tamāla Kṛṣṇa and Balimardana, to purchase land in Māyāpur. Six days had passed, however, and still they had neither returned nor sent word. He had told them not to return until they had completed the transaction, but six days was more than enough time. He was anxious, thinking constantly of his two disciples.

A breeze arrived, carrying the fragrance of *nīm* trees through the open window. The night was becoming cool, and Prabhupāda wore a light *cādar* around his shoulders. Absorbed in thought, leaning against the white bolster pillow, he paid little attention to the familiar sights in his room. A clay jug with drinking water sat beside him, and a potted *tulasī* plant sat upon a small, wooden pedestal. The electricity, off most of the day and night, was now on, and moths and other insects hovered around the bare bulb overhead. A lizard patrolled the ceiling, occasionally darting forward near the light to capture an insect.

Why were Tamāla Kṛṣṇa and Bali-mardana taking so long? It had been more than just a wait of six days; he had been trying to obtain land in Māyāpur for years. And this time the prospects had been excellent. He had clearly instructed Tamāla Kṛṣṇa and Bali-mardana, and now they should have returned. The delay could mean a complication, or even danger.

The land they were trying for was a nine-*bigha* plot on Bhaktisiddhānta Road, less than a mile from the birthsite of Lord Caitanya Mahāprabhu. The Sek brothers, Muslim farmers who owned the plot, had been asking a high price. Only recently had a Calcutta lawyer familiar with Navadvīpa been able to seriously negotiate a fair price. The Sek brothers had settled for 14,500 rupees, and Prabhupāda had authorized withdrawal of the funds from his bank in Krishnanagar. Thus Tamāla Kṛṣṇa and Bali-mardana had left Māyāpur, while Prabhupāda had remained in Calcutta, carrying on with his affairs but thinking often of the activities of his disciples in Māyāpur. Their mission was very important to him, and he kept them in his mind, personally blessing them with his concern.

As Prabhupāda sat, rapt in thought, the only sounds were the usual sounds of the night: mice within the walls, a *brahmacārī* snoring on the veranda, and in the distance the night watchman making his rounds, his stick striking the street. There were no cars, and only an occasional wooden ricksha clattered along the potholed street.

Prabhupāda wondered if perhaps his boys had been robbed. Before sending them off, he had shown Tamāla Kṛṣṇa how to carry money around his waist in a makeshift cloth money belt. But it had been a great deal of money, and robberies were not uncommon around Navadvīpa. Or perhaps there had been some other delay. Sometimes in land negotiations involving large sums of money, the court would require that a clerk record the denomination and serial number of every note exchanged. Or perhaps the train had broken down.

Suddenly Prabhupāda heard footsteps on the stairs. Someone opened the outer door and now walked along the veranda just outside. A soft knock.

"Yes, who is it?"

Tamāla Kṛṣṇa entered and prostrated himself before Śrīla Prabhupāda.

"So, what is your news?"

Tamāla Kṛṣṇa looked up triumphantly. "The land is yours!"

Prabhupada leaned back with a sigh. "All right," he said. "Now you can take rest."

* * *

London
August 1971

Prabhupāda had asked the Indian high commissioner for the United Kingdom to petition Prime Minister Indira Gandhi to attend ISKCON's upcoming cornerstone-laying ceremony in Māyāpur. Already Prabhupāda had instructed all his G.B.C. secretaries to attend the ceremony, and he had asked the devotees to invite many prominent citizens of Calcutta. Writing to his disciples in India, he said that if they could not get Indira Gandhi to come, they should at least get the governor of Bengal, Sri S. S. Dhavan.

Meanwhile, Prabhupāda was meeting in London with several of his disciples experienced in architecture and design; he wanted them to draft plans for his Māyāpur project. Nara-nārāyaṇa had built Ratha-yātrā carts and designed temple interiors, Raṇacora had studied architecture, and Bhavānanda had been a professional designer, but Prabhupāda himself conceived the plans for the Māyāpur buildings. He then told his three-man committee to provide sketches and an architect's model; he would immediately begin raising funds and securing support in India for the project. To the devotees who heard Prabhupāda's plans, this seemed the most ambitious ISKCON project ever.

While taking his morning walks in Russell Square, Prabhupāda would point to various buildings and ask how high they were. Finally he announced one morning that the main temple in Māyāpur should be more than three hundred feet high! Māyāpur's monsoon floods and sandy soil would create unique difficulties, he said, and the building would have to be built on a special foundation, a sort of floating raft. A civil engineer later confirmed this.

The first building, Prabhupāda said, should be a large guesthouse, four stories high, and his design, although not strictly conforming to any one school of architecture, resembled most that of Rajasthan. He wanted a pink-and-rust colored building with many arches and a wide marble veranda on each floor except the ground floor. The building should run east-west, so that the sun would pass lengthwise over it and not shine directly into the building's broad front. Southerly breezes would cool the guesthouse in summer. The building should be equipped with electric fans and lights, modern toilets and showers, and the rooms should be furnished, spacious, and well ventilated.

This guesthouse should be built as soon as possible, Prabhupāda said; then other buildings would follow. He wanted residential buildings for five hundred devotees, a large *prasādam* hall seating several thousand, a kitchen complex, and a *gośāla* (a shelter for the cows that would pasture in nearby fields). In time ISKCON would acquire adjoining land and develop parks with flower gardens, trees and shrubs, fountains, walkways, and arbors.

The main building, the colossal Māvāpur Chandrodaya

Mandir, was to be no less than three hundred feet high and costing perhaps tens of millions of dollars. Prabhupāda's description astounded the architects as well as the devotees; it sounded grander than the United States Capitol or St. Peter's Cathedral. The temple's central dome would house a three-dimensional model of the universe. The design, however, would be based on the Vedic description and would depict not only the material universe but also the spiritual universe.

Entering the main hall, a person would look up and see the planets situated just as *Śrīmad-Bhāgavatam* describes, beginning with the hellish planets, then the middle planets, wherein the earth is situated, then the heavenly planets of the demigods, and then Brahmaloka, the highest planet in the material world. Above Brahmaloka, the observer would see the abode of Lord Siva, and above that the spiritual sky, or *brahmajyoti*. Within the spiritual effulgence of the *brahmajyoti* would be the self-illuminating Vaikuṇṭha planets, inhabited by eternally liberated souls. And highest of all would be the supreme planet of Kṛṣṇaloka, where God in His original eternal form enjoys His pastimes with His most confidential devotees.

The temple would also house a miniature palace in which the Deities of Rādhā and Kṛṣṇa would reside, surrounded by silks and pillars of silver, gold, and jewels. The Māyāpur Chandrodaya Mandir and the Māyāpur city would be ISKCON world headquarters.

And why such a fabulous architectural wonder as this in such an obscure part of the world? The answer, Prabhupāda explained, was that Māyāpur was actually not obscure; it seemed so only from the mundane perspective. To mundane vision, that which was central *seemed* remote. The soul and the next life seemed remote, while the body and immediate sense gratification seemed central. By establishing the Temple of Human Understanding in Māyāpur, Śrīla Prabhupāda would be directing the materialistic world's attention back to the true center.

Any sincere visitor would be charmed by the beauty of the ISKCON Māyāpur project and would perceive that here indeed was the spiritual world. And the devotees living in

Māyāpur, by remaining constantly immersed in singing Hare Kṛṣṇa *kīrtana* and discussing the philosophy of Kṛṣṇa consciousness, would be able to convince any intelligent visitor that the teachings of Lord Caitanya Mahāprabhu were the highest truth. The devotees would explain the philosophy of the Absolute Truth, which would enable visitors to comprehend actual spiritual truth beyond sectarian religious dogma. Furthermore, the continuous Hare Kṛṣṇa *kīrtana* and the blissful devotees engaged in a wide variety of services to Lord Kṛṣṇa would demonstrate that bhakti yoga was the simplest, most direct process for meditating on the Supreme Personality of Godhead. While staying in ISKCON's Māyāpur city, a person would quickly become a devotee of the Lord and begin chanting and dancing in ecstasy.

Śrīla Prabhupāda was demonstrating how the world could be spiritualized by linking material things with the Supreme Personality of Godhead, Kṛṣṇa, through bhakti yoga. And why shouldn't such spiritual feats surpass the achievements of the materialists?

* * *

Śrīla Prabhupāda was back in India, touring and preaching with his disciples. After a successful ten-day *paṇḍāl* festival in New Delhi—several hundred thousand had attended—he decided to take his disciples on a short excursion to Vṛndāvana. His preaching tours had taken him to such places as Amritsar, Surat, Indore, Gorakhpur, Allahabad, and Benares, but never to Vṛndāvana. With so many of his disciples gathered in Delhi for the festival, however, he considered it an opportune time to travel to nearby Vṛndāvana.

When Prabhupāda arrived in Vṛndāvana a Mr. G. L. Saraf accommodated him, his secretaries, and the women in the party at his home, Saraf Bhavan. The rest of the devotees stayed in a nearby *dharmaśāla*.

Prabhupāda had come to Vṛndāvana for more than just a pilgrimage; he had come to try to secure land for ISKCON.

When in 1967 he had come to Vṛndāvana from America, he had come to recuperate, but even then he had looked for a place in Vṛndāvana for his disciples. He had tried to establish an American House, a center where his disciples could live in Vṛndāvana's ideal atmosphere and receive training in Kṛṣṇa conscious culture and then go out and preach. But after two months of little prospect for establishing his American House, he had left.

This time, however, he was coming to Vṛndāvana as that city's famous ambassador to the world, renowned for propagating the glories of Rādhā-Kṛṣṇa and Vṛndāvana in the West. The success of the Hare Kṛṣṇa movement was being widely publicized in India, as Prabhupāda and his band of foreign disciples traveled from city to city holding *kīrtanas*, lecturing from *Śrīmad-Bhāgavatam*, and telling of Kṛṣṇa consciousness in the West. So when Prabhupāda arrived in Vṛndāvana with forty disciples, the entire town heralded his presence.

* * *

The land was in Ramaṇa-retī. Prabhupāda noted that the property on the outskirts of Vṛndāvana was located on busy Chatikara Road, a main thoroughfare into Vṛndāvana and a traffic route to Agra and the Taj Mahal. The land was also adjacent to the Vṛndāvana *parikrama* path, where millions of pilgrims passed annually, circumambulating Vṛndāvana and visiting its temples and holy places.

Ramaṇa-retī (literally "charming sand") was mostly forest, with a few *āśramas* and abandoned fields. Celebrated as a favorite spot of Kṛṣṇa's, where He and His brother Balarāma and Their cowherd boyfriends had played five thousand years ago, Ramaṇa-retī abounded in transcendental love of God, which is the special atmosphere of Vṛndāvana.

Although various city officials had casually mentioned that the city might donate land, Prabhupāda took more seriously a Mr. S.'s offer. Mr. S. explained that although other sadhus had been asking for the land, he and his wife had not yet decided; they wanted to give it to a group who would build a Rādhā-Kṛṣṇa temple there as soon as possible. When Prabhupāda assured Mr. S. he would do so, Mr. S. vowed that the land was now Prabhupāda's.

Prabhupāda had heard such promises before, and they had often proved false. But considering this offer serious, he appointed disciples to remain in Vṛndāvana to draw up a deed with Mr. S.

* * *

From 1965 until 1970 Śrīla Prabhupāda had concentrated mainly on establishing Kṛṣṇa consciousness in America. His plan had been that if the Americans turned to Kṛṣṇa consciousness, the rest of the world would follow. Although his preaching to the English-speaking people had begun in India, some sixty years of single-handed endeavor there had convinced him that Indians were either too absorbed in politics, too ignorant of their spiritual heritage, or too crippled by poverty to seriously accept Kṛṣṇa consciousness. Therefore he had not been successful.

But in the United States success had come. Clearly, America was the prime field for implanting Kṛṣṇa consciousness. Yet Prabhupāda found the West uncultured and uncivilized. If a trace of civilization remained anywhere, he would often say, it was in India, the heart of the original Vedic culture.

By 1970 he had demonstrated through his extensive traveling and preaching that he intended to establish the Kṛṣṇa consciousness movement not only in the U.S. but all over the world—especially in India. Even accepting that preaching in the United States and preaching in India were equally important, still the preaching in the United States was going well without Prabhupada's constant, direct management; what he had begun, his American disciples could continue.

But in India Prabhupāda could not allow his disciples to manage ISKCON. He saw how often and how easily the Indians were able to cheat his disciples. Half of ISKCON's work in India was being spoiled, he said, due to his disciples' being cheated. If they put on a *paṇḍāl* program, they might end up paying several times the standard cost. The only way for ISKCON to develop in India would be under Prabhupāda's direct management.

Beginning in 1970 with a small band of American disciples, Prabhupāda had traveled from place to place in India as a model sannyasi, opening a great new field for ISKCON. Now he wanted to construct big temples in India—three in particular: one in Vṛndāvana, one in Māyāpur, and one in Bombay. As early as 1967 he had attempted to make an American House for his disciples in Vṛndāvana. Māyāpur, being the birthplace of Lord Caitanya, was especially important; and Bombay was India's major city, "the gateway to India." As with most of Prabhupāda's big plans, even his close disciples couldn't fully comprehend the scope of his vision. But Prabhupāda knew what he wanted, and he knew it all depended on Kṛṣṇa. Gradually he began to unfold his plans.

* * *

Bombay
November 1971

For a year the devotees had been living at the Akash Ganga address, two apartments on the seventh floor of a building in the heart of Bombay. But Prabhupāda was not satisfied with this. He wanted land in Bombay, to build on and to expand He was determined. Instead of his usual morning walks, he would take long rides in his car to observe various parts of the city.

Because many of the ISKCON life members lived in aristocratic Malabar Hill, Prabhupāda's disciples thought it a good place for a temple. On several occasions Prabhupāda rode to the top of Malabar Hill and walked around various properties, considering certain large buildings as possible temples. But for one reason or another he judged them all unacceptable.

Then in November, a Mr. N. offered to sell ISKCON five acres in Juhu, practically on the shore of the Arabian Sea. As soon as Śrīla Prabhupāda approached the land, he remembered having seen and considered it years before. In August of 1965, during the weeks just before he had left for America, he had been staying at Scindia Colony. In the evenings he had gone to the home of Scindia Steamship Company owner Mrs. Sumati Morarji in Juhu, where he had read and explained *Śrīmad-Bhāgavatam* for her and her guests. Several times he had passed this very property and had thought what a good location it would be for an *āśrama* and a Rādhā-Kṛṣṇa temple. Although his attention had been absorbed in the task of leaving India, he had still considered the Juhu land. Now he was again in Juhu, reconsidering the same land he had noticed years before. He took it as a reminder from Kṛṣṇa.

The land was overgrown with tall grasses and bushes, and many coconut palms stood throughout. In the back of the property were several tenement buildings. The land bordered on Juhu Road, the main traffic artery back to Bombay, eighteen miles to the south. A broad expanse of beach on the Arabian Sea was a brief walk away.

The location was good—peaceful, yet not remote. Several five-star hotels bordered the nearby beach, and developers were beginning work on other hotels and apartment buildings. When Prabhupāda walked along the beach, he liked even more the idea of buying the land. Rich men had weekend homes on the beach, and thousands of Bombayites would be out enjoying the beach on Sundays. Daily, hundreds of Juhu residents used the long, broad seashore for morning walks before going to work. Almost always people were strolling or gathering here, and yet the beach was clean. The mild waves and open skies were inviting. The locale was ideal not only for hotels, but for a Kṛṣṇa conscious center.

Prabhupāda wanted the Juhu land, and although his disciples continued to show him houses in Malabar Hill, he didn't change his mind. His disciples wanted whatever he wanted, yet they had trouble developing enthusiasm for a property so far from the city, and with no available housing or temple facility.

Mr. N., the owner of the five-acre plot, had set a reasonable price and seemed friendly and sincere. Yet risks were involved in such transactions, and in this case, Prabhupāda even found reasons for suspicion. Through his lawyer, he learned that Mr. N. had previously entered into an agreement to sell this same land to the C. Company but had later cancelled the agreement. The C. Company had then filed suit against Mr. N. for breach of contract. If the Bombay High Court decided in the C. Company's favor, the land would be awarded to them. When Prabhupāda's secretary questioned Mr. N. about this entanglement, Mr. N. assured him the C. Company could not win the suit, but that in any case, ISKCON could withhold a certain portion of their payment until the litigation with C. was settled.

Mr. N. was a well-known figure in Bombay. Formerly the sheriff of Bombay (an honorary judicial police position), he was now publisher-editor of one of the largest daily English newspapers in Bombay. He was wealthy, owning several properties in Juhu and Bombay, and influential—not a man one would want to oppose. To purchase the Juhu land under the present circumstances required boldness.

In late December Prabhupāda met with Mr. and Mrs. N., openly expressing his appreciation of the Juhu land, yet admitting he had very little money. Mr. N., however, seemed inclined toward Prabhupāda and said he wanted to sell him the property. Quickly they reached a verbal agreement.

Prabhupāda and Mr. N. agreed on a down payment of 200,000 rupees; after making the down payment, ISKCON would immediately receive the conveyance. ISKCON would pay the remaining balance of 1,400,000 rupees later, in regular installments. Prabhupāda negotiated further regarding the down payment, offering to pay 50,000 rupees now and another 50,000 later, at which time ISKCON would be allowed to move onto the land. As soon as they paid the remaining 100,000 rupees, the down payment would be complete, and Mr. N. would give them the deed. Mr. N. agreed.

Śrīla Prabhupāda was always one to think carefully over such business transactions. He had said that if a businessman tells you, "Sir, for you I am making no profit," you should know he is lying. Therefore, even in ISKCON's early days in New York City, when a real-estate shark had posed as a well-wisher of the devotees, Prabhupāda had been suspicious. He had, in fact, cheated the devotees, despite Prabhupāda's warnings to them. Now, as then, Prabhupāda was suspicious. But he wanted the Juhu land and would take the risk.

While devotees around the world delighted to hear Prabhupāda's plan for a Bombay center, devotees in Bombay had mixed feelings. To envision a temple rising from what was little more than a jungle tract was not easy. Nor was it easy to envision the five-star ISKCON hotel Prabhupāda spoke of. The tenement buildings in the rear of the land were fully occupied, and according to Indian law, the tenants could not be removed. If the devotees moved onto the land, they would have to erect temporary housing, maybe even a temporary temple, and the land was mosquito-ridden and teeming with rats. Juhu was a small, almost isolated neighborhood, without wealthy ISKCON supporters. Although Prabhupāda (and land speculators) predicted that Juhu would grow, at present it was only a village of about two thousand. To reside at Juhu would be a drastic contrast to the comfortable Akash Ganga Building in downtown Bombay.

Tamāla Kṛṣṇa explained to Prabhupāda, "We are Westerners. We cannot live like this. We need doorknobs and running water."

"Don't you want to become purified?" Prabhupāda replied.

When the Bombay devotees learned of Śrīla Prabhupāda's response to Tamāla Kṛṣṇa, the words "Don't you want to become purified?" went deep into their hearts. They knew that Prabhupāda was asking them to become more austere, and that it was for their ultimate benefit. They began to regard moving to Juhu as a formidable spiritual challenge rather than a drudgery. Developing the Juhu property was important to their spiritual master, and it was something greater and more wonderful than they at present realized.

* * *

Although Prabhupāda was making all the managerial decisions, he wanted the G.B.C. secretaries to take on the responsibility for these practical affairs. He thought it better to use his energy in writing and translating books. "If you G.B.C. do everything nicely," he told his secretary Śyāmasundara, "then my brain will not be taxed, and I can utilize my time completely to produce further books. I can give you *Vedas, Upaniṣads, Purāṇas, Mahābhārata, Rāmāyaṇa*—so many. There are so many devotional works in our line by the Gosvāmīs. This administrative work is taking too much time. I could be discussing philosophy. My brain is being taxed day and night. Because of this I'm neglecting my real work."

Aside from directly managing the Indian projects, Prabhupāda was answering as many as a dozen letters daily from devotees around the world. "Why do they keep writing, asking so many questions?" he asked his secretary.

"The devotees prefer to ask you personally," Śyāmasundara said, "because their G.B.C. men don't always know the right answer."

"They know everything by now," Prabhupāda replied. "I have given you everything. If they don't know the answer, they can find it in my books. Now I am an old man. Let me settle down to philosophy. All day reading letters, doing business, all night signing letters—this is not right. I want to be free from these things. The G.B.C. can do everything now."

But it wasn't possible. As soon as Prabhupāda would sense that one of his devotees was being cheated, he would immediately become actively involved. And his disciples continued to write him regarding important business and managerial decisions. Nor would he discourage them. His desire for retirement and exclusive literary work remained, but it seemed to be only a wishful thought, a dream. If ISKCON were to develop, then there seemed little scope for his retirement.

* * *

Māyāpur
February 1972

Prabhupāda had postponed the Māyāpur cornerstone-laying ceremony until Gaura-pūrṇimā (the appearance day of Lord Caitanya), February 29, 1972. He had requested a big festival, with a *paṇḍāl* and free feasting for guests. His disciples from all over the world would attend.

> I want very much to hold this function this year with all of my students. . . . It is a very important day and it will be a great service to Srila Bhaktivinoda Thakur and to His son Srila Bhaktisiddhanta Sarasvati Thakur. So please arrange for this program.

When inspecting the living accommodations for the devotees, Prabhupāda found spacious white canvas tents—one for the men and one for the women—with fluorescent lighting inside. A large *paṇḍāl* tent stood in the center of the other tents, and a small tent in the rear served as a kitchen. Immediately surrounding the small compound were rice fields. The ground, therefore, was slightly moist, and the wet fields bred large mosquitoes, which emerged at sunset. Conditions were primitive, but many of these devotees were the same disciples who had traveled for a year and a half in India, sometimes living in dirty *dharmaśālas* with bare rooms and sometimes living in cold tents. The devotees had not come to Māyāpur to be comfortable but to serve Prabhupāda. In future years, by the result of their efforts, many, many devotees would be able to gather comfortably in Māyāpur in the spacious buildings Prabhupāda was planning.

Well aware that Westerners were unaccustomed to the austerities of living in India, Prabhupāda wanted to provide facilities so his disciples could feel comfortable and be able to focus their stay in India on spiritual life, without distracting inconveniences.

Prabhupāda's dwelling was a simple thatched Bengali hut about twelve feet square, with a dirt floor. A thin partition divided the main room from the servants' quarters. In front was a small veranda, and in back a garden, where Prabhupāda could sit and take massage. Also in back were a hand pump for bathing and an outhouse. When the devotees apologized for offering Prabhupāda such a humble residence, he replied that he liked the natural simplicity. "Even if you build me the biggest palace," he said, "still I would prefer to live

While living so simply in Māyāpur, Prabhupāda spoke of his vision of a grand project yet to come. Although the Deities of Rādhā-Mādhava were installed in a tent, he spoke of a marble palace. He also spoke of first-class accommodations for guests and devotees, although as yet he had little to offer. Living simply and happily in his thatched hut, he gathered his disciples together and told them of his plans. At his request, devotees had built a small model of the proposed first major building, and there were also drawings of the proposed Temple of Human Understanding. He wanted to build a Māyāpur city, he said, with quarters for each of the four social classes of the *varṇāśrama* institution.

The five-day Gaura-pūrṇimā festival featured twenty-four-hour *kīrtana,* with groups of devotees chanting in two-hour shifts. Each morning the main body of devotees would form a *kīrtana* procession and go out visiting Navadvīpa's holy sights: the *nīm* tree under which Lord Caitanya was born, the house of Śrīnivāsa Ācārya, where Lord Caitanya and His associates had performed nocturnal *kīrtana,* the spot where the Kazi had tried to stop Lord Caitanya's *saṅkīrtana,* the residence of Bhaktivinoda Ṭhākura. (Often Bhaktivinoda Ṭhākura had stood in front of this house, Prabhupāda told the devotees, and looked out across the Jalangi toward where Śrīla Prabhupāda now had his land.)

Throughout the day and especially in the evenings, the devotees would gather on the stage of the orange-striped *paṇḍāl,* while Rādhā-Mādhava stood at stage center within a traditional Bengali *siṁhāsana* of carved banana stalks covered with colored foil and flower garlands. Prabhupāda would have his disciples do most of the public speaking, with Acyutānanda Swami, lecturing in Bengali, as the main speaker.

Hundreds of people came and went in a steady stream, and the devotees distributed Bengali, English, and Hindi *Back to Godhead* magazines. In the evenings they would present a slide show or film. Prabhupāda was especially pleased to watch the *prasādam* distribution from his window, hundreds of villagers sitting in long rows, eating *kicharī* from round leaf plates. "Continue this forever," Prabhupāda told his disci-

Even without a building, Prabhupāda's preaching in Māyāpur was significant. While other nearby *maṭhas* were also observing Gaura-pūrṇimā—mostly by hosting Calcutta widows who paid a fee to live a few days in a temple and visit the holy places of Navadvīpa—Prabhupāda's *paṇḍāl* program was the most vigorous celebration and drew the most visitors. The birthplace of Lord Caitanya Mahāprabhu, Prabhupāda said, had no meaning without preaching. Except for this time of year, very few people visited Māyāpur.

"Which is more important," Prabhupāda asked, "Lord Caitanya's birthplace or His activities? It is His activities, His *karma*. His activities are more important than His *janma*, or place of birth." The activities of Lord Caitanya were chanting Hare Kṛṣṇa and distributing love of God to all people, and this should be the activity of devotees in Māyāpur.

On Gaura-pūrṇimā day, ten of Prabhupāda's sannyasi Godbrothers visited to participate, along with Prabhupāda's disciples and hundreds of visitors, in the dedication and cornerstone-laying ceremony. Prabhupāda was gracious and friendly toward his Godbrothers, and he was gratified that they could all sit together to dedicate the world headquarters of the International Society for Krishna Consciousness.

Sitting on a cushion next to the sacrificial arena, chanting on *japa* beads, Prabhupāda initiated six Bengali devotees and awarded the sannyasa order to a young American disciple. Then Prabhupāda's Godbrothers spoke, each expressing appreciation for Prabhupāda's work in the West.

Finally they all gathered around the pit, five feet square and fifteen feet deep. Certain articles had been collected to be placed inside the pit in accordance with the scriptures: five kinds of flowers, five kinds of grains, five kinds of leaves, five kinds of metal, five kinds of nectar, five kinds of colors, five kinds of fruit, and five kinds of jewels. Prabhupāda's Godbrother Purī Mahārāja descended a ladder into the pit to put coconuts and banana leaves in a pot and to place this, along with flowers, onto the altar of bricks.

Next Prabhupāda entered the pit, carrying a box with a gold, ruby-eyed *mūrti* of Ananta Śeṣa. Earlier that morning in his hut Prabhupāda had confidentially shown a few disciples the *mūrti.* "This is Lord Ānanta," he had said, "the serpent bed on which Lord Viṣṇu rests. He will hold the temple on His head." Prabhupāda now placed Ānanta Śeṣa on the altar of bricks and climbed back on the ladder. Then on Prabhupāda's blissful invitation, everyone began to toss in offerings of flowers and money, followed by handfuls of earth.

After the five-day festival, Prabhupāda left Māyāpur for Vṛndāvana, where he planned to hold another groundbreaking ceremony. The Māyāpur land was still completely undeveloped, and Prabhupāda urged his disciples in India to continue collecting the necessary funds.

> We are making a very gorgeous plan at Mayapur, and if you all together can give shape to this plan it will be unique in the whole world. It will be a world center for teaching spiritual life. Students from all over the world will come, and we shall revolutionize the atheistic and communistic tendencies of rascal philosophers. So we must be responsible for this great task. Not for a single moment shall we be without ISKCON thoughts. That is my request to you all.

* * *

To close the transaction for the land in Ramaṇa-retī, Prabhupāda and Mr. S. met at the Magistrate's Court in Mathurā. In the presence of lawyers they completed the formalities. Prabhupāda saw it as Kṛṣṇa's grace that he had acquired a good plot of land in Vṛndāvana, and writing to his G.B.C. secretaries in America, he asked them to send as many men as possible to help in the new project. He described his intentions "for raising up a very excellent center, to revive the spiritual life for Vṛndāvana on behalf of Rūpa and Jīva Gosvāmīs."

Prabhupāda told Kṣīrodakaśāyī, one of his Indian-born disciples, "I want on this occasion huge *prasādam* should be prepared, and every man in Vṛndāvana should be invited to take *prasādam*." Two days later, with a hundred people attending, Prabhupāda held the cornerstone-laying ceremony at Ramaṇa-retī. Again he descended into the ceremonial pit and placed the Deity of Ananta, on whose head the temple would rest.

But late that night the land was attacked. An elderly Indian widow, with local fame as a sadhu, became very angry that Mr. S. had not given her the land, which she had several times requested. During the night she sent *guṇḍās* to dismantle the brick foundation of the ceremonial cornerstone and to desecrate the pit, which had just that day been filled with flowers and religious objects. The *guṇḍās* dug open the hole, threw garbage into it, and stole the "Posted" sign announcing the land's new ownership.

Prabhupāda was in his room in the Rādhā-Dāmodara temple when he heard what had happened. He became angry and told his disciples to show the deed to the police. That night several policemen guarded the land, and when the hired *guṇḍās* came again, the police warned that if they caused any more trouble they would be arrested. And that was the end of that.

Prabhupāda had several times said that by becoming a devotee, one gains many enemies. The incident also served to confirm Prabhupāda's conviction that ISKCON's taking possession of the land should be followed as quickly as possible by construction of a temple. They should at least encircle the land with a fence, build small huts, and live on the land while preparing for temple construction.

Tejas: *"This will be the Kṛṣṇa-Balarāma temple," Prabhupāda said. We didn't really know what was going on. We all thought it was far away. It was really the boondocks, Ramaṇa-retī. Nobody was out there. It was such an isolated place, and there were lots of dacoits living out there. We thought, "If we're going to have a temple out here, no one will ever come." But Prabhupāda said, "Wherever there is Kṛṣṇa, everyone will come."*

Prabhupāda's secretary, Śyāmasundara, wrote to a Godbrother about the newly acquired Vṛndāvana property.

> Earlier in the day, before breakfast, Prabhupada sewed up the 4,800 sq. yd. gift plot in Ramana Reti where Krishna used to sport with Friends in the forest, about 10 minutes walk from Radha-Damodara. Prabhupada surveyed the land (with the rope from his mosquito net), bargained for, drew plans for, drew up the deed for, went to Mathura magistrate's court for and signed, sealed, and delivered in an instant. Prabhupada has asked me to request you that AT LEAST FIFTY (50) MEN FROM THE U.S. MUST COME TO INDIA IMMEDIATELY!!! At last we have got a solid programme in India: Huge projects at Mayapur, Vrindaban and Bombay. All the lands are acquired, arrangements made, and everything by Prabhupada. But only a few of us men are here to struggle with an immense task—the biggest by far within the Society, of developing these three places, and believe me these three projects are more dear to Prabhupada than any yet contemplated.

* * *

In the month while Prabhupāda was away from Bombay (he had left on February 10) the payment of fifty thousand rupees was duly made. Slowly at first, a few devotees moved to the Juhu land, living in a tent. At night the rats and mosquitoes would disturb the devotees' sleep. While attempting to clear the overgrown weeds, they came upon empty liquor bottles and overflowing sewage. Without Prabhupāda, their resolution grew weak.

But then Brahmānanda Swami, whom Prabhupāda had put in charge of his Bombay project, returned from Calcutta, where he had been with Śrīla Prabhupāda. Brahmānanda Swami was inspired, and he gave the Bombay devotees new impetus. They would have to clear the land and raise a *paṇḍāl* right away. Brahmānanda had never put on a *paṇḍāl* program before, but he hired a contractor to build several *chātāi* (palm frond) houses for the devotees and a festival tent. Even before the construction could begin, however, the devotees would have to thoroughly clear the land.

Mr. Sethi, a neighbor and life member, hired a work crew

to cut down the weeds and vegetation, and several life member friends in Bombay also came forward to assist. Mr. N. offered to help by sending one of his assistants, Mr. Matar, to organize the hired laborers in clearing the fields. The devotees also worked in preparation for Prabhupāda's return.

Śrī Śrī Rādhā-Rāsavihārī, the Rādhā-Kṛṣṇa Deities Prabhupāda had installed in Bombay in 1971, arrived at ISKCON's Hare Krishna Land in a taxi, riding across the laps of several devotees. They had moved before, and this time Their residence was a tent. When Prabhupāda had left orders that Rādhā-Rāsavihārī should move to Juhu as soon as the down payment was made, some of the devotees had questioned him: Why should the Deity move before the facilities were proper? Shouldn't They wait until the temple was built? "Once the Deities are installed on a piece of property," Prabhupāda had replied, "no one will remove Them."

More than anyone else, Prabhupāda was aware of the proper worship to be offered to Rādhā-Rāsavihārī, but his emphasis now was on securing the land. How else, he reasoned, could he eventually give Rādhā-Rāsavihārī a royal throne and temple unless They Themselves first established Their right of proprietorship by taking up residence at Hare Krishna Land? The arrival of Rādhā-Rāsavihārī at Juhu also meant increased difficulties for the devotees, who now had to struggle to maintain the morning *pūjā* and cook six daily offerings in the meager kitchen. Even Rādhā-Rāsavihārī's tent was insubstantial and swayed in the wind.

Śrīla Prabhupāda, however, saw the move as a necessary, transcendental tactic. But because he was asking Lord Kṛṣṇa Himself to accept these inconveniences, he prayed to the Deity, "My dear Sir, please remain here, and I shall build a beautiful temple for You."

By the time Prabhupāda returned to Bombay, Rādhā-Rāsavihārī were installed on the stage of the *paṇḍāl.* Attendance at the festival was not as great as it would have been in downtown Bombay—no more than five hundred people came a night—but Śrīla Prabhupāda was satisfied. This festival was on their own property, and this was only the beginning.

Within a few days of his arrival at Juhu, Prabhupāda was ready to hold the ground-breaking and cornerstone-laying ceremony—another tactic for securing possession of the land. But it was more than a tactic, as he wanted a temple constructed as soon as possible. Rādhā-Rāsavihārī should not remain standing in a tent but should be protected by a silver-and-teakwood *siṁhāsana* on a marble altar. They should be surrounded by deities of the two *gopīs* Lalitā and Viśākhā, and Their temple should have marble domes more than a hundred feet high. Thousands should come daily for *darśana* and *prasādam.*

One morning, in the midst of the festival activities, the devotees of Hare Krishna Land joined Prabhupāda in a simple cornerstone-laying ceremony. They had dug a deep ceremonial pit and surrounded it with bricks. Prabhupāda descended and placed the Deity of Śeṣa. Then, sitting on a simple platform, Prabhupāda accompanied the *kīrtana* by playing a brass gong, while one by one the devotees came before him and threw dirt into the pit, filling it, while smoke rose from the sacrificial fire.

Prabhupāda was planning an extensive world tour, traveling eastward to Australia, Japan, Hawaii, the U.S., and perhaps Mexico and Europe. It might be as long as half a year before he would return to India, and he wanted things to progress smoothly in Bombay without him. A few days before his departure, however, he learned from Brahmānanda Swami that the preaching was deteriorating in Nairobi in Brahmānanda's absence. Prabhupāda agreed that Brahmānanda should return to his duties there.

Again, Prabhupāda had to choose a new Bombay manager, and this time he chose Girirāja, a young *brahmacārī* and leading preacher in making ISKCON life members. Prabhupāda reasoned that since the essence of management was to collect donations and make life members, and since Girirāja was expert at that, then even though he was young and otherwise inexperienced, he had the most important qualifications. Prabhupāda had already found Girirāja to be simple and submissively dedicated to helping him develop Hare Krishna Land.

During Prabhupāda's stay in Bombay, Hans Kielman, a young architect from Holland, had come to hear the lectures and had become interested in Kṛṣṇa consciousness. Prabhupāda convinced Hans to become a devotee and to help build the Hare Krishna city in Bombay. Under Prabhupāda's direction, Hans at once began to make architectural drawings for the buildings.

Prabhupāda said Girirāja and the others would have to collect sixty-four lakhs of rupees for the construction. The devotees had no idea how they would raise even a fraction of that amount, but Prabhupāda gave them some ideas. He talked to them about enlisting the support of influential men by using the *bheṇṭ-nāma* system, whereby a person purchases the use of a guest room for life. And there were other ways.

But the immediate step was to get the land. They had possession of the land, but before building they should have the deed. Since Mr. N. was already overdue in delivering the deed, Prabhupāda told Girirāja to press him to comply with the written agreement and deliver the deed at once.

* * *

Prabhupāda had the extraordinary ability to bring a spiritual vision into physical reality, to change a part of the material world into spiritual energy so that even a common man could perceive the spiritual reality. This was Prabhupāda's constant effort. Often a transcendentalist hesitates to deal with the material world, fearing he may become spiritually weakened. The Vedic injunctions, therefore, warn the transcendentalist to avoid associating with money and materialistic persons. But Prabhupāda, following the principles taught by Śrīla Rūpa Gosvāmī, saw that everything material had the potential of being used in the service of Kṛṣṇa and thus of regaining its spiritual nature. Following this principle, an expert devotee, although apparently acting within the material sphere, could remain always in touch with the spiritual energy. For such a devotee, nothing was material.

In the Vedic scriptures the great devotee Nārada Muni, because of his ability to convert materialistic men into devotees, is referred to as *cintāmaṇi,* touchstone. Just as *cintāmaṇi* is said to convert iron into gold, so Nārada could transform a beastlike hunter into a pure Vaiṣṇava. And as Nārada is glorified in the *Vedas* for accomplishing such feats in bygone ages, so Śrīla Prabhupāda is a similarly potent touchstone in the present age. Again and again he showed by his straightforward application of Kṛṣṇa consciousness that he could change a materialist into a completely renounced, active devotee of the Lord. And now, after recruiting a number of devotees from maya's camp, he wanted to engage them in transforming as much as possible of the material world into living spirit. By his transcendental, visionary words, he was attempting to convert stone and human energy into glorious, spiritual temples.

While ambitious materialists sometimes criticize transcendentalists as unproductive, Prabhupāda, because of his constant activity, could never be so accused. Rather, people would criticize him as being a capitalist in the dress of a sannyasi. But such criticisms never deterred Prabhupāda; he was carrying out the desires of the previous *ācāryas.* He had written this conclusion in his *Śrīmad-Bhāgavatam* even before coming to America in 1965.

> Therefore, all the sages and devotees of the Lord have recommended that the subject matter of art, science, philosophy, physics, chemistry, psychology and all other branches of knowledge should be wholely and solely applied to the service of the Lord.

Prabhupāda wanted to convert significant portions of the material world into the spiritual world. In attempting to construct a spiritual city in Juhu, he realized he was launching a major attack against *māyā.* Within a few months so many complications and headaches had already disturbed his plans, and more would come; the battle was just beginning.

* * *

Leaving Bombay, Śrīla Prabhupāda began a world preaching tour, taking with him a small entourage of disciples. He visited Singapore, Sydney, Melbourne, Auckland, Tokyo, and Honolulu. He stopped briefly at his center in Portland, Oregon, and then flew to Paris and Glasgow. He then returned to the U.S., where he visited the New Vrindaban farm community in West Virginia and, after more than five months of vigorous touring, his Western world headquarters in Los Angeles.

From Los Angeles he wrote to the devotees in Bombay, reassuring them that the Juhu land was not just a trouble spot but a special place where a great plan would be carried out. It was worth fighting for.

> . . . now I am anxious to hear if the conveyance deed has been signed and what are the contents. Kindly send me the copy duly signed as quickly as possible. This will give me great relief. As soon as the conveyance has been signed you may begin the building work immediately. I am coming to India soon, at least by October, and I want to see that the building projects in Bombay, Mayapur and Vrindavana are going on nicely. This Bombay project is one of our most important projects in the whole world and I am looking to you and the others there in Bombay to see that it is done very magnificently.

Prabhupāda repeatedly instructed the managers in Bombay not to deviate from the terms of the purchase agreement. The devotees should press Mr. N. to the original agreement.

Prabhupāda was worried that he had not heard from his lawyer, Mr. D. Two weeks before, he had telegrammed both Mr. N. and Mr. D., asking for reports on the delays, but he had received no replies from either of them. He had since written to another lawyer, a friend in Bombay, asking about the delay, and in Los Angeles he received the reply: Mr. D. was no longer his attorney. A couple of days after receiving this shocking news, Prabhupāda received a formal letter from the office of Mr. D., informing him of the same.

Of all the recent news from Bombay, this was the most disturbing. Prabhupāda began to see how Mr. N. had been devising a devious plot from the beginning. It was not just a matter of slowness or bureaucratic delay; Mr. D. had been in league with Mr. N. They were cheaters. So now it was going to be a real fight. ISKCON would have to go to court and file criminal charges against Mr. N. There was no avoiding the fight, but Prabhupāda still felt that his position was legally very strong.

Before leaving Los Angeles, he thought of a further tactic. He wrote to Girirāja that he should put a notice in the newspaper advising the public that ISKCON had signed an agreement for purchasing Mr. N.'s land at Juhu.

Although Prabhupāda had appointed G.B.C. secretaries to oversee the Kṛṣṇa consciousness movement in various parts of the world, he was the real G.B.C. secretary of India. Wherever he traveled, therefore, he remained partial to those projects. He was setting the perfect example of a G.B.C. secretary. While conscientiously tending to practical affairs, he remained always transcendental—fully dependent on Kṛṣṇa and always preaching.

* * *

October 6

During his brief visit to Berkeley, Prabhupāda met with a group of professors from the University of California and also installed Rādhā-Kṛṣṇa Deities in the Berkeley temple. But still he was meditating on Bombay. He wrote to Tamāla Kṛṣṇa Goswami,

> The Bombay dealing has been muddled by the tactics of Mr. N. and Mr. D. Giriraja is in trouble. He is a child in these worldly dealings, so immediately go to help him. . . . But you must be careful to pay the money in the court (registrar's office) and not in the hand of Mr. N. or his solicitor. . . . Settle up the things properly, otherwise let us go to the court for specific action, either civic or criminal against the tactics of Mr. N.

Prabhupāda decided to send Karandhara, whom he considered expert, to help in Bombay. He also wanted to send Śyāmasundara, but Śyāmasundara had gone to London regarding a large country estate George Harrison was donating. Prabhupāda notified Śyāmasundara, however, that once the London transaction was completed, he should go to Bombay.

Prabhupāda was ready for the fight. He would not be cheated.

During his return trip to India, Prabhupāda again visited his center in Honolulu. Then on October 11 he went for the first time to Manila, where a small number of disciples had arranged preaching programs for him, both in the temple and at the Hotel Intercontinental.

In Manila Prabhupāda carefully considered his position regarding the Juhu property and concluded that he would come out victorious. He listed the points of his argument in a letter to Girirāja.

> 1. We have fulfilled all the conditions as purchaser.
> 2. Mr. N. has purposefully delayed with a motive to cheat us as he had done with some others in this connection.
> 3. But this time he cannot cheat us because we are in possession of the land and our Deity Radha-Krishna is installed there.
> 4. Therefore we must immediately go to the court for enforcing him to execute the conveyance immediately.
> 5. Even if the court case goes on for a long time, still our business there cannot be stopped.
> 6. Without going to the court, we cannot make any compromise with him.
> 7. But I think we can arrange the full amount of 14 lacs to get out this rascal out of the scene.
> 8. But we cannot do it without going to the court otherwise we shall become a party for breaking the purchase agreement. Therefore we have to go to the court before making any compromise.

* * *

Vṛndāvana
October 17, 1972

Prabhupāda had come to Vṛndāvana to observe the Kārttika season (from October 16 to November 14). He planned to lecture daily at the *samādhi* of Rūpa Gosvāmī in the courtyard of the Rādhā-Dāmodara temple, speaking from *The*

Nectar of Devotion, his own translation of Rūpa Gosvāmī's book *Bhakti-rasāmṛta-sindhu.* On his Western tour he had invited devotees to join him for Kārttika in Vṛndāvana, and now a few dozen devotees from America, Europe, India, and other parts of the world had gathered to be with him.

He was concerned with developing his Vṛndāvana project, so rather than immediately rushing to Bombay, he had come here first, sending some of his leading disciples to tackle the problems in Bombay. Now, like a general engaged on a different front, he awaited word from his lieutenants in Bombay. He moved into his two small rooms at the Rādhā-Dāmodara temple, while his disciples stayed nearby in the former palace of the Mahārāja of Bharatpur, an old building near the Yamunā.

Tamāla Kṛṣṇa Goswami, Śyāmasundara, and Karandhara arrived in Bombay. Things had worsened, Girirāja informed them. When Mr. N. had seen the notice in the newspaper publicly advising that ISKCON had entered into an agreement for the Juhu property, he had become furious. Girirāja had gone to him with folded hands and bowed down before him, but Mr. N. would not be appeased. He had gone back on all his promises and had canceled the sales agreement, on the plea that the devotees had not obtained the deed within a six-month period. The two-lakh down payment, he had claimed, was now his, and the devotees should vacate the land immediately.

Mr. N. had shut off the water supply to Hare Krishna Land. Several days later, a hoodlum had shown up at the entrance to the property, brandishing a machete whenever devotees passed by. A friend of Mr. N. had printed a handbill ascribing scandalous behavior to the American Hare Kṛṣṇa devotees and was having it distributed at the nearby Vile Parle train station. Although a few devotees had left and others wanted to, about thirty devotees still remained in Bombay.

The first thing to do, Karandhara said, was to find a new lawyer, and he went to Bombay's most prominent solicitors and hired a specialist in land transactions and conveyances. Next, the leading devotees and their solicitor met with Mr. N. in his office. Mr. N. was stubborn and uncooperative, and the ISKCON lawyer was threatening. A court battle seemed inevitable.

Tamāla Kṛṣṇa Goswami, Karandhara, Bhavānanda, and Śyāmasundara talked together, and the more they talked, the more they began to see the entire Juhu scheme as impossible. Even without Mr. N.'s treachery, just to live on the land was very difficult. The devotees and the Deities had such poor living facilities that the roof leaked and the cement floor was crumbling. Rats, flies, cockroaches, village dogs, and mosquitoes infested the place—with even an occasional poisonous snake. Devotees were always contracting tropical diseases, especially malaria and hepatitis.

So although ISKCON's new lawyer was prepared to take the case to court. the devotees were hesitant. Mr. N. had said that they—not he—were criminals, because they had not gotten permission from the charity commissioner; they were on his land illegally. He said he would sue for damages. He even seemed to be on the verge of some violent action. Considering all angles, the leaders whom Prabhupāda had entrusted to solve the Juhu entanglement decided that ISKCON should relinquish the land. Drafting a joint letter to Śrīla Prabhupāda, they had Śyāmasundara hand-deliver it to him in Vṛndāvana.

Sitting in his room in the Rādhā-Dāmodara temple, Śrīla Prabhupāda read the letter from Bombay. Although hundreds of miles away, the occurrences there were beating on his heart in Vṛndāvana. He took out his copy of the agreement signed by Mr. N. Then he called his secretary and began dictating a letter to his leaders in Bombay.

He began his letter like a lawyer, answering logically, point by point. One reason his disciples had given for wanting to give up the land was that the charity commissioner had refused them permission. In that case, Prabhupāda reasoned, they should try to get back the money and give up the land. But it appeared that the charity commissioner's permission was *delayed,* not denied—a small matter. Although Mr. N.

had mentioned a six-month time limit for obtaining the charity commissioner's approval, Prabhupāda pointed out that the original agreement mentioned no such time limit.

Another reason Prabhupāda's men had given for wanting to relinquish the land was that, according to Mr. N., they had failed to obtain the conveyance within six months, as per the original sales agreement. Prabhupāda replied that, according to the clause in question, "it is *our* option to rescind the contract within six months, not the vendor's." But the real point was that Mr. N. had accepted checks worth one lakh rupees as down payment within the six-month period, and therefore the sales agreement was completed.

> . . . we consider that he has completed the conveyance and we do not want to rescind but we shall close the deal immediately, finished, that's all. He's trying to avoid this issue by tricks, and he has dominated you and you are little afraid of him, and he has fooled you to think he is in superior legal position so that you will give him some money. But this is cheating. We shall not give him any more money. Don't pay him any more. First of all bring a criminal case against him. . . . So why you should be disappointed and afraid of him? Our position is very, very strong.

If Mr. N. was threatening violence, that also was not grounds for quitting the land. The devotees were on the land legally and should seek police protection.

> Therefore I say that you boys cannot deal very well in these matters, because you are too timid. Now whatever you like you may do. Immediately criminal case should be taken, that you are not doing because he is bluffing you. He says big words and makes threats and you believe him foolishly and do like he says. That I shall not do.

Prabhupāda's conclusive advice was that the devotees go to the magistrate and tell him, "We gave Mr. N. money, and now he is threatening violence to drive us away." They should not be afraid.

*   *

Prabhupāda was eager to begin construction on his Ramaṇa-retī property, and the news from Bombay didn't distract him from his purpose. Every day he would have the devotees hold a *saṅkīrtana* procession from the Rādhā-Dāmodara temple to the property at Ramaṇa-retī. He would also go out occasionally to see the site, still nothing more than grass huts, a wire fence, and a small stock of building materials. Subala, the disciple in charge of construction, was slow and reluctant, and Prabhupāda sent for Tamāla Kṛṣṇa Goswami to come from Bombay and take charge. Early one morning Subala left the land at Ramaṇa-retī, where he had been staying, and approached Śrīla Prabhupāda on the roof of the Rādhā-Dāmodara temple. "Prabhupāda," he said, "I am having so much difficulty. I don't have time to read, I can't chant my rounds properly, I can't think of Kṛṣṇa. I'm always thinking of how this contractor is cheating us, or I'm thinking of signing checks for labor and materials. It's just too much. All these things on my mind are stopping me from thinking of Kṛṣṇa."

"Do you think Arjuna was simply meditating on Kṛṣṇa on the battlefield of Kurukṣetra?" Prabhupāda replied. "Do you think Arjuna was sitting in yogic trance, while on the battlefield Kṛṣṇa worked? No, he was fighting. He was killing for Kṛṣṇa. He was thinking of all the soldiers he had to kill for Kṛṣṇa.

"Thinking of the checkbook, thinking of the men, thinking of the contractors—this is also like Arjuna's thinking. This is Kṛṣṇa's service. You should not worry about thinking of Kṛṣṇa directly. Arjuna wasn't sitting before Kṛṣṇa in a trance, meditating on His form. He was engaged in Kṛṣṇa's service. Similarly this is Kṛṣṇa's service, and you should engage. Your life is full of Kṛṣṇa's service, and that is very good."

As far as possible, Prabhupāda engaged each disciple in a certain service according to the particular disciple's psychophysical nature. But everyone had to take up some kind of work for Kṛṣṇa. Since Prabhupāda desired to build a temple in Vṛndāvana, then whoever would help him do it, whether they were trained or not, or whether it was their tendency or not—whoever offered him assistance—would become very dear to him and to Lord Kṛṣṇa.

All over the world devotees were working hard to develop ISKCON projects. Their means of income was from the rapidly growing distribution of Śrīla Prabhupāda's books and, to some degree, from their Spiritual Sky incense business. As yet Prabhupāda had no architectural plan for his Vṛndāvana project, but he determined to gather from his Book Fund and from devotees enough money for materials and labor. One day he went to the building site and asked a devotee to mix a little cement, and with his own hand, he laid down the first concrete for the foundation.

* * *

Hyderabad
November 11, 1972

Prabhupāda had come to Hyderabad for a *paṇḍāl* program. Big crowds attended his lectures, and wherever he went, even while getting into and out of his car, people surrounded him to touch his lotus feet. Although Hyderabad had been suffering from drought, a few days after Prabhupāda's arrival rains came. One newspaper suggested that the *harināma-kīrtana* Śrīla Prabhupāda and his devotees performed so enthusiastically must have ended the drought. Prabhupāda agreed.

He also met with Mr. N., who was visiting Hyderabad from Bombay. Śyāmasundara had a cordial relationship with Mr. N., because Mr. N. had been fond of his three-year-old daughter, Sarasvatī. So he went to Mr. N. and convinced him to speak to Prabhupāda. Mr. N. agreed, but being suspicious that Prabhupāda might try to use mystic power to persuade him to do something against his will, he brought a guru with him, thinking the guru would counteract Prabhupāda's spiritual power.

Mr. N., his guru, and Śyāmasundara all came to the home of Panilal Prithi, where Prabhupāda was staying. Prabhupāda met informally with his guests, conversing with them over *prasādam,* until he yawned, and Mr. N.'s guru said, "Oh, Swami, you must be very tired. We should not disturb you now. You should rest, and we may talk later."

"Oh, yes," Prabhupāda replied, "I am very tired."

So Mr. N. and his guru excused themselves and retired to the adjoining room.

After a few minutes Prabhupāda called Tamāla Kṛṣṇa Goswami into his room. "When someone asks you if *you* are tired," Prabhupāda said, "it means *he* is tired. If you go into the other room, you will see that they are sleeping." He instructed Tamāla Kṛṣṇa to carefully awaken Mr. N. without disturbing his guru and bring him in.

Tiptoeing into the room, Tamāla Kṛṣṇa found both Mr. N. and his guru asleep on the beds. He went over to Mr. N., touched his arm, and said quietly, "Mr. N., Mr. N., wake up. Prabhupāda would like to speak with you. Come quickly." Mr. N., being roused from his slumber, obediently walked into Prabhupāda's room, forgetting his guru friend.

For two hours Prabhupāda talked with Mr. N., and by the end of the discussion they had worked out a new sales agreement. Tamāla Kṛṣṇa and Śyāmasundara, working in a separate room, drafted and typed the documents, while Prabhupāda and Mr. N. settled the final legal points. Then Mr. N. signed the agreement, while his guru friend continued sleeping soundly.

Later that day Tamāla Kṛṣṇa confided to Śrīla Prabhupāda, "I am so disturbed by these dealings that I can't chant my rounds properly."

"That is natural," Prabhupāda replied. "Sometimes when I am disturbed, I also."

"But I can see that I am making spiritual advancement, even so," Tamāla Kṛṣṇa admitted.

Prabhupāda nodded.

"I used to think how to avoid difficult situations," Tamāla Kṛṣṇa said. "But now I think I should not run away from them."

"Yes," Prabhupāda said, "we should welcome these. They give us an opportunity to advance more."

Śyāmasundara and Tamāla Kṛṣṇa Goswami flew back to Bombay with Mr. N. that afternoon. According to the new terms, ISKCON would pay Mr. N. the five lakhs of rupees for a government tax, and in return Mr. N. would execute the deed. But there was also a new time limit—three weeks—and the devotees would have to work fast. Prabhupāda himself would soon come to Bombay to settle the matter once and for all.

* * *

Bombay
November 25, 1972

Although Prabhupāda had come to Bombay with hopes of finishing the land transaction, Mr. N. was still delaying, despite the new agreement. Obviously his stalling was simply part of his plan to cheat ISKCON. Śrīla Prabhupāda waited many days in Bombay, finally departing for a *paṇḍāl* program in Ahmedabad. He left behind instructions for his disciples to get the deed on the new terms or else to take back the original two lakhs of rupees paid as the down payment.

While Śrīla Prabhupāda was away, however, Śyāmasundara, Tamāla Kṛṣṇa Goswami, and the others began talking about how even if they could one day get the deed to the Juhu property, to develop Hare Krishna Land the way Prabhupāda had envisioned would be practically impossible. Śyāmasundara argued that even if they got the land, how could they really expect to build a big temple and hotel out here in the jungle? It just wouldn't work. Meanwhile, from Ahmedabad Prabhupāda continued to wage his Bombay campaign, and he requested Mr. N. and Mr. D. to come to Ahmedabad to try and make a settlement. They declined.

In Bombay the devotees learned that if they wanted to get back their down payment as well as the money they had deposited toward the five-lakh gains tax, then they would have to cancel the new agreement. They were confused, and their time was running out.

One morning one of Prabhupāda's disciples, Viśākhā-devī dāsī, arrived in Ahmedabad from Bombay. Prabhupāda called for her and told her to return to Bombay immediately with a message. Out of concern that his leaders in Bombay not make a wrong decision and decide to relinquish the land, he told her to tell them that they should not under any circumstances cancel the agreement with Mr. N. "Actually," he said, "this is not a woman's job, but everyone else here is either engaged in the *paṇḍāl* or has not been with us long enough to do this task."

Viśākhā took the next train out of Ahmedabad and arrived in Bombay the following morning. But what Prabhupāda had foreseen had already happened: the devotees had canceled the sales agreement. They were convinced that to get the land would be a mistake, and their lawyers had agreed, pointing out that if the devotees wanted to retrieve their money, they should cancel the agreement immediately. When the devotees heard Prabhupāda's message from Ahmedabad, confusion reigned. They now had no legal standing, no claim to the land. And they had failed to carry out Prabhupāda's desire! Girirāja phoned Prabhupāda in Ahmedabad to tell him what had happened.

"Bhaktivedanta Swami here," Prabhupāda said as he took the telephone. Girirāja was saying that a devotee had come from Ahmedabad with a message. "Yes, yes," Prabhupāda said, "what is the point?" Finally Girirāja blurted out that they had canceled the sales agreement. Prabhupāda was silent. Then in a voice that expressed both anger and resignation, he said, "Then everything is finished."

CHAPTER SIX

Let There Be a Temple: Part II

"I shall be the last man to give up Hare Krishna Land to the rogue Mr. N.," Prabhupāda wrote to a life member just before leaving Ahmedabad for Bombay. Prabhupāda was now immediately planning how to rectify his disciples' mistake. No money had yet been transferred, so perhaps it was not too late.

Mr. N. could not possibly understand why Prabhupāda was so determined in his fight to keep the Juhu land. Not that Prabhupāda had kept his motives hidden, but only a devotee can understand the mind or actions of another devotee. Mr. N. was dealing with Prabhupāda just as he had dealt with C. Company. He had cheated them, and now he would cheat ISKCON. He could only surmise that Prabhupāda and his disciples were driven by the same motive as he himself, the only motive he could understand: material possessiveness.

Actually, even Prabhupāda's disciples were having difficulty understanding Prabhupāda's unbreakable determination. Prabhupāda's main motive was to preach Kṛṣṇa consciousness in Bombay. Śrīla Prabhupāda said, "My Guru Mahārāja ordered me to preach Kṛṣṇa consciousness in the West, and I have done that. Now I want to preach in India." Bombay was the most important city in India—the gateway.

And within Bombay, Kṛṣṇa had somehow led Prabhupāda to this land, where he had begun preaching and had brought the Deities of Rādhā and Kṛṣṇa. In Prabhupāda's eyes, the land was suitable for the large, gorgeous temple and international hotel he had planned.

Bombay was an important city and required grand temple worship, large festivals, mass *prasādam* distribution, and a variety of Vedic cultural programs. The Juhu land seemed ideal for a school, a theater, a library, apartments—a Hare Kṛṣṇa city. So how could Prabhupāda retreat from this rogue who was trying to cheat him? There would always be persons opposed to Kṛṣṇa consciousness, Prabhupāda said, but that did not mean the devotees should give in. A preacher had to be tolerant, and sometimes, when all else failed and Kṛṣṇa's interest was at stake, he had to fight.

Another reason Prabhupāda refused to give up this particular plot of land was that he had promised the Deities, Rādhā-Rāsavihārī. He had invited Kṛṣṇa here and prayed, "Dear Sir, please stay here, and I will build You a beautiful temple."

So if using the land for missionary work was the obvious or external reason for Prabhupāda's determination to keep his Hare Krishna Land, then the internal reason was his personal commitment to Their Lordships Śrī Śrī Rādhā-Rāsavihārī. Prabhupāda's fighting spirit to keep the land was so keen that he sometimes appeared to be fighting for fighting's sake. He sometimes even compared Mr. N. to the demon Kaṁsa in *Śrīmad-Bhāgavatam*, who had repeatedly tried to kill Kṛṣṇa. Just as Kaṁsa had employed many minor demons in his attempts to kill Kṛṣṇa, so Mr. N. had employed demoniac agents like lawyers, friends, and hoodlums. Kṛṣṇa's killing of demons like Kaṁsa was His pastime, or *līlā*—He enjoyed it. And Prabhupāda, as the servant of Kṛṣṇa, was fully absorbed in this fighting. He was vigilant, militant. When Mr. N. bluffed or frightened the devotees, causing them to back down, Prabhupāda held his ground. He took naturally to the fight; Kṛṣṇa and Kṛṣṇa's mission were being challenged.

Prabhupāda was acting as the protector and the parent of the Deities and of ISKCON Bombay. As he had described in *The Nectar of Devotion,* many great devotees have an eternal relationship with Kṛṣṇa as His protector. When as a child Kṛṣṇa had fought the serpent Kāliya, Kṛṣṇa's mother and father had been plunged into transcendental anxiety. They had seen their child entangled in the coils of the serpent and, fearing for Kṛṣṇa's life, had wanted to protect Him. The eternal mother and father of Kṛṣṇa always worry that Kṛṣṇa may meet with harm, and when danger appears to come, their natural anxiety increases many times. In this way they show the most intense love for Kṛṣṇa. Śrīla Prabhupāda's mood was to protect Rādhā-Rāsavihārī and also his Kṛṣṇa consciousness movement. Although he knew that Kṛṣṇa was the supreme protector and that nobody could oppose His will, out of a protective desire to spread Kṛṣṇa's glories he feared that the demon Mr. N. might harm Kṛṣṇa.

Prabhupāda's feelings of anxiety and protectiveness extended to his disciples also. He saw them as children, with little worldly experience; they did not know how to deal with rogues and could be easily tricked. But if the son was gullible, the father would have to be shrewd and strong to protect his family. As protector of the devotees and of Kṛṣṇa's mission, Prabhupāda wanted to establish good housing so that his disciples could serve Kṛṣṇa in comfort—even elegance. Prabhupāda's spiritual master, Bhaktisiddhānta Sarasvatī, had taught the same thing when he had said that preachers of Kṛṣṇa consciousness should have the best of everything, because they are doing the best service to Kṛṣṇa. Prabhupāda was therefore determined to establish his Hare Kṛṣṇa city in Bombay. He did not take the attitude of a naked mendicant, who cares for nothing of this material world. He felt responsible for his thousands of disciples, and therefore he took on so many anxieties.

Mr. N. could not know what motives were driving Śrīla Prabhupāda. Nor could he imagine the ramifications of opposing Kṛṣṇa and Kṛṣṇa's pure devotee, even though the danger of such a position had been explained in India's most famous classics, *Bhagavad-gītā*, *Śrīmad-Bhāgavatam*, and *Rāmāyaṇa*. Prabhupāda was fighting on the side of Kṛṣṇa; therefore, Mr. N. was opposing the Supreme Personality of Godhead.

* * *

By Prabhupāda's disciples' cancellation of the agreement, ISKCON's legal position had been weakened. But Prabhupāda had faith that if the devotees just maintained possession of the land, their position would remain strong. At the same time, he urged the devotees to preach more. They should not think that without a temple they could not preach, so he arranged for another big Bombay *paṇḍāl* festival downtown, which proved to be a great success, with twenty thousand attending nightly.

Important guests like Mr. R. K. Ganatra, the mayor of Bombay, made introductory speeches, and the devotees also took an active part, organizing, advertising, cooking and distributing *prasādam,* distributing Śrīla Prabhupāda's books, and preaching at a question-and-answer booth. The *paṇḍāl* festival served to lift the devotees out of the doldrums of their protracted legal fight and the austerity of their living at Juhu.

During the last week of January 1973, Prabhupāda met with Mr. N. at the residence of Mr. Mahadevia. Although Prabhupāda's lawyers had filed a criminal case against Mr. N., Prabhupāda wanted to attempt an out-of-court settlement. He had always been gracious and charming with Mr. N., and Mr. N. had always appeared responsive and polite. But this time was different. Gone were the smiles and friendly words. The two were remaining barely civil to each other. After a few minutes, Prabhupāda asked his disciples to leave the room.

Speaking in Hindi, Mr. N. began accusing Prabhupāda and the devotees of being connected with the CIA. "I will come on Monday," said Mr. N. tersely, "with a check for two lakhs to pay back your down payment."

"All right," Prabhupāda replied. "If you don't want to part with your land, then we will leave. But think before you do this."

Mr. N. continued his accusations. "You people are calling yourselves the owners of the land, but you are just a big disturbance to the whole area, getting up at four and all this . . ."

"We do not claim to be the owner," Prabhupāda replied. "Kṛṣṇa is the real owner. I am not the real owner. Kṛṣṇa is already there on His land. Why are you bothering us so much? Simply take the money and give us the land. Or, if you want us to vacate, then prepare the check." Prabhupāda had been speaking with restraint, but now his tone became angry. "Bring out your check, and we will vacate tomorrow morning. No, we will vacate tonight! Give us our money back. Have you the money?"

Mr. N. shouted, "I will remove the Deities myself! I will break the temple and remove the Deities!" Mr. N. then stormed out of the room.

That week Mr. N. was hospitalized after a severe heart attack. Two weeks later he died.

Mrs. N., although not as legally astute as her late husband, carried on the fight, and her lawyers, eager to collect their fees, pursued even more intently than she the litigation to drive out ISKCON. In April 1973, at ISKCON's instigation, ISKCON's case came before the High Court. There were tactical delays, however, and month after month passed with no decision.

Prabhupāda did not commit himself to construction on the land, because he had no deed and no assurance of one. He toured the West, returned to India, but still nothing had happened to resolve the matter. Life in ISKCON Bombay was peaceful, but progress remained stunted, the outcome uncertain.

Then one day, without warning, Mrs. N. launched a violent attack. On the morning of June 1, while the devotees were attending to their routine duties, a truck drove onto the Juhu property. A demolition squad had come to dismantle the temple. Somehow Mrs. N. had convinced an official in the city government to authorize demolition of the temple, a modest structure of brick and steel-reinforced concrete. When Girirāja attempted to show the officer in charge a letter establishing ISKCON's rights, the man ignored the letter and signaled for the demolition to begin. Soon more trucks arrived, until nearly one hundred demolitionists, working with blowtorches and sledgehammers, swarmed over the property.

The demolitionists mounted ladders and began breaking the roof of the temple hall with sledgehammers. Others used torches to cut through the steel supports. The plan of the demolition squad was to knock out the steel supports of the *kīrtana* hall and proceed methodically toward the Deity house, wherein Rādhā-Rāsavihārī stood. The devotees tried to stop the demolition, but policemen soon appeared on the scene and, working in pairs, would grab the dissenters by the legs and arms and carry them away. Police dragged the women away by the hair, while tenants on the land looked on. Some were glad to see the demolition, although others were sympathetic. Out of fear of the police, however, no one moved to help the devotees.

One devotee, Manasvī, ran to a telephone and called Mr. Mahadevia, who, along with his friend Mr. Vinoda Gupta, rushed to Hare Krishna Land, to find the police dragging off the last protesting devotee by the hair. She had been trying to close the doors to the altar to protect the Deities when three policemen had wrestled her away. Mr. Mahadevia rushed to the house of a sympathetic tenant, Mr. Acarya, and phoned his brother Chandra Mahadevia, a wealthy businessman and friend of Bal Thakura, the leader of one of the most influential political parties in Bombay.

Mr. Chandra Mahadevia informed Bal Thakura of the emergency: at the instigation of a Hindu and under the order of a Hindu municipal officer, a Hindu temple of Lord Viṣṇu was being demolished. Mr. Thakura in turn informed the municipal commissioner, who denied knowing of any order to demolish the temple and who in turn phoned the local ward office that had sent out the demolition squad. The ward office sent a man to stop the demolition. The officer arrived around two p.m., just as the demolition squad had cut through the last pillars and were dismantling the roof above the Deities. The order to stop the demolition was given to the ward officer in charge, who then stopped the demolition squad.

Prabhupāda was in Calcutta at the time of the attack, and when the devotees reached him by phone, he told them to organize the local ISKCON sympathizers and life members and protest the attack by mass publicity. They should also expose the persons responsible. This would be very effective against Mrs. N. and her party.

Prabhupada mentioned various life members he thought would help. Mr. Sada Jiwatlal, the head of the Hindu Viswa Parishad, should help with publicity, since his organization was a defender of Hindu dharma and was meant for handling such cases as this. Mr. Sethi should help in preventing further violence. This episode, Prabhupāda said, had been part of Kṛṣṇa's plan; the devotees should not be afraid.

The next morning a photo of the demolished temple appeared on the front page of the *Free Press Journal* with the headline "UNAUTHORIZED TEMPLE DEMOLISHED BY MUNICIPAL AUTHORITIES."

Devotees began counteracting the bad publicity. Mr. Sada Jiwatlal turned his downtown office into an ISKCON office, and he and the devotees began the campaign. Despite the unfavorable propaganda, many Indians were shocked at the violence, and the municipal corporation unanimously condemned those officials responsible for the attack on a Hindu temple. Devotees, working from six a.m. to nine p.m. at Sada Jiwatlal's office, phoned the newspapers, wrote letters and circulars, and contacted possible sympathizers.

Mr. Vinoda Gupta, a member of the Jan-Sangh political party, which favored maintaining India's Hindu culture, joined with Kartikeya Mahadevia and others to form a "Save the Temple" committee. Mr. Gupta published his own leaflet declaring ISKCON to be a bona fide Hindu organization. As Girirāja met with and elicited the support of government officials, many of Bombay's leading citizens, appreciating the authenticity of the Hare Kṛṣṇa movement, began to show sympathy and offer assistance.

Thus the plan of Mrs. N. and her lawyers backfired. Although they had been thinking they were dealing with only a mere handful of young foreigners, they soon found themselves facing many of Bombay's most influential citizens.

Śrīla Prabhupāda predicted that the results would be positive. A few days after the incident he wrote:

> The demolition of our temple by the municipality has strengthened our position. The municipality standing committee has condemned the hasty action of the municipality, and has agreed to reconstruct the shed at their cost. Not only that, the temporary construction shall continue to stay until the court decision is there as to who is the proprietor of the land. Under the circumstances we should immediately reconstruct the Deity shed. Barbed wire fencing should be immediately done to cover the naked land. And if possible, immediately in front of the Deity shed, a temporary pandal should be constructed, with our materials. If it is so done, then I can go to Bombay and begin Bhagawat Parayana, to continue until the court decision is there. This is my desire.

The devotees began to see the entire course of events as Kṛṣṇa's mercy, since many life members were now rendering valuable service to Prabhupāda and Lord Kṛṣṇa. In the past Prabhupāda had stayed in the homes of many life members, preaching to them and their families, convincing them of his sincerity and of the noble aims of his movement. These friends and members—like Bhagubai Patel, Beharilal Khandelwala, Brijratan Mohatta, Dr. C. Bali, and others—were acting not simply out of Hindu sentiment but out of deep respect and affection for Prabhupāda.

Girirāja, working with Sada Jiwatlal, tried to convince the municipal council to authorize the rebuilding of the temple structure. While doing so, however, he discovered that Mrs. N. had that very day (a Friday) filed for a court injunction preventing ISKCON from rebuilding. Justice Nain told Girirāja that he did not want to grant Mrs. N.'s request and that he would hear the devotees' case on the following Monday. This meant that the devotees had from Saturday morning to Monday morning, two days, to rebuild the temple.

The devotees reasoned that, although they had no actual permission to rebuild the temple, there was as yet no law to stop them. If Justice Nain ruled against them, then to rebuild would be very difficult. They decided, therefore, to use the weekend to rebuild. Mr. Lal, a former contractor, helped arrange materials: bricks, mortar, asbestos sheets. Mr. Sethi offered a crew of laborers. At eight p.m. on Friday the masons began their work, continuing throughout the night despite the rain. And on Monday morning, when the judge learned of the new temple, he declared, "What is built is built. No one can destroy the temple."

When Prabhupāda heard the news, he considered it a complete victory. The temple had been rebuilt, and public opinion was swinging strongly in ISKCON's favor.

* * *

Māyāpur
June 1, 1973

Although the Māyāpur building was not yet completed, Prabhupāda had come there to reside. He took two adjoining rooms, one as his study and one as his bedroom, on the second floor. Meanwhile, construction work continued in the temple room and in other parts of the building. On his first day there, a storm struck, with massive black clouds and high winds. The storm was brief, however, and damage was minimal.

> I have just now come to Mayapur and am very hopeful to regain my strength and health on account of being in this transcendental atmosphere. Every moment we are passing here in great delight.

In the evening the temple *pūjārī*, Jananivāsa, would come to Prabhupāda's room with a clay pot of red coals and frankincense and fan the frankincense until the room was filled with smoke. This was to drive out insects, but Prabhupāda also considered it purifying.

Although he was sometimes disturbed by the workers' hammering, he found the atmosphere otherwise peaceful. Only a few devotees were staying there, and Prabhupāda gave his attention to translating or to speaking with guests and to the devotees in charge of developing his Māyāpur center. He would express his desires especially to Bhavānanda Māhāraja and Jayapatāka Mahārāja, and worked his will through them.

The devotees living in the building with Prahupāda considered themselves menial servants in Prabhupāda's personal house. Of course, all the buildings in ISKCON belonged to Prabhupāda, yet in Māyāpur that sense was intensified. Generally the devotees in each particular center would raise money to support their center, but Prabhupāda personally took charge of getting funds for Māyāpur. He had begun a Māyāpur-Vṛndāvana Trust Fund of donations from his disciples and interest from bonds and security deposits. If money was misspent, energy misused, or the building damaged in any way, Prabhupāda would become very concerned. Now that he was personally on the scene, he often walked about, giving detailed instructions and demanding that discrepancies be corrected. The pink and reddish building was like a huge transcendental ship, and Śrīla Prabhupāda, as captain, would walk the wide verandas, giving strict orders to all mates for keeping everything shipshape.

Prabhupāda felt affection and deep gratitude for those devotees dedicating their lives to the Māyāpur project. One night he called Bhavānanda to his room and began asking him about the devotees. Suddenly Prabhupāda began crying. "I know it is difficult for all you Western boys and girls," he said. "You are so dedicated, serving here in my mission. I know you cannot even get *prasādam*. When I think that you cannot even get milk and that you have given up your opulent life to come here and you do not complain, I am very much indebted to all of you."

Bhavānanda: *The marble workers lived in some* chātāi *houses right near the construction site. There was a hand pump just outside the building, and that's where we took our bath and where the workers got the water for the cement. Some distance off were two toilets—one for the men, one for the women. It was just two holes in the ground, and each hole surrounded by a* chātāi *wall. The storms and the rain would come, and we would have to sludge through the mud in the fields to go to the toilets. There were snakes all over the place. It was wild! It was a construction site. No one lives on a construction site, but we did. Śrīla Prabhupāda made us move there. It was good for us. No bathrooms, nothing—just open floors with concrete.*

Although the devotees endured the austerities of living at the Māyāpur center construction site, they sometimes felt it was too difficult. But Śrīla Prabhupāda never considered it too difficult, and he would encourage the devotees. "Māyāpur is so wonderful. You can live on the air and water alone."

The surrounding grounds were rice fields, and to get to the temple building from the entrance of the property—a distance of more than two hundred yards—devotees would have to walk on paths made by ridges of earth that separated one rice field from another. The kitchen, which was made of tarpaulin and bamboo, was located near the entrance to the property.

The devotees had to live without electricity much of the time, since the power supply was often cut off. They would use kerosene lamps at night, and Prabhupāda said the lamps should be taken apart every day, the wicks trimmed, and the glass washed. "In the future," he said, "you should grow castor plants and crush the seeds and take the oil for burning."

Prabhupāda told the devotees how to build simple dwellings. He also wanted them to build a wall with a gate along the front of the property. They should build small rooms—*hutments*, he called them—against the wall. Devotees could stay in these simple cottages. They should plant coconut and banana trees.

Even with the building incomplete, many guests were coming, especially to talk with Prabhupāda, who patiently spent many hours each day speaking about Kṛṣṇa consciousness with guests who came to inquire about his movement or who came only to talk about themselves and their own philosophy. Sometimes he would remark that an individual had wasted his time, but he never stopped anyone from seeing him. One wealthy Hindu man, Mr. Brijratan Mohatta, and his wife, a daughter of multimillionaire R. D. Birla, visited Prabhupāda from Calcutta. Śrīla Prabhupāda took care in properly hosting his guests, and he personally reviewed the menu and briefed his disciples on serving Mr. Mohatta and his wife. Offering *prasādam* was an important part of the Vaiṣṇava's etiquette, and Śrīla Prabhupāda always stressed that the devotees immediately offer *prasādam* to visitors.

"You should always be able to offer water, hot *purīs* and eggplant *bhājī* (fried eggplant), and sweets," Prabhupāda said. Even when guests appeared shy, Prabhupāda would insist they take a full meal. Mrs. Mohatta, even though a member of one of the wealthiest families in India, was satisfied with the simple hospitality Śrīla Prabhupāda and his disciples offered. The room she and her husband stayed in was unfinished—the slate floors hadn't been polished, and construction work was going on all around—and the devotees could only offer them a mattress on the floor with a pillow; yet they appeared to be quite satisfied and appreciative.

Bhavānanda: *Śrīla Prabhupāda introduced us to many of the details of Indian culture at Māyāpur. In 1970, in Los Angeles, he had asked me to sew sheets together to make a covering for the rug in his room. And then he had gotten down on his hands and knees right next to me, and we had smoothed out the wrinkles in the sheet.*

So he had us do that same thing in Māyāpur, where we put

mattresses from one end of the room to the other with bolster pillows against the wall. "Now you have white sheet covers," he said, "and you change these every day." When Bengali gentlemen visited Śrīla Prabhupāda in his room, they would sit on these mattresses around the edge of the room, their backs against the bolster pillows.

It was very aristocratic. The whole mood was that he was the mahant, *the master of the house, the* ācārya. *But also the aristocratic Bengali gentlemen saw that he was reestablishing the old aristocratic mood from the early 1900s or 1920s. It was from Prabhupāda's old days with the Mullik family, and it was rapidly dwindling. At that time you couldn't find a semblance of the old culture anywhere, because all those families had become degraded, and their wealth was gone.*

During this summer visit, Prabhupāda further revealed his vision for ISKCON's Māyāpur development. The devotees were already aware that the plan was vast and would cost millions of dollars. They now had one building, but this was only the beginning. In the total plan, this building was almost insignificant. Prabhupāda spoke about a colossal temple, its great dome rising above a transcendental city. This Mayapur Chandrodaya Mandir would house the greatest planetarium in the world, depicting the universe as it is described in the Vedic literature.

To execute such a project, Prabhupāda wanted to train his disciples in the Vedic arts, now dying in Bengal. Bhaktisiddhānta Sarasvatī had been greatly interested in using dioramas to depict the *līlā* of Kṛṣṇa and Lord Caitanya, and now Prabhupāda wanted his own disciples to learn the art by studying under local Māyāpur artists.

In June Baradrāja, Ādideva, Mūrti, and Īśāna arrived to begin to learn the art of doll-making. Prabhupāda also wanted a disciple to learn to make *mṛdaṅgas,* and a potter began coming every day to teach Īśāna how to mold and fire the clay shells. The devotees converted Prabhupāda's original straw cottage into a workshop, and Prabhupāda began inviting other disciples to come to Māyāpur.

> Mayapur is already wonderful, being the transcendental birthplace of Lord Krishna. By utilizing Western talents to develop this place, certainly it will become unique in the world.

The Māyāpur city, Prabhupāda said, would be the fulfillment of the desires of the previous *ācāryas.* The city would grow to a population of fifty thousand and would become the spiritual capital of the world. With its gigantic temple in the center and separate quarters for *brāhmaṇas, kṣatriyas, vaiśyas,* and *śūdras,* the city would be a model for all other cities. The day would come when the world's cities would be ruined, and humanity would take refuge in cities modeled after Māyāpur. The development of Māyāpur would mark the beginning of a Kṛṣṇa conscious world. Thus the influence of Śrī Caitanya Mahāprabhu would increase, and His prediction would manifest: "In every town and village My name will be chanted."

Prabhupāda said that Māyāpur should eventually become more easily accessible—by bridge from Navadvīpa, by motor launch up the Ganges from Calcutta, and from all parts by air. In Bengal millions were by birth followers of Lord Caitanya, and they would recognize and take up Kṛṣṇa consciousness as the pure form of their own culture. There is a saying: What Bengal does, the rest of India follows. So if Bengal became reformed and purified by the Kṛṣṇa conscious example of American Vaiṣṇavas, then all India would follow. And when all India becomes Kṛṣṇa conscious, the whole world would follow. "I have given you the kingdom of God," Prabhupāda said to his Māyāpur managers. "Now take it, develop it, and enjoy it."

* * *

June 27, 1973

From Māyāpur Śrīla Prabhupāda went to Calcutta. He wrote to Tamāla Kṛṣṇa Goswami,

> . . . There is a suggestion by Shyamsundar that I may go to London for meeting very important men there in the new house

> given us by George. . . . But I want to make some definite settlement of Bombay affairs before I return to Europe or America. If there is a suitable place for me to stay for a few days in Bombay I can go there immediately and from there I may go to London.

While considering his itinerary, Prabhupāda passed some days in the Calcutta temple on Albert Road. He was very free about allowing people to see him, and his room was often filled with local Bengalis as well as his own disciples, seated on the white sheet before him. In the evenings he would go, even when it meant riding for miles through congested parts of the city, to spend an hour in someone's home, preaching Kṛṣṇa consciousness.

Śrīla Prabhupāda's sister, Bhavatarini (known as Pisīmā to Prabhupāda's disciples), would also visit the Calcutta temple to see her beloved brother and, as usual, to cook for him. One day, however, a few hours after eating her *kachaurīs,* Prabhupāda felt sharp pains in his stomach. He closed his doors and went to bed. His followers became very concerned. When his servant, Śrutakīrti, came into the room, he found him tossing.

"Śrīla Prabhupāda, what's wrong?"

"My stomach," Prabhupāda replied. "That coconut *kachaurī*—it was not cooked."

The seizure continued all night, and several devotees continually massaged Prabhupāda's body, especially his stomach. But with every breath he would moan. Pisīmā was standing by, but Prabhupāda's disciples feared her presence, thinking she might want to cook something else for him, even in his illness.

Prabhupāda asked that the picture of Lord Nṛsiṁha be taken from the altar and put beside his bed. Some devotees feared that Prabhupāda might be about to pass away. The next morning, when the illness continued, the devotees called for the local *kavirāja* (Āyur-Vedic doctor).

The old *kavirāja* came and diagnosed Prabhupāda's illness as severe blood dysentery. He left medicine, but it was ineffectual. Later, when Prabhupāda called Bhavānanda to his room and requested fried *purīs* with a little *paṭala* (an Indian vegetable similar to a small squash) and salt, Bhavānanda protested; such fried foods would be the worst thing for him. Prabhupāda said that this was the blood dysentery cure his mother had given during his childhood. He then called for his sister and, speaking to her in Bengali, told her to prepare *purīs* and *paṭala*. A few hours after taking the food, Prabhupāda again called Bhavānanda; he was feeling better. "My mother was right," he remarked.

A lengthy telegram arrived from Śyāmasundara, glorifying the preaching opportunities that awaited Prabhupāda in London, where he would be picked up at the airport in a helicopter and flown to the main event—the greatest Ratha-yātrā ever held. The parade would proceed down Picadilly Lane, climaxing under a large pavilion at Trafalgar Square.

"Let me strike while the iron is hot," he said. "I think that is an English maxim. If you do that, then you can keep the iron in shape. In the West, people are fed up. So we want to give them spiritual enlightenment."

Prabhupāda had immediately convinced his disciples with his forceful statements. "There are two misleading theories in the West," he continued. "One is that life comes from matter, and the other is that there is no life after death—you can just enjoy this life. They say everything is matter. So as this Kṛṣṇa consciousness movement grows, the Communists will be curbed down. People say they are trying for unity, but they have no brains to see how this will achieve unity. They have formed a big complicated League of Nations and now United Nations, but they all fail. But this simple method of Ratha-yātrā—all over the world it is spreading. *Jagannātha* means 'Lord of the universe.' So Lord Jagannātha is now international God, through our ISKCON. Therefore, I want to go to the West and give them these things."

Although Prabhupāda appeared physically unfit to immediately fly to London to the active preaching that awaited him, his disciples submitted, accepting this as another miracle by Kṛṣṇa.

* * *

London
July 7, 1973

Paravidha: *It was Ratha-yātrā day. I saw Prabhupāda coming into the temple, and he didn't look very strong. I was really amazed, but I could understand that his strength was something spiritual.*

Dhruvanātha: *At the parade site we were waiting to receive Śrīla Prabhupāda at Marble Arch, where the procession starts. The* vyāsāsana *was nicely decorated, and everybody was expecting Prabhupāda simply to sit on his* vyāsāsana *on the cart and just ride through the streets, just as he had done in the other Ratha-yātrās. So it was to our great amazement and joy that when Prabhupāda came, he refused to sit on the* vyāsāsana. *He indicated that he would dance and lead the procession.*

Yogeśvara: *They brought stairs up so Prabhupāda could mount the* ratha *cart and sit down on the* vyāsāsana. *But he waved them off and just started walking with the chariots, leading the dancing.*

Dhīraśānta: *I twisted my ankle and couldn't walk, so I rode on the cart. Therefore I could see Prabhupāda very clearly. Revatīnandana Mahārāja was chanting into the microphone from the cart, but after about fifteen minutes of the procession Prabhupāda told the devotees to tell Revatīnandana Mahārāja and the others to come down and lead the* kīrtana *in the street with him.*

Revatīnandana: *When Prabhupāda saw his* vyāsāsana *on the cart, he said, "No, I am just a devotee. I will go in the procession." We had a big, great* kīrtana. *Haṁsadūta led, I led, Śyāmasundara led—different devotees traded off, leading this fantastic* kīrtana. *And Prabhupāda was right in the middle of the* kīrtana *with his* karatālas *the whole time. He was dancing back and forth and jumping up and down and dancing.*

Rohiṇī-nandana: *The cart was going quite slowly. Prabhupāda walked about twenty or thirty yards ahead of the cart, leading the procession. Meanwhile the* kīrtana *was coming from the* ratha *cart through microphones. Prabhupāda called them all down, and he got them all around himself, and they were chanting Hare Kṛṣṇa. Every so often he would turn around and raise both his arms very majestically in the air and say, "Jaya Jagannātha!" Sometimes we would get a little further ahead, so then he would turn around and wait for the cart to come on. Sometimes he was dancing, and sometimes he would stand, raising his hands in the air.*

Śāradīyā dāsī: *Prabhupāda would dance, and then after a few feet he would turn around and look up at the deities with his arms raised. Then he would dance for a few moments, meditating on the deities, and then he would turn around and go on. In this way he danced the entire way. The devotees held hands in a circle around him to protect him from the crowd. It was a wonderful, transcendental affair. Prabhupāda was looking up at the deities, and all the devotees were behind him.*

Sudurjaya: *Prabhupāda surprised us. We didn't know if he was sick or not, feeling weak and dizzy or not. Sometimes he looked very ill, and sometimes he looked like an eighteen-year-old boy. He surprised us. He had his cane in his hand but raised it in the air as he danced. After a while, Śyāmasundara came up to me and said, "Listen, he's not going to make it. Prabhupāda is very ill. I want you to follow in a car. Be within thirty seconds' reach so we can put Prabhupāda in the car immediately." Prabhupāda was going down Park Lane, and from time to time they couldn't pull the cart fast enough to keep up with him. He would turn back, raise his hands, and say, "Haribol!" Several times he did this. He was going so fast that he had to wait. The devotees were dancing, the weather was beautiful, and the crowd was wonderful.*

Dhruvanātha: *The passersby were rooted to the spot, looking at Prabhupāda. A man of that age simply dancing and jumping in the air like a young boy was the most amazing sight! And then every five minutes or so Prabhupāda would turn around and look toward Jagannātha. The devotees would clear the way so no one blocked his sight, and he had a perfect view of Jagannātha, Balarāma, and Subhadrā. But after a while the police came and motioned that we couldn't keep stopping like this. We had to keep the whole thing going, because the traffic jams were becoming critical. Devotees were crying and chanting and dancing, and there was much commotion.*

Śrutakīrti: *When Prabhupāda was dancing, the bobbies kept on coming up and looking for someone official. Finally they came to me and said, "You'll have to tell your leader to sit down. He's causing too much of a disturbance. Everyone is becoming wild, and we can't control the crowd, you know." So I said, "All right." But I didn't say anything to Prabhupāda.*

So then they came again and said, "You must tell him he'll have to sit down." So I said, "All right," and I tapped Prabhupāda. The whole time he had been in ecstasy, dancing before the cart and encouraging everyone else to dance. He would motion with his hands and encourage the devotees to keep dancing. He kept the momentum of the festival. So I said, "Prabhupāda, the policemen want you to sit down. They say you are creating havoc in the parade." Prabhupāda looked at me, turned, and kept on. He completely ignored it and kept on dancing. And they couldn't do anything. Prabhupāda wouldn't stop, and the police wouldn't say anything to him.

Paravidha: *I was distributing* Back to Godhead *magazines along the whole parade route. I was exhausted, and I was having a lot of trouble keeping up with the procession. But Prabhupāda was just there, and he was dancing like a young boy. I was amazed at his spiritual energy.*

Dhruvanātha: *When we came to Picadilly Circus, Prabhupāda suddenly stopped the whole procession. Picadilly Circus, of course, was just packed with people. For about three minutes Prabhupāda stopped the procession and just danced and danced with the devotees all around him.*

Rohiṇī-nandana: *When we got to Picadilly Circus, Prabhupāda really started to dance. He was leaping off the ground. The cart was stopped. It was very similar, actually, to the description in the* Caitanya-caritāmṛta *of how Lord Caitanya would lead the Ratha-yātrā procession. So the cart was stopped, and then Prabhupāda would wait for it to catch up.*

Yogeśvara: *When we finally arrived at Trafalgar Square*

and Prabhupāda saw the big tent and the other arrangements the devotees had made, he held up his hands again. He had been dancing and walking the entire route of the parade. It must have been at least an hour that he had been walking and dancing—all the way from Hyde Park to Trafalgar Square.

Rohiṇī-nandana: *When Prabhupāda got to Trafalgar Square, he immediately sat down on the plinth of Nelson's Column on a little* vyāsāsana *and delivered a lecture about the holy name of Kṛṣṇa. This was directly after his marathon of chanting and dancing.*

The next day's papers carried favorable news coverage of the festival, and Prabhupāda wrote of it to a disciple in Los Angeles.

> You will be glad to know the Ratha-yatra in London was very successful. The Daily Guardian had a picture on the front page of our cart and stated that we were competition to the monument in memory of Lord Nelson in Trafalgar Square. My health is good and I am taking daily walks and speaking at the class in the morning.

In another letter Prabhupāda wrote:

> Our festival here was very well received and I was so much encouraged by the whole thing that I was able to walk and dance the entire way from Hyde Park to Trafalgar Square.

The devotees had invited many prominent British citizens to meet Śrīla Prabhupāda, and the responses were good. Economist Ernst Schumacher promised to visit, as did philosopher Sir Alfred J. Ayer. When Śyāmasundara informed Prabhupāda that Mr. Ayer was well known, Prabhupāda replied, "What is his philosophy?"

"Well," Śyāmasundara replied, "he doesn't believe in the existence of God."

"I will give him evidence," Prabhupāda replied. "I will ask him what he means by 'the existence of God.' I will ask him to make a list of the deficiencies of God's existence." Prabhupāda liked to meet with philosophical men and "corner them and defeat them."

Historian Arnold Toynbee was old and invalid; therefore Prabhupāda agreed to visit him at his residence. Interested in discussing life after death, Dr. Toynbee asked Prabhupāda about karma. Most people, he said, were afraid of death. Prabhupāda agreed and added that according to a certain astrologer, one of India's recent leaders had taken birth as a dog. "So they are afraid they will go down," he said. When Toynbee asked if karma could be changed, Prabhupāda replied yes, but only by bhakti, devotion to God.

George Harrison approached Prabhupāda in a submissive mood similar to that of Prabhupāda's disciples. Prabhupāda and George took *prasādam* together, a special lunch of *samosās, halavā,* vegetables, sour cream, and *purīs.* While they were enjoying the *prasādam,* Prabhupāda mentioned that certain Vṛndāvana *paṇḍās* (professional guides at a holy place) eat too much. Once one ate so much that he was practically dying, but he assured his son, "At least I am dying from eating, and not from starving. To die of starvation is unglorious." Prabhupāda smiled as he talked with George, gratefully acknowledging his donation of the Manor. "Have you seen my room?" Prabhupāda asked. "It is actually your house, but my room."

"No," George protested, preferring the mood of a humble disciple, "it is Kṛṣṇa's house and your room."

When George confided to Prabhupāda that by taking to Kṛṣṇa consciousness he was losing friends, Prabhupāda told him not to worry. He read to George from the *Gītā,* where Kṛṣṇa explains that He can be known only by devotional service.

"In the future," said George, "ISKCON will be so large it will require executive management."

Prabhupāda: "I have divided the world into twelve zones with twelve representatives. As long as they keep to the spiritual principles, Kṛṣṇa will help them."

Before leaving, George assured Prabhupāda that he would help him increase his temples. Later Prabhupāda commented, "George is getting inward hope from Kṛṣṇa."

Through George Harrison, another famous pop singer and musician, Donovan, was drawn to come and see the renowned leader of the Hare Kṛṣṇa movement. Donovan, accompanied by a musician friend and their two girl friends in miniskirts, sat in awkward silence before Prabhupāda. Prabhupāda spoke: "There is a verse in the *Vedas* that says music is the highest form of education." And he began to explain how a musician could serve Kṛṣṇa. "You should do like your friend George," Prabhupāda said. "We will give you the themes, and you can write the songs." Prabhupāda said that anything, even money, could be used in the service of Kṛṣṇa.

"But money is material," Donovan's girl friend interrupted.

"What do you know what is material and what is spiritual?" Prabhupāda said. He turned to Donovan: "Do you understand?" Donovan humbly replied that he was thickheaded but trying. Donovan's girl friend then leaned over and whispered something in his ear, whereupon Donovan stood up and said, "Well, we have to go now." Prabhupāda insisted that at least they first take some *prasādam.*

As soon as the guests left, Prabhupāda and his disciples began to laugh. Prabhupāda said, "She was thinking . . . " and he encouraged his disciples to finish the sentence.

"Yes," said Yogeśvara, "she was thinking that if Kṛṣṇa gets him, then she will lose him."

Prabhupāda so much liked preaching to important guests that he wanted to continue doing so wherever he traveled. "Wherever I shall go now," Prabhupāda wrote in a letter to a disciple, "this policy of important men being invited to talk with me about our Kṛṣṇa consciousness movement should be implemented."

A month passed at the Manor, and still several weeks remained before Janmāṣṭamī and the Deity installation. So when Bhagavān requested Prabhupāda to come for a visit to Paris and install Rādhā-Kṛṣṇa Deities, Prabhupāda agreed.

* * *

Paris
August 9, 1973

The devotees had arranged an official City Hall reception for Śrīla Prabhupāda. In the presence of the mayor of Paris and his government entourage, Śrīla Prabhupāda said that if the government leaders do not teach the citizens genuine God consciousness, then they are not responsible leaders. Reporting this talk in the next day's paper, a news writer stated that the swami even criticized Napoleon Bonaparte.

Bhagavān: *We had just moved into our new temple at 4 Rue Le Sueur, Paris, and we had received forty-eight-inch Rādhā and Kṛṣṇa Deities. Prabhupāda had Pradyumna chanting the* mantras *and pouring the substances on the Deities while Prabhupāda himself looked on from his* vyāsāsana, *giving directions. I was assisting, and at one point I turned around and saw Śrīla Prabhupāda standing right next to me, taking the substances in his own hands and smearing them over the lotuslike face of Śrīmatī Rādhārāṇī. After the Deities were installed on the altar, Śrīla Prabhupāda came up and offered the* ārati, *and I assisted him by handing him the articles.*

After the installation we went up to Śrīla Prabhupāda's room and very anxiously requested him to please give a name for the Deities. He sat back in his chair and said that the Deities will be known as Rādhā-Paris-īśvara. He then went on to say that in India people look to England for education and to Paris for sense gratification. He began to laugh and said that Kṛṣṇa has come to Paris in order to get some gopīs, *some French girls, because the faces of the women in Paris are considered the most beautiful. "Rādhārāṇī is so beautiful," Prabhupāda said, "just like a Paris girl. And Kṛṣṇa has come here to find out this most beautiful of all the* gopīs. *So He is Paris-īśvara."*

* * *

Śrīla Prabhupāda arrived in London, where he received an emergency phone call from Bombay. Girirāja wanted him to come and personally settle with Mrs. N. the purchase of the Juhu land. Girirāja had consulted a new lawyer, Mr. Bakhil, who felt that Prabhupāda must be present for there to be a settlement. Another ISKCON lawyer, Mr. Chandawal, also advised that Śrīla Prabhupāda come immediately to Bombay. Girirāja, therefore, had telephoned Prabhupāda, begging him to please come and settle the matter with Mrs. N. once and for all. Prabhupāda agreed. He would remain in London until Janmāṣṭamī. Then he would return to Bombay.

Bombay
September 15, 1973

The day after his arrival, Śrīla Prabhupāda met with Mrs. N.'s solicitors and heard their offers. The situation had begun to look hopeful, and yet the conclusion eluded them. Mrs. N. had become changed by the public reaction to her attempt to demolish the temple. If Prabhupāda would pay the full balance of twelve lakhs of rupees for the land in one payment, she told her lawyer, she would agree. Prabhupāda was agreeable, but did not want to arrange to collect his money until he was certain that Mrs. N. was actually serious.

Mr. Asnani, a Bombay lawyer and ISKCON life member, regularly met with Mrs. N., persuading her to cooperate with Prabhupāda. Her lawyers concurred. Yet after Prabhupāda had been in Bombay for several weeks, no meeting with Mrs. N. had taken place. Once Mr. Asnani went to bring Mrs. N. to meet with Prabhupāda, but she was not feeling well. Day after day, Mr. Asnani would tell Prabhupāda, "Mrs. N. will come tomorrow." Prabhupāda became disappointed at the procrastination, and seeing this, his secretaries told Mr. Asnani that although they knew he meant well, they were inclined to have their other lawyers handle the case. Mr. Asnani asked for another forty-eight hours to close the deal and execute the conveyance.

Mrs. N. was at her other home, where she had just recovered from her illness, when Mr. Asnani visited. "Mataji," he begged, "my Guru Mahārāja is leaving tomorrow. If you don't come tonight, the problem with the land will go on another year." Mrs. N. agreed, and around nine p.m. she and Mr. Asnani arrived at the home of Mr. Bogilal Patel, where Śrīla Prabhupāda was holding a program of *kīrtana* and *Bhāgavata* discourses. Prabhupāda was on the roof preparing to lecture, but hearing that Mrs. N. had arrived, he interrupted the meeting and came down to his room to talk with her. They talked briefly, and Prabhupāda excused himself and returned to the roof to lecture.

Around midnight, he returned to his room again, accompanied by his servant and secretary. Mrs. N. was still waiting. She burst into tears and bowed at Prabhupāda's feet. "I am sorry for everything I've done," she sobbed. "Please forgive me." She promised to do whatever Prabhupāda wanted.

Prabhupāda looked at her compassionately and understood her heart. "You are just like my daughter," he said. "Don't worry. I will take care of you. I will see to all of your needs for the rest of your life." And Prabhupāda said he still accepted the very terms she had proposed: that he pay the remaining balance of twelve lakhs plus fifty thousand rupees compensation for the delay.

At six-thirty on the evening of November 1, Śrīla Prabhupāda was seated at his low desk between two windows, his back against the wall. Mrs. N. and her lawyers, the registrar, Mr. Asnani, Mr. and Mrs. Sethi, and about eight devotees were also present, and the full room grew warm and stuffy. Mrs. N. sat at Prabhupāda's right as the registrar prepared the papers for signing. Śrīla Prabhupāda sat gravely. The room was silent except for the sound of papers rustling and a pen's scratching. Preparing and signing the conveyance papers took more than twenty minutes. Prabhupāda paid Mrs. N., who then signed the conveyance. The land was legally ISKCON's.

Girirāja: *The room was hushed during the signing, and everyone felt as if a momentous event was taking place—just as if two great world powers were signing a treaty. After Mrs. N. signed the document, everyone silently watched the papers being passed. She started to cry. Tamāla Kṛṣṇa*

Goswami asked her why she was crying, and Mrs. N. replied that just that day Mr. Matar had come and told her he had found a buyer for the land for many more lakhs than we were paying. Actually, as we were watching Mrs. N., we were thinking that she must be remembering all the events that had taken place, the wrongs she had done, the death of her husband. It was very intense, like a combination of months of struggling. So for Prabhupāda, the devotees, and Prabhupāda's well-wishers their dreams and desires and efforts over the past many years were being fulfilled.

Śrīla Prabhupāda asked that the devotees inform the newspapers, and he invited everyone into the hall outside his room for a feast. Mats were rolled out in two lines, and devotees brought leaf plates and placed them in front of everyone. The devotees began serving the various dishes to the two rows of seated guests.

Prabhupāda was standing. "Now let us start," he said, as he supervised the serving. The devotees had prepared several courses: rice, *dāl,* many varieties of *pakorās* (such as potato, cauliflower, and eggplant), potato *sabjī, papaḍs, burfī,* wet cauliflower *sabjī, laḍḍus, camcam* (a milk sweet), vermicelli *khīr, halavā,* and a lime drink. It was a festive and happy occasion.

Mrs. Warrier (a tenant on Hare Kṛṣṇa Land): *The devotees were all saying "Jaya!" after the signing, and all of them were very happy. Then Prabhupāda gave a lecture about the Bombay project. He gave an idea to all the people of how it would be all marble. Some were asking how it would be possible for everything to be marble, and Prabhupāda explained that it was possible and could be done. He was visualizing the project and everyone was thrilled to hear the way he was describing it. It would be like one of the seven wonders of the world. People would be attracted from all over to come and see it. It would be a landmark in Bombay. Prabhupāda explained the whole project as if he saw it in his mind's eye, and he said that after it was constructed it will be more than what we could visualize. It would be fantastic!*

Śrīla Prabhupāda on the Bowery, photographed by Fred McDarrah of *The Village Voice*, June 1965.

The street entrance to 94 Bowery.

26 Second Avenue: *"It had been a curiosity shop, and someone had painted the words Matchless Gifts over the window."*

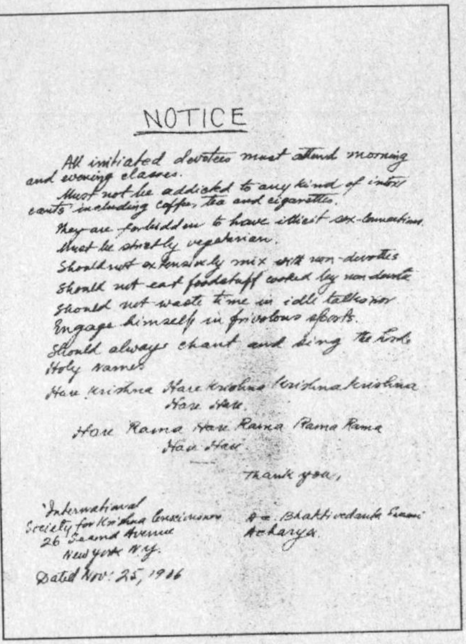

NOTICE

All initiated devotees must attend morning and evening classes.

Must not be addicted to any kind of intoxicants including coffee, tea and cigarettes.

They are forbidden to have illicit sex-connections.

Must be strictly vegetarian.

Should not extensively mix with non-devotees

Should not eat foodstuff cooked by non devotee

Should not waste time in idle talks nor

Engage himself in frivolous sports.

Should always chant and sing the Lord's Holy names.

Hare Krishna Hare Krishna Krishna Krishna
Hare Hare.

Hare Rama Hare Rama Rama Rama
Hare Hare.

Thank you,

International Society for Krishna Consciousness
26 Second Avenue
New York N.Y.

A.C. Bhaktivedanta Swami
Acharya.

Dated Nov: 25, 1966

Śrīla Prabhupāda posted this notice in the storefront.

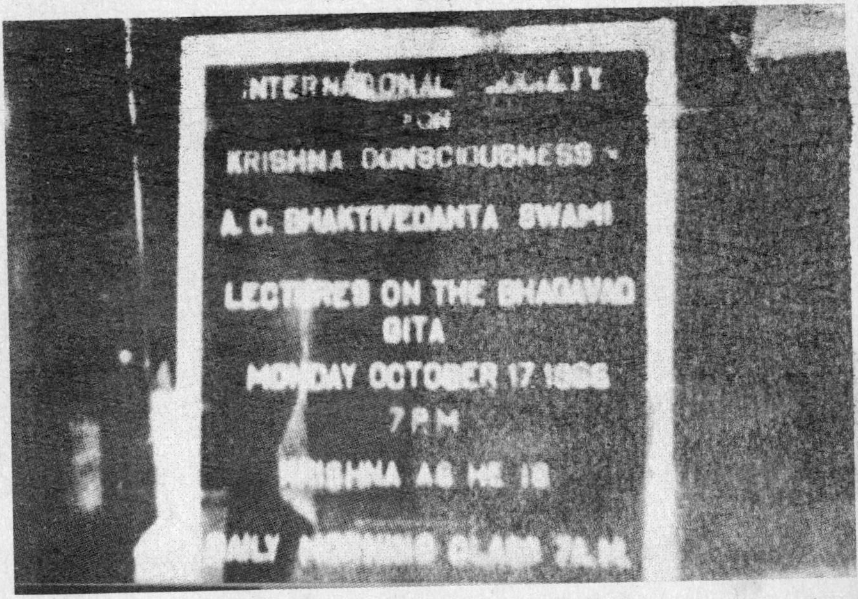
KRISHNA CONSCIOUSNESS
A. C. BHAKTIVEDANTA SWAMI
ON THE BHAGAVAD
GITA
7 PM

One of the Śrīla Prabhupāda's first expenditures at 26 Second Avenue was the purchase of this sign for announcing the classes.

In the storefront Śrīla Prabhupāda taught the ABC's of Kṛṣṇa consciousness, lecturing from *Bhagavad-gītā* and leading the group chanting of Hare Kṛṣṇa.

ı the storefront. From left to right: Dāmodara (with glasses), Jadurāṇi, Gargamuni (playing rum), and Brahmānanda.

The photo from *The New York Times*, October 10, 1966: *"Swami's Flock Chants in Park to Find Ecstasy."*

The East Village Other's coverage of Śrīla Prabhupāda's first kīrtana in Tompkins Square Park.

The poster advertised Śrīla Prabhupāda's appearance at the Mantra-Rock Dance.

Śrīla Prabhupāda on the Lower East side, winter 1966.

rīla Prabhupāda chants in Golden Gate Park.

Śrīla Prabhupāda with some of his San Francisco disciples, in 1968.

Śrīla Prabhupāda outside the television studio in Amsterdam, November 1969.

Installation of Rādhā-Londonīśvara, December 14, 1969.

Gala welcome for Śrīla Prabhupāda in Bombay, September 29, 1970.

Śrīla Prabhupāda's with Sumati Morarji, head of the Scindia Steamship Company.

Śrīla Prabhupāda in front of St. Basil's Cathedral.

Śrīla Prabhupāda walks in Red Square, Moscow, June 1971.

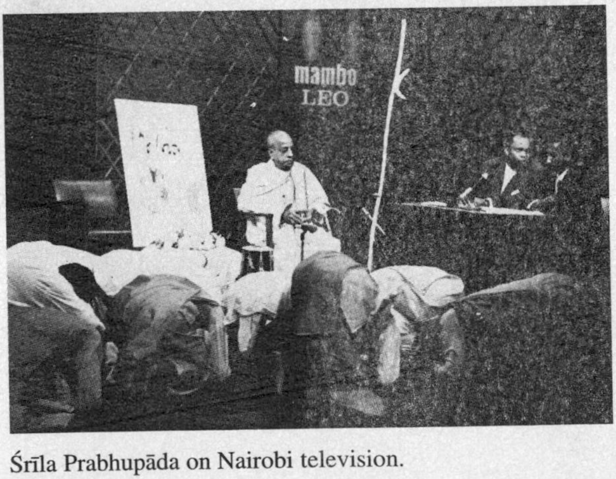

Śrīla Prabhupāda on Nairobi television.

ṛīla Prabhupāda and Karandhara dāsa meet with Dai Nippon executives to discuss the rinting of Prabhupāda's books, Tokyo, April 1972.

rīla Prabhupāda awards *sannyāsa* to Hridayananda, Satsvarūpa, Rupānuga and Bali-ardana, May 1972.

The cornerstone-laying ceremony, Juhu, Bombay, March 1972.

Śrīla Prabhupāda performs an initiation ceremony i the temple room of the Mayapur Chandrodaya Mandir, 1973.

Śrīla Prabhupāda at the London Ratha-yātrā, July 1973.

Śrīla Prabhupāda offers first *āratī* to Śrī Śrī Rādhā-Paris-īśvara after Their installation in Paris, August 1973.

he *āratī* during the installation of Śrī Śrī
ādhā-Gokulānanda at Bhaktivedanta
lanor, England, on Janmāstamī, 1973.

Śrīla Prabhupāda arrives in Geneva, May 31, 1974.

Śrīla Prabhupāda holds informal meetings on the roof of his quarters in Bombay, summer of 1974.

The cornerstone-laying ceremony for the grand temple in Bombay.

Śrīla Prabhupāda with members of the Rādhā-Dāmodara bus party in Chicago, July 1975.

rīla Prabhupāda tours the new offices of the Bhaktivedanta Book Trust in Los Angeles, une 1975.

Śrīla Prabhupāda receives (from left to right) Sushill Muni, Yogi Bhajan and Swami Chidananda, Berkeley, July 1975.

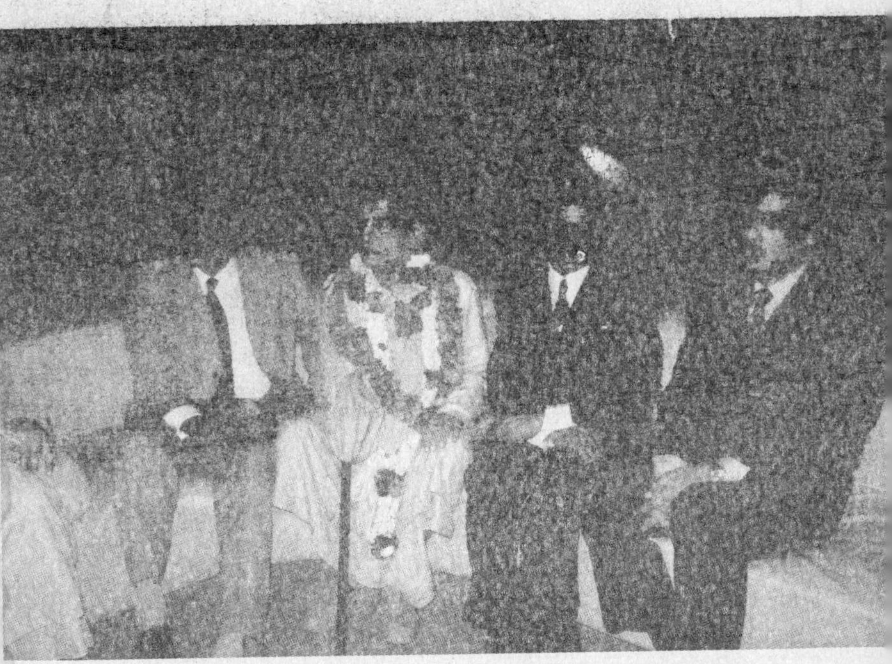

Śrīla Prabhupāda speaks with guests during his tour of Africa, October 1975.

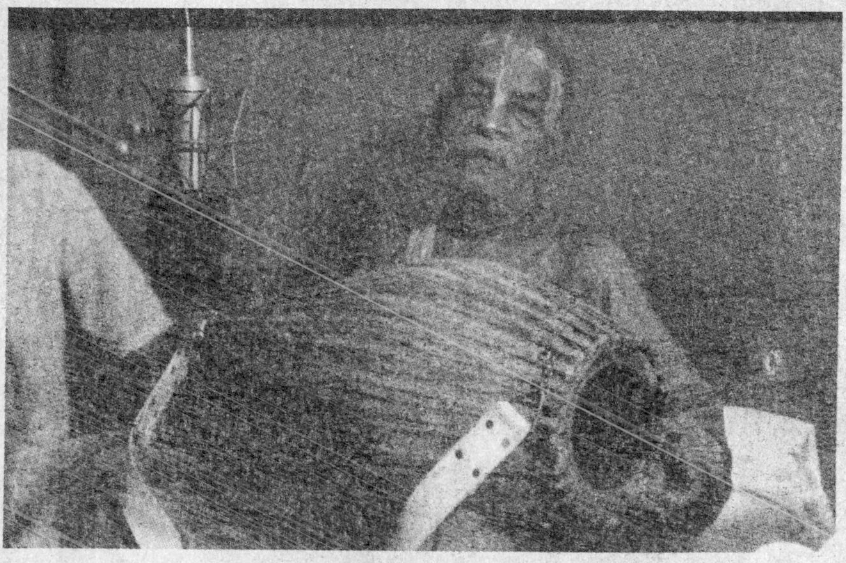

Śrīla Prabhupāda sings *bhajanas* in the Los Angeles recording studio.

Śrīla Prabhupāda passing out cookies in the Los Angeles temple.

Śrīla Prabhupāda examines the newly published Fifth Canto of the *Śrīmad Bhāgavatam.*

hupāda in the last Bombay *paṇḍal,* April 1977.

After the late feast, when everyone had departed, Prabhupāda returned to his room. Leaning back at his desk, he exclaimed, "It was a good fight!"

* * *

Vṛndāvana
March 1974

Śrīla Prabhupāda was meditating on constructing his Krishna-Balaram Mandir. In April of 1972 he had asked his disciple Hans Kielman (now Surabhi), who had drawn the plans for the Bombay center, to execute drawings, basing the design on Indian Renaissance architecture. Prabhupāda liked the Govindajī temple, located near the original Govindajī temple constructed by Rūpa Gosvāmī. He liked its open courtyard surrounded by many arches and its front steps leading up to the Deity *darśana* area. He suggested that some features of the temple be incorporated into his temple. Surabhi, with the assistance of a Vṛndāvana architect, executed the plans, and Prabhupāda approved.

> This will be the grandest temple in Vrindavana. Many high-class gentlemen in Delhi who are also devotees will relish the chance to live with us on weekends and it will be for them just like Vaikuntha. You must construct something wonderful. Otherwise it will be a discredit to you American boys. That will absolve the position of America and India. And this Vrindavana project is one of the most important of ours in ISKCON.

Although Guru dāsa had been careful to keep in touch with Prabhupāda by mail, he had neglected certain important matters in Vṛndāvana, such as digging a well and getting city approval—things Prabhupāda had repeatedly asked for. In the summer of 1972 Prabhupāda wrote,

> From the beginning I said I simply wanted a temple built in Vrindavana just like Govindaji's temple. And there have been

so many letters, but that has not been done. Never mind, now I like that plan of Surabhi's.

To build a temple in Vṛndāvana should not be so difficult, Prabhupāda thought, and he became impatient with the delays. Concerned that the devotees and architects not make the building too costly, he said that they should go ahead with the plans he had approved, even if the building were to be a little cheaper than in the original plan. He was concerned that a competent disciple oversee the work so that ISKCON didn't get cheated.

As early as April of 1972, Prabhupāda had asked that the Deities in Vṛndāvana be Kṛṣṇa and Balarāma. "Kṛṣṇa may be black, Balarāma of white, and the pose in the back of the *Back to Godhead* magazine is very nice." He asked that a sign be put out front announcing, "Shri Krishna Balaram Mandir."

One reason Prabhupāda chose Kṛṣṇa and Balarāma as the presiding Deities was that most of the Vṛndāvana temples were of Rādhā and Kṛṣṇa; ISKCON's temple would be unique in Vṛndāvana. Another reason was that the ISKCON land was located in Ramaṇa-retī, an area of forest and soft sands where Kṛṣṇa and Balarāma had enjoyed Their childhood pastimes five thousand years ago. To celebrate and worship the youthful sports of Kṛṣṇa and Balarāma in Ramaṇa-retī was fitting.

Although thousands of years had passed since Kṛṣṇa's advent in Vṛndāvana, the same atmosphere and many of the same sights and sounds still prevailed. Peacocks ran across the sands or sat on rooftops or in trees. The cooing and chirping of pigeons and cuckoos and the sweep of the parrots' green wings were eternal sounds and sights of the Vṛndāvana forest.

In establishing a temple of Kṛṣṇa and Balarāma, Prabhupāda wanted to offer the peaceful, transcendental atmosphere of Ramaṇa-retī to all people, including visitors from abroad, commuters from Delhi, and his own disciples. Already he had received a letter from a major international travel agency requesting that he provide accommodations for tourists so that the ISKCON guesthouse could be included in official tours of spiritual India. People were always coming to India to tour the holy places; unfortunately most of the places were unauthorized or overrun by cheaters. ISKCON's center, therefore, would be very important. Prabhupāda wrote,

> Have a European preaching center, and try to enlist all the tourists and hippies who come to Vrindavana. Give them nice prasadam and engage them in chanting, cleaning the temple, and reading our books, give them all facility for becoming devotees.

After Prabhupāda's 1972 visit during Kārttika, he was away from Vṛndāvana for more than a year, directing things through correspondence. With the Kṛṣṇa consciousness movement growing quickly on all continents, he had many places to visit. Still, his three main projects—Bombay, Vṛndāvana, and Māyāpur—were his major subjects of correspondence and his greatest financial investments.

One day, during the massage, Prabhupāda confided to his servant, "Most men are retired at my age. I do not want to manage anymore. I just want to do some writing." Prabhupada asked if there was some place in the world he could go for six months, a place where he would be all alone, where no one would come to disturb him and where he would not get any mail.

Prabhupāda's servant suggested Tehran. Prabhupāda considered it, then suggested New Vrindaban. He spoke of Mohandas Gandhi, who could not even sleep at night because people were always after him, even though he traveled incognito.

That very day a letter came from Bhagavān in Paris, inviting Prabhupāda to tour his ISKCON centers in Europe. Immediately Prabhupāda was enlivened at this invitation. He said he would go.

"But earlier today," his servant said, "you wanted to go away and be alone."

Prabhupāda laughed. "That will not be possible for me in

this lifetime. Better I keep traveling and die on the battlefield. For a warrior, it is glorious to die on the battlefield. Is it not?"

* * *

Guru dāsa had sent a letter to all ISKCON centers inviting devotees to attend the opening of the Krishna-Balaram Mandir in Vṛndāvana. He had invited life members from Bombay and Calcutta and had reserved cars for them on the trains. Prabhupāda also was inviting his disciples to come to Vṛndāvana for Janmāṣṭamī. Lecturing before hundreds of devotees in Los Angeles, he said, "I invite all of you to come to Vṛndāvana to the opening of the Krishna-Balaram Mandir."

Prabhupāda had also mailed invitations to his Godbrothers, and when one of them accepted the invitation, Śrīla Prabhupāda replied, assuring him of accommodations and suggesting the easiest way to travel from Calcutta to Vṛndāvana.

On July 15, only ten days before Prabhupāda's proposed arrival in Vṛndāvana, he wrote almost identical letters to his sannyasi disciples, inviting them to come and resolve the many personal matters and items of business that had been pending during his busy tour.

Except for Guru dāsa, however, none of the devotees in Vṛndāvana thought that the building would be ready by the scheduled grand opening. Work was going on slowly, as usual, and except for the Deity hall area, the land was still a construction site. There were no altars, no Deities. Tejas thought Guru dāsa so feared displeasing Prabhupāda that he could not bear to admit that the building would not be ready. The date had been set, and Prabhupāda did not want excuses. "It has to be done by Janmāṣṭamī," he wrote. "There is no question of delay." Guru dāsa admitted that the temple construction wouldn't be *completely* finished by Janmāṣṭamī, but he reasoned that the opening ceremony could still take place, even if the final touches on the temple weren't done.

Because there was no regular G.B.C. secretary for India, Prabhupāda did not receive accurate reports on the Vṛndāvana temple construction. Several months earlier, Tamāla Kṛṣṇa Goswami had left his position as G.B.C. secretary for India and had gone to preach in the West. Three months had passed before Prabhupāda had appointed a replacement, Karandhara, but now, after only a few weeks, Karandhara was resigning. Guru dāsa's version, therefore, was the only one Prabhupāda had received. The end of July grew near, and devotees prepared to travel to Vṛndāvana—for a fiasco.

* * *

Vṛndāvana
August 4, 1974

When Prabhupāda's car pulled up at the ISKCON property in Ramaṇa-retī, a group of devotees greeted him with *kīrtana* and flowers. Some twenty-five devotees from temples around the world had already gathered for the grand opening celebration, and along with the Vṛndāvana devotees they crowded happily around Śrīla Prabhupāda. No formal walkways had been constructed, and Prabhupāda walked through the half-constructed walls, past piles of sand and bricks, making his way toward the Deity house. Even here the lack of ornamentation and finishing was apparent, and rubble lay all around.

"What is this?" Prabhupāda demanded as he toured the construction site. "There is nothing here. Where is the temple? You told me the temple was finished." Guru dāsa, Surabhi, Guṇārṇava, and others directly responsible were unable to answer. Their faces went white.

Prabhupāda was furious. "How can you open this?"

The visiting devotees also began speaking among themselves: "It's not ready. How can we open?"

"But Prabhupāda," said one devotee, "devotees from all over the world are coming."

"Stop them immediately!" Prabhupāda said. "There will be no opening."

Prabhupāda had burst the bubble, the illusion that they would be ready for the grand opening. Prabhupāda's anger was frightening, and the devotees who surrounded him were no longer carefree and joyful. "You were going to open this temple?" Prabhupāda scoffed.

"The altar is ready," said Harikeśa, who had come from Japan to attend the opening. "We can install the Deity and—"

"You cannot open this temple!" Prabhupāda shouted. "This temple is not completed!"

Prabhupāda then walked into his house, followed by the Vṛndāvana managers and a few other leaders. Whoever could keep his distance from Prabhupāda in this mood considered himself spared. Surabhi's wife ran off to pray to Kṛṣṇa—afraid of Prabhupāda's ferocity.

In his room Prabhupāda's anger only increased. He yelled at Guru dāsa for mismanagement. He yelled at Surabhi. He yelled at all of them. No one dared to offer suggestions or excuses. There was nothing to do but turn white and become depressed. Prabhupāda suddenly inquired whether the temple could be opened, despite the mess.

"Can you have the Deity rooms ready at least?" He turned to Surabhi. "This is an insult to our Society. What will people think? We have announced it everywhere!"

"Nobody actually knows about it, Śrīla Prabhupāda," Surabhi replied fearfully, exposing himself for another blast.

"Oh?" Prabhupāda somewhat changed his tone. "You have not made any propaganda about it? No invitations?"

"Not yet, Prabhupāda. Not to the people in Vṛndāvana. They do not expect it to open, because everyone who has been here can see that it is not possible to open. They know it's not ready."

"This is a farce," Prabhupāda scowled. "It is a fiasco." Disgusted, he looked at his Vṛndāvana managers. "We have to open. How can we open on Janmāṣṭamī?"

"Śrīla Prabhupāda," Surabhi said, "the doors are not ready. They are still cutting the wood." Prabhupāda inquired about the Deities from Yamunā, who explained that Their paraphernalia had been purchased but that the thrones were not ready.

"What is your opinion?" he asked her.

"I am totally unqualified to speak," Yamunā said, "and

although I have no right to speak, I see it as almost impossible to actually open the temple. There is no *pūjārī.*"

With a sense of finality and failure, Prabhupāda said, "Then we won't do it. But we have invited so many people from all around the world to come, and I was not informed of this. Now you all decide.

"*When* can we open?" Prabhupāda asked. "Can we open on Diwali?"

"October, Śrīla Prabhupāda."

"How about Bhaktisiddhānta Sarasvatī's appearance day?" a devotee suggested. "That's at the end of December."

Prabhupāda was silent, looking displeased. Surabhi spoke up. "It will take six, actually seven months." Then Prabhupāda chose the day of Rāma-navamī, in April; the opening could coincide with the annual gathering of devotees in Māyāpur and Vṛndāvana.

Ultimately, Prabhupāda's anger with his disciples was incidental, the reaction due them for their foolishness. It was also a way of instructing them and testing them. But deeper was Prabhupāda's transcendental impatience and frustration that his devotional service in Vṛndāvana was still not manifested. He wanted a wonderful temple for the glory of the Kṛṣṇa consciousness movement, a temple that would establish Kṛṣṇa consciousness all over the world. It was an offering to his spiritual master, and he had promised it to Kṛṣṇa. But still it was not completed.

As for Prabhupāda's disciples' failure to do the job, Prabhupāda had to take the burden and the agony of that failure. His disciples were his instruments in his service to Kṛṣṇa. If the instruments didn't work properly, then he suffered, just as when one's arms and legs fail to function, the whole body suffers. His disciples' failure to carry out his desires was his loss. In this way, he felt transcendental lamentation over their failure to open the Krishna-Balaram Mandir on Janmāṣṭamī day.

Prabhupāda's disturbance, though transcendental, was nonetheless real; it was not feigned merely for instructing. Nor could the devotees cheaply "cheer up" their spiritual master. For Prabhupāda's disciples to properly assist him, they would have to understand his transcendental mood and serve him accordingly. Prabhupāda wanted practical, down-to-earth service from his disciples. They should not expect to serve him sentimentally but should work hard. Devotional service was dynamic. Prabhupāda wanted his disciples to help him with his projects to serve his Guru Mahārāja—projects which, if successful, could save the world from misery.

Getting concrete was a big problem. Surabhi, Guṇārṇava, Tejas, and others were always meditating and striving, "How to get cement?" Yet it seemed no cement was available in the whole of India, as month after month they waited for government permission. Daily, since Prabhupāda's arrival for the so-called temple opening, the devotees had been traveling by bus and ricksha to Mathurā to see if cement—even a few bags—was available.

Sometimes they were cheated. One shipment of twenty bags had been cut with other materials, and when they used it in casting a column, it remained soft for four days and finally crumbled. When at last enough cement arrived to complete the work, the devotees felt sure it had happened only because of Śrīla Prabhupāda's presence.

Prabhupāda had Guṇārṇava count every bag of cement as it arrived. From eight in the morning until nine-thirty at night the shipment kept coming on trucks, each truck with four coolies to carry the heavy bags on their backs into the storage shed. Guṇārṇava stood outside all day with pad and pen, marking the receipt of each bag. Śrīla Prabhupāda came out of the house several times and watched gravely. In the evening when they were finished, he called Guṇārṇava in. "So how many bags?" Prabhupāda asked, and Guṇārṇava gave the exact figure.

"Everything is locked away now?" Prabhupāda asked.

"Yes, Śrīla Prabhupāda."

Prabhupāda talked about the cement as if talking about a shipment of gold.

* * *

During February and March of 1975, Śrīla Prabhupāda toured widely again, traveling eastward via Tokyo and Hawaii to Los Angeles. While traveling, he received word that Governor Reddy had accepted the invitation to attend the Vṛndāvana temple opening on Rāma-navamī. He also received an encouraging report from Surabhi, assuring him that this time the temple opening would definitely take place. "I am encouraged that you expect to have everything completed on time," Prabhupāda wrote. "This I want."

Next Prabhupāda traveled to Mexico City, Mexico, and Caracas, Venezuela. He continued to travel quickly, stopping in Miami, Atlanta, Dallas, and New York—all within a month of his departure from India. He then went to London, stopped in Tehran, and returned to India on March 16. It was Prabhupāda's eighth trip around the world in ten years.

* * *

Māyāpur
March 23, 1975

For this year's festival, almost five hundred devotees from around the world had gathered, and Prabhupāda—while taking his morning walks in the nearby fields, while entering the temple of Rādhā-Mādhava, or while lecturing from the *Caitanya caritāmṛta* was the central attractive feature. Each morning after giving the class, he would circumambulate the temple room, followed by his disciples. A brass bell hung from the ceiling on either side of the Deities' altar, and Prabhupāda, while circumambulating the Deities, would go up to one of the bells and ring it several times, pulling the rope while the *kīrtana* continued wildly. Then, with cane in hand, he would walk around the back of the Deity altar and emerge on the other side to ring the other bell.

The devotees would jump up and down close around him, singing Hare Kṛṣṇa, Hare Kṛṣṇa, Kṛṣṇa Kṛṣṇa, Hare Hare/ Hare Rāma, Hare Rāma, Rāma Rāma, Hare Hare. Smiling with great pleasure, Prabhupāda would continue the length of the temple room to the first bell again and strongly ring it. After half a dozen such blissful circumambulations, he would leave the temple, while the *kīrtana* continued to roar. Coming out into the bright morning sunshine, he would walk up the broad staircase to his room.

Prabhupāda again supervised the annual meeting of his Governing Body Commission and personally approved or modified all their decisions. ISKCON was indeed growing, but as Prabhupāda had told his friend, the aged Gopala Acarya, in Madras, "Kṛṣṇa and Kṛṣṇa's institution are non-different. If the devotees are thinking of Kṛṣṇa's institution, they will not forget Kṛṣṇa."

By insisting on the devotees' participation in the annual Indian pilgrimage, Prabhupāda was solidifying the spiritual basis of ISKCON, his transcendental institution. To gather his devotees like this was the reason he had prayed and struggled to erect centers in the *dhāmas*. He wanted to extend the purifying shelter of Māyāpur and Vṛndāvana to all his followers, now and in the future. Bit by bit, the plan was coming together; the whole world was being saved by Lord Caitanya's movement.

* * *

Vṛndāvana
April 16

When Śrīla Prabhupāda arrived to finally conduct the Krishna Balaram Mandir opening, he was pleasantly surprised to see the three tall domes rising over the temple. The domes had been constructed entirely during the eight months since his last visit. The four-story international guesthouse had also been completely built during his absence. Surabhi had supervised workers in day and night shifts to get everything done on time.

The tall central dome and two side domes, one over each altar, were magnificent. Their graceful form led the mind to higher thoughts and suggested an existence beyond the material world. The strength and beauty of the domes reminded one that beneath resided the Deity of the Supreme Lord. A temple was to enlighten people, to remove their nescience, and the domes eloquently spoke of this purpose. They could be seen for miles, rising boldly above the landscape of Vṛndāvana, proclaiming the worship of Kṛṣṇa and Balarāma.

Each dome was topped by a copper *kalasa* consisting of three balls (representing the lower, middle, and higher planets), and at the top, the eternal Sudarśana *cakra,* the spinning wheel-weapon of Lord Viṣṇu. The Sudarśana *cakra* was Kṛṣṇa Himself, and just to see this glorious symbol atop the *mandira* made the devotees feel victorious and satisfied. Even the guests could not help but regard it with awe. Atop the Sudarśana *cakras* were copper victory flags.

As Prabhupāda toured the completed building, he continually looked up at the domes. "Oh," he said, "the domes have come out very nice. What do you think?" He turned to the devotees accompanying him.

"They are magnificent!" said one devotee.

"Yes." Prabhupāda smiled. "Everyone is telling how nice Surabhi is doing." Prabhupāda turned to Surabhi, who had gone with little sleep for weeks. "But I can't say that. Only me—I am criticizing you, because that is my job. I have to always criticize the disciple."

No less than six hundred devotees from ISKCON centers around the world had come to Vṛndāvana as part of the annual Indian pilgrimage. The high point was to be the installation of the Deities and the opening of the temple. Final preparations were going furiously—cleanups, decorations, cooking. Many important life members and guests had come and were staying in their private rooms in the forty-room guesthouse. Prabhupāda's vision had finally come to pass. He had created probably the most beautiful and opulent temple in Vṛndāvana—certainly the one most alive with dynamic devotion and preaching spirit—and along with it had built one of the best local hotels, for visitors with an eye for *kṛṣṇa-bhakti.*

Touring the grounds, Prabhupāda walked into the sunken courtyard, its marble floor clean and dazzling. This was no rented house in America, something built for another purpose—it was a temple, like the temples in Vaikuṇṭha described in the *Śrīmad-Bhāgavatam.* "It is heaven on earth," Prabhupāda said. "I think it surpasses all the temples in India."

Prabhupāda stood smiling before the *tamāla* tree, its venerable branches spread throughout one corner of the courtyard, and he recounted how there had been a discussion of cutting it down and he had prevented it. *Tamāla* trees are associated with the pastimes of Śrīmatī Rādhārāṇī and are very rare. In Vṛndāvana there were perhaps only three: one here, one at Sevā-kuñja, and one in the courtyard of the Rādhā-Dāmodara temple. That the *tamāla* tree was growing so luxuriantly, Prabhupāda said, indicated that the devotees were performing genuine bhakti.

Convinced that the temple was actually ready, Prabhupāda entered his residence, just between the temple and the guesthouse. Many details demanded his attention, and many visiting disciples were present.

Thus in Ramaṇa-retī, in a place where there was no temple, a pure devotee desired, "Let there be a temple, and *sevā,* devotional service." And what had once been an empty lot was now a place of pilgrimage. Such is the power of the desires of the pure devotee.

CHAPTER SEVEN

Uniting Two Worlds

San Francisco
July 5, 1970

Śrīla Prabhupāda was attending the 1970 Ratha-yātrā in San Francisco. The day was cold and windy, and about ten thousand people had joined Lord Jagannātha's procession through Golden Gate Park. Śrīla Prabhupāda had danced in the street with thousands of participants during the parade, addressed a large crowd in an auditorium by the beach, and looked on as his disciples had distributed a free vegetarian *prasādam* feast to thousands. But when a devotee arrived with a half-dozen advance copies of Volume One of *Kṛṣṇa, the Supreme Personality of Godhead,* Śrīla Prabhupāda appeared especially pleased.

Surrounded by devotees and curious festival-goers, Śrīla Prabhupāda held one of the books, admiring the front cover, with its full-color picture of Rādhā and Kṛṣṇa. The volume was big, almost seven-and-a-half by ten-and-a-half inches, and its dust jacket shone, silver with large bright red letters: "KṚṢṆA." It was a transcendental wonder in Śrīla Prabhupāda's reverent hands.

Onlookers could barely restrain themselves from pressing in against Śrīla Prabhupāda to peer over his shoulders. And they *didn't* restrain their exclamations when Prabhupāda smiled and opened the volume. He examined the illustrations, the print, the paper, and the binding. "Very nice," he said. He fixed his attention on a page, reading. Then he looked up and announced that this greatly valuable book, *Kṛṣṇa,* had just arrived and that everyone should read it. Holding one book in his hand, with the other copies stacked before him, he said that anyone who so desired should come forward and buy a copy.

People began clamoring, and hands with ten-dollar bills thrust forward, while voices cried out, begging for a copy. And Prabhupāda promptly sold every book, not even keeping one for himself.

For the devotees, Śrīla Prabhupāda's selling of the *Kṛṣṇa* book was the most spectacular event of the Ratha-yātrā festival. They pored over the purchased books in groups, discussing Kṛṣṇa's pastimes and the effect they would have on the people of America.

Brahmānanda told how in 1967 Prabhupāda had given away his advance copy of *Teachings of Lord Caitanya* in his room at 26 Second Avenue in New York City. Just before that book had arrived, Śrīla Prabhupāda had been sitting and talking with Satyavrata, a disciple who had previously stopped coming to the temple due to petty quarreling with his Godbrothers. When the copy of *Teachings of Lord Caitanya* had arrived, Śrīla Prabhupāda had lovingly inspected it and had then offered it to Satyavrata as a gift.

Brahmānanda had been astounded to see Śrīla Prabhupāda give away his only copy of the book. Having helped publish the book, Brahmānanda knew how painstakingly Prabhupāda had written it and how he had anxiously waited one year for the book to finally see print. Yet once it had arrived, he had immediately given it away, and to a disciple who was not even in good standing. Satyavrata had taken the book, thanked Śrīla Prabhupāda, and left, never to be seen again.

Although Śrīla Prabhupāda wanted his disciples to be as eager to distribute Kṛṣṇa conscious literature as he was, none of them knew how to do it. Distributing a magazine and asking for a small donation was one thing—but a big, hardbound book? When the entire shipment of *Teachings of Lord Caitanya* had arrived in New York in April of 1967, the devotees had hired a truck, picked up the books at the dock, and unloaded them at 26 Second Avenue. They had then shipped them to ISKCON centers in Los Angeles, San Francisco, Boston, Montreal, and elsewhere. And there they remained.

Some devotees had tried placing ads in magazines and leaving books in book stores on consignment. But the books didn't sell. How to sell these big, hardbound books remained a mystery—until something significant happened, an accidental discovery.

One day in 1971, while driving back to the temple after chanting in downtown San Francisco, two *brahmacārīs* stopped at a local service station for gas. When the attendant came to the window for money, one of the devotees showed him a *Kṛṣṇa* book. The attendant seemed interested, and the two devotees began preaching the glories of Kṛṣṇa consciousness. When they suggested he take the book as payment for the gas, he agreed.

Astonished at what had happened and inspired by their success, the two *brahmacārīs* went the next day with several *Kṛṣṇa* books and stood in front of a grocery store. And again it happened; this time they sold two books.

Keśava, the San Francisco temple president, phoned his G.B.C. supervisor (and brother), Karandhara, in Los Angeles to tell him what had happened. "It's like a miracle!" Keśava exclaimed. Karandhara encouraged him to experiment further, and soon the San Francisco temple had half a dozen men going from door to door showing the books to people in their homes. When Buddhimanta began selling as many as five books in a day, the devotees in other temples, especially in Los Angeles, San Diego, and Denver, wanted to follow his example. And whoever tried it and sold a book became caught up in a euphoric excitement.

The experience and testimonies of devotees selling Śrīla Prabhupāda's books describe a special taste, distinct from the happiness young men might ordinarily experience by stumbling upon a sales technique and finding themselves on the verge of making a lot of money. The difference is that the devotees' book distribution, being devotional service to Kṛṣṇa, produces an ecstasy that is transcendental, an ecstasy far beyond even the greatest material happiness.

Ordinary business and the business of selling Kṛṣṇa conscious literature are as different as material life is from spiritual life. And anyone observing spiritual life from the material point of view will not understand it. Bhaktisiddhānta Sarasvatī had compared such empirical attempts to understand the ecstasy of Kṛṣṇa consciousness with attempts to taste honey by licking the outside of the bottle.

The young men and women beginning to distribute books in America knew that Śrīla Prabhupāda, by giving them Kṛṣṇa consciousness, had saved them from hellish life, and they wanted to help him give Kṛṣṇa consciousness to others. And such preaching, by distributing his books, was ecstasy, spiritual ecstasy.

By mid-1971, the temples were selling hundreds of *Kṛṣṇa* books a week. Karandhara, Prabhupāda's Book Fund manager, began sending *saṅkīrtana* newsletters to the North American temples and to Śrīla Prabhupāda. By listing the monthly results of each temple's book distribution, the newsletters incited competition. Karandhara's December 1971 newsletter summed up the mood of the year and urged the devotees to increase.

> Recently, in an all out program to sell books, the San Francisco Temple has been averaging 20 Krishna Books per day distribution. What is their technique? Keshava Prabhu says, "Simply we make it our priority activity. All you have to do is want to do it and then try as hard as you can. Everywhere we go, we carry BTGs and Krishna books," he says, "on street SKP, door to door, to the laundromat, to the store, everywhere." We have been taxing our brains in so many fancy and complicated ways to try to increase sales, but as it has been experienced, nothing is more successful than simply taking the books personally in hand and going door to door with this Causeless

> Mercy. Just consider, how many hours a day do we spend specifically trying to distribute Srila Prabhupada's literature, which is the dearmost thing to him?

The crowning touch to end the year's *saṅkīrtana,* however, came not from the newsletter but from Prabhupāda himself, who wrote to Keśava, the "king" of *Kṛṣṇa* book distribution.

> I have been receiving so many reports about how my disciples from the San Francisco Temple cannot be surpassed by anyone in distributing my books. Sometimes they are selling as many as 70 Krishna books daily. So if this is true, then certainly when I return to the U.S. I must come and stay in your Temple. By distributing my books profusely you are giving me great encouragement to translate. And you are all helping me to fulfill the order which Guru Maharaja gave me. So I am so much grateful to you, and I am sure Krishna will bless you a million times over for doing this work.
>
> I hope that you and all my beloved disciples in San Francisco Temple are in strong health and jolly mood.

Copies of this letter went out to every ISKCON center. Prabhupāda had always given his blessings to all the devotees, but never before could anyone recall his saying a devotee would get Kṛṣṇa's blessings "a million times over"!

Although a letter from Prabhupāda usually instructed a specific devotee, the instruction often had universal application; and Śrīla Prabhupāda's letters made clear his disciples' top priority: book distribution.

> I am very pleased to hear that you are increasing in your distribution of our books and magazines. This is a good sign that your preaching work is also strong. The more you increase your strength in preaching, the more you will go on selling books. I want especially that my books be distributed widely.

Prabhupāda's ambition was to replace mundane literature with transcendental. At least in every home there should be one piece of Kṛṣṇa conscious literature, he reasoned, because if a person read only one page, his life could be turned toward perfection. "If one percent of the readers become devotees," he wrote, "that will change the world." Whereas mail-order advertisers were satisfied with a five-percent response, Śrīla Prabhupāda spoke of an even smaller percentage—one percent—whom he thought could become pure devotees in response to receiving a book. Lord Kṛṣṇa also confirms this in *Bhagavad-gītā:* "Out of many thousands among men, one may endeavor for perfection, and of those who have achieved perfection, hardly one knows Me in truth." To make the world Kṛṣṇa conscious, therefore, would require that millions of pieces of transcendental literature be distributed.

Śrīla Prabhupāda wanted his disciples to understand *why* they should distribute his books, and he instructed them through his letters.

> Who God is can be summed up in only five words—Krishna is the Supreme Controller. If you become convinced of this and preach it enthusiastically, success is assured, and you will be doing the greatest service for all living entities.

He wrote to Jayādvaita,

> These books and magazines are our most important propaganda weapons to defeat the ignorance of maya's army, and the more we produce such literature and sell them profusely all over the world, the more we shall deliver the world from the suicide course.

To Jagadīśa he wrote,

> I am encouraged to see your report of books sold, because it proves that you consider it your responsibility to see that more and more people are reading our literature. Actually, this is the solid basis for our preaching work—no other movement has got such profuse authority for preaching. And if someone reads our Krishna conscious philosophy, he becomes convinced.

Prabhupāda continued to insist that all major Kṛṣṇa conscious programs be maintained, including Deity worship, chanting Hare Kṛṣṇa in public, and holding outside lectures.

All programs were important. But book distribution, whenever possible, should accompany the other programs. To a sannyasi whose main program was public lecturing, Prabhupāda wrote,

> Distribute books, as many as possible. If anyone hears some philosophy from us, that will help him. But if he purchases one book, that may turn his life. So selling books is the best preaching activity. Sell books, hold the kirtan in public places like schools and colleges, preach.

And in a letter to Bhagavān dāsa in France, he stressed the same thing: "What will your three minutes' preaching do? But if they buy one book, it may turn their life."

* * *

Another breakthrough for book distribution came at the end of 1972. The previous year devotees had taken advantage of the Christmas season by selling *Kṛṣṇa* book door to door, but no one had been aware just how significant the Christmas season could actually be.

Rāmeśvara: *It was on December 22, 1972, that we accidentally discovered the Christmas marathon in Los Angeles. Of course, we noticed a great increase in the number of people going into the stores, and the stores were staying open sometimes until midnight. I was standing in front of a Burbank Zody's. We were having an intense competition with prizes in Los Angeles, and it was building up to a feverish pitch.*

So after distributing madly all day long, I had collected about $350 and had distributed 650 magazines. It was about ten o'clock at night. I was convinced this was the new world's record in ISKCON and that nobody was possibly going to beat me this day. Even though the store was open until twelve, business had started slowing off, and I was thinking, "Maybe I should go back. Undoubtedly everyone is back already. No one has ever stayed out past eight o'clock. They'll all be waiting up for me. I shouldn't keep them waiting up." So in this way my mind was convincing me to go back.

By eleven o'clock the store was completely dead. I got in the car and started driving back. On the way back I passed another Zody's, called Hollywood Zody's, on Sunset and Western. I was torn whether to stop or not, because that store was crowded and was going to be open until midnight. But I decided to return to the temple because I thought all the other devotees were probably already back and were just waiting up to see how many books I had distributed. So I just kept on driving.

I finally arrived at the temple at about ten minutes to twelve, and I burst into the saṅkīrtana *room. But the only person there was the secretary, Madhukaṇṭha. I said, "Oh, no. Everyone went to bed?" He said, "No, nobody is back yet." I was the first one back! That was the discovery of the first Christmas marathon. It was completely unplanned. No one had ever instructed anyone to stay out that late. We just did it spontaneously.*

Finally, at about one-thirty in the morning, all the devotees had returned, and we were all sitting around looking at the saṅkīrtana *map. We couldn't sleep, we were so excited to go out. We were thinking, "Where can we find plenty of conditioned souls to distribute books to?" Our noise and raucous laughter was like a drunken party, and it woke up Karandhara, who was sleeping in his office in the next room. He came stumbling in, wiping the sleep from his eyes, but when he saw us and saw what was going on, he burst out laughing and sent us all to bed, saying, "Get ready for tomorrow." So in this way we performed the three-day marathon—December 22, 23, and 24.*

No one had ever distributed as many books before in the history of our movement. A big day had been considered to be somewhere between twenty-five and forty books. But we were distributing between five thousand and six thousand pieces of literature a day for a three-day period. One temple had distributed almost eighteen thousand pieces of literature in just three days.

When Prabhupāda received news of the book distribution in Los Angeles and elsewhere in the United States, he was very pleased, and amazed. Although involved with many affairs from throughout the world, he put them aside and relished the overwhelming victory of book distribution in America. Immediately he called in his personal secretary and dictated letters.

> My dear Ramesvar,
>
> I beg to acknowledge receipt of your letter dated December 27, 1972, and with great happiness I have read your figures of amount of books sold during three-day period, December 22–24, 1972. It is scarcely believable that more than 17,000 books could have been sold by one temple in three days! That indicates to me that people are at last becoming a little serious about this Krishna Consciousness movement in your country. Otherwise, why they should buy our books? But they can see that our boys and girls, devotees, are so much sincere and serious to distribute the message of Krishna Consciousness, they are at once struck by seeing them, and therefore they appreciate and purchase. This is unique in the world. So I am so much pleased upon all of the boys and girls in Los Angeles and all over the world who are understanding and appreciating this unique quality of our transcendental literature, and voluntarily they are going out to distribute despite all circumstances of difficulty. By this effort alone they are assured to go back to home, back to Godhead.

The same day Prabhupāda dictated a letter to Karandhara.

> I could never have thought it was possible to distribute so many of our literatures. Therefore I can understand it is simply Krishna's blessing us for your sincerely working on His behalf. Actually, that is the secret of my success, not that personally I have done anything wonderful, but that because those who are helping me are sincere. They have done the work. That is the reason for our success all over the world where others have failed. A little sincerity is very difficult thing in this age of hypocrisy and bluff, but I am so fortunate that Krishna has sent me all of you nice boys and girls who are sincerely working. Please convey to all of them my deepest appreciation.

Śrīla Prabhupāda's letters acknowledging the Christmas marathon and assuring the devotees that they would go back to Godhead sent the book distribution movement flying into the new year with great momentum. Devotees continued to find new ways and places to distribute books. New records were constantly topping the old, and the devotees were making still higher projections for the future.

Praghoṣa: *I was coming regularly to the Detroit temple for classes in the evening, and I was doing some odd work to help the devotees prepare the temple. Every night I would be painting, and I would watch the devotees coming back from* saṅkīrtana. *They seemed very ecstatic and enlivened, and I was always a little curious about what they did out there that made them come back like this. I would be up on my ladder, painting and listening to them talk as they sat on the floor drinking hot milk. They would talk about how they had knocked on one man's door and this had happened and then that had happened—it was very attractive to me.*

After I moved into the temple and had been a devotee about a week, someone asked me if I would like to go out and try distributing books. So I went out, wearing a dhoti and tilaka *and using a straightforward presentation, walking up to people, giving them a card and a book, telling them about the contents of the book, showing them Prabhupāda's picture, and asking for a donation. The exhilaration I got from that was just incredible. It became extremely blissful to go out and do this. None of us could actually put a finger on why it was so ecstatic.*

We used to lie awake at night. All the brahmacārīs *stayed in one big room, and we would lie there on the floor in our sleeping bags, whispering to each other: "What did you say to the people out there?" There would be all these different conversations going on in the room at night, with the lights out and everyone talking, trying to relate how we were presenting Prabhupāda's books.*

Tripurāri: *My association with Śrīla Prabhupāda was always more or less in separation and in the field. While many of the older devotees were trained personally by Prabhupāda, I never got that training. I was trained by Śrīla Prabhupāda more from within my own heart. I think that's the case with all of our book distributors. They have a very intimate sense of feeling for Prabhupāda, but they never had much personal contact. Their intimacy and real sense of knowing Prabhupāda very closely was because of that service which Prabhupāda said was his life and soul—seeing that the books went out.*

* * *

In the summer of 1973 the devotees found that at concerts they could distribute hundreds of *Kṛṣṇa* books in a few hours. The *Kṛṣṇa* book, available now as a paperback trilogy with a foreword by George Harrison, was especially attractive to young people. In July, Rāmeśvara wrote to Prabhupāda in London, telling him that the Los Angeles temple was distributing two thousand *Kṛṣṇa* books a week and that at one concert devotees had distributed six hundred books in two hours.

The devotees in Los Angeles decided that Tripurāri and a few other leading *saṅkīrtana* men should travel from temple to temple and share their experience. Rāmeśvara wrote to Prabhupāda, "This is the mercy of Śrī Śrī Rukmiṇī-Dvārakādhīśa [the Deities of the L.A. temple] that we can send out so many devotees to other centers. It is the real opulence of New Dvārakā." Śrīla Prabhupāda replied on August 3.

> There is no doubt about it, to distribute books is our most important activity. The temple is a place not for eating and sleeping, but as a base from which we send out our soldiers to fight with maya. Fight with maya means to drop thousands and millions of books into the laps of the conditioned souls. Just like during the war time the Bombs are raining from the sky like anything. . . .
>
> I like also your program of sending out your best men to teach the others. That is the actual progress of Krishna Consciousness, to train others. Continue this program so that in the future every devotee in our movement will know the art of distributing books. This is approved by me.

Sura: *Vaiśeṣika was selling books in the airport with me. He would walk up to people and say, "Well, how are you doing, sir? All glories to the* śrī-kṛṣṇa-saṅkīrtana *movement, the prime benediction for humanity at large, which cleanses the heart." He was repeating the* Śikṣāṣṭaka *prayers of Lord Caitanya right out of the book, and yet he was selling books. The books had pictures of Kṛṣṇa and devotional scenes on the cover, and sometimes some devotees couldn't understand how people could relate to these books. But Prabhupāda wanted them distributed. And he was saying that we should preach on the merit of the book. When a devotee asked Prabhupāda what we should say to distribute the books, Prabhupāda replied* kṛṣṇe sva-dhāmopagate, *which is the verse that says the* Śrīmad-Bhāgavatam *is as brilliant as the sun and it has arisen just to give people religion in this age of darkness. So we were also repeating that verse and distributing books on faith.*

We would go out and see the people actually becoming struck by Kṛṣṇa consciousness. They would see that the devotees were very sincere and serious, and they would become impressed. Daily on saṅkīrtana *we would see people appreciating Prabhupāda's books. There was also harassment, but Prabhupāda had talked about it, that there was always difficulty. So everything was there from Prabhupāda to confirm whatever realizations we had. Śrīla Prabhupāda said a book salesman would sometimes have difficulty because he'll be sometimes accepted and sometimes rejected. But he tolerates.*

In the airport we met professors, lawyers, all kinds of people who would stop and talk. They would challenge, and we would constantly have to defend Prabhupāda's books and his movement and speak up on behalf of Prabhupāda, more so than when we were just kids out on the parking lots talking to women and begging fifty cents for a pack of incense. We were presenting Prabhupāda's books to the scholars, coming into contact with Māyāvādīs, scientists, businessmen, people who were very sharp, in Chicago, New York, Los Angeles, and San Diego. People there were very sharp and hard. And just by having to spiritually combat them and defend the movement, we became more mature in our understanding of Prabhupāda's books and how to present them in such a way that we could convince even people who didn't want to be convinced. We had to study Prabhupāda's books.

* * *

Book distribution took another great stride forward when Tamāla Kṛṣṇa Goswami, Śrīla Prabhupāda's zonal secretary in India for four years, returned to the U.S. Joining with his friend Viṣṇujana Swami, he helped form the Rādhā-Dāmodara *saṅkīrtana* party, traveling in a bus with Rādhā-Kṛṣṇa Deities to distribute books and hold festivals all over the U.S.

Śrīla Prabhupāda showed special interest in the Rādhā-Dāmodara party and approved loans from the BBT for the purchase of more buses, thus creating a *saṅkīrtana* army traveling in renovated Greyhound buses. By the end of 1974 the Rādhā-Dāmodara party had three buses, vans, and numerous men. Prabhupāda called the buses "moving temples," and he urged the Rādhā-Dāmodara devotees to continue their program, with certainty that they were pleasing Lord Caitanya. "I am glad that you have understood the importance of my books," Prabhupāda wrote, "therefore I am stressing it so much. Let everyone take these books."

Śrīla Prabhupāda encouraged the Rādhā-Dāmodara party to expand to hundreds of buses and thus fulfill the mission of Śrī Caitanya Mahāprabhu to bring Kṛṣṇa consciousness to every town and village. When a tight transcendental competition arose between the Los Angeles temple, Tripurāri's BBT party, and the Rādhā-Dāmodara party, Prabhupāda watched and approved it with pleasure.

Another party forming in 1974 was the BBT library party. It began with Hṛdayānanda Goswami's sending some *brahmacārīs* from his traveling party to sell books at prestigious universities in New England. Then in 1974 it became the BBT library party, backed up by a professionally organized sales office in Los Angeles. At that time the men started to sell entire sets of Śrīla Prabhupāda's books, including the published and yet-to-be-published volumes of the seventeen-volume *Caitanya-caritāmṛta* and the sixty-volume *Śrīmad-Bhāgavatam*. Even in their first attempts they met with great success.

Śrīla Prabhupāda had long cherished this idea, and even before coming to America he had gone to libraries in India with copies of his *Śrīmad-Bhāgavatam* First Canto. By his efforts in New Delhi, the United States Library of Congress had obtained copies of those early volumes. Now his desire to see his books placed in all the U.S. libraries and universities was becoming a reality. Rāmeśvara, the BBT supervisor, wrote in a newsletter to all the temples,

> Srila Prabhupada has become more and more interested about this program and is making it one of our most important priorities. His Holiness Satsvarupa das Goswami, who presently is GBC secretary serving as Srila Prabhupada's personal secretary, is being sent back to the U.S. by His Divine Grace to personally lead and organize this BBT Library Program.

Under Satsvarupa's guidance, the party crisscrossed the United States, selling dozens of standing orders each week to university libraries, including those of Yale, Harvard, Columbia, Princeton, and Stanford. Within a few months professors began writing favorable reviews, and many ordered Prabhupada's books for their college courses. After placing complete sets of books in the majority of American and Canadian libraries, the BBT library party shifted its operations to Europe and India, meeting with the same success.

Dr. Alex Wayman, professor of Sanskrit at Columbia University, wrote,

> It has been my great pleasure recently to have read the *Śrīmad-Bhāgavatam* in the superb edition authorized by A. C. Bhaktivedanta Swami Prabhupāda. The consummate care and devotion to the Sanskrit word and its precious meaning are evident on every page. I am sure this monumental work will go far to bring the sublime message of the *Bhāgavatam* to numerous Westerners who otherwise would miss this opportunity.

Prabhupāda was pleased with the recognition coming from Western scholars and often showed their reviews of his books to his guests. "I very much like this program of the standing orders," Prabhupāda wrote. "Try to increase it up to fifty thousand such orders from the libraries."

When Śrīla Prabhupāda became ill for several weeks in September of 1974, the book distribution reports were his best medicine. "Whenever I get report of my books selling," he wrote to the library party, "I feel strength. Even now in this weakened condition I have got strength from your report." And during the same illness he wrote to Rāmeśvara,

> Regarding the book sales figures, please endeavor in this way. This is the only solace of my life. When I hear that my books are selling so nicely, I become energetic like a young man.

Śrīla Prabhupāda recovered his health, and by the end of 1974 his BBT was also in extraordinary health, with the temples again competing in a furious Christmas marathon. The BBT office in Los Angeles reported to Prabhupāda that approximately 387,000 hardbound books had been sold during the year, a 67% increase over the previous year. And almost 4,000,000 *Back to Godheads* had been sold, an 89% increase. The American BBT sold to the individual temples a total of 6,668,000 pieces of literature, a 60% increase.

Such news made Śrīla Prabhupāda "become energetic like a young man," and Prabhupāda and his book distribution movement headed into 1975 with all signs of increasing—doubling and tripling—the already astounding figures of 1974. Moreover, the new BBTs in other countries around the world were also expanding.

Śrīla Prabhupāda had created his Bhaktivedanta Book Trust in 1972 as an independent entity to ensure that his books could continue being produced and distributed. The BBT would operate exclusively for the benefit of the International Society for Krishna Consciousness, and yet it would exist independently.

The trust document stated that the trustees should divide the money from the sale of books to ISKCON temples into two funds: one for printing books and one for purchasing ISKCON properties and building temples. Prabhupāda believed that if this fifty-fifty formula were followed, Kṛṣṇa would assure the success of ISKCON. Repeatedly he would refer to this formula in conversations and letters, even in his purports on *Śrīmad-Bhāgavatam.*

Śrīla Prabhupāda gave his BBT trustees authority to make printing plans, and the trustees would then consult him for approval. He would set the standards and guidelines for his BBT trustees to follow; only after consulting him could they institute changes.

And to changes Prabhupāda was particularly averse. He would choose the book size, determine the artwork, and make suggestions about the size of a particular printing, about shipping policies, about sales to temples—about almost every aspect of the BBT's publishing activities. Even when certain temples did not remit their payments to the BBT, Prabhupāda would become involved.

> It is not good if such big temples who are setting the example for the whole Society do not pay their bills. This is most irregular. I am trying to retire from the administrative affairs, but if the presidents and GBC men make such disturbances, then how can I be peaceful? Things should be maintained automatically, then it will be peaceful for me.

He was a strict manager. "According to Vedic instruction," he said, "fire, debt, and disease should never be neglected. They must be extinguished by all means."

Śrīla Prabhupāda saw book distribution as (among other things) the basis for an economically sound ISKCON. Other businesses could also operate, but book-selling was the best for it combined preaching with a good source of income. As he wrote to one of his temple presidents,

> I am very encouraged by the report of how nicely our books are being distributed. This is our main business all over the world. If

> you give full attention to this, there will never be any shortage of funds.

And on another occasion,

> Regarding the society's leaders emphasizing business, you should understand what is the meaning of business. Business means to help the preaching. Preaching needs financial help, otherwise, we have no need for business. So far as I understand, our book business is sufficient to support our movement.

* * *

By steadfastly distributing Śrīla Prabhupāda's books, the members of the Kṛṣṇa consciousness movement were experiencing the essence of loving service to Kṛṣṇa in separation, which is the highest spiritual ecstasy. "Don't try to see God," Śrīla Prabhupāda's spiritual master had often said, "but act in such a way that God sees you." In other words, by submissively acting on the order of the servant of the servant of the servant of Kṛṣṇa, Prabhupāda's disciples were sure to attract Kṛṣṇa's loving attention.

The quickest way to catch Kṛṣṇa's attention, Śrīla Prabhupāda said, was to direct another person to Kṛṣṇa consciousness. The book distributors, therefore, felt a special reciprocation with their spiritual master, and this impelled them to go on serving and distributing.

Sañjaya: *Philosophically we saw that going out and distributing books was what our spiritual master wanted us to do. We knew that. That was clear to us. We also had a real sense of idealism—that these books and magazines would change the world. Once you come to Kṛṣṇa consciousness, you actually see how crummy the world really is, how really contaminated things are, how envious people are, and how horrible material life is. You can see that. You don't feel that you yourself can change it, but you feel that whoever gets one of Prabhupāda's books and looks at it will be changed in a spiritual way. There was no question about it. We also felt a big change would come in the world in the future as Kṛṣṇa consciousness spread. Prabhupāda also said that if people just touch one of these books their lives will change. Our faith was in the books and Śrīla Prabhupāda.*

Keśava Bharatī: *When you pass out a book, there is a certain reciprocation from Prabhupāda. There was a dramatic difference in our internal experience when a person would take a book compared to just taking some incense or something. We would actually experience Prabhupāda's association all day by distributing those books. We didn't feel left out just because certain devotees were physically closer to Prabhupāda. Book distributors always got strong enlivenment. We would read about Haridāsa Ṭhākura going out and rolling on the ground and begging people to chant. That kind of thing would inspire us.*

Vaiśeṣika: *We used to think how Prabhupāda was spending so much time behind a dictating machine just writing these books. We would meditate on how he would sleep just a few hours a day and minimize everything else to write these books. So we were also trying to cut down our other activities and just go out and distribute books. Prabhupāda said a devotee should be in the mood of the six Gosvāmīs, so we were singing those prayers every day. We felt a real connection. Even in the beginning a devotee told me, "Where is Prabhupāda, do you know?" And then he said, "He's in his books." That mood was always there. We always felt that connection.*

Jagaddhātrī-devī dāsī: *When I was distributing Prabhupāda's books, I understood that that was the most pleasing thing I could do for him. I was helping him to fulfill his spiritual master's instructions, and so he was pleased. And he was even more pleased if I did it nicely. I always used to hear the story about how Bhaktisiddhānta Sarasvatī would be happy if someone went out and distributed even one magazine, because it's actually the* mood *of* saṅkīrtana, *of going out and* trying *to give mercy to the conditioned souls, that counts.*

I always wanted to do welfare work. I like the feeling of doing something for people. So this is the summum bonum of helping people. You are helping them to go back to Godhead.

So that was my motivation. And we automatically become purified by bringing other living entities to Kṛṣṇa.

Lavaṅga-latikā-devī dāsī: *Having heard Śrīla Prabhupāda speak and knowing that he was always reading from these books, the* Śrīmad-Bhāgavatam, *and that he was preaching that you have to distribute this knowledge to others made it all very simple. That is, you just knew that this was Śrīla Prabhupāda's desire. He was always telling us that he was giving us this knowledge and that once you have this knowledge, you have to distribute it to others. Śrīla Prabhupāda came to America to preach with his disciples. So we must do it, because it's Prabhupāda's desire. He spent so much time translating these books to be distributed. You just want to distribute to others, and you want people to have these books in their homes.*

* * *

Vṛndāvana, India
April 20, 1975

Śrīla Prabhupāda installed the Deities for the grand opening of the Krishna-Balaram Mandir. Almost a thousand disciples were present, and the governor of Uttar Pradesh was the guest of honor. After years of hard endeavor, the grand opening was a climactic triumph for Śrīla Prabhupāda and his movement. While still standing at the altar after having offered the first *ārati* to Kṛṣṇa and Balarāma, Prabhupāda addressed the crowd, explaining that this was an international temple, where people from all over the world could come to worship and take shelter of Gaura-Nitāi, Kṛṣṇa-Balarāma, and Rādhā-Kṛṣṇa.

Later that evening, Śrīla Prabhupāda sat in his room with a few G.B.C. men. The buttons on his *kurtā* open because of the heat, his legs and bare feet extended under the low table, he relaxed, and his men sat close around him in the dim light of the desk lamp. It was a milestone, he said, but still they had to go forward, not merely savor their success. Many things were still required to make the temple and guesthouse operative.

Śrīla Prabhupāda was thinking beyond Vṛndāvana. "This temple construction is so important," he said, "that I'm willing to spend many lakhs to open a temple like this. And yet as important as it is, the book production is even more important." This was a significant reaffirmation of the priority of book production; even while in the midst of this splendid temple opening, he was stressing that book production was more important.

Śrīla Prabhupāda seemed displeased, however, because for months his *Caitanya-caritāmṛta* had been delayed by his Sanskrit editor. He said with a scowl that although he had finished the *Caitanya-caritāmṛta*, it remained unpublished. He had also completed all four volumes of the Fourth Canto of *Śrīmad-Bhāgavatam* and was beginning the Fifth, yet only one volume of the Fourth Canto had been published.

One of the devotees present, not understanding Prabhupāda's point, remarked that since Prabhupāda was going next to Hawaii he would be able to write there in peace and quiet. Prabhupāda replied that he was not encouraged to write when his manuscripts were not being published.

The BBT Press, after several years in New York, was about to relocate to Los Angeles, where Rādhāvallabha would be production manager and Rāmeśvara, the BBT supervisor, would be able to more closely oversee the Press operations. Rāmeśvara, unaware of the delay in publishing the *Caitanya-caritāmṛta* manuscript, learned of it now, in Vṛndāvana. He promised Prabhupāda that he would immediately get the Press set up in Los Angeles and begin producing *Caitanya-caritāmṛta.*

That Śrīla Prabhupāda had completed the entire *Caitanya-caritāmṛta* manuscript in eighteen months during 1973 and 1974 was a remarkable feat, because in those same months he had been intensely engaged in many affairs of management while constantly traveling. He had confronted major problems with leaders who had left their posts, he had personally attended to G.B.C. duties in India, and he had dealt with other ISKCON managerial affairs. He had authorized many large BBT loans and had approved the expansion and development of ISKCON in all areas of the world, in addition to responding regularly to large volumes of mail, speaking daily to guests, and giving *Bhāgavatam* lectures wherever he went. His only time for writing had been on arising at one in the morning, when he had persistently worked two or three hours each day.

Los Angeles
June 20, 1975

On arriving in Los Angeles, Śrīla Prabhupāda received a joyous welcome. He was accompanied by leading sannyasis and G.B.C. secretaries, including Kīrtanānanda Swami, Viṣṇujana Swami, Brahmānanda Swami, Tamāla Kṛṣṇa Goswami, and others. Later, sitting in his room—one of his favorites in all of ISKCON—he spoke only briefly about the backlog of unprinted books. He seemed mildly disturbed but said little. He was very pleased, however, to see the temple and the Deities of Rukmiṇī-Dvārakādhīśa.

In his short arrival speech he had explained why he was so urgently pressing his disciples to produce his books. "I have no personal qualification," he had said from the plushly upholstered *vyāsāsana,* "but I simply try to satisfy my guru, that's all. My Guru Mahārāja asked me that, 'If you get some money, you print books.' So there was a private meeting, talking. Some of my important Godbrothers also were there—it was in Rādhā-kuṇḍa. So Guru Mahārāja was speaking to me that, 'Since we have got this Baghbazar marble temple, there has been so much dissension. And everyone thinking who will occupy this room or that room. I wish therefore to sell this temple and the marble and print some books.' Yes, so I took up this from his mouth, that he is very fond of books. And he told me personally, 'If you get some money, print books.' Therefore I am stressing on this point—Where is book? Where is book? So kindly help me. That is my request. Print as many books as possible in as many languages as possible, and distribute throughout the whole world. Then the Kṛṣṇa consciousness movement will automatically increase."

The next morning, while walking on Venice Beach, Śrīla Prabhupāda delivered an extraordinary ultimatum. Surrounded by devotees, he walked along, poking the sand softly with his cane. "These seventeen volumes unpublished," he began, "are a great problem for our movement."

"Yes, Prabhupāda," Rāmeśvara responded, attentive and concerned. The other devotees also nodded, commiserating. Something must be done.

"Yes," Prabhupāda continued, "they must be published immediately."

"Yes, Prabhupāda," Rāmeśvara replied obediently.

"So I think they can be printed in two months," Śrīla Prabhupāda said conclusively.

Rāmeśvara wasn't sure he had heard correctly. The Press had only just opened. The artists didn't even have lights in their rooms. Two months was illogical, impossible. Now was the moment to tell Śrīla Prabhupāda the plan for increased production. Rāmeśvara stepped closer.

"Śrīla Prabhupāda," he began, "we've been meeting about this, and now that the Press is finally here and established, I think we can increase production four times. We think that now we can go from producing one book every four months to producing one of your books every month." Now both Rāmeśvara and Rādhāvallabha were walking together beside Śrīla Prabhupāda, with Tamāla Kṛṣṇa Goswami and Brahmānanda Swami walking on his other side.

"One book every month," Śrīla Prabhupāda said, as if thinking out loud and considering it. "That means over one year. It is not fast enough." The other devotees looked over at Rāmeśvara and Rādhāvallabha, who glanced at each other.

"You have to do all the books in two months' time," Śrīla Prabhupāda said again. They had clearly heard it this time, and the two managers were stunned in disbelief.

"Śrīla Prabhupāda," Rāmeśvara said, "I think that's impossible. Maybe we can go faster . . ."

Śrīla Prabhupāda suddenly stopped walking. Planting his cane firmly in the sand, he turned to Rāmeśvara and said, without anger but very gravely, "*Impossible* is a word found in the fool's dictionary."

Suddenly Rāmeśvara realized his spiritual life was on the line. To say "impossible" now would mean he had no faith in Kṛṣṇa's representative, no faith in the power of God. He must throw away his material estimations and rational common sense.

While Rāmeśvara and Rādhāvallabha stood speechless, Śrīla Prabhupāda resumed walking, accompanied by the others. The two devotees hurried to catch up, but now everyone looked at them as if to say, "Come on. Stop doubting. You have to do it." Rāmeśvara asked Śrīla Prabhupāda if he could discuss this with the other devotees at the Press and then report back. "Oh, yes," Prabhupāda replied, "whatever is required." Rāmeśvara and Rādhāvallabha dropped back, while Śrīla Prabhupāda and the others continued down the beach.

All through the morning program in the temple, Rāmeśvara and Rādhāvallabha tried to concentrate on chanting their *japa* and on Prabhupāda's class, but all they could think of was arranging for the production of seventeen volumes in two months. And by the time they met with the Press workers, they had become convinced it could be done. It was as if some mystical power was going to descend. Somehow or other it could be done. So they presented the plan and convinced the other workers.

"It can be done," Rāmeśvara said later, talking with Śrīla Prabhupāda.

"Hmmm," Śrīla Prabhupāda replied.

But there were some conditions, Rāmeśvara said. For the Bengali editing to go smoothly, the editors would have to be able to regularly consult Śrīla Prabhupāda. Immediately Prabhupāda agreed, adding that he was prepared to stay in Los Angeles as long as necessary to insure that they met the two-month deadline. Another condition Rāmeśvara raised was that the artists would be working as quickly as humanly possible, but the paintings might not be of the best quality. "A blind uncle is better than no uncle," Śrīla Prabhupāda said. When Rāmeśvara mentioned that the artists would have many technical questions, Prabhupāda agreed to make time to answer them. He also agreed that photographs of Indian holy places connected with Caitanya *līlā* could be used to supplement the paintings.

After their meeting with Śrīla Prabhupāda, Rāmeśvara and Rādhāvallabha felt that they had a chance. They left Śrīla Prabhupāda's room, running down the stairs. The marathon was on!

* * *

Although Śrīla Prabhupāda had said he would stay in Los Angeles, he soon decided to follow his original travel plans. Feeling compelled to see to the welfare of his disciples around the country, he left on a tour of thirteen ISKCON centers in the U.S. and Canada. Less than a month later, however, he returned to Los Angeles to see if his Press workers were keeping their vow of producing seventeen volumes in two months.

Śrīla Prabhupāda was pleased with the sincerity of his disciples. Seventeen books in two months he had asked them to produce, and they, rather than try to explain to him why this was impossible, had taken the order so seriously that they could not conceive of rejecting or changing or modifying it. Instead of modifying the order, they had modified their lives. They had gone beyond the realm of routine work into the realm of extraordinary effort. As a result, both they and Prabhupāda felt great satisfaction. As Prabhupāda said, it was all an arrangement for the satisfaction of Lord Caitanya and the previous *ācāryas*.

Śrīla Prabhupāda decided to take another U.S. tour, visiting Laguna Beach and San Diego and then going on to Dallas. From there he would visit New Orleans and the nearby ISKCON farm in Mississippi. Then on to Detroit, Toronto, Boston, and New York, eventually traveling to Europe and India.

From Prabhupāda's point of view, his touring was imperative for spreading Kṛṣṇa consciousness. As he had said in his arrival address at Berkeley during his last tour, "I am traveling all over the world, twice, thrice in a year. My duty is to see that my disciples, who have accepted me as guru, may not fall down. That is my anxiety."

Prabhupāda's concern was for his disciples, but also for all people. Distressed by the fallen and ignorant state of humanity, specifically in the West, he wanted to help the English-speaking world, as his spiritual master had ordered. This had been his spirit two years ago in Calcutta, when he had risen from his sickbed and flown to London to take part in the Ratha-yātrā. This was his great desire: to preach in the West, where people were so strongly under the grip of speculative philosophies, denying God and glorifying sense enjoyment. The mass of people would not easily change their ignorant ways, but if he could make only one person a pure devotee, he said, then his work would be successful.

Prabhupāda would work intensively with his important India projects for a few months, but then would always return to the West to again tour and preach. Both were required—developing his projects in India and touring the West.

* * *

Detroit
August 2, 1975

Alfred Ford, the great-grandson of Henry Ford, had become attracted to Kṛṣṇa consciousness through meeting some of Śrīla Prabhupāda's disciples in Detroit and through reading *Bhagavad-gītā As It Is*. He had adopted the principles of Kṛṣṇa consciousness, begun regularly chanting sixteen rounds, and was now Śrīla Prabhupāda's initiated disciple, Ambarīṣa. Today Ambarīṣa was at the airport, behind the wheel of a white Lincoln Continental limousine, waiting to meet Śrīla Prabhupāda. On seeing Śrīla Prabhupāda approach, Ambarīṣa got out of the driver's seat and offered obeisances. He opened the back door of the limousine for Śrīla Prabhupāda, shut it, and returned to his seat, just like a menial chauffeur.

"We devotees also have a car," said Prabhupāda as they drove away, "but we are going to the temple and distributing books with it. Anything can be used for Kṛṣṇa. Here is a rich man's son, Alfred Ford. We are giving him a little spiritual teaching, and he is happy."

Another of Śrīla Prabhupāda's Detroit disciples was Elisabeth Reuther, now Lekhāśravantī-devī dāsī, the daughter of labor leader Walter Reuther. Ambarīṣa told Prabhupāda that the Fords and the Reuthers had been enemies, but now two of their descendants were peacefully working together in Kṛṣṇa consciousness. Śrīla Prabhupāda was pleased with the humility of these two disciples, and while he gave them some special status, he did not dote on the fact that they were from such famous families. Ambarīṣa and Lekhāśravantī saw themselves as humble servants of the Vaiṣṇavas.

On the way to the temple, Prabhupāda's car passed a large, modern building displaying flags of many nations and a large sign: "World Headquarters, Ford." One of the devotees turned to Ambarīṣa and asked, "Is this where you work?"

From the back seat, Prabhupāda spoke up. "No, he is the proprietor."

As they passed by a big urban redevelopment project, Prabhupāda asked, "What is this?"

"This is known as Detroit's Renaissance Center," said Ambarīṣa.

"They will never have a renaissance," Prabhupāda replied.

The Detroit temple was located in an old brick house with the temple room in the third-floor attic. The lease was soon due to run out, and Govardhana, the temple president, was looking for a new place. He showed Prabhupāda photos of likely buildings, one of them a mansion of the late auto industry millionaire Lawrence Fisher. The place was probably too expensive, Govardhana said, and was located in a bad neighborhood.

But Prabhupāda was interested. In fact, whatever the devotees cited as bad, Prabhupāda would say was actually good, or at least could easily be rectified. As for the high crime rate in the area, he said, "You'll have nothing to fear. Just chant

Hare Kṛṣṇa and distribute *prasādam*. Invite all the neighborhood people, thieves, and rascals to take *prasādam* and chant, and you won't have any thefts."

Devotees emphasized that Detroit was the crime capital of the U.S. and that the poor slum area where the mansion was located was known for drug trafficking, robberies, and murders. But Śrīla Prabhupāda repeated that they should not be afraid. "I lived in the Bowery," he said, and he described how the bums used to urinate on his front door and lie across the doorway. But when he would come to enter the building, they would get up and say, "Yes, sir. Come on, sir."

"Get the place," Prabhupāda said, "and chant Hare Kṛṣṇa there twenty-four hours a day. If a thief comes, we will say, 'Yes, first take *prasādam*, and then take whatever you want.' What do we have?"

Śrīla Prabhupāda went to see the mansion with Govardhana, Ambarīṣa, and several G.B.C. men. They were met by the owner and a lady who introduced herself as the real estate agent.

As the owner guided them on a tour, Prabhupāda came to like the estate even more. The palatial building was situated on four acres surrounded by a high stone wall. There were gardens and walkways, now in disrepair, as well as fountains and a swimming pool. Some of the devotees thought the place gaudy, with its extravagant 1920s decor, but Śrīla Prabhupāda saw the great potential.

As soon as he entered the vestibule and saw the ornate Italian tiles and marble archways, he began to smile. The group entered the lobby, its high ceiling covered with classically sculptured leaves, rosettes, and hand-painted plaster flowers. Next they entered the ballroom, with its marble floor and high, vaulted ceiling painted to resemble an early-evening blue sky with clouds and stars. Special lighting gave the effect of natural starlight. At the end of the hall, three marble arches exactly resembled the design Prabhupāda had given for the Deity altars in his temples. Three altars could be installed there and the ballroom made into a temple with very little renovation. Prabhupāda did not comment to the owner on the ballroom's suitability, but to the devotees it was obvious.

The tour then proceeded to the boat well, an indoor water garage capable of holding several yachts. The boat well opened into a channel, which opened into the nearby Detroit River. Prabhupāda mentioned that the devotees could get a boat for their preaching.

As Prabhupāda and his entourage entered one gorgeous room after another, they saw the many carved stone columns, hand-painted floor and wall tiles from Italy and Greece, and ceilings ornamented with gold-leafed figures. Rare antique crystal chandeliers adorned many of the rooms. There were living rooms, library rooms, a dining room, a billiards room, a music room, two master bedrooms, other bedrooms—all extravaganzas. "Each room is worth the entire price," said Prabhupāda privately to the devotees.

The owner spoke of Mayan, Moorish, Spanish, Greek, and Italian influences, and pointed out that the two hand-carved spiral columns in the dining room were salvaged from an ancient European palace. Wherever Śrīla Prabhupāda looked, he saw opulence: an indoor marble fountain, a wall of iridescent tiles, hand-painted cornices. Even the large bathrooms were extraordinary, with glamorous imported tiles and gold-plated accents.

The introductory tour completed, Prabhupāda, his followers, the owner, and the real estate agent sat together at an umbrella-covered patio table by the swimming pool. Already Śrīla Prabhupāda had mentioned to his disciples that the owner should donate the building for ISKCON's missionary purposes, and he had told Brahmānanda Swami to make the request. Since the owner had not mentioned the price, Prabhupāda spoke up.

"So, we are beggars," he began. He was serious, and yet he spoke with an air of humor. Ambarīṣa and Upendra hid their faces in embarrassment. "We have no money," Prabhupāda continued boldly. "Therefore, we are asking you, please give us this building."

The owner glanced incredulously at his real estate agent and then laughed nervously. "It's out of the question," he said. "I can't do that."

The agent was also taken aback and upset. "He can't do that," she whispered.

"I can't give it to you," explained the owner, "because I have taken a loss in maintaining this property. So I have to make my money back. This property represents a major part of my income."

"Then," said Prabhupāda, "how much do you want?"

"Well," the man replied, "I have to get at least $350,000."

None of the devotees dared say anything. Prabhupāda thought for a moment and then said, "We will give you $300,000 cash."

"I'll have to think about it," the man replied.

The real estate agent got to her feet, saying that a transaction like this is usually not done straight to the owner. But Prabhupāda ignored her and spoke with the owner about how lovely the mansion was. Prabhupāda then got up and took a short walk in the garden with his men.

Govardhana asked Prabhupāda if he'd liked the place, and Prabhupāda said, "Yes, who would not like such a building?"

"Ambarīṣa doesn't like it," said Govardhana.

"Oh?"

Ambarīṣa said he thought the mansion was maya.

"Yes," said Prabhupāda, "but maya is also Kṛṣṇa. We can use anything in Kṛṣṇa's service."

Leaving the garden path and returning to their cars, Prabhupāda asked Ambarīṣa, "So, is this possible?"

"Yes, Prabhupāda. This is possible."

As soon as they returned to the temple, Ambarīṣa and Lekhāśravantī conferred. Her inheritance was limited, but she was able to give $125,000. Ambarīṣa had to come up with the balance.

The next day the owner came to see Śrīla Prabhupāda. The man was accompanied by two women, and they all appeared a little intoxicated. He had come to say that he accepted the offer. Prabhupāda smiled and reaffirmed his intention to buy.

Afterward, Śrīla Prabhupāda openly showed his blissfulness about the purchase. "Just see," he said, "I didn't have one penny, and yet I offered him $300,000 cash. And now Kṛṣṇa has provided the money."

As Prabhupāda had told the estate owner, "I am a sannyasi. I have no money." And after collecting $300,000 from his disciples, he still had no money. Within a few days he left for Toronto, taking nothing for himself. Everything was Kṛṣṇa's, to be used in Kṛṣṇa's service.

* * *

In Toronto Śrīla Prabhupāda's North American tour was suddenly interrupted. A telegram from Tejas in New Delhi announced that if Prabhupāda wanted an interview with Indira Gandhi, he would have to come at once. The telegram contained no details, and his secretary was unable to reach the Delhi temple by phone. But Prabhupāda didn't need to hear anything more. When an auspicious opportunity arose, he said, a devotee should act at once.

Harikeśa planned the trip so they could stop in Montreal overnight. From Montreal they would fly to Paris, where Prabhupāda could rest before going on to Delhi. As word of Prabhupāda's imminent departure spread, several devotees in Toronto tried to see him for last instructions about their projects. Rāmeśvara also phoned from Los Angeles, pressing Harikeśa to ask Prabhupāda a list of last-minute editorial questions regarding the Fifth Canto of *Śrīmad-Bhāgavatam*. The questions, however, concerning the *Bhāgavatam's* explanation of the structure of the universe, Prabhupāda rejected as unintelligent. He ordered the BBT to simply print the books as they were.

Not only was the prospect of meeting with Prime Minister Gandhi prompting Prabhupāda's return to India, but so were his uncompleted projects, especially Hare Krishna Land in Bombay. Brahmānanda Swami said he thought Prabhupāda had been looking for such a chance to end his Western tour and get back into personally managing the projects in India. Prabhupāda had just dictated a letter to Surabhi in Vṛndāvana, expressing disappointment that things could not get done without him.

> You are all simply writing letters to me. Without my personal presence there you cannot do anything. Simply correspondence. Anyway, be careful there is no underhanded dealing in

this transaction [purchasing land]. It is very much risky, so be careful. Please send me a regular report of the Bombay construction. I am very much anxious and will be glad to receive your regular report.

New Delhi
August 22, 1975

At 9:15 in the morning, Śrīla Prabhupāda and several of his leading disciples arrived at the prime minister's home, where they were confronted by a formidable security check. Two days before, the prime minister of Bangladesh had been assassinated, and Mrs. Gandhi was rumored to be next. Armed soldiers, therefore, surrounded her residence. The guards at the outer gate decided that the foreigners could not go in; Śrīla Prabhupāda alone could enter. While one guard opened the gate, another ushered Śrīla Prabhupāda into a car, which carried him to the prime minister's front door.

Meanwhile, the devotees waited in anxiety by the outer gate. Always some disciples would accompany Prabhupāda wherever he went; his disciples worried, almost like doting parents, that he might need their assistance.

In tiny, cramped handwriting, Śrīla Prabhupāda had noted down in a small address book a list of points he wanted to discuss with Mrs. Gandhi.

1. Grant immigration for 500 foreigners.
2. All M.P.'s initiated brahmanas.
3. Sanjaya the King.
4. Close slaughterhouses.
5. Chanting.
6. Meat-eaters—at home. No public meat-eating.
7. Prostitution punishable.
8. No religious group except Bhagavad Gita as it is.
9. All government officers must join kirtan at least twice a day.
10. Support Krishna consciousness all over the world.

The most pressing item was at the head of the list: Mrs. Gandhi should grant permanent visas to Prabhupāda's Western disciples in India. Just a few weeks before, some of the foreign devotees in Māyāpur had been asked to leave the country. For years Prabhupāda had been asking for permanent visas whenever he met governors, members of Parliament, or other men of influence. Devotees were constantly being asked to leave the country to renew their six-month visas. The travel costs incurred and the disruption of the devotees' services seriously hampered ISKCON's work in India; therefore, Prabhupāda wanted Indira Gandhi to sanction up to five hundred foreign disciples to stay permanently in India.

The other points of Śrīla Prabhupāda's list were scriptural directions for how the prime minister could make her leadership Kṛṣṇa conscious, in the spirit of the great *rājarṣis* of the Vedic age. These were the same tenets of God conscious leadership he preached wherever he went, and he had deep conviction that if the world's leaders would apply them, an era of peace, prosperity, and happiness would dawn. Indira Gandhi had a tendency toward authoritative control, so she should exercise it in terms of Vedic directions. Then her rule could become most effective and beneficial.

A government official opened the door to Śrīla Prabhupāda's car, ushered him into the house, and brought him before the prime minister. As Prabhupāda entered the room, Mrs. Gandhi stood up. Although she greeted him cordially and offered him a seat, he could immediately detect that she was distracted, fearful for her life. She openly admitted it, and added that this was not, therefore, a good time for their meeting. Prabhupāda felt that she would have preferred not to meet at all, but was allowing it only because she had promised. Her agreeing to see him, he felt, was an indication that she had some attraction for spiritual life, but he understood that on this visit at least, he could not introduce the extensive advice he had been contemplating

Mrs. Gandhi complimented Śrīla Prabhupāda on the work he was doing all over the world. "They are good boys," he replied, and he asked if she could arrange for permanent visas. She agreed, but again mentioned her present anxiety. They soon ended their talk, and Śrīla Prabhupāda left.

A few days later, while still in New Delhi, Śrīla Prabhupāda received a letter from Rāmeśvara. The BBT in Los Angeles was miraculously fulfilling Śrīla Prabhupāda's order to publish seventeen volumes in two months. The composers, editors, artists, and workers had ecstatically finished their marathon—on schedule! When the first books had come back from the printers and had been offered on the altar of Rukmiṇī-Dvārakādhīśa, the devotees had cried in transcendental bliss, chanting again and again the mantras to Śrīla Prabhupāda. They were feeling the potency of the order of their spiritual master and seeing themselves as instruments in carrying out what had once seemed an impossible request.

> Today our composer finished the last volumes of Caitanya-caritamrta. By Wednesday next week, August 20th, all volumes will be at the printer. Now they are just starting to compose the Fifth Canto, and the entire canto will definitely be at the printer by Vyasa-puja day.

After promising delivery of books by October at the latest, the letter was signed by about sixty devotees: "Your unworthy servants at ISKCON Press." On their behalf, Rāmeśvara stated,

> We have lost all desire to do anything except be engaged in producing and distributing your transcendental books by the millions in every town and village.

Śrīla Prabhupāda wrote back the next day from Delhi.

> Regarding your desire for all twelve Cantos, you will get it, rest assured. Your so much ardent desire will be fulfilled by Krishna.

On August 21, the appearance day of Lord Balarāma, Rāmeśvara sent Śrīla Prabhupāda a telegram.

> BY THE MERCY OF LORD BALARAMA, NITYANANDA, THE LAST VOLUME OF CAITANYA-CARITAMRTA IS LEAVING TODAY FOR THE

PRINTER. BY YOUR MERCY AND DIVINE ORDER IT IS DONE.

Although Śrīla Prabhupāda traveled on to Vṛndāvana, the devotees were able to dispatch advance copies of all fifteen volumes to him by his eightieth birthday on August 31. Just after Prabhupāda observed the ceremony in the temple, a devotee arrived in Vṛndāvana with the final six volumes of the *Caitanya-caritāmṛta.*

With great relish and satisfaction Śrīla Prabhupāda examined the books. He was pleased with the artwork and quickly became absorbed in reading the pastimes of Lord Caitanya. He felt so inspired he remarked to the devotees in Vṛndāvana that he was thinking of stopping all touring and just staying in Vṛndāvana and translating. The reciprocation of the devotees at ISKCON Press was so sincere that it increased Śrīla Prabhupāda's desire to reciprocate with them. He wrote to "My dear Ramesvara and company,"

> You have taken seriously the publishing and also the distribution of these books, and that is the success of our mission. You have taken seriously this work and I know that my Guru Maharaja is pleased with you because he wanted this. So by this endeavor you will all go back home, back to Godhead.

In a few short years, Śrīla Prabhupāda had seen the publishing facilities of ISKCON evolve from the small, hand-operated A. B. Dick printing press at his first storefront temple in New York to the sophisticated BBT operation in Los Angeles, equipped with the latest computer typesetting machines and staffed with a devoted, hardworking crew of managers, editors, proofreaders, artists, photographers, designers, layout artists, and phototechnicians. Whereas in India, before he had gone to the West, Śrīla Prabhupāda had struggled alone for months to organize the printing of a single volume of his *Śrīmad-Bhāgavatam* translations, he now saw his loving disciples rushing his manuscripts into print as fast as he could produce them. Moreover, they were simultaneously translating them into a variety of languages all over the world.

Vṛndāvana
September 13, 1975

On Rādhāṣṭamī Śrīla Prabhupāda laid the cornerstone for a large *gurukula* building adjacent to the Krishna-Balaram Mandir. He said that when it was built, the devotees should accommodate five hundred students there from all over the world. Through the gorgeous temple, the guesthouse, and soon the *gurukula,* Śrīla Prabhupāda intended to draw as many people as possible to the shelter of Kṛṣṇa in Vṛndāvana. For this end he was willing to sacrifice everything, even his peaceful writing. And for this end he also demanded his disciples to sacrifice.

Constant travel, Śrīla Prabhupāda said, was becoming more and more inconvenient—one reason for his return to India. But he was by no means stopping; unless he traveled, his movement could not remain vital and healthy. So he was prepared, despite inconvenience, to continue touring. Disciples never stopped inviting him to travel, and recently Puṣṭa Kṛṣṇa Swami had asked him to come to South Africa. When Prabhupāda agreed, Puṣṭa Kṛṣṇa had quickly arranged ten festivals and other engagements in Durban and Johannesburg, covering a period of three weeks in October.

Devotees on the predominantly Hindu island of Mauritius had also requested Prabhupāda to visit, mentioning that the prime minister wanted to meet him. Prabhupāda agreed. Leaving Vṛndāvana—making brief stops in Delhi, Ahmedabad, and Bombay—he was off to Africa.

Mauritius
October 24

Prabhupāda had come to Mauritius to meet with the prime minister. As a friendly gesture, the prime minister had sent a chauffeured car for Śrīla Prabhupāda's use during his stay. One day Prabhupāda was leaving to take a ride in the countryside, but as he was about to enter the car on the right side, Puṣṭa Kṛṣṇa Swami suggested, "Śrīla Prabhupāda, come to the other side. It's safer." And Prabhupāda complied. For half an hour they rode through the beautiful countryside, past sugarcane fields, mountains, and the ocean. At one point, they stopped and walked along a cliff beside the sea. When they returned to the car, Brahmānanda Swami opened the right-side door and Prabhupāda said, "No, the other side is safer," just as Puṣṭa Kṛṣṇa had previously suggested.

A few minutes later, as Prabhupāda's black Citroen was rounding a curve, a Volkswagen suddenly appeared, heading toward them in the same lane. Prabhupāda was seated behind Puṣṭa Kṛṣṇa, and Brahmānanda was seated behind the driver. The moment before the Volkswagen had appeared, Śrīla Prabhupāda had sat up, cross-legged, planting his cane against the floor of the car to support himself.

As the Volkswagen rushed toward them, the chauffeur braked, swerving to the left, but the Volkswagen swerved in the same direction. There was a head-on collision. Puṣṭa Kṛṣṇa's head hit the windshield, cracking the glass. The driver's head also slammed against the glass, and his face was covered with blood.

In the back seat, Śrīla Prabhupāda remained sitting, his face set gravely. Brahmānanda, in shock, suddenly embraced Prabhupāda, as if to protect him, although the danger had already passed.

Brahmānanda then jumped out of the car to try and flag down a motorist, and Puṣṭa Kṛṣṇa got out and opened the back door, where he found Śrīla Prabhupāda with his face bruised, his leg bleeding, and pieces of glass scattered at his feet. Prabhupāda didn't speak or indicate how he felt. Suddenly Puṣṭa Kṛṣṇa realized that the car, disabled on a curve, was in a dangerous position, so he joined Brahmānanda in the road to caution motorists and to try to get someone to stop.

The Citroen and the Volkswagen were totaled, and the man and woman in the Volkswagen were both injured. Motorists soon stopped, and when the injured persons had received help, Prabhupāda and the devotees got into a car and rode back to the temple.

Harikeśa was waiting anxiously, wondering why Śrīla Prabhupāda was so late, when suddenly Prabhupāda entered, walking very stiffly, saying nothing. When Harikeśa saw all three were injured, he cried out, "My God! What happened? What happened?" But Śrīla Prabhupāda just walked to his quarters and sat down, silent. A devotee brought bandages for the obvious injuries: Prabhupāda's chin, hand, and leg, and Puṣṭa Kṛṣṇa's and Brahmānanda's heads.

Śrīla Prabhupāda had said nothing since the accident. Finally he spoke: "*Asann api kleśa-da āsa dehaḥ.*" And he translated: " 'As soon as you accept this material body, there are so many difficulties.' We were sitting peacefully in the car, and the next moment—crash." He talked briefly about the collision, and Brahmānanda Swami told how just before the accident Prabhupāda had braced himself with his cane, preventing perhaps more serious injuries.

"Get some resin and turmeric," Prabhupāda said. "Mix it together with a bit of lye, and heat it." Prabhupāda was again speaking—*Bhāgavata* philosophy and practical medical remedies. It remained a frightening event, however, and Prabhupāda asked the devotees to have *kīrtana.* Kṛṣṇa had saved them, he said. Considering that both cars had been destroyed, the injuries were negligible.

Prabhupāda sat like a battle hero, anointed in three places with the yellow poultice, while Harikeśa read aloud from *Caitanya-caritāmṛta*—"The Disappearance of Haridāsa Ṭhākura."

Then Śrīla Prabhupāda began talking about the dangers of traveling, questioning the advisability of his extensive touring. His mission of translating *Śrīmad-Bhāgavatam* and other Vaiṣṇava literature was too important for him to be risking his life traveling in automobiles. He had been considering a visit to Nairobi before returning to Bombay, but now he said he would cancel his visit. He said he had never wanted to leave Bombay, but because they had made so many arrangements in Africa, he had come. Perhaps the accident was a sign that he should go back to India.

The next morning, with Brahmānanda Swami and Puṣṭa Kṛṣṇa Swami hobbling along, Prabhupāda went on his morning walk as usual, although he favored his injured knee. Again he discussed with his disciples whether he should go on to Nairobi or return to India. Cyavana, the president of ISKCON Nairobi, argued that Prabhupāda should go to Nairobi. The devotees there were expecting it, he said, and they had made arrangements. If Prabhupāda canceled now, he would probably not come back for a long time. Others, however, argued that there was no question of asking Śrīla Prabhupāda to keep going now, after this traumatic accident; he should go directly to Bombay.

Prabhupāda heard both opinions, but he was more affected by the consideration of disappointing the devotees in Nairobi than of recuperating after the accident. He decided to go to Nairobi.

But after only a few days in Nairobi, Prabhupāda became anxious to return to India. Reports were reaching him about mismanagement in Bombay and about building materials being stolen from the property through a conspiracy involving the workers, the storekeeper, and the *chaukidhars.* When Śrīla Prabhupāda heard this, he became so morose he stopped translating. He even stopped eating. Although thousands of miles from Bombay, he was feeling the pain more than any of the devotees there. Many of them, in fact, were not even aware that the theft was taking place. When Brahmānanda Swami asked Prabhupāda why he wasn't eating, he replied, "How can I eat when my money is being stolen?"

Bombay
November 1

Śrīla Prabhupāda's plane from Nairobi arrived in Bombay at one a.m., yet even at such an early hour he was greeted at the temple by a gathering of intimate life members, disciples, and even some of the tenants on the land. When the group followed him to his room, he confided that he had had a serious accident, and he even showed them the scar on his knee. He said he was relieved to be back. In a letter from Bombay he wrote,

> The accident was very disastrous, but still Krishna saved. . . . Perhaps I may stay here for some time for finishing our temple construction on this land.

Śrīla Prabhupāda immediately got to work. He fired the engineer, whom he held responsible for the poor, slow work and stolen building materials. At first Prabhupāda had tried to avoid hiring a construction company by having Surabhi oversee the whole project, assigning work to various subcontractors. But that wasn't working.

Śrīla Prabhupāda wanted a change, but there was no clear alternative. "We have come to Kṛṣṇa consciousness for a life of eternal bliss," he said to Surabhi. "But instead of eternal bliss, I am suffering eternal anxiety." He appealed to Surabhi, Girirāja, and the others to do something.

One day a life member, a construction engineer, visited the site and told Śrīla Prabhupāda the temple and hotel could easily be completed in six months. Prabhupāda then berated Surabhi, who said that six months' time was not enough. "Now I am nowhere," thought Surabhi. "I'm losing my service."

Then another life member, Mr. Omkar Prakash Dir, the chief engineer with E.C.C., one of India's largest, most reputable construction companies, came to the Sunday feast and examined the work. Appalled at the poor quality, he said that after two or three years it would fall apart.

Girirāja, impressed with the idea of hiring Bombay's biggest, most competent construction firm, spoke with Prabhupāda, who was also interested. At first Surabhi resented that the work was being taken out of his hands, but after meeting with Mr. Dir he also liked the proposed change.

The contract was made with E.C.C., and Mr. Dir presented a progress chart, detailing each phase of the work and showing when it would be completed. Śrīla Prabhupāda was pleased with their professional methods, despite the higher cost. Now the work would be done as professionally and as quickly as possible, and this was what mattered most.

Prabhupāda stayed for the greater part of November, and the construction progressed quickly. There was no question of cutting corners to save a little money, Prabhupāda explained to Surabhi. The temple had to be a beautiful jewel, so that people from all over India would want to come and stay. During the Vṛndāvana construction Prabhupāda had emphasized, "Why so much? Why not just simple?" But now he was stressing, "Why not more?" The temple should be opulent and ornate, with marble everywhere. The hotel should be the finest, with beautifully furnished rooms and an elegant restaurant. And the air-conditioned theater building should be one of the best in Bombay.

"Why not marble on the floors?" asked Prabhupāda, speaking of the hotel rooms.

"It's going to be very expensive," said Surabhi.

"Don't worry about the money," Prabhupāda said. "Can we put marble on the floor? Then do it." Surabhi did it, but tried to save money by putting a cheaper stone in the hotel hallways. When Prabhupāda saw it, he was displeased. It should have been all marble, he said.

Funds for the Bombay construction came primarily from the sale of books in America, and Śrīla Prabhupāda was regularly receiving reports. On November 18, Rāmeśvara sent a telegram with some of the good news.

> ONE MILLION COPIES OF BTG JUST PRINTED. DEVOTEES GONE WILD. PROMISED TO DISTRIBUTE ALL WITHIN ONE MONTH. SPANISH GITA JUST OFF THE PRESS BRINGING HUNDREDS OF MILLIONS TO YOUR LOTUS FEET. ALL POSSIBLE BY YOUR MERCY ONLY.

When the temple president from ISKCON Denver wrote asking about starting a jewelry business, Śrīla Prabhupāda wrote back, disapproving.

> Why are they doing business? This creates a bad atmosphere. We shall only do one business and that is book-selling. That's all. As soon as you become karmis after business, then spiritual life becomes damaged. This business should not be encouraged anymore. Doing business and not sankirtana, that is not at all

good. Sankirtana is very good, but grihasthas under condition can do other business, only if they give at least 50 percent. But sankirtana is the best business.

Prabhupāda envisioned that book distribution could not only finance Bombay construction but could also support his even more ambitious plans for Māyāpur. He approved a plan whereby all the various BBTs would contribute a minimum of ten percent of their yearly income toward the construction of ISKCON's international projects in India, especially the planned Mayapur city, with its towering Temple of Understanding. Such cooperation among the BBTs in different countries would help keep the growing Kṛṣṇa consciousness movement unified. Book distribution was good business, and it was the best preaching. It was Prabhupāda's formula—American money combined with India's spiritual culture—and he encouraged Rāmeśvara to motivate the *saṅkīrtana* in the U.S.A. in accordance with this principle.

America has the money, so this is cooperation between the blind men and lame men. It will make good relations between India and America. The next chance I have for meeting with Indira Gandhi I shall inform her about how much foreign exchange we are sending. After receiving your encouraging assurance that as book distribution increases, the amount BBT sends will also increase, we are now going to attempt a Kurukshetra project and the Jagannath Puri project. For the time being we are spending in India, but eventually we will spend everywhere. This will greatly enhance the Americans' spiritual position.

Always remain dependent on Guru and Krishna and your progress will always be assured.

Ever since the BBT Press marathon in the summer of 1975, the Press had continued to keep up with Śrīla Prabhupāda's writing. A sweet, transcendental competition had developed between Prabhupāda, his Press, and the book distributors. In November of 1975, Prabhupāda had written to one of the leading book distributors,

> The BBT says that they are publishing at the speed of my translating and that you will distribute at the pace of publishing. That's nice. But still I am ahead in my translation work. They owe me now the sixth canto of Srimad-Bhagavatam. I am working already on the seventh canto.

In recent months, however, Śrīla Prabhupāda's literary output had been diminishing, mostly because of his involvement in management.

Actually, the word *translating* is incomplete in describing Śrīla Prabhupāda's writing. Translating involved only the verses and synonyms, but Prabhupāda's deepest meditations—what he referred to as his "personal ecstasies"—were his Bhaktivedanta purports. Composing the purports, as well as translating the verses, came best when he could think about them throughout the day, not just when he turned on his dictating machine at one a.m. He was translating the extremely grave and complex Vedic knowledge into a modern context, thus making it understandable to Western readers. And it was a great, demanding task.

To best speak to the people of the world through his *Śrīmad-Bhāgavatam* writings, Śrīla Prabhupāda required a very conducive situation. After the Māyāpur festival, therefore, he formulated an itinerary that, in about a month's time, would bring him to Hawaii. There he expected to find an atmosphere beneficial for his literary work.

Hawaii
May 3, 1976

After brief visits in several Indian cities, as well as stops in Melbourne, Auckland, and Fiji, Śrīla Prabhupāda arrived in Hawaii on schedule. Immediately he began to increase his writing.

He had been in Honolulu about a week when he announced one morning, walking along Waikiki Beach, that he expected to finish that night the last purport to the Seventh Canto. When Hari-śauri expressed his happiness to hear this, Prabhupāda replied, "Oh, I can finish very quickly, but I have to present it for your understanding. It requires deep thought, very carefully, to present it for the common man."

Immediately Prabhupāda turned to the Eighth Canto, beginning with a prayer: "First of all, let me offer my humble, respectful obeisances unto the lotus feet of my spiritual master, His Divine Grace Śrī Śrīmad Bhaktisiddhānta Sarasvatī Goswami Prabhupāda." Prabhupāda explained that his spiritual master had instructed him at Rādhā-kuṇḍa in 1935 to stress book production more than temple construction. He had followed that instruction, beginning with his starting *Back to Godhead* magazine in 1944, and in 1958 he had begun *Śrīmad-Bhāgavatam.* As soon as he had published three volumes of *Śrīmad-Bhāgavatam* in India, he had started for the U.S. in August 1965.

Prabhupāda said he was making the *Bhāgavatam* understandable for the common man. This did not mean his writings were lacking in substance; they were pure substance. But in the essential spirit of the *Bhāgavatam* itself, Prabhupāda was omitting anything extraneous and distracting, selecting from the commentaries of previous *ācāryas* whatever would best impel his readers to pure devotional service.

Overwhelmingly, those university scholars who seriously read Prabhupāda's books appreciated the faithful quality of his *paramparā* rendering. Reviews came from all over the world.

> ". . . For those who have no access to the Sanskrit language, these books convey, in superb manner, the message of the *Bhāgavatam.*" Dr. Alaka Hejib, Department of Sanskrit and Indian Studies, Harvard University.
>
> ". . . It is a deeply felt, powerfully conceived, and beautifully explained work. I don't know whether to praise more this translation of the *Bhagavad-gītā,* it's daring method of explanation, or the endless fertility of its ideas. I have never seen any other work on the *Gītā* with such an important voice and style. . . . It will occupy a significant place in the intellectual and ethical life of modern man for a long time to come." Dr. Shaligram Shukla, Professor of Linguistics, Georgetown University.
>
> ". . . For the first time we possess a readily accessible edition

for this great religious classic that will provide opportunity for scholars in Indian literature and followers of the Kṛṣṇa consciousness tradition alike to compare the original text with a modern English translation and become acquainted with the deeper spiritual meaning of this work through the learned commentary of Śrī Bhaktivedanta.

". . . Anyone who gives a close reading to the commentary will sense that here, as in his other works, Śrī Bhaktivedanta has combined a healthy mixture of the fervent devotion and aesthetic sensitivity of a devotee and the intellectual rigor of a textual scholar. At no point does the author allow the intended meaning of the text to be eclipsed by the promotion of a particular doctrinal persuasion.

". . . These exquisitely wrought volumes will be a welcome addition to the libraries of all persons who are committed to the study of Indian spirituality and religious literature whether their interests are sparked by the motivations of the scholar, the devotee, or the general reader." Dr. J. Bruce Long, Department of Asian Studies, Cornell University.

"This English edition translated by A. C. Bhaktivedanta Swami Prabhupāda is superb. It contains the original Sanskrit and Bengali verses with their English transliterations, synonyms, translations, and elaborate purports, easily bearing testimony to the author's profound knowledge of the subject." Dr. O.B.L. Kapoor, Emeritus Chairman and Professor, Department of Philosophy, Government Postgraduate College, Gyanpur, India.

Prabhupāda's making *Bhāgavatam's* message "available," therefore, did not mean mere simplification. It meant urgently addressing the reader to give up the world of illusion and take to the eternal liberation of Kṛṣṇa consciousness.

Modern society, however, was so degraded that a preacher could no longer appeal to the authority of Vedic scripture—no one would accept it. Śrīla Prabhupāda's writings, therefore, dealt with such theories as the origin of life by chance, Darwinian evolution, and chemical evolution. And he defeated them all with strong logic, establishing that life comes from life, not from dead matter.

Prabhupāda's writings also combatted the false teachings of bogus yogis, gurus, and "incarnations," who had appeared like a tidal wave of falsity in Kali-yuga, both in India and in the West. His writings criticized modern political institutions also, analyzing why monarchies fell, why democracy was also failing, and how dictatorship would increasingly harass the citizens. The governments' policies of abusive taxation and their propaganda to bring people to the cities to work in the factories, abandoning simple, agrarian life, were all discussed in the light of the scriptures.

In his travels, Śrīla Prabhupāda had observed the rampant degradation of human society: sexual liberation, the latest fads in intoxication, and the vicious crimes of animal slaughter and meat-eating. A *Bhagavad-gītā* purport dealt specifically with the threat of nuclear holocaust.

> Such people are considered the enemies of the world because ultimately they will invent or create something which will bring destruction to all. Indirectly, this verse anticipates the invention of nuclear weapons, of which the world is today very proud. At any moment war may take place, and these atomic weapons may create havoc. Such things are created solely for the destruction of the world and this is indicated here. Due to godlessness, such weapons are invented in human society; they are not meant for the peace and prosperity of the world.

Prabhupāda's criticisms were strong and authoritative, befitting a true *ācārya;* his uncompromising spirit was appealing. He was not a timid scholar pointing out some obscure historical references. Yet underlying his writing, a humble tone of request spoke to the heart. As the servant of the servant of Kṛṣṇa, he asked everyone to please take up Kṛṣṇa consciousness and be restored to his original, constitutional position of eternity, bliss, and knowledge.

As Prabhupāda had originally left his writing at the Rādhā-Dāmodara temple in Vṛndāvana to preach in the West, so he could leave his writing retreat in Hawaii for preaching. In any case, he was prepared to continue writing wherever he went. All along he had planned to stay in Hawaii only for a month, not permanently. His disciples needed to see him for strength and inspiration, and as long as he had life and breath, this was his purpose.

* * *

Prabhupada wanted to first visit his Los Angeles center, now a large, thriving community of devotees. He would see their new temple room, with its marble arches and gallery of gorgeous transcendental paintings, and observe the opulent worship of the Deities Rukmiṇī-Dvārakādhīśa. He would see the latest technological applications of Kṛṣṇa consciousness at Golden Avatara recording studios and at the FATE museum, which utilized multimedia dioramas to depict the teachings of the *Bhagavad-gītā.* He would sit in his garden and hear *Kṛṣṇa* book and walk on Venice Beach discussing scientific theories with Dr. Svarūpa Dāmodara. And, of course, he would increase the already swelling waves of book distribution. One day in the car he had said, "My books will be the lawbooks of human society for the next ten thousand years."

* * *

New York City
July 9, 1976

Jayānanda was driving the car. Tamāla Kṛṣṇa Goswami and Rāmeśvara Swami were also there. They had picked up Śrīla Prabhupāda and Hari-śauri at La Guardia Airport, and as they proceeded toward Manhattan, Prabhupāda asked, "Things are going on here nicely?"

Tamāla Kṛṣṇa replied that everything had really just begun; the devotees were still moving into their twelve-story building in Manhattan and were making the final arrangements for Ratha-yātrā. "You will see that all of the work is just in progress," he said.

"Yes," said Śrīla Prabhupāda, "manage nicely. Kṛṣṇa is giving us everything. There is no scarcity. If we simply sincerely work, Kṛṣṇa will give us intelligence—everything. By His mercy everything is available. That is Kṛṣṇa. He can give you anything."

As their car approached the colossal Brooklyn Bridge, Śrīla Prabhupāda inquired, "That is Brooklyn Bridge, I think? Sometimes I was coming here and sitting down near the bridge."

"Near the water?" asked Tamāla Kṛṣṇa. They were fascinated to hear of Śrīla Prabhupāda's early activities alone in New York. "You were sitting near the water?"

"Yes, that river," said Prabhupāda. "Because I was on that Bowery Street. It is not very far away. So I was coming, walking there, and sitting under that bridge and thinking, 'When I shall return to India?'" He laughed. He asked about other places, almost like inquiring about old friends—the Fulton Street subway station and Chambers Street.

Tamāla Kṛṣṇa told Prabhupāda that the ISKCON center was not far from the Empire State Building and that he would be able to get a nice view of it from his room on the eleventh floor. "Our building," said Tamala Kṛṣṇa, "is right in the midst of the theater, restaurant, and entertainment section of the city."

"In New York," said Prabhupāda, "I feel a little at home, because first I came here. I was loitering on the street here and there. From 1965 September to July 1967, continually I stayed in New York."

"Tamāla Kṛṣṇa Mahārāja gave a class this morning," said Rāmeśvara Swami. "He was explaining that we cannot understand the good fortune of this city, that you have come here."

"Yes, when I decided that I shall go to a foreign country," said Prabhupāda, "I never thought of going to London; I thought of coming here. Generally they go to London, but I thought, 'No, I shall go to New York.'"

"Very progressive," Tamāla Kṛṣṇa commented.

"I do not know," Prabhupāda laughed. "It is Kṛṣṇa's dictation. I could have gone. London was nearer. But I thought, 'No, I shall go to New York.' Sometimes I was even dreaming that I had gone to New York."

As they passed through various neighborhoods, Śrīla Prabhupāda recalled the old days. He mentioned Dr. Misra's *yoga* studio and his room at 100 Seventy-second Street, where his tape recorder and typewriter had been stolen; the West End Superette, where he would buy fruit.

"Sometimes I think I was coming to this part," said Prabhupāda, looking out the window, "—aimlessly. Yes, sometimes walking on Second Avenue."

As they drove down Fifty-fifth Street, the devotees pointed out to Prabhupāda the ISKCON building, with the words Hare Krishna written in gold letters down the side. A large yellow banner showing a devotee of Lord Caitanya performing *saṅkīrtana* flew from the front of the building, and a stylish awning, emblazoned "Hare Krishna Center," extended onto the sidewalk. At the sight of Prabhupāda's car, hundreds of devotees at the entrance began to cheer and chant his name.

It was the largest gathering of ISKCON devotees since the Māyāpur festival. Many had come from distant places to be with Śrīla Prabhupāda, and more than six hundred devotees were staying in the building. The *kīrtana* was tumultuous. Standing before the Deities of Rādhā-Govinda, Prabhupāda appeared pleased. A picture of Lord Jagannātha, Balarāma, and Subhadrā was on the third altar, and Prabhupāda said he was anxious to see them on Ratha-yātrā day.

As Prabhupāda sat on the large green *vyāsāsana,* he was at first too moved with emotion to speak. "First of all I must thank you all for bringing me in the new temple," he began. "Because when I first came, my ambition was to start a temple here in New York, and I was seeking the opportunity." He described some of his first, almost helpless, attempts to buy a twenty-five-by-one-hundred-foot space in Manhattan; but he had been unable to get any money.

"I had no place," he said. "What to speak of a temple, I had no residential place even. So in that condition I was thinking of returning to India. Practically every week I was going to the shipping company. So it is a long history, that I came here with determination to start a temple in New York first. But at that time, ten years before, in 1965, it was not possible. But by the grace of Kṛṣṇa and by the grace of my Guru Mahārāja, you have got this place. So I must thank you very much for organizing this temple."

During Prabhupāda's ten-day stay in New York, the devotees remained in a triumphant, euphoric mood. For the Ratha-yātrā the devotees had permission from the City to have the parade down Fifth Avenue. Prabhupāda had said that New York was the most important city in the world and that a skyscraper would be a beacon of Kṛṣṇa consciousness for the world. So now ISKCON had its skyscraper in Manhattan, its Ratha-yātrā parade down Fifth Avenue, and Prabhupāda's personal presence.

The Ratha-yātrā procession, with its three fifty-foot-tall carts, began at Grand Army Plaza on Fifth Avenue and proceeded downtown. Young men, girls in saris, Indians, New Yorkers—hundreds—tugged at the ropes, pulling the gigantic chariots. With silken towers billowing yellow, green, red, and blue in the wind, slowly and majestically, the carts sailed south. The parade was complete with beautiful weather, hundreds of chanting and dancing devotees, and thousands of onlookers. And the route was some fifty blocks down Fifth Avenue, "the most important street in the world," to Washington Square Park.

At Thirty-fourth Street Prabhupāda joined the procession. As he came forward to board the chariot of Subhadrā, the devotees converged around him, amazing the policemen and other onlookers with their spontaneous adoration of Kṛṣṇa's representative. Although the inner meaning of Ratha-yātrā is the *gopīs'* desire for Kṛṣṇa to return to Vṛndāvana, these devotees were more absorbed in Śrīla Prabhupāda's return to New York.

It was a gorgeous, appropriate climax to Prabhupāda's ten years of preaching in New York City. When he had first come he had had no money, no place of his own to live, and no place for people to congregate and hear about Kṛṣṇa. Now he was riding in splendor down Fifth Avenue at the Ratha-yātrā festival, and his Rādhā-Govinda Deities had a skyscraper. In 1965 he had been alone on the street, but now he was accompanied by six hundred disciples, loudly singing the holy names and benefiting millions of conditioned souls.

When the procession arrived, Washington Square Park was crowded with people. A temporary stage had been erected, and Śrīla Prabhupāda and the Deities took their places. Kīrtanānanda Swami introduced Prabhupāda before the crowd, and Prabhupāda stood up to speak.

In the evening the parade and festival received good coverage on all major TV stations, and the next morning, pictures and articles appeared in the newspapers. Prabhupāda particularly liked the *New York Daily News* centerspread, where several photos bore a large caption: "Fifth Avenue, Where East Meets West."

"Send this cutting to many places," Prabhupāda said. "Send it to Indirā Gandhi. This title is very nice. This is the point. 'East meets West.' As I always say, the lame man meets the blind man. Together they do wonderful, and apart they cannot do anything. *He* is lame, and *he* is blind. But if they join together—Indian culture and American money—they will save the whole world."

Śrīla Prabhupāda heard from the *New York Times* article, which stressed how the parade included hundreds of Indians "who were pleased to see they could keep faith even in New York City." The article quoted "an Indian immigrant" as saying, "We love New York City, America. It's the most beautiful place in the world. No other country will give such freedom for our own ceremony."

"That's a fact," Prabhupāda said, "that I always say. The *Times* first published about my activities when I was in Tompkins Square Park."

At the festival site, *prasādam* had been served to seven thousand people. And even when the devotees had walked back uptown with the carts late at night, hundreds of people had followed and chanted. The devotees were already talking about how to improve the festival for next year. They could have a press box, and Prabhupāda suggested they rent a small building downtown and call it Guṇḍicā.* Lord Jagannātha

---

*The temple in Orissa, India, where Lord Jagannātha traditionally stays each year during His Ratha-yātrā pastimes.

could stay there for one week. Then the devotees should have another procession and festival, with Lord Jagannātha returning to the temple on Fifty-fifth Street.

"Last night," said Tamāla Kṛṣṇa Goswami, "all night we were cleaning up the grounds at the park. So one woman who lives next to the park said, 'In all my years of living here I've never seen such a wonderful festival held.' And on CBS television, the official who's in charge of the park said, 'We are very proud to be able to say that this park was founded hundreds of years ago when America was religious and that spiritual life is still present in Washington Square Park.' "

"So why not ask the mayor to construct a temple there?" said Śrīla Prabhupāda. The devotees all laughed. But Prabhupāda thought such things were certainly possible.

Śrīla Prabhupāda's health was worsening, as often happened when he traveled extensively. Particularly in New York his health began to suffer. His itinerary was to continue on to London, Paris, Tehran, Bombay, and then to Hyderabad, where he would conduct the opening ceremony of a new ISKCON temple. Senior devotees entreated him to rest awhile before going to England and India. He had spent a very pleasant day at the ISKCON farm in Pennsylvania, and the devotees suggested he go there for two or three months to rest, recover his health, and write. Every day they would beg him to please stay. When he heard that the G.B.C. members in New York had unanimously recommended he not immediately travel, he said, "All right. I will not travel."

But he could not be bound by the G.B.C., however—only by Kṛṣṇa. He already had his plane tickets, and he remained set on traveling.

On the morning of Prabhupāda's departure, a few devotees came to his room to make a last attempt, begging him not to travel. He said nothing, though he was obviously set on leaving. His servants were packing his bags and everything was ready to go. Nevertheless, even as he left his room and got on the elevator, a few men followed, still suggesting he not go.

"Prabhupāda, please reconsider," said Rāmeśvara Swami. Śrīla Prabhupāda had remained jolly so far, despite his physical weakness, and despite his disciples' pleading. But now his face changed.

"Don't travel," one devotee said. And another added, "Just stay. Sit down and rest."

Prabhupāda turned, and his eyes were very deep. More than ever he seemed not of this material world. "I want the benediction to go on fighting for Kṛṣṇa up to the last breath," he said, "just like Arjuna."

Everyone remained silent, and the important instruction burned into their memories. The elevator opened on the main floor and hundreds of waiting devotees chanted and cheered as Śrīla Prabhupāda walked to his car.

CHAPTER EIGHT

The Last Instruction

Bombay
January 9, 1977

Śrīla Prabhupāda started his morning walk before dawn. He and the devotees knew their way well through Hare Krishna Land to the public road, and once off the property, they turned left then right and began walking down the block leading to the beach. The sky began to lighten. At first they could not visibly distinguish land from sea from sky. But gradually subtle nuances of color revealed the horizon, and they could see the vast plain of the Arabian Sea stretching to meet an even greater sea of sky, where last stars twinkled and faded. As Prabhupāda and his small group walked along the broad beach, they were flanked on their left by a line of leaning palms and on their right by a rumbling surf.

Śrīla Prabhupāda wore a gray woolen *cādar* around his shoulders, a saffron silk *kurtā* and dhoti, and peach-colored canvas shoes. He used a cane, leaning not heavily on it, but lightly. With each brisk step he would point the cane ahead, poking it into the sand and lifting it again, rhythmically marking the pace. He walked erectly and held his head high.

A long line of Bombayites, many of them wealthy Juhu residents on their morning stroll, appeared, and a few coconut-*walas* set up their carts, cutting off the tops of choice coconuts in anticipation of their first customers. Śrīla Prabhupāda liked to walk at this time of morning, and weather permitting, he would do so no matter where he was in the world. Juhu Beach, however, was one of his favorite places to walk.

Along the way, he and his disciples were joined by Dr. Patel, in white shirt and pants, and several of his friends, mostly doctors and lawyers.

Suddenly Prabhupāda spoke. "There's a very big conspiracy against us."

"By the church?" guessed Dr. Patel.

"Not by the church," said Prabhupāda.

"By the society?"

Prabhupāda uttered a thoughtful "Hmm," then added, "Now they are determined to cut down this movement." He didn't give any details, and neither Dr. Patel nor the others could fully draw out what was on his mind. Whatever it was, said Dr. Patel, no conspiracy against Kṛṣṇa consciousness could take place in India.

"I wanted to start this movement in India," Prabhupāda replied. "I requested so many friends, 'Give me just one son.' But nobody agreed. They said, 'Swamiji, what will be the benefit by this if I make my son a Vaiṣṇava or a *brāhmaṇa*?' They do not give much importance to the movement. They are planning how to stop this movement in so many ways."

Always a faithful Indophile, Dr. Patel replied, "The Americans are always like that, always making propaganda."

"There is good and bad in every place," said Prabhupāda. "Kṛṣṇa says, *manuṣyāṇāṁ sahasreṣu*. Out of thousands of persons hardly anyone is interested in perfecting his life. This is Kali-yuga."

About five minutes before seven, Śrīla Prabhupāda left the beach and walked back to Hare Kṛṣṇa Land. As he approached, he saw the massive towers of the ISKCON hotel and the even taller and grander temple domes. The buildings were unfinished, but most of the construction had been done. The temple domes still had to be covered with marble, and all the buildings needed numerous finishing touches. Prabhupāda was anticipating the opening, but the construction head, Surabhi Mahārāja, spoke of delays. The opening date, therefore, remained indefinite.

Prabhupāda had had trouble ever since he had first tried to purchase the land from Mr. N. in 1971, and obstacles had plagued all his attempts for permission to build. Now the triumph of installing the Deities Rādhā-Rāsavihārī in one of the most gorgeous temples in all of India was near. Śrīla Prabhupāda was continuing his worldwide travels and pushing his movement ahead on all fronts, yet he regularly returned to Bombay. He could see when the workers were delaying, and he understood that they were sometimes cheating, although his own men weren't always aware. This time, as before, he would stay for awhile, give advice, and then move on.

Rādhā-Rāsavihārī were still being worshiped in the temporary shelter the devotees had erected in 1971. The magnificent temple building now loomed behind that humble shed, proclaiming that soon Rāsavihārī would move into His new palace.

On returning to the ISKCON property, Śrīla Prabhupāda came before the Deities and beheld once again Their charming beauty that made him sometimes indicate that of all Deities, these were the dearest to him. His promise to Rādhā-Rāsavihārī that he would build Them a beautiful temple was soon to become a living reality, but he sometimes expressed doubt as to whether he would live to see it. He was now eighty-one and was bothered by certain persistent illnesses.

Of course, the warnings of death were nothing new to Śrīla Prabhupāda, as he had had serious bouts with illness from the beginning of his preaching in the West in 1965. Yet despite his frequent remarks about retiring, his disciples found it difficult to imagine. Yes, they should by all means complete the work as soon as possible and open the Bombay temple, and yes, they should assure Prabhupāda that he could retire and eventually complete his *Śrīmad-Bhāgavatam.* But of course, Kṛṣṇa would allow him to remain with them and see the completion of at least these two projects.

Each month, one of Śrīla Prabhupāda's G.B.C. men stayed with him to serve as his secretary and to receive direct training and personal association. The secretary for January 1977 was Rāmeśvara Swami. Prabhupāda was genuinely pleased and enlivened when, early in the morning, Rāmeśvara entered his room, having flown straight from Los Angeles to Bombay. Prabhupāda considered Rāmeśvara an expert ISKCON manager, especially in printing and distributing Kṛṣṇa conscious literature, which was Prabhupāda's priority in preaching.

When Śrīla Prabhupāda asked Rāmeśvara Swami for news, he reported how the Kṛṣṇa consciousness movement was being attacked in America. Śrīla Prabhupāda was already aware of this, and it was, in fact, the "conspiracy" he had referred to on his morning walk. An anticult movement was now aggressively active and lumping the Hare Kṛṣṇa movement in with other new movements. Śrīla Prabhupāda was well aware of the "deprogrammers' " activities—kidnapping of devotees and intensively coercing them. And he had shown that he was not afraid of it. He assured the devotees that Kṛṣṇa would protect them and that the outcome would ultimately be in their favor.

The most significant battle, one that had concerned Śrīla Prabhupāda for several months, was a legal case in New York, where the temple president, Adi-keśava Swami, was being charged with employing mind control to keep the devotees in the temple. The parents of two adult devotees had pressed charges after hired deprogrammers had failed to break the two devotees' determination for Kṛṣṇa consciousness. In a spirit of anticult crusade, an assistant attorney general was prosecuting, using all the legal and governmental facilities at his disposal. Although civil libertarians were outraged and assured the devotees that the opposition could never win, the implications of the case were fearful nevertheless. The case challenged the very right of the Hare Krishna movement to exist as a bona fide religion and challenged the right of adult devotees to remain in the movement against the wishes of their parents. Also at issue was whether members of the Hare Krishna movement were members by their own choosing or were being kept in the movement by psychological manipulation, "brainwashing." When Śrīla Prabhupāda first heard of this case, his reply in a letter from Vṛndāvana had been like a clarion call to battle against the forces of illusion.

> Regarding the point about whether our movement is bona fide, you can use the following arguments. *Bhagavad-gita* has got so many editions. Our books are older than the Bible. In India there are millions of Krsna temples. Let the judges and juries read our books and take the opinion of learned scholars and professors. Regarding the second point about the parents' jurisdiction over their children, here are some suggestions. Do the parents like that their children become hippies? Why don't they stop it? Do the parents like their children to become involved in prostitution and intoxication? Why don't they stop this?
>
> They are now feeling the weight of this movement. Formerly they thought, "These people come and go," but now they see we are staying. Now we have set fire. It will go on. It cannot be stopped. You can bring big, big fire brigades but the fire will act. The brain-wash books are already there. Even if they stop externally, internally it will go on. Our first-class campaign is book distribution. Go house to house. The real fighting is now. Kṛṣṇa will give you all protection. So, chant Hare Kṛṣṇa and fight.

Sitting with Śrīla Prabhupāda in Bombay, Rāmeśvara Swami informed him that a nationwide committee of professors and theologians had come to the defense of Kṛṣṇa consciousness in the New York case and that many lawyers and psychologists were sympathetic.

Prabhupāda explained that the greatest shock for the materialists was that the Kṛṣṇa consciousness movement strongly opposed illicit sex, meat-eating, and intoxication. To them, for a person to give up these things was so shocking that they could not accept it was happening because of a genuine spiritual experience. Referring to a previous case, Śrīla Prabhupāda said, "In Germany they also accused that the old man is sitting in Los Angeles, and he has engaged all these young boys in collecting money for him. They are thinking that way, that I have some mind control power, and I have engaged these men—they are getting money, and I am enjoying."

Śrīla Prabhupāda recalled how, as early as 1969, when his temple in Los Angeles had purchased a few cars and the number of devotees had begun increasing, the neighbors had become envious. Prabhupāda said that he had invited them to also come and live in the Kṛṣṇa consciousness community, but that their reply had always been no. Prabhupāda said that the more the opposition created a turmoil, the more Kṛṣṇa consciousness would become famous. He also reasoned that people were reacting to his very strong preaching.

"You do not understand how to face the opposing party," Śrīla Prabhupāda explained. He was in an animated, argumentative mood, enthusiastic to show his disciples how to defeat the opposition. He had sometimes described his own spiritual master as *siṁha* ("lion") guru, and they now saw him in a similar fighting spirit. "The more opposition there will be," he said, "the more we have to defend."

"In regard to brainwashing," said Rāmeśvara, "they claim that our life-style tends to take the devotee and isolate him from the world."

"Yes," said Prabhupāda, "we hate to mix with you. No gentleman tries to mix with loafers. Crows will not like to live with the ducks and white swans, and white swans will not like to live with crows. That is natural division. Birds of the same feather flock together."

Rāmeśvara: "They have a list of five or six conditions, and they say if all these conditions are present, then it is a suitable atmosphere for brainwashing. They say we are imposing those conditions on our members."

Prabhupāda: "Yes. We are brainwashing from bad to good. That is our business. We are washing the brain from all rascaldom. Your brain is filled up with all rubbish things—meat-eating, illicit sex, gambling. So we are washing them. Don't you cleanse your room? Is that bad? So if you wash your room very clean, who blames you? But you are so rascal that you charge us, 'Why are you washing away this garbage?' We are washing out the garbage, and you are protesting. This is your intelligence. But intelligent men wash away the garbage. That is the law of civilization, to cleanse. That we are doing.

"According to Vedic civilization you are actually untouchable. Now we have come to touch you. Therefore wash—first you must wash. According to Indian civilization the dog is untouchable, but he is your best friend. So you are not touchable. Therefore, we have to wash your brain. Unless your brain is washed, you cannot understand Kṛṣṇa. Man is known by his company. You sleep with dog, you eat with dog, your best friend is dog, so what you are? You must be washed, scrubbed."

Rāmeśvara: "But this is their argument, that the standard in America is that you become learned in different fields—science, music, art, and literature. This standard of culture and education is coming from the idea of the Renaissance in Europe. But in our Hare Kṛṣṇa movement we are isolating ourselves from these things and simply reading one set of literature—Kṛṣṇa."

Prabhupāda: "This other is not culture. As soon as you change, that means it is not culture. It is *mano-dharma*, mental concoction. Yes, we want to stop your nonsense. That is our mission. Those who are intelligent, they have taken. And you also take."

Rāmeśvara: "They say that if we claim our members are gentlemen, then why is it that they go to the airport and bother so many people?"

Prabhupāda: "They are not bothering. They are educating. When a thief is advised, 'Kindly do not become a thief,' he takes it as botheration. But it is good advice."

Rāmeśvara: "They say it is invasion of privacy. Every man has the right to think the way he wants."

Prabhupāda: "Yes. Therefore I have got the right to think like this and to sell books."

Rāmeśvara: "So if I do not want to hear your philosophy, why do you impose it?"

Prabhupāda: "It is not imposing. It is good philosophy. We are canvassing: 'Take it. You will be benefited.' And they are being benefited. Those who are reading, they are being benefited. And why are you advertising—big, big signboards: 'Please come and purchase'? Hmm? Why are you imposing your so-called goodness on us? Why are you doing?"

Back and forth the battle went, hour after hour, Rāmeśvara unleashing all the arguments against the Kṛṣṇa consciousness movement, and Śrīla Prabhupāda defeating them. Prabhupāda called the arguments "childish" and "foolish," and he strongly criticized the materialistic demeanor from which they sprang. By *śāstra* and logic he proved that the nondevotee has no good qualities and is less than an animal because of his lack of God consciousness. Such a person, he said, was in no position to criticize, and his criticisms only showed ignorance of the real purpose of human life.

Prabhupāda was absorbed in defending the Kṛṣṇa consciousness movement. He relished fighting on behalf of Lord Caitanya. He was speaking, of course, mainly for the benefit of his disciples, but beyond that, he was expressing his compassion for all beings and his dedication to the Kṛṣṇa consciousness movement.

Rāmeśvara: "But the Christians say that, according to the Bible, if God wanted us to believe in Kṛṣṇa He would have told us on Mount Sinai, and He would have told us through Jesus Christ. Jesus said, 'I am the only way.' "

Prabhupāda: "That's all right. But Jesus Christ did not explain more to you because you are rascals. You cannot follow even his one instruction, 'Thou shalt not kill.' It is not the foolishness of Jesus Christ. But because you are so rascal, you cannot understand him. Therefore he avoided you rascals. Because whatever he said, you cannot follow. So what you will understand? Therefore he stopped speaking."

Rāmeśvara: "I think we've used up all our arguments."

"Actually," Śrīla Prabhupāda concluded, "their arguments are not very sound. Therefore it is simply a plan of Kṛṣṇa to help give us some prominence. It will make us more well known." Opposition, he said, was just an opportunity to preach. But to deal properly with the legal cases and other serious opposition, the devotees would have to know *how* to preach. And they would have to be spiritually strong. He was readying his men, speaking to them day and night.

Bhubaneswar
January 1977

After one month, another of Śrīla Prabhupāda's G.B.C. men, Satsvarūpa dāsa Goswami, replaced Rāmeśvara Swami as Prabhupāda's secretary for the month. "Śrīla Prabhupāda," Satsvarūpa asked one evening while sitting with Prabhupāda in his quarters, "when I first came here Rāmeśvara Mahārāja said that you had been speaking of how Kṛṣṇa consciousness would rise to power in the United States, and I find it hard to have that vision, since now it is just the opposite."

"It is true," said Śrīla Prabhupāda, "but now it has only taken its roots. You have to water and protect it, then you will get fruit. You have to give it protection. People must hear about us by our books, and we have to talk about the books."

"So it is not that it will happen overnight?"

"No," said Śrīla Prabhupāda. "Gradually it will grow. The seed is there. Now protect it by introducing more and more books in every house."

Again, Prabhupāda referred to the upcoming New York court case. "At least tell them to read our books," he said. "This is our statement. Our defense is that you first of all read these books and then give your statement. Finish this, and then give your judgment. Give them all these eighty-four books."

Śrīla Prabhupāda became excited by the thought of the judges and lawyers reading all his books. He was completely serious, and he insisted the devotees get the authorities to read the books as legal evidence. Śrīla Prabhupāda continued, "Kṛṣṇa says, *sarva-dharmān parityajya:* 'Surrender to Me and give up all other religion.' Now the question may arise, 'Why we shall surrender?' Then you can argue and go on for three years. The whole thing will come out: What is God? What is creation? What is your position? Why you should surrender? And so on, and so on, so on. What do you think?"

"Yes, we should introduce the books as much as possible," said Satsvarūpa. "I'll write a letter to New York and tell them to emphasize this."

"Bring all these books in the court," Prabhupāda said. "One time in Calcutta there was a big lawyer named Mr. Ghosh. So on one case he brought so many books for argument. The judges were friends, so they very mildly criticized him, 'Oh, Mr. Ghosh, you have brought the whole library?' 'Yes, my lord,' said Mr. Ghosh, 'just to teach you law.' " Śrīla Prabhupāda laughed and repeated, " 'Yes, my lord, just to teach you law.' "

Prabhupāda wanted his disciples to apply the same logic in the New York case. If the judge objected and said, "Why have you brought so many books to bother me?" the devotees should reply, "You have to hear. It may take twelve years to hear, but you have to hear. This is the law." It sounded difficult, but the devotees knew they would have to try. This was Śrīla Prabhupāda's specific instruction for handling the case.

"We have to say," said Prabhupāda, "we never tried to brainwash. We have done exactly according to *śāstra,* authority. Here is the evidence. We have not manufactured anything. So they must read all the books. I think you should take defense in that way."

"Our defense statement is already written there in the books," said Hari-śauri.

"Certain sections?" asked Satsvarūpa. "Or should we say that they have to read all the books?"

Prabhupāda shouted, "All! Line to line. Our defense is eighty-four volumes."

"But they'll say," said Guru-kṛpa Swami, " 'If we read all these books, we'll become brainwashed too.' "

"That is my duty," said Prabhupāda. "You are trying to brainwash me, and I am trying to brainwash you. This is going on. That is the tussle. It is wrestling. You are trying your strength. I am trying my strength. Otherwise, where is there fight? You have got right to not agree with me. I have got right to not agree with you. Now let us settle."

Māyāpur
February 7, 1977

More than eighty Bengali *gurukula* boys, along with some one hundred other devotees, greeted Prabhupāda with a *kīrtana* at the front gate of the Māyāpur Chandrodaya Mandir. The entire ISKCON land seemed to be blooming with flowers, and the freshly painted temple building shone like the first reddish rays of dawn. The new building, a long residential building, was almost completed. "Back to home, back to Godhead," Prabhupāda said softly, as his car entered the gate and slowly proceeded toward the temple.

Later, while sitting in his room on the second floor, Śrīla Prabhupāda complimented the devotees for making the grounds so beautiful and clean. Hundreds of flowers decorated his room like a gorgeous garden. "These flowers are your first success," said Prabhupāda. He sat back, relaxed with the special pleasure and satisfaction he felt when in the atmosphere of his beloved Māyāpur. "For Kṛṣṇa's service," he said, "you submit some plan, and He's very glad. We want some flowers for Kṛṣṇa's service, and Kṛṣṇa is supplying. *Everything* we want for Kṛṣṇa, not for our sense gratification. For Kṛṣṇa we can endeavor multifariously—that is the contribution of Bhaktisiddhānta Sarasvatī."

Later, Śrīla Prabhupāda went to oversee the new building—the longest building in West Bengal, Jayapatāka Swami said—more than seven hundred feet. Śrīla Prabhupāda said it looked like a train. He inspected all the rooms one by one and emphasized that they must be ready in time for the festival. Walking along the veranda he remarked, "Oh, it is just like Fifth Avenue."

The next few days were quiet. Prabhupāda would sit taking his massage in the late morning on the roof amid hundreds of potted plants. Leaning on the rail of the veranda outside his room one day, he looked down onto the lawn where one of the women was picking flowers for the Deities. "This is temple," he said, "—always something going on. And with each flower picked, she advances in spiritual life a little more." Prabhupāda particularly liked that the Mayapur Chandrodaya Mandir was always being expanded and improved. He liked to look out from the veranda and see guests arriving, devotees working, and new plans manifesting.

But Prabhupāda's ill health persisted—an imbalance of *pitta* and *vāyu* (bile and air), he said. One morning when his servant asked him how he felt, he replied, "Very bad." But sometimes after a "very bad" morning, he would feel much better.

The devotees did not think of Prabhupāda's illness in a material way, but it caused them anxiety. Over the years he had gone through various health crises, and the devotees knew these illnesses were transcendental, directly controlled by Kṛṣṇa. In 1974, when he had been very ill in Vṛndāvana, he had said that the cause was his disciples' not strictly following the rules and principles of Kṛṣṇa consciousness. His disciples knew they had to strictly follow his orders if they actually cared for his health. He would go on taking risks—accepting more disciples, traveling and preaching—but his disciples had to avoid acting in ways that would disturb his health. Mostly the devotees preferred to think that Prabhupāda's health would soon improve. And Śrīla Prabhupāda himself did not dwell on the subject; he was too absorbed in spreading the Kṛṣṇa consciousness movement.

A few days after his arrival, Śrīla Prabhupāda journeyed by car and ferry to Navadvīpa to visit the *āśrama* of his Godbrother Bhaktirakṣaka Śrīdhara Mahārāja. But while walking up the steep stone steps, Prabhupāda's legs suddenly gave way, and he collapsed. Fortunately, Hari-śauri was close enough to catch him. It was the second time Prabhupāda had collapsed in less than two weeks. Both times he had been actively preaching, and both times he had continued on his way with no mention of what had happened.

One morning just after breakfast, Prabhupāda was on his veranda looking out across the land of Māyāpur. Turning to Hari-śauri, he said, "Actually it does not matter even if I die immediately. I have given the basis of everything, and now if they simply manage things nicely and follow whatever programs I have begun, then everything will be successful." Hari-śauri was disturbed to hear such statements, and he remained speechless. Then Prabhupāda added, "But still I would like to finish this *Śrīmad-Bhāgavatam.*"

With Gaura-pūrṇimā only about a week away, thousands of Bengali pilgrims were attending the ISKCON center each night. They streamed into the temple room for *kīrtana* and *darśana* of Rādhā-Mādhava and then went to see the ISKCON photo exhibit. It was the biggest and best-organized Māyāpur festival ever. Despite the opposition in America, Lord Caitanya's movement was flooding the world with the waves of *saṅkīrtana,* and this gathering of more than five hundred devotees from every continent was a powerful testimony to the good health of the growing Kṛṣṇa consciousness movement.

Rāmeśvara Swami returned with the latest figures of Prabhupāda's book production. In the English language alone Śrīla Prabhupāda had published 43,450,000 pieces of literature. And the total production of Prabhupāda's books in 23 languages, including Russian, was 55,314,000, more than 90% of which had already been distributed. Rāmeśvara also presented Śrīla Prabhupāda with a new book just off the press, the Ninth Canto, Part One, of *Śrīmad-Bhāgavatam.* Rādhāvallabha reported that the next printing of *Bhagavad-gītā As It Is* would be so large that the paper required to print it would have to be carried on 76 train cars. Prabhupāda and the devotees laughed at the astounding figures.

Prabhupāda thanked the devotees for their hard work. "This is the blessing of my Guru Mahārāja," he said. "He wanted it. And because we are trying to do this, he is giving us all blessings."

Śrīla Prabhupāda continued to be very active: encouraging devotees, writing, preaching. Soon after the busloads of devotees arrived, however, he became very ill again. His busy schedule became a strain, but he continued.

The G.B.C. men began their annual three days of meetings, and each evening they would meet with Prabhupāda. He heard their proposals and, after making some corrections, approved them. The final item on the G.B.C.'s list of resolutions was that all ISKCON temples hold twenty-four-hour *kīrtana,* in view of Prabhupāda's sickness. The devotees had also done this in 1974 when Prabhupāda had been ill. "Yes," Prabhupāda said when he heard the resolution, "chanting is the only cure for all diseases."

Almost two weeks later, while Śrīla Prabhupāda was still in Māyāpur, the news of the New York court decision appeared on the front page of *The Times of India.* On receiving it, Tamala Kṛṣṇa Goswami immediately brought a copy to Prabhupāda in his room and, at Prabhupāda's request, read it out loud.

HARE KRISHNA MOVEMENT IS BONA FIDE RELIGION

> Washington, March 18. The Hare Krishna movement was called a "bona fide religion" yesterday by the New York High Court Justice who threw out two charges against the officials of the movement of "illegal imprisonment" and "attempted extortion." The charge had been preferred by an angry parent that his son, as well as another disciple, had been held by the movement illegally and that they had been brainwashed. "The entire and basic issue before the court," said the Justice in dismissing the charges, "is whether the two alleged victims in this case and the defendants will be allowed to practice the religion of their choice and this must be answered with a resounding affirmative." Said Mr. Justice John Leahy, "The Hare Krishna movement is a bona fide religion with roots in India that go back thousands of years. It behooved Merril Kreshower and Edward Shapiro to follow the tenets of that faith and their inalienable right to do so will not be trampled upon. The separation of church and state must be maintained. We must remain a nation

> of laws, not of man. The presentment and indictment by the Grand Jury was in direct and blatant violation of the defendants' constitutional rights." The Justice said that it appeared to the court, "The people rest their case on an erroneous minor premise to arrive at a fallacious conclusion. The record is devoid of one specific allegation of a misrepresentation or any act of deception on the part of any defendant." The Justice said, "The freedom of religion is not to be abridged because it is unconventional in beliefs and practices or because it is approved or disapproved by the mainstream of society or more conventional religions. Without this proliferation and freedom to follow the dictates of one's own conscience in this search of approach to God, the freedom of religion will be a meaningless right as provided for in the constitution. In the attempt, be it direct, well-intentioned or not, presents a clear and present danger to this most fundamental basis and eternally needed right of our citizens—freedom of religion." The Hare Krishna movement has been under pressure from various groups and this judgment is expected to stop some of the harassment in which it has been subjected in recent months.

"My mission is now successful," said Śrīla Prabhupāda. "In 1965 I went there. This is now recognized after twelve years. I was loitering in the street alone, carrying the books. Nobody cared . . . Kṛṣṇa is wonderful always. He is the most wonderful person, and He can do anything wonderful."

Śrīla Prabhupāda continued to make appreciative remarks about the judge's decision. He said he had feared the case might have taken fourteen years, and yet it had not even taken fourteen hours. Kṛṣṇa was so wonderful.

* * *

March 22

The senior devotees in Māyāpur felt Śrīla Prabhupāda was too ill to travel and that he should remain there and recuperate. Besides, reports from Bombay were conflicting. Surabhi Swami, knowing that Prabhupāda's quarters weren't finished, wanted more time, so he wired Prabhupāda, requesting him not to come. But Girirāja and others had been arranging a lecture program for Śrīla Prabhupāda at a pandal in Azab Maidan in Bombay, and Girirāja had written inviting Prabhupāda. Prabhupāda considered the opportunities for preaching and decided to go. He had his secretary send a telegram from Māyāpur to Bombay.

> PRABHUPADA ARRIVING TUESDAY AT 1350 HAVE ROOMS READY IN WHATEVER CONDITION.

But on Prabhupāda's arrival in Bombay, he was so weak that he could not walk down the steep stairs from the airplane, and airline personnel arranged for him to be lowered to the ground by hydraulic lift. Once he was on the ground, several devotees assisted him in walking. Although he appeared frail, he smiled brightly when he saw the devotees waiting for him at the airport.

Hare Krishna Land was intense with activity as some two hundred workers plied their various skills in constructing the temple-hotel complex, under the direction of Surabhi Swami and his assistants. A dozen men were cutting redstone slabs to cover the concrete superstructure of the hotel; almost fifty marble workers were chipping away with hammers, making decorative columns and arches in the temple; and masons and interior finishers were working on the theater building. Much of the work was completed, yet everything still appeared bare, like bones without flesh. The hotel had no windows or doors and, of course, no furniture or curtains, and the temple was mostly an unfinished structure. The work crews were moving quickly, concentrating especially on Śrīla Prabhupāda's quarters on the top floor of one of the hotel towers.

As Śrīla Prabhupāda entered his beautiful quarters at Hare Krishna Land, he remarked that no one could outdo Surabhi Swami. "I think I haven't such place to live anywhere else in the world," he said. "Los Angeles and New York are big, big cities, and London, Paris—but nobody can present such a luxurious royal palace."

Seeing how the one large room was arranged to facilitate

his different activities, Śrīla Prabhupāda said, "This is like my room at the Rādhā-Dāmodara temple. In one corner I am writing, in another corner I am sitting, in another corner I am taking *prasādam.*" The comparison was odd, since the Rādhā-Dāmodara place was a tiny cell, yet Śrīla Prabhupāda saw them as related: the beginning in Vṛndāvana and the apex in Bombay. In either place, he was the same person, humbly taking a little *prasādam,* writing his books, and ambitiously planning for spreading Kṛṣṇa consciousness.

Śrīla Prabhupāda discussed with several of his disciples and Dr. Sharma about his daily routine in Bombay. He said he would come down for a *darśana* of the Deity and would lecture once a week, on Sunday. On special occasions he would see a visitor in his quarters, but rarely. "Generally," he said, "people come to visit and say, 'How are you? How are you feeling?' And he takes a half hour even. So what is the use of wasting time like that, 'How are you?' Everyone knows that I am not feeling well."

"So they can come to the temple room in the morning," said Tamāla Kṛṣṇa Goswami.

"Yes," said Prabhupada. "If they actually want to see me, I am going there. They can see me for a half hour. And for talking, there is no need of talking, 'How are you? How are you feeling?' This is not talking."

"Instead," said Gargamuni Swami, "they can buy some of your books downstairs."

"Yes," said Prabhupāda, nodding approvingly. "This is a waste of time. I want to stop this, to answer all these things, 'How are you?' " By saving his time and energy, he said, he could work on his book-writing. Devotees assured him that everyone would appreciate this schedule and would be happy that he was working on the Tenth Canto.

"I think I shall be able to work from today," Prabhupāda declared. "Now I have got very nice place, full freedom. So there will be no difficulty."

That Prabhupāda would not take any morning walks went without saying. Everyone closely involved with Śrīla Prabhupāda had come to accept a new way of living, with no morning walks and very few classes. Someone suggested that

Prabhupāda might like to walk on the roof, but even that seemed to be too difficult.

Certain managerial affairs Prabhupāda would try to avoid, although often to no avail, such as concerning the delays in completing the construction work at Bombay. He could hear the sounds of the work, and sometimes it was noisy, but it was the slowness that perturbed him. Sometimes he would sit silently for hours and then remark to his servant or secretary that he was very upset by the delays. "You are sincere workers," Prabhupāda told the devotees in charge, "but no intelligence. I can see that this construction work is not going on. Am I to close my eyes? I can do that, but I am a sensible man. How can I close my eyes? They are all giving their excuses."

Śrīla Prabhupāda had no regular doctor. From time to time a *kavirāja* might show up to give a diagnosis and some medicine. But Prabhupāda wouldn't take it very seriously. He didn't consider these *kavirājas* very qualified, and if the medicine tasted bitter or produced any bad effect, he would stop taking it. Everything was up to Kṛṣṇa, and a doctor couldn't change that. Prabhupāda mentioned the relative merits of Āyur Vedic and homeopathic medicines, but like any other mundane topic, medicine was something he showed little interest in.

The days went by peacefully, with mild, pleasant breezes always passing through Śrīla Prabhupāda's room. His intelligence was always sharp and alert, and yet his health did not improve. Bhavānanda Goswami had come from Māyāpur and had been intimately serving Śrīla Prabhupāda, but he had to return to Bengal for important preaching duties. Śrīla Prabhupāda said there was no doubt that Bhavānanda was the best at giving massage and taking personal care of his spiritual master. But the personal servant's duties were not as important as preaching.

Śrīla Prabhupāda would repeatedly mention that the ISKCON leaders should prepare to carry on without his direct management. One day he was recalling some of the incidents of his first year in New York City, when suddenly he began speaking of the future. "Don't spoil it," he said. "Now it is up to you, my senior men. I can part away from you. My health is not good. I am old man. It is not surprising. Now you G.B.C., young boys, you are American, expert. You have all intelligence. So you don't spoil it. Let the movement go forward more. You have a lot of nice places. Don't be anxious for. And even if I go, where is the harm? I have given my ideas and direction in my books. Just you have to see it. I think I have done my part. Is it not? Do you think so or not?"

"Yes, you have done everything. Still, we want the whole *Bhāgavatam,* Śrīla Prabhupāda."

"That will be done," said Prabhupāda. "Even it is not full, there is no loss. You are competent. You can take charge. Now you can take charge of all the money, and let me remain free from management. My only request is, don't spoil it. I have sometimes chastised so that it may not be spoiled."

Prabhupāda said that for him to see that things were going on nicely under his ISKCON leaders would make him happy. "And I will go on writing books. That will be all right?" He said there was no need for him to eat any more. Since he was not physically active, there was no purpose in taking a lunch of *capātīs* and rice.

Girirāja expressed that it was the pleasure of Prabhupāda's devotees to see him eat and relish *prasādam.* But Śrīla Prabhupāda disregarded this and said the brain could be kept active just by a little fruit or even milk.

These moods—Prabhupāda speaking of retirement and fasting, even hinting of passing away—were only occasional moods. They were very real, practical, and sober, but he would soon turn to other things, promising his continual involvement with his disciples, his movement, and the world. After a brief spell of such talking, he would again be commenting fiercely on the follies of the scientists and politicians.

Śrīla Prabhupāda occasionally talked of traveling to a place better for his health. It was May, and Bombay was hot. Soon the monsoons would come. He had considered going to Kashmir, because the air and water were reputedly good for health; but no suitable accommodations could be found there, and the weather was too cool. Then one day he received a visit from Sriman Narayan, the former governor of Gujarat.

"You should take care of your health," said Sriman Narayan. "I hope you get better."

"Oh, this is just an old machine," Prabhupāda laughed. "The more you cure it, the more it gets worse. But my work never stops. That keeps on going. My main work is to write these books, and that is going on." Several other Indian guests were present, and they at once began recommending good places for health: Srinagar, Kashmir, Dehradun, Masouri, Simla, Hardwar.

"Yes, the water in Hardwar is good," said Sriman Narayan, "but better than that would be in Hṛṣīkeśa, where the Ganges flows. Whatever places are on the bank of the Ganges, the water will be very good. Let us arrange for that." From that moment, going to Hṛṣīkeśa became a definite plan, and Prabhupāda prepared to leave Bombay within a week.

* * *

The first week in Hṛṣīkeśa was idyllic, heavenly, with perfect weather and hopes of Prabhupāda eating and recovering. But on the eighth night, a violent storm hit, and with the storm came a drastic turn in Prabhupāda's health. He said the end was near, and he asked to go immediately to Vṛndāvana, in case Kṛṣṇa wanted him to depart from the world very soon.

The devotees in Hṛṣīkeśa had been in high spirits, and so had Śrīla Prabhupāda. While crossing the Ganges by boat, Prabhupāda had requested drinking water to be fetched from the center of the river. He had liked the lodge provided by his host, and he had even gone into the kitchen to show his disciples how to cook. Word had spread through the pilgrimage-tourist town that A. C. Bhaktivedanta Swami was present, and Prabhupāda had agreed to hold a *darśana* from five to six p.m. daily. The room had always been crowded at that hour with forty to fifty people, including Western hippies and seekers as well as Indians on pilgrimage and vacation. Although Śrīla Prabhupāda's voice had been extremely faint, he had spoken with force, stressing *Bhagavad-gītā* as it is.

When an American hippie had questioned him skeptically, Prabhupāda had replied, "You cannot understand, because you are crazy." And when a lady had put forward materialistic welfare work as the highest good, Prabhupāda had replied, "Your compassion is as valuable as blowing on a boil to heal it."

Only a few disciples were with Prabhupāda in Hṛṣīkeśa, and they had deemed it was a wonderful treat. Not only had Prabhupāda directed the cooking, but he had told stories while cooking. He had said that only a lazy man couldn't cook, and then he told a Bengali story—the story of a lazy man—to illustrate. There was a king who decided that all lazy men in his kingdom could come to the charity house and be fed. So many men came, all claiming, "I am a lazy man." The king then told his minister to set fire to the charity house, and all but two men ran out of the burning building. One of the two men said, "My back is becoming very hot from the fire." And the other advised, "Just turn over to the other side." The king then said, "These are actually lazy men. Feed them."

But on the evening of May 15, Śrīla Prabhupāda could neither sleep nor work at his dictation. The storm, a harbinger of the monsoon season, knocked out all electric power in Hṛṣīkeśa. Since the fans were not running and the window shutters had to be closed because of the wind, the room became very hot.

At five in the morning Śrīla Prabhupāda called for Tamāla Kṛṣṇa Goswami and said he was feeling weak. Tamāla Kṛṣṇa massaged Prabhupāda for an hour. Even at dawn the wind did not let up, and sand was blowing.

The storm and power failure continued the next night. Tamāla Kṛṣṇa asked Prabhupāda about the swelling in his hands and feet, and Prabhupāda replied, annoyed, "Why you are bothering? It is *my* body, and I am not disturbed." But then he added, "From the material point of view, it is not good. Please consider how everything may be turned over to the G.B.C., so that in my absence everything will go on. You may make a will, and I will sign it." He was talking definitely about things that before he had only alluded to.

Suddenly, at one-thirty a.m., Prabhupāda rang his bell, and Tamāla Kṛṣṇa and Kṣīracora-gopīnātha responded. From beneath his mosquito net, he said, "As I was telling you, the symptoms are not good. I want to leave immediately for Vṛndāvana." If it was time for him to pass away, he said, then let it be in Vṛndāvana. Since he wanted to leave immediately, the devotees stayed up all night, packing and preparing to leave. Train reservations were not available, however, so they decided to go by car.

* * *

As they turned off the Delhi–Agra Road, Śrīla Prabhupāda saw for the first time the stone marker, "Bhaktivedanta Swami Marg." They soon met up with Guṇārṇava, who was waiting on a motorcycle and who joyfully sped ahead to tell the devotees at the Krishna-Balaram Mandir that Śrīla Prabhupāda was here. At the gate of the temple a big *kīrtana* party, including all the *gurukula* children, was gathered to greet Prabhupāda with chanting and dancing. Four devotees carried Prabhupāda in a palanquin to the temple hall, where he offered his respects to the two Lords, Kṛṣṇa and Balarāma. After the *ārati* ceremony honoring Śrīla Prabhupāda, Prabhupāda spoke briefly to the assembled devotees.

"If death takes place," he said, "let it take place here." Seeing his demeanor and hearing him speak these unexpected words, some of the devotees in the room began to cry. "So," he continued, "there is nothing to be said new. Whatever I have to say, I have spoken in my books. Now, try to understand it and continue your endeavors. Whether I am present or not present, it doesn't matter. As Kṛṣṇa is living eternally, similarly, the living being also lives eternally, but *kīrtir yasya sa jīvati.* One who has done service to the Lord lives forever. So, you have been taught to serve Kṛṣṇa. So with Kṛṣṇa, our life is eternal. The temporary disappearance of this body, it doesn't matter. The body is meant for disappearance. So live forever by serving Kṛṣṇa."

After one day in Vṛndāvana, Śrīla Prabhupāda wrote,

> I was staying in Hrsikesha hoping to improve my health, but instead I have become a little weaker. Now I have come back to my home, Vrindavan. If anything should go wrong, at least I will be here in Vrindavan.

Śrīla Prabhupāda called for Tamāla Kṛṣṇa Goswami. "There are two things," he said "—trying to survive and to prepare for death. It is better to plan for the worse. Arrange to always have three or four men with me. Have *kīrtana* and read *Bhāgavatam* all the time. Now I am trying to take little food. Parīkṣit Mahārāja would not even take water."

Seeing Śrīla Prabhupāda's mood, Tamāla Kṛṣṇa mentioned the need for a will, and Prabhupāda agreed.

The writing of the will would not be done with the attitude that the end had come, but in the spirit of "preparing for the worst." It also meant finishing things so they would not have to be done at the last minute. Prabhupāda was concerned that his movement continue securely, with all ISKCON properties in the possession of his disciples within the institution and all his instructions made clear for the future. These matters should be dispatched now in a will, and the G.B.C. men should gather in Vṛndāvana to make these last arrangements and to be with him.

Tamāla Kṛṣṇa wanted to double check to see that Prabhupāda actually wanted all the G.B.C. men from all over the world to come. It would be costly and demanding, so he wanted to be sure that Prabhupāda really wanted it. When Śrīla Prabhupāda assured him that he did, Tamāla Kṛṣṇa, who saw his service as responding to whatever Śrīla Prabhupāda desired, also spoke in favor of the idea.

"Because they love you," said Tamāla Kṛṣṇa, "I am sure they will all want to come and be with you."

"Your love for me," said Śrīla Prabhupāda, "will be shown by how much you cooperate to keep this institution together after I am gone."

The word was sent to all G.B.C. secretaries worldwide. Śrīla Prabhupāda might depart very soon, and he wanted them to be with him in Vṛndāvana. As soon as possible, the G.B.C. men left their duties and came to him.

The G.B.C. men met and decided that aside from Prabhupāda's will, which would secure the ISKCON properties, and aside from making all the bank accounts within ISKCON secure, there were also a few questions which they should put before Prabhupāda before it was too late. These questions, such as how future disciples would be initiated, would have to be answered; otherwise they would become a source of speculation and havoc after Śrīla Prabhupāda's departure.

A selected committee from the G.B.C. came before Śrīla Prabhupāda as he sat up in bed in the main room downstairs. Satsvarūpa dāsa Goswami was to be the spokesman, but he felt shy and uneasy. To come directly before Śrīla Prabhupāda and ask about what should be done after his passing away might seem impertinent. But it was necessary. Śrīla Prabhupāda himself had requested that the G.B.C. come to Vṛndāvana to take care of exactly this kind of business.

"Śrīla Prabhupāda," said Satsvarūpa, "we were all asked by the rest of the G.B.C. to come to ask some questions. These are the members of the original G.B.C. as you first made it out. Our first question is about the G.B.C. members. We want to know how long should they remain in office?"

Śrīla Prabhupāda spoke slowly and deeply. "They should remain for good. Selected men are chosen so that they cannot be changed. Rather, if some competent men are found, they should be added."

Satsvarūpa asked what to do if a G.B.C. member gave up his post, and Prabhupāda said that the G.B.C. body should elect another man. "Our next question," Satsvarūpa proceeded, "concerns initiation in the future, particularly at that time when you are no longer with us. We want to know how a first and second initiation would be conducted."

"Yes," said Śrīla Prabhupāda, "I shall recommend some of you." What he had already described many times throughout his Bhaktivedanta purports was now being implemented: his disciples would become gurus and accept disciples of their own.

Satsvarūpa next asked about the BBT. "At present," he said, "no translated works are to be published without your seeing and approving them. So the question is, is there any system for publishing works in the future, works that you may not see."

"That we have to examine expertly," Prabhupāda replied.

He accepted the principle that future works could be translated from Sanskrit, but he cautioned, "But amongst my disciples, I don't think there are many who can translate properly."

Śrīla Prabhupāda went on to describe the special qualifications for translating Sanskrit Vaiṣṇava literature. It would take a realized soul, he said. "Otherwise, simply by imitating, A-B-C-D, it will not help. My purports are liked by people because it is presented as practical experience. It cannot be done unless one is realized."

Śrīla Prabhupāda had already given the outline for his will to Tamāla Kṛṣṇa Goswami. The G.B.C. would be the ultimate governing authority in ISKCON. Three trustees would be assigned to each ISKCON property. The G.B.C. was to make a thorough draft and make the will legal.

For Śrīla Prabhupāda, a will meant protection for his ISKCON. As Śrīla Prabhupāda had explained, a devotee has not a tinge of self-interest—everything is for Kṛṣṇa. But in his purity he must not be naive. ISKCON was a large, growing organization of properties and monies intended one hundred percent for use in the devotional service of Kṛṣṇa. Śrīla Prabhupada called on the G.B.C. to be vigilant.

At times like this, it became especially clear that the day was approaching when Prabhupāda's children would have to grow up and lead, manage, protect, and expand his society on their own. These might well be their last chances to learn directly from him and to be close with him for chanting the holy name and dedicating themselves utterly to carrying out his desires for ISKCON.

A few days later the final version of the "Declaration of Will" was notarized in the presence of a lawyer. The G.B.C. men, each of whom had pressing leadership and administrative duties within their respective zones, began to feel the need to return to their posts. When some of them expressed their plans to return to their areas of work, Prabhupāda gave his permission. They had been together for a week, and now, one by one, they began to disperse. Within another week most of them had left Vṛndāvana. Śrīla Prabhupāda and his small staff remained, and the constant chanting continued, performed by the devotees of the Krishna-Balaram temple.

* * *

As June came in Vṛndāvana, the weather remained very hot. The sky, which had been a clear blue, turned hazy as the first moisture arrived. Between noon and four p.m., the ground was too hot for bare feet, and the residents of Vṛndāvana would stay home, confining most of their activity to either the morning or the late afternoon and evening. Even eating was excluded from the midday hours, since the heat killed the appetite. The Yamunā was shallow and hot, giving little relief. The cows were gaunt from lack of grass and feed, and occasional hot, searing winds raised dust clouds. Flies and mosquitoes died in the air. One of the few pleasant features of summer was the fragrance of *bel* flowers that climbed along the walls around Prabhupāda's garden, somehow thriving in the dry heat.

In the first days of June, Śrīla Prabhupāda experienced some hope of recovery. He asked to resume his morning rides, and when being brought down to the car, he said, "Soon I will get down and walk myself." His old friend from Allahabad, Dr. Ghosh, came and diagnosed his disease as anxiety for the devotees of the Kṛṣṇa consciousness movement. Śrīla Prabhupāda agreed. But he didn't follow the doctor's orders, since they included having his blood pressure checked regularly and taking various medicines and special treatments. But by receiving massages from his servants, he felt he was improving. At this rate, he said, he would be all right after a month and a half. But he stressed, "I am not leaving Vṛndāvana until I am well."

* * *

July brought the rainy season to Vṛndāvana. Clouds began building from the beginning of the month, and by mid-July it would be raining daily. The perfumed odor of the *kadamba* flower was heavy in the air, and after a rain, the *nim* blossoms would give off their onionlike aroma. The peacocks, with their full-feathered tails, became ecstatic, dancing, cooing, and calling. Sometimes a sudden rainstorm would come even while Śrīla Prabhupāda was sitting on his bed or at his dictating desk in an unsheltered part of the veranda, and his servants would rush out to move him inside as quickly as possible. Sometimes when rain prevented his using the garden he would recline instead on the little porch overlooking the garden. But at least the 120-degree heat was broken, and the days became more bearable.

Prabhupāda quietly rested and continued his day's routine, waiting to see what Kṛṣṇa desired. He would often wake about six a.m. and open his eyes to see Tamāla Kṛṣṇa at his bedside. He would then extend his hands, indicating that he wanted to sit up in bed. Tamāla Kṛṣṇa or another servant would then lightly stroke Śrīla Prabhupāda's back while Śrīla Prabhupāda spoke his mind.

Very few devotees were visiting Vṛndāvana, and guests were rarely allowed to see Prabhupāda. His health was not improving, nor did it seem to be at a crisis point as it had been in May. But because he was hardly eating anything, he was not building his strength. His main treatment consisted of hearing *kīrtana*, *Śrīmad-Bhāgavatam*, and *Caitanya-caritāmṛta*.

July was a good month for Śrīla Prabhupāda's work on *Śrīmad-Bhāgavatam*. He continued dictating very early in the morning and in the afternoon, completing chapters Eight and Nine of the Tenth Canto. It was his great pleasure to do so. Working on *Śrīmad-Bhāgavatam*, he was completely transcendental to his physical condition, despite the accompanying heart palpitations and despite his faint voice and general weakness. Even to sit was difficult, and yet once he began working, nothing could stop him.

Speaking into the hand microphone of his dictating machine, oblivious of his bodily condition, Prabhupāda described patiently and methodically how Nanda Mahārāja's family priest, Gargamuni, performed the name-giving ceremony for baby Kṛṣṇa. In his purports, Śrīla Prabhupāda often spoke from his personal experiences and realization.

Sometimes sitting in the predawn open air on the second-floor veranda and sometimes in the humid heat of bright afternoon, Śrīla Prabhupāda worked, describing the limitless Vedic knowledge, just as his predecessors, the Gosvāmīs and Kṛṣṇadāsa Kavirāja, had done when worshiping Kṛṣṇa and Lord Caitanya while living in Vṛndāvana. Śrīla Prabhupāda, however, was the first great *ācārya* to make Kṛṣṇa conscious literature available to persons of all countries throughout the world, regardless of birth status or previous character. Even as he composed the latest chapters of *Śrīmad-Bhāgavatam,* thousands of young men and women were working on his behalf to preach the Vedic message to the world. His disciples were, in fact, keenly aware of how Śrīla Prabhupāda was producing the Tenth Canto purports in Vṛndāvana, and they prayed to Lord Kṛṣṇa that he be allowed to continue for many years, so that he could complete the entire *Śrīmad-Bhāgavatam.*

Śrīla Prabhupāda was concerned that what he wrote be published and distributed; it was his service to his Guru Mahārāja. And he received great satisfaction in hearing that book distribution was still expanding all over the world. Harikeśa Swami, the G.B.C. of northern and eastern Europe, reported that he was printing a very large quantity of books in thirteen languages. After hearing only the beginning of this report, Śrīla Prabhupāda exclaimed, "All the blessings of Bhaktisiddhānta Sarasvatī Mahārāja on you! You are the most important grandson of Bhaktisiddhānta Sarasvatī. Go on doing like this."

In a similar mood, Śrīla Prabhupāda pushed his G.B.C. secretary for India, Gopāla Kṛṣṇa, to produce Hindi books faster and in greater quantities. Whenever Gopāla Kṛṣṇa came to visit Śrīla Prabhupāda without a new publication, Prabhupāda would reprimand him for his slowness. Gopāla

Kṛṣṇa therefore began a policy of visiting Prabhupāda only when he had a new book to present. In mid-July, when Gopāla Kṛṣṇa brought a copy of *Śrīmad-Bhāgavatam,* First Canto, Part Two, in Hindi, Śrīla Prabhupāda accepted it happily and said, "Twice now unless he brings some book he won't come, because every time I criticize him: 'Where is the book? Where is the book?' "

Toward the end of July, Prabhupāda's health seemed to be worsening again. And again he mentioned that the end might come at any moment.

Tamāla Kṛṣṇa had been acting as Śrīla Prabhupāda's personal secretary for six continuous months, and he had become Prabhupāda's eyes and ears and his spokesman, especially in dealing with ISKCON management. And he had also become a personal confidant, assisting Śrīla Prabhupāda in his transcendental moods. As a sincere servant, he now began suggesting a different remedy. Śrīla Prabhupāda had recently been feeling and expressing intense devotion towards his disciples in their preaching. Taking this as a cue, Tamāla Kṛṣṇa suggested that if Prabhupāda could travel to the West and be with his disciples there, he would find new life.

"But if I die," said Prabhupāda, "I want to do so in Vṛndāvana." Tamāla Kṛṣṇa replied that Śrīla Prabhupāda should not think of dying. If he would go on a tour of the West, see the devotees there, take *prasādam* made from food grown on the ISKCON farms, then certainly he would respond to such devotion and regain his appetite and strength.

Tamāla Kṛṣṇa gave encouragement: "When you get there, with so many devotees who are giving their lives for spreading Kṛṣṇa consciousness and assisting you, it will really be enthusing. And you won't have to speak so much. It's your presence—your seeing the devotees and their seeing you. So in that sense, it won't be exhausting. It's a good climate now, too—August—in London. It's a very good time."

Prabhupāda turned to Upendra and said, "His words are making me feel different. Just hearing, I become enthusiastic."

"Śrīla Prabhupāda," said Tamāla Kṛṣṇa, "by going West I know you will recover."

"May Kṛṣṇa fulfill your words," said Śrīla Prabhupāda.

July of 1977 had begun a special time for pious Hindus, and the people of Vṛndāvana spent extra time in reading scriptures and visiting holy places. So by the end of July, when the trees and bushes were freshening with green leaves, pilgrims came in crowds to Vṛndāvana and to the Krishna-Balaram Mandir. Despite the mud and the rain, many of the people were in a jubilant mood, relieved from the oppressive heat and anticipating Jhulana-yātrā, the swing festival of Rādhā-Kṛṣṇa. Jhulana-yātrā was Vṛndāvana's biggest festival and would occur in mid-August this year.

The local newspapers were giving reports on Śrīla Prabhupāda's health, and a genuine concern for his well-being prevailed throughout Vṛndāvana and surrounding villages. Therefore, because of the festival season as well as out of concern for Śrīla Prabhupāda, many people were coming to the Krishna-Balaram Mandir. Those who came around nine a.m. got to see Śrīla Prabhupāda when he went for his morning *darśana* of the Deities.

Śrīla Prabhupāda still had no appetite and had scarcely eaten during the past six weeks. He was no longer regular in his times for sleeping, taking massage, or sitting up and translating. Feeling himself to be at a critical period, he had given permission for the devotees all over ISKCON to recite a simple prayer: "My dear Lord Kṛṣṇa, if You desire, please cure Śrīla Prabhupāda." He would regularly go before the Deities each morning. Wearing his dark sunglasses and sitting erect in the rocking chair, he would hold his palms together in a gesture of prayer, while two men, one in front and one behind, carefully carried the rocker from Prabhupāda's room into the temple room. They would set the chair down first before the Deities of Gaura-Nitāi, then before Kṛṣṇa-Balarāma, and then before Rādhā-Śyāmasundara. Then they would carry him to a central spot in the courtyard, under the *tamāla* tree, and set his chair down on the black and white checkered marble floor.

Śrīla Prabhupāda would sit facing Kṛṣṇa and Balarāma, and the devotees would sit down around him and begin a *kīrtana*. As the *kīrtana* began, two *gurukula* boys would rise and come in front of him, where they would begin dancing with arms upraised, their cotton *cādars* swinging back and forth. Prabhupāda would usually not speak or even smile, but after a few minutes he would give his garlands to a devotee, who would place them around the necks of the dancers. Soon two other young boys would come forward, and the first boys would garland them with the garlands they had received from Śrīla Prabhupāda and sit down. For half an hour, the dancing and singing continued. Guests to the temple would gather, many of them offering money at Prabhupāda's feet, which rested on an embroidered silk cushion.

Śrīla Prabhupāda was gaining resolve to go to the West. "If I can work a little more," he said, "our society will be very strong. I want to see that what I have done is made still stronger."

Prabhupāda's talk of travel, however, coincided with increasing weakness. He talked less. When Tamāla Kṛṣṇa tried to encourage him to translate, he replied, "When I get inspiration, I will take it up. Don't try to force me. I am going through a difficult time and am now feeling restless. It is not mechanical."

The Jhulana-yātrā pilgrims were mostly villagers. Many were from Rajasthan, the men and women wearing bright colored clothes and the women wearing heavy gold and silver bangles and bracelets, which clanked as they walked barefoot on the roads. The numbers of mendicant sadhus also increased, and they became a common sight, with their ash- or clay-covered bodies marked with brightly colored *tilaka*. The Yamunā had flooded in many places and was too swift for bathing or swimming. Thousands of visitors came to the Krishna-Balaram Mandir, which was now one of the most popular temples in all of northern India. The evening *ārati* at Krishna-Balaram was so crowded that resident devotees couldn't attend but could only stand in the back of the courtyard at the edge of a packed, jostling crowd. Some of the *gurukula* boys would greet the guests with Hindi *Back to*

Godhead magazines, each boy selling two or three hundred magazines a night. Śrīla Prabhupāda was glad to hear this.

A report came from Abhirama in Calcutta that Śrīla Prabhupāda's passport had finally been secured and the American Consulate in Calcutta would help in getting the green card for the U. S. Tamāla Kṛṣṇa ran upstairs and told Śrīla Prabhupāda, "There is very good news." Śrīla Prabhupāda was lying down in bed, but when he heard the news he began to slowly clap his hands, saying, "Give me good news and keep me alive!" He began to think ahead to London. "The Rādhā-Kṛṣṇa Deities there are so nice," he said. "Rādhā-Londonīśvara—an innocent boy, He is." Śrīla Prabhupāda thought of the Bhaktivedanta Manor. "That lawn before my room is magnificent," he said. "I think good time is coming."

* * *

When Prabhupāda arrived in London his disciples there were shocked. They had never imagined that he would be so thin or that anyone could travel in such condition. For the devotees who had been at the airport to meet him, it had been a heart-rending experience. Even those who had heard the reports of Prabhupāda in Vṛndāvana were not emotionally prepared for such a change. Prabhupāda was as transcendental as ever, or even more than ever, but the devotees were shocked at first to see him so different. Now he appeared like a powerful sage who had been undergoing long austerities for the benefit of humankind and who had become transcendental to his body, although living within it. Śrīla Prabhupāda's visit to London gave the devotees great hope for his recovery.

Śrīla Prabhupāda looked forward to traveling to America shortly after Janmāṣṭamī, which would fall on September 6, two weeks from the date of his arrival in England. "I want to live a little longer," he said, "to make everything more perfect."

"Will you do this by enthusing the devotees by staying with them," asked Tamāla Kṛṣṇa, "or is there a specific program?"

"A specific program," said Śrīla Prabhupāda. "I want to introduce *varṇāśrama*. A our Pennsylvania farm, the biggest problem of life is solved: food." He considered the establishing of the model Vedic social system on ISKCON farm communities as an important unfinished part of his life's mission. But after Prabhupāda had been in London two weeks, on the day after his birthday celebration, his health suddenly became much worse. This was the first crisis since his coming to England, and suddenly his plans changed. Instead of going on to the United States, as he had planned, he now requested that he be taken back to India. He spoke of Bombay. "If I live a few days more," he said, "let me see the opening of the Bombay temple. We can wait here and then fly to Bombay. I have worked so hard for it. If I see the opening and then die, it will be a very peaceful death. And if I live, then I can come back here."

Śrīla Prabhupāda went to Bombay, but his health was not improving. Finally he announced that he would rather return to Kṛṣṇa-Balarāma in Vṛndāvana than continue staying in such critical condition in Bombay.

"But Śrīla Prabhupāda," said Tamāla Kṛṣṇa, "what will happen to all the devotees here? They have been serving you so sincerely. How will they be able to open the temple without you being here? I mean, all the devotees, when they hear you are going to Vṛndāvana, they will want to come. They won't want to stay here. Then they will all want to leave their posts and come with you to Vṛndāvana."

"Yes, then let them come," said Śrīla Prabhupāda. "I have no objection." Tamāla Kṛṣṇa mentioned that if a thousand devotees might come to be with Prabhupāda, that would slow 'own the ISKCON work all over the world. Prabhupāda again said he had no objection. Tamāla Kṛṣṇa asked whether it was compulsory for the G.B.C. members to come, and Prabhupāda affirmed that it was.

* * *

The devotees at the Krishna-Balaram Mandir were upset to see that Prabhupāda's condition had deteriorated so much in the one month he had been away. His room was as he had left it, except for the addition of a large double bed. He lay down, and they closed the curtains and dimmed the lights. For about five minutes he lay still, with his eyes closed.

"Now you are home, Śrīla Prabhupāda," said Tamāla Kṛṣṇa.

Still Śrīla Prabhupāda lay quietly, not moving. Then slowly he brought his hands to his chest, clasped them together, and said, "Thank you." He seemed relieved.

"Now you are in the care of Kṛṣṇa-Balarāma," said Tamāla Kṛṣṇa.

Śrīla Prabhupāda smiled and nodded slightly. "Yes," he said, *"kṛṣṇa tvadīya-pada-paṅkaja-pañjarāntam,"* indicating King Kulaśekhara's prayer: "My dear Kṛṣṇa, please help me die immediately so that the swan of my mind may be encircled by the stem of Your lotus feet. Otherwise, at the time of my final breath, how will it be possible for me to think of You?"

Although Śrīla Prabhupāda was in a precarious state, he remained completely fixed in thought of Kṛṣṇa in one way or another—Kṛṣṇa's name, His form, His pastimes, or His devotional service. Prabhupāda suggested going to see Kṛṣṇa and Balarāma at nine-thirty, just as he had done before, but his servants advised that he rest today and begin that program tomorrow. "Whatever you desire, I will do," Prabhupāda said.

Tamāla Kṛṣṇa asked Prabhupāda if he wanted the *kavirāja* to come. "As you said, Prabhupāda, for better or worse, some husband must be there."

Śrīla Prabhupāda nodded. "Now manage everything," he said, "and let me think of Kṛṣṇa-Balarāma."

In response to Śrīla Prabhupāda's call, the twenty-three G.B.C. members again began gathering in Vṛndāvana. They arrived heavy-hearted, yet on coming before Śrīla Prabhupāda they were pleased to give him progress reports on their preaching on his behalf. Śrīla Prabhupāda was happy to hear the reports and was as encouraging as ever to his leaders, despite his condition.

Actually, Prabhupāda's calling the G.B.C. men together had been so they could chant for him. Now, more than ever, he wanted the medicine of the holy name, not of the doctors. When he heard that his friend Dr. Ghosh was coming to Vṛndāvana to open a clinic and that he could prescribe treatment, he refused the offer. "These doctors will come and give something to try and save," he said. "I don't want to be saved. Dr. Ghosh may come for the clinic he wants to develop, but not for my treatment." Tamāla Kṛṣṇa asked if they could at least call in some local Vṛndāvana doctors.

"No," said Prabhupāda. "Let us take your advice for *kīrtana* only." Tamāla Kṛṣṇa agreed that *kīrtana* was best, because in that way they were pleading for Kṛṣṇa's help.

"Better you don't pray to Kṛṣṇa to save me," said Śrīla Prabhupāda. "Let me die now."

When Harikeśa had received the call to come immediately to Vṛndāvana, he had been told to "expect the worst." Immediately he had contacted his printer, who was in the process of completing several books, and told him that he must have advance copies by the next day. So by the time he got on the plane for India, he had newly printed volumes of the Second Canto of *Śrīmad-Bhāgavatam* in German, the *Kṛṣṇa* trilogy in German, and a Yugoslavian *Śrī Īśopaniṣad.* Harikeśa went in and showed Prabhupāda the seven new books. Immediately Prabhupāda took the first volume of the *Kṛṣṇa* trilogy and held it up, looking at the cover painting of Rādhā and Kṛṣṇa. Prabhupāda began crying and reached out, trying to stroke Harikeśa's head. Harikeśa reached out and held Śrīla Prabhupāda's hand, thinking himself unworthy of being patted.

"He was rotting here, typewriting," said Śrīla Prabhupāda, referring to when Harikeśa had been his secretary, just before going to preach in Europe. "I said, 'You go.' I had ten servants. You thought that I was degrading you by sending you away. No. Now you understand?"

"Yes, I understand," said Harikeśa, sobbing.

"Here is an intelligent boy, I thought," said Śrīla Prabhupāda. "Why should he rot here, typewriting?" Prabhupāda looked at each book. "Printing and everything first class," he said. He asked how many had been printed, and Harikeśa replied, "One hundred twenty thousand *Kṛṣṇa* trilogies, sixty thousand *Śrīmad-Bhāgavatam* Second Cantos, and ten thousand *Īśopaniṣads.*"

"Can you distribute that *Īśopaniśad*?" Prabhupāda asked.

The devotees in the room knew that Harikeśa had been involved in distributing Śrīla Prabhupāda's books in the Communist countries of Eastern Europe, at great personal risk. This knowledge heightened the already supercharged emotional intensity of the moment.

Harikeśa assured Prabhupāda that they could definitely distribute the book in Yugoslavia.

"Then print more," said Prabhupāda. They continued discussing book production. Books were indeed Śrīla Prabhupāda's life and soul. From Harikeśa's entering with these new books, Prabhupāda had felt a profound ecstasy that had spread to Harikeśa and all the devotees present. Everyone was keenly aware that what they were experiencing was transcendental, a special reciprocation with Śrīla Prabhupāda, and as long as they were sincere, it would not die.

"Now you just have to become better," said Harikeśa. "More healthy."

"Healthy?" said Śrīla Prabhupāda. "I have nothing to do with this body."

Śrīla Prabhupāda was becoming more and more in favor of departing from the world. When Tamāla Kṛṣṇa remarked that Prabhupāda was not drinking much, he replied that he had no inclination.

The devotees with Prabhupāda found it very difficult to adopt his mood of looking forward to his passing away. In their resignation, they became philosophical. Rūpānuga said Prabhupāda could be likened to an ambassador in a foreign country who is finally called back. Jayādvaita said that Prabhupāda had taught his disciples everything and that now he was teaching them how to die. In their talks, the devotees stressed the importance of their cooperating with one another, and they discussed how ISKCON would continue in the future. But it was all depressing.

Nevertheless, they kept returning to the unpleasant but unavoidable realization that Prabhupāda would very soon leave them. With Prabhupāda so clearly indicating that he had decided to definitely leave, the devotees were becoming despondent. At best, a solemn mood prevailed.

Then Śrīla Prabhupāda said they should consult Nārāyaṇa Mahārāja, a disciple of Prabhupāda's sannyasa-guru, for details on how to conduct the ceremony for a departed Vaiṣṇava. He also described where his *samādhi* should be located and asked that after his departure, a feast be served in all the main temples in Vṛndāvana, with ISKCON bearing the expense.

On one level, everything seemed to go on as usual. The October weather was very pleasant. The *gurukula* boys were continuing with their routine, and the Deity worship went on as usual. But in front of the temple, workmen began clearing a space for Prabhupāda's *samādhi*.

Despite an earlier promise to live, Śrīla Prabhupāda said his life was still in Kṛṣṇa's hands—everything was. His free choice did not mean he was absolutely independent. Rather, the pure devotee's attitude is to freely surrender to Kṛṣṇa, whatever happens. In the mood of the *gopīs,* the foremost devotees of Lord Kṛṣṇa, Lord Caitanya Mahāprabhu prayed, "You may handle me roughly in your embrace or make me brokenhearted by not being present before me, but You are always my worshipable Lord, unconditionally."

Because the exchanges between the Lord and His pure devotees are always supremely personal, both the Lord and His devotees express desires and individual will. In His childhood *līlā,* Kṛṣṇa sometimes breaks mother Yaśodā's butter pot, and sometimes He allows her to catch Him and bind Him. In any case, the will of the Lord and the will of the devotees are always one in interest, but they are sometimes expressed in the form of a loving conflict. Similarly, although Śrīla Prabhupāda had promised his devotees that he would stay in the world and defy death, he still remained surrendered to the will of Kṛṣṇa.

Śrīla Prabhupāda had already expressed his surrender in the prayer he had given his disciples to offer on his behalf: "My dear Lord Kṛṣṇa, if You desire, please cure Śrīla Prabhupāda." By the phrase "if You desire," he was reminding his followers of the supreme prerogative of Kṛṣṇa and was asking them to abide by it, although he was also giving them an acceptable way to petition Kṛṣṇa. In a similar case in 1967, he had given his disciples another prayer: "My master has not finished his work." He had said then that Kṛṣṇa had responded to this prayer, granting the wishes of the devotees. Śrīla Prabhupāda himself was responding to the devotees' prayers, and Kṛṣṇa had given him the choice. But as a surrendered soul, Śrīla Prabhupāda waited for further developments, ever sensitive to Kṛṣṇa's desire. As Prabhupāda had said when invited by Kīrtanānanda to come to his palace in New Vrindaban, "Let us see which palace I am going to."

As a loving tension can sometimes exist between the Supreme Lord and His pure devotee, so now a similar tension existed between Śrīla Prabhupāda and his followers. Prior to his disciples' desperate petition at his bedside, Śrīla Prabhupāda had seen his duty as instructing his disciples in how to die. Part of his mission was to set the perfect example in this most important lesson—how to pass life's ultimate test. But now his disciples were asking him to postpone the lesson in dying and stay with them indefinitely in the preaching field. And Prabhupāda had agreed, showing that he had the ability to live if he chose. But sooner or later he would have to return to the lesson of how a person should face the end of life.

One special feature of Śrīla Prabhupāda's activities is his relating intimately to the human condition while at the same time remaining always aloof and transcendental. As a pure devotee, he was not subjected to the law of karma, which awards reactions for pious and sinful deeds. He was not born by the force of karma, nor would he die by force of karma. As stated by Śrīla Rūpa Gosvāmī, "One whose body, mind, and words are fully engaged in devotional service to Lord Kṛṣṇa is a liberated soul, even while living in this world." People often misunderstand the movements of a pure devotee within the material world, just as one, on seeing clouds blowing past the moon, may think the moon itself is moving. The *śāstra,* therefore, warns us never to see the guru as an ordinary man subject to karma.

But Śrīla Prabhupāda, while always transcendental to this world, showed the conditioned souls how they too could come to the stage of liberation by constantly thinking about Kṛṣṇa and serving Him, so that at the time of death they could return to Kṛṣṇa in the eternal, spiritual world. And Prabhupāda's lessons were always practical and universal. Śrīla Prabhupāda's books, for example, were not mere theory but were practical and full of realized knowledge. And Prabhupāda practiced what he preached; his entire life was exemplary. He had been in family life, and even then he had vigorously preached by starting his *Back to Godhead* magazine. In poverty and obscurity he had struggled to start a spiritual movement, and by the grace of Kṛṣṇa and his spiritual master, he had become successful. He had always shown by his humanlike attempts his willingness to bravely take on austerity and face danger. He had shown exemplary spiritual life for all to try and follow. He had gone alone, in old age, to a foreign country and had chanted Hare Kṛṣṇa in a park in New York City, attracting the young men and women of America. Therefore everyone should take his example and try to serve Kṛṣṇa, despite the immediate impediments.

Śrīla Prabhupāda encountered obstacles, yet by his free will and the help of Kṛṣṇa, he surmounted them. This was his wonderful example. It is said that Lord Caitanya, five hundred years ago, made surrender to Kṛṣṇa more attainable than Lord Kṛṣṇa had five thousand years ago. And now, in the twentieth century, Śrīla Prabhupāda has made Kṛṣṇa consciousness possible for people all over the world.

As part of his instruction and example, Śrīla Prabhupāda knew he would have to show people just how to die. He had escaped death a number of times—by Kṛṣṇa's grace, by the prayers of his disciples, and by his own pure and powerful will—to propagate his movement. But from the signs given to him by Lord Kṛṣṇa in 1977, Śrīla Prabhupāda began decisively and conclusively ending his mission in the material world. And among his final duties was his giving complete guidelines on how to die. He was perfectly showing how to do that which everyone has to do, but which is most difficult to do successfully: die.

But a loving conflict was there. Prabhupāda loved his disciples. He also knew they were not yet fully mature. His movement already had great potency and stature in the world, and yet it had many enemies. He was inclined to always protect his devotees, his movement, and all living entities, even the animals. So when his most intimate and faithful disciples pleaded that they could not go on without him, he had turned from showing how to die, agreeing to stay with them and preach. But at what point would they ever be willing to let him go? At what point could he say that the world of maya and the enemies of Kṛṣṇa were all gone? At what point would his disciples become fully mature?

In following his decision to stay, Śrīla Prabhupāda turned himself over to his disciples, allowing them to care for him completely. Those who took part recalled that never before had Śrīla Prabhupāda allowed such intimate dealings between himself and his disciples. The only thing comparable was in New York, in 1966, when he had been very intimate in dealing with the first persons to join him, persons who had known nothing of the etiquette of approaching a spiritual master. But those who were present now and who had also been present then said that these days were even more intimate.

At one point Kīrtanānanda firmly insisted that Śrīla Prabhupāda drink a full cup of juice, even when he said he had had enough. Kīrtanānanda felt awkward, insisting. "I am not like mother Yaśodā that I can do this," he said. "I keep remembering that you are my spiritual master." But Śrīla Prabhupāda allowed himself to be ordered by Kīrtanānanda. Similarly, Bhavānanda, Tamāla Kṛṣṇa, Bhakticāru, Upendra, and other servants coaxed Śrīla Prabhupāda to follow certain diets and cared for his body constantly. The other devotees were reminded of the story of Īśvara Purī, who gave intimate bodily service to his spiritual master, Mādhavendra Purī, when Mādhavendra was in the last stages of his life and apparently invalid. According to the *Caitanya-caritāmṛta,* it was by this menial, bodily service that Īśvara Purī proved his love for his spiritual master and was allowed to become the spiritual master of Lord Caitanya.

Śrīla Prabhupāda had deferred the lessons in dying in favor of giving his disciples an unparalleled opportunity to serve him in pure and simple love. And he allowed this not only for a few, but for whoever came to Vṛndāvana. Many came, and all were allowed to enter Śrīla Prabhupāda's room, massage his body, and sit with him as long as they liked, day and night, chanting the holy name for his pleasure. Śrīla Prabhupāda also recommenced his translating, and this was done openly. Whereas previously he had always worked in solitude, he now encouraged all devotees to come as he lay in bed dictating his Bhaktivedanta purports. A devotee would softly read the Sanskrit text to him, while another held a microphone to his mouth. His voice sometimes barely audible, Śrīla Prabhupāda would speak. Awestruck, the disciples watched as their spiritual master worked. His thoughts were clear, he cited from memory references from various scriptures, and his philosophical exposition was rigorous. Prabhupāda was giving himself completely and declaring it also, telling the devotees present, "Never leave me," and "I cannot live without your company." They had asked him to stay, and he had agreed, consigning himself completely to their care.

Those who were blessed to have this service felt themselves passing over all barriers of reluctance to serve, as well as all barriers of material desire. By intimately serving Śrīla Prabhupāda, they felt the strength of complete surrender and sensed that this would sustain them always, even when Śrīla Prabhupāda eventually did depart from the world.

Prabhupāda also continued speaking, as he had in recent months, about being unafraid of death and being fixed in transcendental knowledge. When receiving a presentation of some of his books recently printed in Portuguese by Hṛdayānanda Goswami, Prabhupāda encouraged him and said, "This is life. The material world is just bones. The bones are not our real life. Our real concern is the living force. The bones may remain or go—it doesn't matter. The real life is sustaining the bones. There is even a history that there was a *ṛṣi* who had only bones. So there is a science by which you can sustain life by only bones. Hiraṇyakaśipu did it."

"You are also doing it, Śrīla Prabhupāda," Tamāla Kṛṣṇa said.

"So take care of the bones as long as possible," said Prabhupāda, "but the real life is here, always remember that. The material world means we are simply all protecting bones and flesh together. But they have no knowledge of what they are."

And when Ātreya Ṛṣi visited Śrīla Prabhupāda and asked that he visit Tehran, Prabhupāda said that he was ready to go, but, "Now you have to take a bundle of bones." These were, of course, the same themes that Prabhupāda had always taught, the same themes that were in his books. But the lessons were more poignant and striking when Prabhupāda applied them to his own situation.

More than one devotee compared Prabhupāda to Bhīṣmadeva, who gave important instructions in his last days. As Bhīṣma felt no pain and delivered learned and loving discourses even from his "bed of arrows," and as Bhīṣma determined by his own free will the time of his departure from the world, so Śrīla Prabhupāda spent his last days oblivious to his physical condition, defying death, and instructing his spiritually innocent sons. But Prabhupāda's sons could no longer stand by and simply hear the philosophical lessons. Prabhupāda had accepted their affection when they had cried for him to stay with them, and now they wanted to express that affection in the only world they understood, a world with Śrīla Prabhupāda living and talking with them, laughing or reprimanding them, as he liked. They wanted him to eat and drink and become physically strong again.

But again Śrīla Prabhupāda seemed to change, and he began refusing food and drink. He had postponed his passing away to exchange lovingly with his disciples, and yet at the same time, by refusing to eat or drink, he was showing his preference for passing away. He admitted, when pressed, that it was an impossible course of action—to live without food or drink. Nor did he expect or want miracles. If he was to get better, it would be by taking nourishment. But for reasons of his own, he would not eat. He said recovery was material, and he didn't want it.

He kept closely in tune with the will of Kṛṣṇa, allowing the holy name to sustain him. The doctors who came were often puzzled, but those who were Vaiṣṇavas understood and respected his prerogative. Prabhupāda's servants made anxiety-filled attempts to induce Prabhupāda to take regular treatment. But Prabhupāda preferred to take only *kīrtana* and *Bhāgavatam,* while at the same time sustaining a willingness to live. He empathized with his disciples' anxiety and patiently explained the puzzling situation they were in. He wanted their care, and he allowed them to try to treat him, knowing that it was bringing them more and more into a surrender of love. But gradually it became more clear that Kṛṣṇa's will was indicating Prabhupāda's departure.

"Śrīla Prabhupāda," Bhavānanda coaxed, always working on the assumption that Prabhupāda could stay if he wanted, "your presence on this planet is the only thing that's keeping the onslaught of the Kali-yuga from really taking effect. We have no idea even what will happen if you leave."

"It is not in my hands," said Śrīla Prabhupāda, with perfect clarity of consciousness. "Kṛṣṇa-Balarāma."

Śrīla Prabhupāda always spoke clearly, logically, and with complete devotion to Kṛṣṇa. Up until the last he dealt with practical matters, forming a Bhaktivedanta Swami Charity Trust for reconstructing ancient temples in Bengal and arranging final details regarding ISKCON properties and monies. Through all dealings he stayed always alert, and he absorbed himself in *kīrtana* and *Bhāgavatam.*

But it became obvious to his disciples that, despite his promise, he was again moving inevitably towards giving the final lesson. He was teaching that love was beyond death, that a disciple's love could call the spiritual master back to the world to stay, and that a pure devotee has the ability to stay in the world beyond his allotted time. Meanwhile, however, he was progressing steadily to the final point. The devotees didn't feel angry with him or cheated that he was doing so. He had told them that he had free will given by Kṛṣṇa. And they also, by their free will, had asked him to stay, and he had agreed. But they knew he was not obliged. If, despite their prayers, Lord Kṛṣṇa was telling Śrīla Prabhupāda that he should come back home to Godhead, what could they do but accept? If Śrīla Prabhupāda was accepting, then they would accept also. Nothing, however, could change the fact of their surrendered love; it had now become a solid pact that could not be vanquished by any material changes. They had passed the test of eternal loving service, and that could not be taken away by death.

Up until the end there were interludes of sweetness as well as displays of Prabhupāda's indomitable mood of fighting for Kṛṣṇa. One day Prabhupāda's sister Pisīmā arrived unexpectedly, and Prabhupāda asked her to cook *kicharī*. At that time Kīrtanānanda was trying to put Prabhupāda on the road to recovery by gradually increasing his liquids, and Kīrtanānanda and the other devotees opposed the idea of his suddenly eating solid foods. But Śrīla Prabhupāda insisted.

"It doesn't matter whether what she cooks does good to me or bad," said Śrīla Prabhupāda. "She is a Vaiṣṇavī. It will be good for me." He then began speaking in an extremely humble way. "Probably I became a little puffed up because of my opulence and success," he said. "Now God has shattered that pride. If you don't have your body, what is there to be puffed up about?"

Bhakticāru protested, "Śrīla Prabhupāda, whatever you have done, you have done for Kṛṣṇa."

"That may be, but in this world, unknowingly you commit offenses."

When Pisīmā heard this, she exclaimed, "No, no, he never committed any offense."

"You cannot ever commit offenses," said Bhakticāru. "You are God's very dear one. How can you commit offenses?"

"I am a little temperamental," said Śrīla Prabhupāda. "I used to use words like *rascal* and so on. I never compromised. They used to call it 'a club in one hand and a *Bhāgavatam* in the other.' That is how I preach. Anyway, make arrangements for my sister."

There were also visits from Śrīla Prabhupāda's Godbrothers, and again Prabhupāda asked forgiveness for his offenses. One time, Niṣkiñcana Kṛṣṇadāsa Bābājī, Purī Mahārāja, Āśrama Mahārāja, Ānanda Prabhu, Puruṣottama Brahmacārī, and about twenty others came and sat next to Prabhupāda's bed.

He was resting when they arrived, and they joined the *kīrtana* until he awoke. When he saw them, he asked to be raised up. Sitting in the center of his bed with his Godbrothers all around, he addressed them.

"All over the world there is a beautiful field to preach Kṛṣṇa consciousness," he said. "I didn't care whether I would be successful or not. People are willing to take. They are all taking also. If we preach together, the saying of Mahāprabhu, *pṛthivīte,* will come true. We have everything. Spread the holy name and distribute *prasādam*. There is a beautiful field. In Africa, in Russia, everywhere they're accepting."

When Prabhupāda began asking his Godbrothers to forgive him, they protested. "You are the eternal leader," one of them asserted. "You rule over us, guide us, and chastise us."

"Forgive all my offenses," Prabhupāda repeated. "I became proud of all my opulence."

"No," said Purī Mahārāja, "you never became proud. When you started preaching, opulence and success followed you. That was the blessing of Śrī Caitanya Mahāprabhu and Śrī Kṛṣṇa. There cannot be any question of your being offensive."

When Śrīla Prabhupāda presented himself as *mahā-patita,* greatly fallen, Purī Mahārāja did not accept it. "You have saved millions of people around the world," he said. "Therefore there is no question of offenses. But you should be called *mahā-patita-pāvana* [the great savior of the fallen]."

Prabhupāda's disciples regarded Prabhupāda's asking for his Godbrothers' forgiveness as a manifestation of his humility. But they were also puzzled. Certainly Prabhupāda's Godbrothers were sincere in saying Prabhupāda had committed no offense. Whatever he had done, he had done for Kṛṣṇa. But Śrīla Prabhupāda was also sincere in asking for forgiveness. That was the beautiful gem of his humility—to ask everyone for forgiveness.

For the purpose of preaching, displaying this gem had not always been the most effective way to spread the merciful teachings of Lord Kṛṣṇa in every town and village. But now it could be displayed. In London and now in Vṛndāvana, Prabhupāda was showing his disciples extra affection and gratitude, without the reprimands usually necessary in training disciples. This attitude of complete humility was a symptom of the highest stage of devotional life. Śrīla Prabhupāda had explained in his books that the *madhyama-adhikārī,* the second-class devotee, makes distinctions between the devotees, the innocent nondevotees, and the demons, whereas the *mahā-bhāgavata,* or first-class devotee, sees everyone except himself as a servant of God. Sometimes, however, the *mahā-bhāgavata* desires to come down from the first-class platform, just to take up the most compassionate service of preaching Kṛṣṇa consciousness. Prabhupāda's disciples had all read of the *mahā-bhāgavata* stage in the scriptures, and now they were seeing it fully displayed, as Prabhupāda referred to himself as the most fallen and asked for everyone's forgiveness.

Śrīla Prabhupāda had heard of the program of his disciple Lokanātha Swami, who was taking a small group of men on a bullock cart and preaching in villages throughout India. Lokanātha had told Śrīla Prabhupāda how in the course of their travels they had recently visited *tīrthas* such as Badarikāśrama and Bhim Kapur. Śrīla Prabhupāda was enlivened to hear this, and he then evolved a transcendental desire to go himself on a cart pulled by bullocks to circumambulate the area of Vṛndāvana. Tamāla Kṛṣṇa and Bhavānanda, who were serving Prabhupāda with increased intimacy, felt themselves unable to support Śrīla Prabhupāda in his desire, since they thought his fragile body could not survive such rough treatment on the roads.

But Śrīla Prabhupāda reasoned that, "Dying on *parikrama* is glorious," and he asked them to take him. A controversy developed among the devotees, as some said Prabhupāda's will to go on *parikrama* should be immediately honored as an order from the spiritual master; he wanted it, and he should not be denied. The doctor, however, assured them that Śrīla Prabhupāda's body would not survive the jostling of the cart. The many devotees who crowded around Śrīla Prabhupāda's bed held different opinions, and Prabhupāda could see this. Following his request, however, Lokanātha went out and hired a cart with bullocks and prepared it for the ride. Lokanātha and Haṁsadūta suggested that the *parikrama* could go to the city of Vṛndāvana or visit the seven main temples of the Gosvāmīs. But then they said that since the next day was Govardhana-pūjā, Prabhupāda could go to Govardhana Hill. Tamāla Kṛṣṇa, Bhavānanda, and Bhakticāru, however, protested adamantly against the *parikrama*.

"One-day experiment," Prabhupāda said. "It is for one day. Rest assured I will not die in one day." He liked the idea of going to Govardhana. "And we shall make our cooking there," he said. Lokanātha Swami, he assured them, was experienced. "Make very good picnic," he said.

After discussing back and forth, the devotees finally decided that early the next morning they would take Śrīla Prabhupāda in a bullock cart to Govardhana. The majority of the devotees then left Śrīla Prabhupāda alone for the night.

Later that night Śrīla Prabhupāda received a visit from Niṣkiñcana Kṛṣṇadāsa Bābājī, who sat with Prabhupāda, chanting and sometimes speaking in Bengali. Suddenly, Tamāla Kṛṣṇa and Bhavānanda came to Prabhupāda's bedside. They were in tears and beside themselves with anxiety.

Prabhupāda understood. "You request me not to go?" he asked.

"Well, Śrīla Prabhupāda," said Tamāla Kṛṣṇa, "I'll tell you, I'm getting so upset sitting in the room upstairs. I was walking around. Two of the devotees told me that this road is so bad that if you go on this road you're going to be jolted back and forth. The road is terrible. I just can't understand, Śrīla Prabhupāda, why it has to be tomorrow that we have to go. Of anybody that wants you to travel, I do. But why do we have to go when you're in this condition? I can't understand it. Why are we throwing everything out the window that we must go tomorrow? I can't understand."

"All right," said Śrīla Prabhupāda softly, immediately agreeing to their proposal that he not go.

"*Jaya,* Śrīla Prabhupāda!" said Bhakticāru, who was also present.

"Thank you, Śrīla Prabhupāda," said Bhavānanda with great relief.

"All right. You're satisfied?"

"Now I am, Śrīla Prabhupāda," said Bhavānanda. "Yes. I was in too much anxiety."

"Never mind. I shall not put you in anxiety."

"Actually, Śrīla Prabhupāda," said Tamāla Kṛṣṇa, "we're so much attached to you that you practically drive us to madness sometimes. Tonight we were becoming mad."

"No, no, I shall not do that," said Prabhupāda. "Bābājī Mahārāja," Prabhupāda turned to Niṣkiñcana Kṛṣṇadāsa Bābājī and said, "just see how much affection they have for me."

"Śrīla Prabhupāda," said Tamāla Kṛṣṇa, "the way you deal with us simply deepens our attachment every moment."

"It is my duty," said Prabhupāda, and the devotees laughed warmly, understanding. Yes, they could understand—that was his duty. By all his actions and dealings, Prabhupāda's intention was to capture spirit souls and deliver them to Kṛṣṇa. His method was loving service, but he did not do it for himself. He was delivering them to Kṛṣṇa. That was his duty.

On November 14, 1977, at 7:30 p.m., in his room at the Krishna-Balaram Mandir in Vṛndāvana, Śrīla Prabhupāda gave his final instruction by leaving this mortal world and going back to Godhead.

His departure was exemplary, because his whole life was exemplary. His departure marked the completion of a lifetime of pure devotional service to Kṛṣṇa. A few days before the end, Śrīla Prabhupāda had said he was instructing as far as he could, and his secretary had added, "You are the inspiration." "Yes," Śrīla Prabhupāda had replied, "that I shall do until the last breathing."

Prabhupāda's "last breathing" was glorious, not because of any last-minute mystical demonstration, but because Śrīla Prabhupāda remained in perfect Kṛṣṇa consciousness. Like grandfather Bhīṣmadeva, he remained completely collected and noble and grave, teaching until the end. He was preaching that life comes from life, not from matter, and he was showing that one should preach with every breath he has. The many devotees who crowded the large room bore witness that up to the very end, Prabhupāda remained exactly the same. There was nothing suddenly incongruous with what he had previously shown and taught them. At the time of his departure, therefore, he was teaching how to die, by always depending on Kṛṣṇa. Prabhupāda's passing away was peaceful. During the evening of November 14, the *kavirāja* asked him, "Is there anything you want?" and Prabhupāda replied faintly, *kuch icchā nahi:* "I have no desire." His passing away was in the perfect situation: in Vṛndāvana, with devotees. A few months previously, a young girl, the daughter of one of Prabhupāda's disciples, had passed away in Vṛndāvana, and when Śrīla Prabhupāda had been asked if she went back to Godhead to personally associate with Kṛṣṇa, he had said, "Yes, anyone who leaves his body in Vṛndāvana is liberated."

Of course, "Vṛndāvana" also means the state of pure Kṛṣṇa consciousness. As Advaita Ācārya had said of Lord Caitanya, "Wherever You are is Vṛndāvana." And this was also true of Śrīla Prabhupāda. Had Śrīla Prabhupāda passed away in London, New York, or Moscow, therefore, his destination would have been the same. As Lord Kṛṣṇa states in the *Bhagavad-gītā,* "One who is always thinking of Me, surely he attains to Me." But because Vṛndāvana-dhāma is the quintessential realm of Kṛṣṇa consciousness within the universe, the ideal place for departure from this world, so it was yet another exemplary feature of Śrīla Prabhupāda's life that he went back to Godhead with Vṛndāvana as his last junction.

Those Vaiṣṇavas who had taken the vow never to leave Vṛndāvana could see that Śrīla Prabhupāda, after sacrificing everything—including the benefit of residing in Vṛndāvana—to deliver fallen souls in the most godforsaken locations of the world, had returned to the holy land of Vṛndāvana and from there had departed for the original abode of Lord Kṛṣṇa in the spiritual sky. As stated in *Śrīmad-Bhāgavatam,* "Anyone who executes service in Vṛndāvana certainly goes back to home, back to Godhead, after giving up his body."

Śrīla Prabhupāda's departure was also perfect because he was chanting and hearing the holy names of God. Thus the Supreme Personality of Godhead was present at Śrīla Prabhupāda's passing just as He was at the celebrated passing away of Bhīṣmadeva, who said, "Despite His being equally kind to everyone, He has graciously come before me while I am ending my life, for I am His unflinching servitor." As Lord Kṛṣṇa came before Bhīṣmadeva, assuring him and everyone else that Bhīṣma was returning back to Godhead on leaving his body, so the Lord in His incarnation of *nāma-avatāra,* the Hare Kṛṣṇa mantra, was present for Śrīla Prabhupāda's departure.

Śrīla Prabhupāda's life had been dedicated to spreading the holy name to every town and village, and for a month he had been surrounding himself with the holy name. For his passing away, he especially wanted to fill the room with devotees chanting Hare Kṛṣṇa, and Kṛṣṇa fulfilled that wish. Śrīla Prabhupāda, therefore, departed under the most favorable circumstances possible—in the most sacred place, Vṛndāvana, surrounded by Vaiṣṇavas chanting the holy name.

An ideal spiritual teacher (*ācārya*) always acts in such a way that others may follow his example. As *Śrīmad-Bhāgavatam* states, these great souls who cross over the ocean of birth and death by taking shelter of the "boat" of the lotus feet of Kṛṣṇa miraculously leave the boat on this side for others to use. And Śrīla Prabhupāda's disappearance, by its perfect example, affords all conditioned souls the means for meeting the greatest of all dangers. An auspicious death is not merely a matter of psychological adjustment, so that one may die without regret or without becoming unduly upset. The real point is that at the time of death the soul must leave the body and take his next birth. Only the Kṛṣṇa conscious soul can leave this world of birth and death and attain an eternal, blissful life in the spiritual world. Therefore one's life is tested at death.

Death means the soul cannot stand to live in the body anymore. Whatever the material cause may be, the situation has become unbearable for the soul. And leaving the body causes great distress. The *śāstras,* therefore, advise us to get free from the cycle of repeated birth and death. Meeting an inauspicious death and being dragged down to a lower birth is the most fearful thing for the living being. So fearful is it that we may try to ignore death altogether. Death is painful because the eternal spirit soul is placed in a most unnatural situation: although he is eternal and should not have to die, he is forced to die because of his connection with the material body. At death, the eternal soul is forced to leave the body for a destination he knows not. Thus he is full of fear and suffering. The pain and fear is usually overwhelming, and one thinks only of material attachments or bodily pain. Therefore King Kulaśekhara prayed, and Prabhupāda often quoted, "Please let me pass away, not in some prolonged contemplation of my bodily death, but just while I am chanting Hare Kṛṣṇa. If I can meditate on You and then pass from this body, that will be perfection."

Over the last months of his life in this world, Śrīla Prabhupāda taught how it is possible to meet death step by step in Kṛṣṇa consciousness. In his last days, he told one of his sannyasis, "Don't think this isn't going to happen to you." Prabhupāda came into this world, on Kṛṣṇa's request, to teach us how to live a pure life of Kṛṣṇa consciousness, and that includes how to finally pass away from this world to attain eternal life. Prabhupāda underwent death in a way that was perfect and glorious, and at the same time in a way which we can all follow. When we have to go, we can cling to the memory of how a great soul left his body—always thinking of Kṛṣṇa, surrounding himself with the medicine of chanting Hare Kṛṣṇa, always desiring to hear about Kṛṣṇa, and practicing detachment from the misery of the material condition. This last lesson was one of the most wonderful and important instructions Śrīla Prabhupāda gave us. He taught by his life, by his books, and at the end by his dying. Education in how to die is meant especially for the human being. An animal dies, and a human being also dies; but a human being is supposed to understand the process of going back to the spiritual world at the time of death. Remaining always fixed and undisturbed in Kṛṣṇa consciousness, Śrīla Prabhupāda expertly taught the process. His passing away, therefore, was a perfect lesson, and one that can be faithfully followed.

While there was nothing lamentable for Śrīla Prabhupāda in his departing from the world and going back to Godhead, it was certainly lamentable for his followers and for the people of the whole world, who became bereft of the presence of their greatest well-wisher and benefactor. Śrīla Prabhupāda had written in a *Śrīmad-Bhāgavatam* purport, "When the mortal body of the spiritual master expires, the disciple should cry exactly like the queen cries when the king leaves his body." At the departure of his own spiritual master, Śrīla Prabhupāda had written, "On that day, O my Master, I made a cry of grief; I was not able to tolerate the absence of you, my guru." And so on November 14, 1977, as the powerful news spread around the world, those who knew and loved Śrīla Prabhupāda were gripped by a fearful, unrestricted grief. They saw everything around them in the overwhelming atmosphere of separation from Śrīla Prabhupāda. They turned for solace to Śrīla Prabhupāda's books.

> However, the disciples and the spiritual master are never separated, because the spiritual master always keeps company with the disciple, as long as the disciple follows the instructions of the spiritual master. This is called the association of *vāṇī*. Physical presence is called *vapuḥ*. As long as the spiritual master is

> physically present, the disciple should serve the physical body of the spiritual master, and when the spiritual master is no longer physically existing, the disciple should serve the instructions of the spiritual master.

Śrīla Prabhupāda's disciples were already carrying out his instructions, but now they would have to do so without the *vapuḥ,* without the opportunity of regularly seeing and being with him. At first this was very difficult for them to face, but those who were sincere soon realized that Śrīla Prabhupāda had, upon his departure, given them the greatest gift of all: service in separation.

Service in separation is the highest realization and ecstasy. This was the teaching of Lord Caitanya Mahāprabhu, in regard to Lord Kṛṣṇa and His foremost devotees, the *gopīs* of Vṛndāvana. When Kṛṣṇa left His beloved *gopīs* and went to Mathurā, never to return to them in Vṛndāvana, the *gopīs* (and all the other residents of Vṛndāvana) wept piteously in separation. They so much loved Kṛṣṇa that they could not live without Him, and to maintain their lives they began to constantly remember and discuss His name, fame, form, and entourage. By constantly remembering Him in love and by anticipating His return to Vṛndāvana, they achieved an ecstasy of *union in separation,* which Gauḍīya Vaiṣṇava scholars declare to be superior even to the ecstasy the *gopīs* felt in Kṛṣṇa's presence. Because Kṛṣṇa is absolute, even remembering Him or chanting His name puts the devotee into direct contact with Him. But because there is simultaneously a feeling of separation from Him, there is an added dimension of inconceivable, simultaneous union and separation. This is the epitome of Kṛṣṇa conscious realization.

Prabhupāda's followers knew this principle of service in separation, technically known as *vipralambha-sevā,* but to most devotees it was a theoretical realization. Before one can feel intense loving separation from Kṛṣṇa, one must first feel intense attraction to Him. But for the conditioned soul who has forgotten and abandoned Kṛṣṇa and has come to the material world under the spell of maya, illusion—for him, "separation" from Kṛṣṇa is based on complete ignorance and forgetfulness.

In coming to spiritual life, a neophyte first begins to awaken to the very existence of God as he overcomes atheistic misconceptions. Next, he comes gradually, through practice, to take up a relationship of service to Kṛṣṇa, through serving the spiritual master. Intense love of Kṛṣṇa in separation is the most advanced stage and cannot possibly be realized in full by the neophyte. Thus service in separation had remained a theoretical teaching to many of Prabhupāda's followers.

But when Śrīla Prabhupāda departed from the world and left his disciples to carry on his mission, they immediately realized union with him in separation. He was gone, but he was still very much present. This realization was not a pretention or a myth, nor was it sentimental psychic phenomena—telepathy, "communion with the dead," or so on. It was a completely substantive, practical, palpable reality, a fact of life. Śrīla Prabhupāda had given them personal service, and now they would continue that service. Prabhupāda was still present through his instructions, and all the nectar of his direct association—all the nectar of Kṛṣṇa consciousness that he had given and shared with them—was still available.

Service in separation for Prabhupāda's disciples was undoubtedly a fact; otherwise, now that they were without his personal presence, how were they able to sustain themselves in spiritual life? The fact that they could continue as before, increase their feelings of devotion, and even increase their serving capacity, meant that Śrīla Prabhupāda was very much still with them. As Śrīla Prabhupāda's last instruction was the lesson of how a human being should die, he now taught, beyond dying, how to practically implement the highest philosophical teaching of Gauḍīya Vaiṣṇavism.

This realization gave the devotees great hope that Śrīla Prabhupāda and the revolutionary life of Kṛṣṇa consciousness he had brought with him were not finished upon his departure. Often when a great personality dies, his contribution collapses; but Śrīla Prabhupāda's presence remained and expanded, sustaining his devotees' lives. He was still in charge.

GUIDE TO SANSKRIT PRONUNCIATION

The system of transliteration for Sanskrit used in this book conforms to a system that scholars in the last fifty years have accepted to indicate the pronunciation of each Sanskrit sound.

The short vowel **a** is pronounced like the **u** in b**u**t, long **ā** like the **a** in f**a**r, and short **i** like the **i** in p**i**n. Long **ī** is pronounced as in p**i**que, short **u** as in p**u**ll, and long **ū** as in r**u**le. The vowel **ṛ** is pronounced like the **ri** in **ri**m. The vowel **e** is pronounced as in th**ey**, **ai** as in **ai**sle, **o** as in g**o**, and **au** as in h**ow**. The *anusvāra* (**ṁ**), which is a pure nasal, is pronounced like the **n** in the French word bo**n**, and *visarga* (**ḥ**), which is a strong aspirate, is pronounced as a final **h** sound. Thus **aḥ** is pronounced like **aha**, and **iḥ** like **ihi**.

The guttural consonants—**k, kh, g, gh** and **ṅ**—are pronounced from the throat in much the same manner as in English. **K** is pronounced as in **k**ite, **kh** as in Ec**kh**art, **g** as in **g**ive, **gh** as in di**g h**ard, and **ṅ** as in si**ng**. The palatal consonants—**c, ch, j, jh** and **ñ**—are pronounced from the palate with the middle of the tongue. **C** is pronounced as in **ch**air, **ch** as in staun**ch-h**eart, **j** as in **j**oy, **jh** as in he**dgeh**og, and **ñ** as in ca**ny**on. The cerebral consonants—**ṭ, ṭh, ḍ, ḍh,** and **ṇ**—are pronounced with the tip of the tongue turned up and drawn back against the dome of the palate. **Ṭ** is pronounced as in **t**ub, **ṭh** as in ligh**t-h**eart, **ḍ** as in **d**ove, **ḍh** as in re**d-h**ot, and **ṇ** as in **n**ut. The dental consonants—**t, th, d, dh** and **n**—are pronounced in the same manner as the cerebrals, but with the forepart of the tongue against the teeth. The labial consonants—**p, ph, b, bh** and **m**—are pronounced with the lips. **P** is pronounced as in **p**ine, **ph** as in u**ph**ill, **b** as in **b**ird, **bh** as in ru**b-h**ard, and **m** as in **m**other. The semivowels—**y, r, l** and **v**—are pronounced as in **y**es, **r**un, **l**ight, and **v**ine respectively. The sibilants—**ś, ṣ,** and **s**—are pronounced, respectively, as in the German word *sprechen* and the English words **sh**ine and **s**un. The letter **h** is pronounced as in **h**ome.

Glossary

Ācārya—one who teaches Kṛṣṇa consciousness by example.
Ārati—a ceremony for worshiping the Deity of the Lord.
Āśrama—a dwelling place for spiritual shelter.
Āyur-Vedic—relating to Vedic medicine.

Bābāji—a renounced, recluse devotee.
Bhajanas—devotional music and song.
Bhakti yoga—devotional service, which links one to the Supreme.
Bhārata-bhūmi—India.
Brahmacārī—a celibate monk.
Brahman—the Absolute Truth supreme spirit, especially the impersonal aspect.
Brāhmaṇa—an intelligent person who understands the spiritual purpose of life and can teach others.
Burfī—a condensed-milk sweet.

Cādar—a shawl.
Caitanya Mahāprabhu—the *avatāra* of Lord Kṛṣṇa in this age whose mission is to teach love of God through the chanting of His holy names.
Capātīs—whole-wheat flatbreads.
Chaukidhars—guards.

Dāl—a spicy *dāl*-bean soup.
Darśana—audience with the Deity or a saintly person.
Deity—an authorized form of the Supreme Lord.
Dharma—one's eternal religion; religious principles.
Dhoti—the standard Indian men's lower garment, a simple wrapped cloth.
Diwali—an annual Indian festival.

Ganja—a marijuana derivative.
Gaudiya Math—Śrīla Bhaktisiddhānta's Vaiṣṇava mission in India.
Gauḍīya Vaiṣṇava—a follower of Lord Kṛṣṇa (Viṣṇu) in the line of Lord Caitanya Mahāprabhu.
Gṛhastha—a devotee in family life.
Guru—a spiritual master or teacher.
Gurudeva—an affectionate address to one's spiritual master.
Gurukula—the school of the spiritual master.

Halavā—a sweet and buttery grain preparation.
Haribol!—a greeting or exclamation meaning "chant the names of Hari (Kṛṣṇa)!"

Japa—soft private chanting of Hare Kṛṣṇa.

Kacaurīs—a spicy fried pastry.
Karatālas—small hand-cymbals.
Karma—fruitive action, for which there is always a reaction, good or bad.
Kavirāja—an Āyur-Vedic doctor.
Khādī—homespun cotton garments.
Khīr—sweetened condensed milk.
Khicarī—a simple preparation of *dāl* beans and rice.
Kīrtana—glorification of God, especially by chanting His holy names.
Kṣatriya—one in the administrative and protective occupation.
Kurtā—a kind of simple men's shirt.

Laḍḍus—a chick-pea-flour candy.
Lakh—one hundred thousand.
Līlā—spiritual pastimes of the Supreme Lord or his pure devotee.

Mahā-mantra—the great chanting for deliverance:
Hare Kṛṣṇa, Hare Kṛṣṇa, Kṛṣṇa Kṛṣṇa, Hare Hare
Hare Rāma, Hare Rāma, Rāma Rāma, Hare Hare.

Mandira—temple.
Mantra—a chanted sound vibration that liberates the mind.
Maṭha—mission; missionary organization.
Māyā—the illusory energy of the Supreme Lord.
Māyāvāda—the impersonal philosophy.
Mlecchas—meat-eaters.
Mṛdaṅga—a sacred clay drum used in *kirtana.*
Mūrti—a cast or sculpted Deity form.

Pakorās—deep-fried batter-covered vegetables.
Pān—a kind of intoxicant.
Paṇḍāl—a large and often decorative tent.
Pandit—a scholar.
Papaḍs—large, thin *dāl*-flour chips.
Paramparā—disciplic succession.
Parikrama—circumambulation of holy places.
Prasādam—vegetarian food spiritualized by first being offered to the Supreme Lord for His enjoyment.
Pūjā—worship according to authorized ceremony.
Pūjārī—a priest who serves and worships the Deity.
Puris—puffy, fried white-flour wheat breads.
Puṣpānna rice—a fancy rice with fried curd pieces.

Rājarṣis—saintly kings.
Rāma(candra)—the incarnation of the Supreme Lord as the ideal king.
Rāma-navamī—the appearance day of Lord Rāmacandra.
Ṛṣi—a sage.

Sabjī—a vegetable preparation.
Sādhu—a saintly person.
Samosās—a fried spicy-vegetable pastry.
Saṅkīrtana—congregational *kīrtana* or public glorification of the Supreme Lord.
Sannyāsa—the final renounced order of life.
Sannyāsī—one in the final renounced order of spiritual life.
Sari—the standard garment of Indian women.
Śikhā—the remaining tuft of hair on a Vaiṣṇava's shaven head.

Śūdra—one of the laborer class.

Tilaka—sacred clay markings on the body of a Vaiṣṇava.
Tīrthas—holy places.
Tulasī—the plant most sacred to Lord Kṛṣṇa.

Upaniṣads—a branch of Vedic scriptures.

Vaiṣṇava—a devotee of Viṣṇu, or Kṛṣṇa.
Vaiśya—a farmer or merchant.
Varṇāśrama—the Vedic institution dividing the human population into four social orders and four spiritual orders.
Vedic—pertaining to human culture based on the *Vedas*.
Viṣṇu—Kṛṣṇa's first expansion for the creation and maintenance of the material universes.
Vṛndāvana—a sacred village that was Kṛṣṇa's childhood home.
Vyāsāsana—a seat for the spiritual master.

Yāmunācārya—a prominent Vaiṣṇava.
Yoga—any of various spiritual disciplines meant for purification and ultimate realization of one's position as servant of God.

THE AUTHOR

Satsvarūpa dāsa Goswami was born on December 6, 1939. In July 1966, he met His Divine Grace A. C. Bhaktivedanta Swami Prabhupāda, and he became his initiated disciple in September of that year. Satsvarūpa dāsa Goswami began contributing articles to *Back to Godhead,* the magazine of the Hare Kṛṣṇa movement, and later became its editor in chief. In August 1967 he went to Boston to establish the first ISKCON center there. Satsvarūpa dāsa Goswami was one of the original members selected by Śrīla Prabhupāda to form the Governing Body Commission of ISKCON in 1970. He remained as president of Boston ISKCON until 1971, when he moved to Dallas and became headmaster of Gurukula, the first ISKCON school for children.

In May 1972, on the appearance day of Lord Nṛsiṁhadeva, he was awarded the sannyasa (renounced) order by His Divine Grace Śrīla Prabhupāda and began traveling across the United States, lecturing in colleges and universities. In January 1974 he was called by Śrīla Prabhupāda to become his personal secretary and to travel with him through India and Europe. In 1976 he published *Readings in Vedic Literature,* a concise account of the Vedic tradition. The volume is now being studied at various universities. In 1977 Śrīla Prabhupāda ordered him to accept the duties of initiating guru, along with ten other senior disciples. In addition to his duties as a Governing Body Commissioner and an initiating guru, he has written many books, including the multivolume *Śrīla Prabhupāda-līlāmṛta* and this book, *Prabhupāda.*

Other Books
by Satsvarūpa dāsa Goswami

Śrīla Prabhupāda-līlāmṛta
(an unabridged biography in 6 volumes):

A Lifetime in Preparation
Planting the Seed
Only He Could Lead Them
In Every Town and Village
Let There Be a Temple
Uniting Two Worlds

Readings in Vedic Literature
Handbook for Krishna Consciousness
He Lives Forever
Śrīla Prabhupāda Līlā (Chapters 1–8)
Letters from Śrīla Prabhupāda (Vol. 1)
Japa Reform Notebook
The Voices of Surrender and Other Poems
Remembering Śrīla Prabhupāda (Vols. 1–6)
Life with the Perfect Master
Vaiṣṇava Behavior / The Twenty-Six Qualities of a Devotee
In Praise of the Mahājanas
Prabhupāda Nectar (Vols. 1–3)
Living with the Scriptures (Vol. 1)
The Worshipable Deity
Reading Reform

For further information, contact the address below.

The Gita-nagari Press
10310 Oakland Rd.
Potomac, MD 20854
(301) 983-3386